West African
Narratives
of Slavery

West African Narratives of Slavery

Texts from
Late Nineteenth-
and Early
Twentieth-Century
Ghana

Sandra E. Greene

Indiana University Press

BLOOMINGTON AND INDIANAPOLIS

This book is a publication of

Indiana University Press
601 North Morton Street
Bloomington, Indiana 47404-3797 USA

iupress.indiana.edu

Telephone orders   800-842-6796
Fax orders   812-855-7931
Orders by e-mail   iuporder@indiana.edu

⊖ *The paper used in this publication meets the minimum
requirements of the American National Standard for
Information Sciences—Permanence of Paper for Printed
Library Materials, ANSI Z39.48-1992.*

Manufactured in the United States of America

Library of Congress Cataloging-in-Publication Data

Greene, Sandra E., [date]-
West African narratives of slavery: texts from late nineteenth-
and early twentieth-century Ghana /Sandra E. Greene.
p.   cm.
Includes bibliographical references and index.
ISBN 978-0-253-35607-9 (cloth : alk. paper)—ISBN
978-0-253-22294-7 (pbk. : alk. paper) 1. Slave narratives—
Ghana—History and criticism. 2. Slavery—Ghana—History.
3. Slave trade—Ghana—History. I. Title.
HT1394.G48G74 2011
306.3'620922667—dc22
2010035373

1 2 3 4 5 16 15 14 13 12 11

To Ethel

To Ethel

CONTENTS

CONTENTS

ACKNOWLEDGMENTS

This book would not have been possible without the assistance and support of a wide range of individuals and institutions. I am especially grateful to the many research libraries and their staffs whose collections and personal assistance made it possible to make the documents included here available to a wider public. To the Bremen Staatsarchiv and the Norddeutsche Mission in Bremen Germany; the Center for Research Libraries in Chicago; Northwestern University Library and the Garrett Theological Seminary Library in Evanston, Illinois; Yale University Library in New Haven, Connecticut; Cornell University Library in Ithaca, New York; the Basel Mission Archives in Basel, Switzerland; and the librarians at the National Humanities Center in North Carolina, I thank you. Translations of the German and Ewe texts are a central part of this study. For their translation work I am grateful to Kodjopa Attoh, Anna Parkinson, Rüdiger Bechstein, Paul Agbedor, Jasper Ackumey, and K. A. Mensah. I also thank the many undergraduate and graduate students as well as my Cornell University professorial colleagues whom I enlisted throughout the years to help with the translation of the German language sources that I consulted so as to contextualize the documents presented here. This group includes Kora Bättig von Wittlesbach, Jessica Bauman, Timothy Haupt, Sean Franzel, Chris Muenzen, and Herbert Deinert, among others. I thank Michelle Moyd, who was a wonderful research assistant, and Kodzo Gavua, who has been very supportive of my work on Yosef Famfantor. Ange Romeo-Hall was immensely helpful in proofreading the entire manuscript. Many individuals read one or more draft versions of the chapters of this book: Dagwami Woubshet, Judith Byfied, Daniel Magaziner, Johanna Crane, Jeremy Foster, Carina Ray, and Tamara Loos. Martin Klein and Joseph Miller read the entire manuscript and provided most helpful comments. To them I am also most grateful. As with most projects that extend over many years, I am sure I have failed to mention everyone who was helpful. To them I apologize, but know that I am grateful to you even if your name does not appear here. Of course, I am ultimately responsible for any mistakes that may have inadvertently found their way into the book.

Perhaps the most challenging aspect of this project was that during the entire period I was writing the book and preparing it for publication, I was simultaneously dealing with a particularly stressful family illness. Without the support of many friends and family, I would simply have been unable to complete this project. To my parents, siblings, nieces, and nephews, to many of the friends already mentioned as well as Sung Gook and Hye Kim, Vincent Tsiag-bey, Maria Cristina Garcia, Sherman Cochran, Alice Bellagamba, and Carolyn Brown, to Durba Ghosh, Robert Travers, and Barry Strauss, I cannot express enough how grateful I have been for your support.

A NOTE ON THE TRANSLATIONS

All the texts that are analyzed here required some form of translation. Four of the five narratives were written (or contained sections that were penned) in the Ewe language. These include the life history of Aaron Kuku, the biography of Yosef Famfantor, segments of Paul Sands's diary, and the oral narratives about the Atorkor kidnappings. One of the narratives, the biography of Lydia Yawo, was written and published in German. Another document, an account of the history of Atorkor that I appended to the Atorkor oral texts, was also published in German.

A great deal has been written about the translation process, whether it involves texts of great literary value (a group that does not include the narratives presented here) or ones that are more technical or prosaic in orientation. Debates rage about the capacity to truly transfer meaning from one language to another, whether or not to take a literal or free approach to the translation process, whether or not to focus on particular linguistic units (sentences and phrases) only or also to translate these elements in relation to larger cultural contexts. None of these concerns are discussed here. Instead I focus on the particular issues faced by the translators of the texts included in this study of West African narratives of slavery. All the translators sought to be as faithful as possible to the source texts, converting into the English language the meanings, phrasing, and the spirit of the original texts. In many instances, they encountered no problems at all. Difficulties did arise in some instances, however. The discussion here will focus on those areas that proved to be challenging to one degree or another. First, however, it is important to say something about the translators themselves. I begin with the Ewe translators.

The Ewe language is spoken largely in both Ghana and Togo, but also in those parts of the world where one can find native Ewe speakers. It is taught today in the Ghana public schools, but rarely do Ghanaians have an opportunity to achieve great competence in the written form of the language. Schools texts are largely designed for the elementary grades, and even instruction at this level has varied over time as different Ghana governments have offered changing levels of support (or none at all) for local-language education. The availability of texts for a larger reading public has also varied over time. From the late nineteenth century through at least the 1960s, Ewe language publications were produced for a small but interested reading public. Since the 1970s, the increasing costs of production have undermined publishers' abilities to produce affordable local-language materials for a relatively small Ewe reading public. One of the consequences of this situation is that individuals who are specifically trained in reading the language in both its historic and contemporary form are relatively rare. Those trained more specifically in the art of translation are even rarer. Thus, in seeking translators of the Ewe texts presented here, I have had to rely on individuals whose mother tongue is the Ewe language but who have had varying degrees of experience with the study of the language and the translation process. The Aaron Kuku narrative was translated by Kodjopa Attoh, a native Ewe speaker who is intimately familiar with the language as it is spoken in Ho and Kpando, but who is not a trained translator. In contrast, Paul Agbedor, who translated the Yosef Famfantor text, is both a native Ewe speaker and a professor of Ewe linguistics, specializing not in the theories and practice of translation, however, but in Ewe syntax, phonology, and semantics. Jasper Ackumey, who translated the Ewe-language passages in Paul Sands's diary, is a researcher associated with the University of Ghana, with no specific language training although he is fluent in two of the major languages of southern Ghana, Twi and Ga, as well Ewe and is a native speaker of the Ewe dialect spoken by Sands. K. A Mensah, a high school teacher at the time he translated the oral interviews about Atorkor into English, is fully fluent in English and Ewe, but has also had no formal training in translation. All expressed confidence in their translations, not only because the texts are fairly prosaic, but also because they rarely relied solely on their own knowledge of the language. Virtually all consulted other Ewe speakers. They also relied on their understanding of the context in which the text was produced to help them deduce its meaning. They consulted D. Westermann's 1928 Ewe-English dictionary, a text which has its own problems but which proved especially useful for finding the meanings of terms that are no longer in use. In the case of the oral interviews, when I asked Mensah if he was sure his translations captured all that the interviewees said, he responded by rethinking how he had translated an interview. All made decisions; all cross-checked their translations with others.

In completing their work, the translators faced a number of challenges. In his translation of the Kuku narrative, Paul Agbedor encountered a passage in which the Ewe word for sibling was used to describe Kuku's relationship with someone by the name of Adanuvor. This term, however, did not identify Adanuvor's gender. The only hint came from the text itself. Adanuvor was said to have helped Kuku's mother prepare rice for the family. Because such tasks were traditionally assigned to girls, I suggested that we avoid the awkward phrasing of continually describing Adanuvor as a sibling, but instead assume she was a girl. In the translation offered here, the English version of the text uses the term sibling, but readers will also find the pronouns "she" and "her" used in reference to Adanuvor.

The meaning of certain antiquated terms also proved elusive. Attoh, for example, was unfamiliar with the term *akla* (fried bean paste), which Tsekpo used in his biography of Famfantor. The meaning of this word was determined with the help of Kenneth Krieger, a speaker of the Anlo dialect of Ewe, and by consulting the Westermann dictionary. Certain phrases also proved to be challenging. One such phrase involved a passage in which Tsekpo described Famfantor posing a question to himself about his children. Famfantor had just determined that he could no longer trust his in-laws. This, in turn, prompted his wife's family to take her from him. Not only did his in-laws remove his wife, however, they also decided to leave him with their children. According to Tsekpo, Famfantor responded by asking himself: "*afika yeakplɔ ɖeviawo ayi mahã?*" This phrase literally means "where could I take the children?" If translated in this way, however, it would not make sense given the larger context in which this phrase was to appear in the English translation. There was no prior reference to Famfantor going anywhere or the need for him to move his children to a different location. A more appropriate translation would recognize that the locational questioning term "afika" (where is something or someone?) was used to highlight the fact that he felt the need to take his children to a place other than his own home where they could be properly cared for. Yet Famfantor could not return to the family that had enslaved him. He was not on good terms with them anymore. He also could not take them on his trading trips; they were too young. Yet he had no other family in the area. A better translation of the phrase "*afika yeakplɔ ɖeviawo ayi mahã*" would recognize that in this case the term "afika" referred not just to location but also to the question of how we would take care of his children. How was he to care for them? All this was implied in the question that Tsekpo posed about Famfantor's dilemma. Accordingly, Attoh translated the phrase to read "what will I do with the children?"

Yet another issue was faced by Jasper Ackumey, who provided the translations of the Ewe-language passages in Paul Sands's diary. Much of the diary consisted of lists of names with a few terms identifying their status and origins. But there were other passages that were more substantive and that were initially difficult to decipher because the spelling, the grammar, and the phrasing was so different from contemporary spoken or written Ewe. Ackumey used his considerable language abilities to decipher these more difficult passages.

The only other documents presented here that were translated from the Ewe language are two of the oral traditions about the village of Atorkor. These interviews, with Togbi Awusu II and Togbi Axovi, were conducted in 1988 with K. A. Mensah serving as translator. At the time these two men were interviewed, it was common practice for researchers to use a tape recorder when conducting interviews. One could always return to the tapes if one's memory or pen failed. Translations could be cross-checked. Several factors led me to eschew this particular practice, however. Some ten years earlier, in 1978–79, when I first conducted interviews in Anlo, I was forced to do so without any recording equipment. At that time the Ghana economy was in such difficult straits that it was virtually impossible to buy batteries to power a tape recorder. In addition, the area had only an intermittent electricity supply. The infrastructure simply did not permit the use of sophisticated or even basic recording equipment. Yet I conducted some wonderful interviews and made sure to go back to the same individuals over and over again to check that the information I had received had indeed been translated correctly. In light of this experience, and, perhaps even more importantly, because the topic of slavery was and still is such a sensitive topic (many informants refused to talk about slavery and the slave trade even without a tape recorder), I opted not to record the interviews I conducted in 1988. Instead I used the same techniques I employed in 1979. The interviews presented here were translated on the spot without being recorded. I trusted K. A. Mensah to provide me with an accurate rendering of the interviewees' words. Their accounts—largely factual in content—were further corroborated by other interviews (not included here).

Two of the texts in this study have been translated from German: the biography of Lydia Yawo, written by Johannes Merz, and an account penned by German missionary Carl Spiess in which he recounts in 1907 the oral information he received about the history of the town of Atorkor. The Lydia Yawo biography was translated by Anna Parkinson, a professor of German languages and literature, who has also had extensive experience doing translation work. The Carl Spiess article was translated by Rüdiger Bechstein in the 1980s, when he was an exchange student at Kalamazoo College. Like the Ewe texts, these were fairly prosaic accounts, with no literary value and largely straightforward wording. The only issue faced by both Parkinson and Bechstein was the need to familiarize themselves with the blackletter typeface of the Fraktur script. This had to be deciphered, which took a bit of work for both Parkinson and Bechstein as readers of modern German texts.

In presenting these accounts, the majority of which are translated here for the first time, it is hoped that readers will take advantage of the opportunity to see for themselves how the formerly enslaved of West Africa and their descendants—those who never left Africa—remembered and talked about their experiences with slavery, the slave trade, and its aftermaths.

A NOTE ON EWE ORTHOGRAPHY

The Ewe language has a number of letters that do not exist in the English language. These include the following:

ọ = the open sound found in the English word taught
ẉ = voiced bilabial fricative
ƒ = voiceless bilabial fricative
ḍ = a voiced retroflex stop
x = a voiceless dorsal-velar fricative, like the "ch"
ẹ = pronounced like the English long "a"

When Ewe words are written in English-language texts, however, practices vary in terms of which orthography is used. Ewe proper names are often written using the English orthography while Ewe-language phrases are written using the Ewe orthography. I follow this particular practice here. Only specific words and phrases in Ewe are rendered using the Ewe orthography. These are also italicized. With regard to proper names, I have attempted to use the most common English-language spelling.

West African
Narratives
of Slavery

Introduction

After more than forty years of sustained research, historians have learned a great deal about the trade in human beings that existed in West Africa between c. 1500 to c. 1870, the era of the Atlantic slave trade. We know that more than twelve and half million individuals were sold for export to the Americas and that countless more were enslaved within West Africa itself. We know where and how slaves were acquired and the relative importance that warfare, kidnapping, legal mechanisms, economic processes, and religious institutions played in generating an enslaved population. We know the West African trade routes that were used to transport slaves to regional and local markets. We know as well the forms of resistance employed by the enslaved and the ways West African slave buyers, sellers, and owners attempted to thwart that resistance.

Yet there is still so much we do not know. This is especially true with regard to the impact that slavery and the slave trade had on the individual. Yes, the slave narratives written by Africans transported to the Americas tell us of the anguish felt by those forcibly removed from their natal homes, the difficulties they faced when marched to distant markets, the horror and shock they experienced when confronted by the life-threatening actions of their captors.[1] We know that some individuals were in a better position to resist than others. In the end, however, as noted by the historians Raymond Dumett and Marion Johnson, each experience was ultimately a personal one, influenced not only by such factors as age at the time of enslavement, gender, and the social and political contexts in which the enslaved found themselves, but also by more personal individual circumstances.[2]

By analyzing the lives of specific individuals enslaved in West Africa, by understanding them as persons whose thoughts and actions were influenced as much by their earlier pre-enslavement experiences as by the time they spent as captives, this study attempts to expand the discussion about the impact of the slave trade and slavery on West Africa by highlighting how West Africans themselves, specifically those who never left the continent, thought about, remembered, and were prepared to discuss their lives in both slavery and freedom. How did they talk about their lives? What did they remember, and what did they choose to forget (some of which we can document using European sources from the period)? What factors peculiar to their own personal circumstances influenced the decisions they made while they were enslaved? And how did the totality of their experiences (those that took place before and after as well as during their enslavement) impact not only their own memories but also the legacies they left their descendants? Equally important, in what ways did the communities from which the enslaved came choose to commemorate or bury this aspect of their past, a history that saw villages and citizens attacked, humiliated, and enslaved?

West African Narratives of Slavery addresses these questions by analyzing five heretofore unpublished or untranslated West African texts that were produced by and about the ex-enslaved and by their descendants and neighbors between the late nineteenth and early twentieth centuries. The narratives come in a number of forms. One is a life history of a man captured and enslaved in the state of Asante in 1870, who dictated his autobiography some forty years later to a German-trained African minister with whom he shared a common language and religion. Two others are biographical accounts. These were also written by missionaries, one a German and the other West African, both of whom had become intimately familiar with the woman and the man about whose lives they wrote. The fourth is a diary, in which the writer discusses his family history and the social difficulties he and his family faced as the descendants of a war captive who had been enslaved more than two hundred years earlier in the community that had become their hometown. The fifth is an oral history, first recorded in the early 1940s, that documents as a collective community memory the kidnapping of a number of men and women by the crew of a passing European slave ship.

In analyzing these texts, I emphasize the importance of understanding the historical, literary, and cultural contexts that influenced the production of each narrative. We know, for example, that many slave narratives (those texts written by or about the formerly enslaved), whether from West Africa or elsewhere, were often recorded and edited by someone other than the individual whose life is being discussed. This is certainly the case for the first three narratives reproduced and analyzed here. In such instances, the enslaved may have shared his or her experiences with an interested listener, but it was the amanuensis, the person who recorded the words, who then selected extracts and shaped the resulting fragments into a narrative. Given this, how should we read such a text? Is it possible to separate the voice of the enslaved from that of his or her amanuensis? Or does this unraveling in some instances undermine the shared effort that was at the very heart of the collaborative production of the narrative? Where the narrative takes the form of a diary by a slave descendant, how does this particular literary form—perhaps better termed a narrative *about* slavery—influence what was said and what was not said, how it was said, and for what purpose? Equally compelling are those oral traditions that recount the loss of individual family members to enslavement. These oral texts—like their literary counterparts—recount the shock and despair that accompanied enslavement. They do so not from the perspective of the enslaved, however, but rather as remembered by those who lost a son or a daughter, a father or a mother, to the trade. But why did they remember in some instances but forget in others? We know, for example, that Britain abolished the slave trade in 1807, but in West Africa during much of the rest of the nineteenth century, the danger of capture and enslavement still infused a range of everyday activities. Warfare persisted. Kidnapping was common. A visit to distant relatives, travel to one's farm, a business transaction gone awry, could well lead to a life in slavery. But not all such incidents were remembered many years later in the oral traditions of the communities from which the kidnapped came. Why? Why were some kidnappings remembered and others forgotten? What factors encouraged the retention of certain memories but the forgetting of others? To answer these questions, I read the five narratives examined here as texts that are far from transparent. They do indeed tell us a great deal about the individual experience of enslavement in West Africa and how West Africans talked about its impact on their lives. But they also reveal that how memories were recorded must be taken into consideration when examining why certain memories were recalled, why others were forgotten, and why some memories were reconfigured to meet the needs of the present. The texts examined here speak to these issues. They provide us with the opportunity to explore the cultural, literary, and historical contexts that produced in the late nineteenth and early twentieth centuries a particular discursive terrain that allowed for the discussion of a topic that most West Africans were (and in many instances are still) not prepared to discuss openly.

*   *   *

Slave narratives—defined here as oral and written texts produced by or in collaboration with the (formerly) enslaved and their descendants about their experiences with the institution of slavery—have long been an important source of information for scholars of African slavery. In 1975, 1983, and 1993, Marcia Wright and Edward Alpers analyzed seven different slave narratives to obtain a better understanding of how the experiences of enslaved women were similar to but also different from that of enslaved men.[3] Others have since followed suit. In 2000 and 2002, for example, Peter Haenger, John Hunwick, and Eve Troutt Powell republished and analyzed several slave narratives from West and North Africa to illustrate how the enslaved themselves remembered the plight of those who were castrated or otherwise physically abused, how those who had been forced into bondage were compelled to engage in the most life-threatening of tasks, and how they continued to suffer the stigma of their slave origins even after they had gained their freedom.[4] Aware that these texts were also necessarily affected by the contexts in which they were recorded, the analyses of these narratives almost always included a discussion of how the narratives were recorded and by whom. In his study of the narrative of Swema, a woman enslaved in mid-nineteenth-century east-central Africa, for example, Alpers noted that her narrative was recorded in Swahili only months after the events documented in her account took place. The text eventually came into the hands of the French missionary Père Anton Horner, who then translated the Swahili narrative into French. In doing so, however, he also rewrote it to "conform to mid-nineteenth century French literary conventions." Its publication was then subsequently managed by yet another person, Monsignor J. Gaume of Paris, who in turn made his own modifications to the text, "frequently changing words and adding and deleting passages in Swema's testimony, while also supplementing it with a considerable amount of linking text between chapters that did not exist in the original manuscript." His purpose: "to give the book added dramatic effect." In discussing the impact of these interventions—the translation from Swahili to French, the structuring to conform to current literary fashion, and the subsequent emendations and deletions—Alpers emphasized that still "there seems to be no basis for questioning the essential reliability of her recorded testimony."[5] Haenger, Wright, and Hunwick and Powell have taken the same approach. They acknowledge that the contexts in which the narratives they analyze were produced may have shaped them in profound ways, but their primary focus has been on verifying their historicity and reliability. They use documentary and oral sources to confirm that the wars described in a particular narrative—conflicts that saw numerous men, women, and children enslaved—did indeed take place at a particular time, that the slaves were transported along one route rather than another, and that the death toll along the route was indeed exacerbated by a drought that we know afflicted the area at the time the slave was transported through that district. But does such an emphasis really allow us to open a window onto the experiences of enslavement from the perspective of the enslaved? I think not.[6]

Studies by scholars of North American slave narratives suggest that one can obtain this more intimate understanding of the slave experience by reading in different ways the very kinds of texts found in West Africa. In order to do this, however, one must take into consideration a set of issues quite different from those that have traditionally informed studies of African slave narratives. They insist, for example, that in reading such texts, one must be particularly attentive to the political and discursive contexts of the times in which slave testimonies were recorded. In her book *The African American Slave Narrative*, for example, Audrey Fisch notes that North American slave narratives published between the 1770s and 1830s were often modeled on popular spiritual autobiographies and conversion narratives. With the rise during this same period of an organized antislavery movement, however, the authors of slave narratives began to be more open in their demands that readers treat Africans as fellow human beings, as emphasized in the more secular writings of Enlightenment thinkers. The 1830s and 1840s saw yet another shift. Slave narratives increasingly emphasized the veracity of the "evidence" they presented in condemnation of the institution of slavery. They did so because of attacks launched by Southern slaveholders who argued that the narratives were fictional.[7] After the abolition of slavery and the end of the Civil War, slave narratives continued to reflect the changing political and economic landscape of North America. "Since ex-slaves no longer needed to denounce slavery to white America," noted William L. Andrews, "the stories of their past no longer carried the same social and moral import." Instead new times demanded a different focus. "The turn-of-the-century American 'scientific' racism, which stereotyped 'the Negro' as degraded, ignorant, incompetent, and servile, demanded that slavery be represented anew, not as a condition of deprivation and degradation, but as a period of training and testing, from which the slave graduated with high honors and even higher ambitions. . . . [For] the slave past, if effectively represented, could provide the freedman and freedwoman with credentials that the new industrial-capitalist order might respect. . . . The agenda of the postbellum slave narrative thus emphasize[d] unabashedly the tangible contribution that blacks made to the South, in and after slavery, in order to rehabilitate the image of the freedman . . . in the eyes of business America."[8]

These observations about the impact of the prevailing discourses of the time on slave narratives do more than simply situate the narrative in its literary context. They also highlight the extent to which the larger cultural and historical landscape shaped the very terms by which the formerly enslaved and their descendants, as well as their amanuenses, made sense of the enslavement experiences. Equally emphasized in the analysis of North American slave narratives are the circumstances surrounding the interview. How much time did a person live in enslavement and when: as a child, into adulthood? In what ways might this have affected what was remembered and what was forgotten? Was the interview recorded verbatim or edited and summarized by the interviewer?

Who was the interviewer and how did his or her identity, interests, and biases affect what the former slave said and did not say?[9] Knowing these details places one in a better position to understand not only *what* someone experienced in slavery but also why certain experiences were discussed and others were not, what local discursive norms influenced how they were prepared to describe their experiences, and the extent to which their voices were muffled, intertwined with, or unaffected by the editorial hand of the amanuensis.

In analyzing the three slave narratives presented here, I employ the many methods developed by historians of African slavery to determine their veracity and what the narratives can tell us about the individual experience of slavery in West Africa. But I also draw quite heavily upon the insights of scholars of North American slavery, especially those that involve the analysis of mediated texts (those that were edited and structured by an amanuensis). In chapter 1, for example, I use a variety of sources to verify the historicity of the events described by Aaron Kuku in his life history. I locate his now-extinct home village of Petewu. I date his capture and reconstruct the painful details of the forced march he endured to Asante. I familiarize myself with the history of the rubber trade in southeastern Ghana to verify his claim that he was indeed in a position to accumulate enough funds from the collection of this commodity to redeem his mother from slavery more than twenty years after they were separated from each other. But I also explore the discursive contexts that influenced both the content and structure of the narratives presented in this study. In my discussion of the biography of Lydia Yawo, a text written in 1877 by Bremen missionary Johannes Merz, for example, I note that Merz—like other Europeans during this period—was deeply influenced by the racist attitudes about Africans that existed at the time. He described the culture into which Lydia was born as "primitive" and inherently violence-prone. Lydia herself he depicted as "fearful" and childlike, who could only be brought to a state of "civilization" by being converted to Christianity. Late nineteenth-century European attitudes about Africans were not the only factors that influenced Merz's narrative, however. As a Christian missionary writing about Lydia to a German Christian audience and as an author who sought to use Lydia's story as a means of recruiting more women missionaries to the field, he opted to write about Lydia's experiences using the genres that were both familiar to and popular with his readers. One was the conversion narrative, the same genre that had deeply influenced eighteenth-century North American slave narratives. Merz would have certainly been intimately familiar with this form. Although its popularity had significantly waned in much of Europe and America by the late nineteenth century, many within Europe—especially those associated with the Pietist faith practiced by the Bremen Mission—considered the conversion narrative central to their self-understanding. Merz, in fact, had been required to pen his own spiritual autobiography before he was accepted as an employee of the mission. So in constructing Lydia's biography, he deployed the same template he himself had used for his own life history. He documented her fitful struggle to move from a state of "error to truth." He emphasized Lydia's movement from living in a state of sin to one of forgiveness."[10]

The conversion narrative was not the only literary form that influenced the way Merz chose to structure his biography. An additional influence appears to have been the captivity narrative. This was a popular literary form that had circulated in Europe and the United States since the late seventeenth century and that had also influenced North American slave narratives.[11] Using the conventions of this genre, Merz described how Lydia was "abruptly brought from a state of protected innocence [and ignorance] to confrontation with the evil of slavery." He documented the suffering she experienced at having to live a "forced existence in an alien society," and he suggested to his readers that her difficult life experiences were critical for her "moral and spiritual" development. By recognizing how Merz used the narrative for his own purposes, by understanding the degree to which he was influenced by contemporary European attitudes about Africa and Africans, by acknowledging the influence of certain discursive forms on his construction of Lydia Yawo's biography, we are better able to differentiate what Lydia opted to share of her experiences with Johannes Merz from how Merz himself manipulated her voice for his own ends.

Unlike Lydia Yawo's biography, the life history of Aaron Kuku and the biography of Yosef Famfantor were written not by Europeans but by Africans, in this case, the Bremen missionary–trained ministers the Revs. Samuel Quist and G. K. Tsekpo, respectively. Having been educated in the same literary traditions as their German missionary colleagues, Quist and Tsekpo were as deeply influenced by captivity and conversion narratives as was Merz. And like Merz, they sought to use the narratives they recorded in support of their faith. Their identities as Africans, however, made them more familiar with and sympathetic to the culture and potential of the individuals whose life histories they recorded. Both Quist and Tsekpo had been born and raised within the Ewe culture of their subjects. Both considered the individuals whose lives they depicted in their texts as not only fellow Christians but also friends and neighbors. One sees no evidence on their part of feelings of cultural, religious, or educational superiority. Instead they exhibited a clear interest in allowing the voices of the formerly enslaved to be heard with minimal mediation. This is particularly evident in how Quist opted to document Aaron Kuku's life history. Kuku described to Quist the number of times in his life he became so despondent he seriously contemplated suicide. The first incident occurred when he was enslaved. He tried to hang himself and was almost successful. This attempt was subsequently followed by five other incidents of suicidal ideation. Quist recorded them all and included them in the narrative he wrote about Kuku's life. When a German colleague published an edited and abridged version for his audience in Germany, however, most of these suicidal episodes were omitted so as not to undermine the notion that Africans were capable of being good Christians and would never contemplate such a sinful act so many times.[12] Quist, on the other hand, writing for an Ewe audience, understood that Ewe discursive norms allowed one to speak more openly about suicide, whether the topic was presented as evidence-based reportage or as a rhetorical device. In constructing Kuku's narrative, Quist's identity as an African familiar with and accepting of local discursive norms certainly influenced how he presented Kuku's account of his own life.

The narratives produced by Quist and Tsekpo are also more revealing in their portrayal of the African family. Their German missionary predecessor, Johannes Merz, used his biography of former slave Lydia Yawo to emphasize her motherly and wifely devotion to counter the racist stereotypes prevalent in late nineteenth-century Germany about the lack of affective bonds within African families, beliefs to which he himself did not subscribe. Quist and Tsekpo—writing in the 1920s—felt no such compunction to use their own narratives in this way.

They were certainly aware of European racism and the damage such attitudes could inflict on West Africans. They and their fellow Bremen-trained, Ewe-speaking ministers had already had firsthand experience with racism as a result of their interactions with the mission. Quist, for example, had been among the few Ewe-speaking West Africans who had been selected to receive additional training in Germany. He studied in the Bremen Mission's school in Westheim, Germany, between 1890 and 1894, with the hope of taking greater leadership in the mission. But, as noted by the historian Werner Ustorf, the head of the Bremen Mission, Michael Zahn, who had authorized the training of West Africans in Europe, "was completely singled-minded in his insistence that the 'cultural stage' of the [Africans] still did not go far enough for them to undertake the evangelization of Africa independently: the white missionary was not only indispensable long-term, but was, like Germans in general, . . . 'more talented that the blacks.'" The school instead was simply to produce better "missionary helpers" who could do "what we expect . . . to obey and serve." Some of the German missionaries posted to West Africa with whom Quist and Tsekpo had to work regularly raised questions about the "cleanliness of the German [educated] Ewes." Others believed Africans were particularly prone to moral lapses and that it would take several generations before they could be considered the equals of their European brethren. Such attitudes influenced disciplinary decisions. If a European missionary was discovered having engaged in inappropriate sexual behavior, information about the incident was squashed and the offender reassigned, often to the United States. If an African worker affiliated with the mission was accused of similar indiscretions, he was simply dismissed.[13] These attitudes were certainly felt by the West Africans affiliated with the mission. Quist actively objected to such beliefs and practices and as a result quickly gained the reputation among his European colleagues and superiors as arrogant and resistant to European supervision. Only with the outbreak of World War One did Quist and his colleague have the opportunity to assume the leadership roles that they had long been denied.

Between 1914 and 1918, troops from the British and French colonies of the Gold Coast and Dahomey, respectively, expelled all the German missionaries affiliated with the Bremen Mission. This left the one Bremen missionary still resident in West Africa, Swiss-born mission head Ernst Bürgi, no choice but to ordain a number of Africans to take the place of those who had been expelled. Quist was among this group. After receiving his ordination in 1915, he quickly assumed a leadership role in the church, taking particular responsibility for revising the church's congregational orders to meet the needs of the now African-led denomination.[14] He also deepened his involvement in the educational activities of the church, redirecting its efforts to meet a set of goals now defined largely by his African colleagues.[15]

These goals—while deeply influenced by the Bremen Mission's emphasis on local-language education—emphasized the ability of Africans (and not just Europeans) to serve as exemplary Christians whose lives could serve as models to be followed by others.[16] It was in this context that Quist recorded the life history of Aaron Kuku. Written in the Ewe language to address a local West African audience, Quist intended his narrative to be used, in part, by the African-run schools of the late 1920s and 1930s to encourage students to recognize and respect one of their own as a devout Christian, whose life experiences offered important lessons. He gave particular attention to the nature of family relations, not to counter European racist notions but to emphasize the importance of family and the need to understand how those who were respected in their communities had chosen to lead their lives under circumstances that were not always loving and supportive. In describing Aaron Kuku's life, for example, Quist made sure he included in his narrative evidence of the affection Kuku had for his wife and mother. Quist's German missionary colleague did the same in his own edited and abridged version of Kuku's life history. But Quist described as well the disagreements and compromises that also characterized Kuku's marriage. More important than countering European racism was the need, in Quist's mind, to show his West

African audience how they could successfully manage family relations in all their complexity. Tsekpo did the same. In his biography of the former slave Yosef Famfantor, he included the fact that Famfantor had great difficulty forgiving his family for having selected him, rather than another relative, to serve as a debt slave on their behalf. Family relations were complex. But it was only Quist and Tsekpo—not their German missionary colleagues—who felt able to represent the full reality of their informants' domestic lives.

Understanding the extent to which the cultural attitudes and concerns of those who recorded and edited slave narratives could influence the content of the texts they published is certainly important for understanding any slave narrative. But other questions remain. What can we really know about an individual former slave's perspective on his or her own life given the extent to which that person's story bears the imprint of another's editing and structuration, no matter who that recorder was? Can one disentangle the voice of the formerly enslaved from that of his amanuensis? This question—addressed only in limited ways by scholars of Africa in their analyses of slave narratives by Africans who never left Africa[17]—has been given considerable attention in studies of North American slave narratives. Written in the many hundreds beginning as early as 1760 and collected through 1938 as part of the Federal Writers' Project of the Works Progress Administration, American slave narratives have become central to the historical analysis of U.S. slavery and the slave trade. Scrutinized throughout the nineteenth and twentieth centuries first for their historical accuracy, they have since become central to our understanding of the experience of being captured and enslaved in Africa, shipped to the Americas, being sold at auction, and forced to make a life on particular plantations and farms, in different regions, during different time periods. Perhaps most important, they have allowed historians to hear the voices of the enslaved over the otherwise overwhelming documentary record produced by owners, sellers, and interested observers. In 1987, however, John Sekora questioned the extent to which so many of these narratives should be understood as texts that truly reflected the individual, the ex-slave, in possession of his or her own life story. He argued, for example, that even though a number of narratives were written in the first person as autobiographies, they were in fact narrated to an amanuensis (often anonymous) who then structured them to become vehicles for purposes defined not by the narrator but by the recorder. Thus, he argued, in many if not most mediated narratives "the selfhood and individuality" of the ex-slave narrator is "deliberately suppressed; the voice of the [recorder] is . . . [the dominant] voice . . . the slave [voice] remain[s] silent."[18]

Sekora's understanding of how one should read slave narratives has not gone unchallenged. In 1990, Angelo Constanzo agreed with Sekora that there are indeed "enormous difficulties . . . encountered whenever scholars attempt to analyze and evaluate slave autobiographies." Issues of self-censorship, the extent to which recorders may have sought to elicit from the narrator only those events that supported the intended purpose of the life story, the fact that it is the recorder who actually did the writing, the editing, and the structuring of the work, all this makes it difficult to see such a text as truly reflective of the way the narrator understood his or her own life experiences.[19] But he also goes on to argue that it is nevertheless possible through careful reading to detect what story the narrator was attempting to communicate. Thus he notes:

> it must have been a heady experience for a slave or ex-slave to be asked to tell his or her story for general use and possible publication in the service of noble causes such as the abolition of slavery, the furtherance of religious conduct, or the humanitarian claims that black men and women are the moral equals of white persons. Because of this exhilarating once-in-a-lifetime experience, the black autobiographers would want to impart an honest and accurate message about the understanding they had of significant, and many times, shocking events. Thus, within the limits of inner and outer censorship . . . the narrators attempted through various implicit or hidden maneuvers to give the true meaning of their lives.[20]

Constanzo's claims are based on his reading of a number of Caribbean slave narratives, in which he detects efforts on the part of the slave or ex-slave narrators to confound the prevailing image of Africa and Africans by presenting a portrait of Africa as culturally advanced and its inhabitants as capable of exercising unusual restraint in the face of provocation.[21] What he does not consider, however, is that the narrator, the slave or ex-slave, might have been able to influence openly the presentation of his or her own story despite his or her amanuensis. As argued by Dwight McBride, one can certainly look for hidden signs embedded in a narrative written and structured by an amanuensis, but one must also be aware that the slave or ex-slave, in presenting his or her story, might have structured it in ways that involved using the amanuensis to achieve their *own* ends.[22]

I use these insights, derived as they are from studies of American slave narratives, to analyze the educated African–recorded ex-slave narratives that exist from West Africa. In examining the life history of Aaron Kuku, for example, I note that Kuku's amanuensis, Samuel Quist, while highly educated in comparison with Kuku, nevertheless spoke the same language as Kuku (even if they communicated in different dialects of the Ewe language) and shared the same faith (Christianity). Born only about seven years apart, they were intimately familiar with the late nineteenth-century and early twentieth-century local cultures and times that had shaped both their lives. In fact, it is *because* they had so much in common and were known to have been quite good friends for a number of years that we get such a full account of what Kuku understood to be the defining moments of his life, as well as the emotions he expressed while recalling these events. Yet they were also different. Quist was from the much more cosmopolitan coastal town of Keta; Kuku was from the rural Liati village of Petewu, about 150 kilometers away. Kuku had only sixteen days of formal education and never learned to write. Quist had been trained not only in the North German Missionary Society (Bremen Mission) primary schools but also had attended the local seminary and then received, as mentioned earlier, further training in Germany at the Bremen Mission's Westheim School. In the end it was Quist, not Kuku, who edited and structured for possible publication Kuku's life history. Accordingly, in my analysis of Aaron Kuku's life history and the other mediated texts presented here, I emphasize the point that knowing the identities and concerns of both the narrators and the recorders is critical for understanding them as texts that are, yes, the product of multiple forces and voices. But they are also ones that allow us to see how the enslaved understood and spoke about their own experiences.

*   *   *

Self-authored texts, in comparison with mediated narratives, are far less problematic in terms of our ability to hear the voices of those directly victimized by the institution of slavery. Yet they too have their own complexities. Take, for example, diaries. Felicity Nussbaum, Dan Doll, and Jessica Munns have noted that this particular genre—although ostensibly the recording of everyday events—presents quite complicated "representations of reality." They are frequently "'composed' days, weeks and even months after the date they were entered." They are "personal reflections . . . [that must be understood as texts] informed at every level by ideologies of self, state, religion and sense of the world." On reading a diary, one must ask who wrote it, for what purpose, and under what influences. How truly representative is it of the larger times and the thoughts and feelings that many felt during the period? How much is it a document of self-justification? How much is it simply a personal recording of events and experiences?[23] Similar questions can be raised about oral histories and traditions. How much does a particular account accurately represent the past, having often been collected not just weeks and months, but in many instances decades after the events discussed? How have the circumstances under which an oral text was collected impacted what was said and what was not? How have such memories been affected not only by the time and circumstances when they were recorded but also by the changes in the way the individuals who retained these memories understood themselves and the world? I address these questions in my analysis of the diary of Paul Sands and of a West African oral tradition about the kidnapping and enslavement of a number of people from the coastal town of Atorkor. I verify the historicity of the events and discuss the historical, social, economic, and political context in which the texts were recorded. I note how peculiar or representative the issues raised by these documents were at the time the diarist wrote about them.

Equally important for reading these two documents, Sands's diary and the Atorkor oral tradition, however, is that neither can be defined as a slave narrative. The author of the diary, Paul Sands, was never enslaved himself. He was instead the descendant of a slave. It was his great-grandmother—not him, not his father or mother, not even his grandparents, but a relative three generations removed—who had been forced into bondage. Not only was he not a slave, he was part of a larger family that defined itself by the number of slaves they themselves owned. Would it not be better to understand this text as an example of the narratives written by wealthy West Africans who took slaveholding for granted, who understood their possession of human chattel as central to their social status and essential for the running of their households and business activities? This is certainly one way to read this text, but I include Sands's diary in this collection because it has a lot to say about how the institution of slavery continued to impact how slave descendants in Africa saw themselves and how this self-understanding, in turn, could influence the way such individuals chose to operate in the world after abolition. Britain officially abolished slavery in the West African territories it claimed as colonies in 1874. These territories included the coastal district of Keta, where Paul Sands was born and raised. Abolition, however, did not extinguish the social stigma locals had long attached to those of slave descent. Distinctions remained. In most families and communities, certain members were considered more equal than others because of the status of their ancestors. Families who held chieftaincy positions often gave priority to appointing someone from among their ranks who was free of the taint of slave origins. During this same period, the late nineteenth century, when Sands began his diary, the institution of slavery also had a profound effect on inheritance decisions. A husband/master might stipulate before his death that the children of his enslaved wives inherit much more of his property than those whose mothers were free, in part because they—unlike their free siblings—had no maternal families to whom they could turn after his death. Thus slavery lived on well after its abolition, not as an active and growing institution but as a hidden thread in the social ranking and inheritance systems of many West African communities. The social and psychic toll this stigma could inflict on slave descendants was great. Paul Sands's diary is a perfect illustration of this fact. In sharing his memories about his childhood, he wrote about the anguish he felt when teased as a child for being the descendant of a slave. From his diary, we also know that one of the ways he sought to handle this stigma was by clearly distinguishing himself and the other free members of his family from those who were of more recent slave origin. It is these concerns, so evident in the diary of Paul Sands, that make his text an important narrative about slavery.

Similar considerations explain my inclusion of an oral tradition from the Ewe-speaking town of Atorkor in this collection of narratives. According to this tradition, several citizens of the village of Atorkor were kidnapped after they boarded a slave ship to provide musical entertainment for the crew. Instead of being paid for their performance, they were instead shackled and taken away to be sold in the Americas. In remembering this incident, the citizens of Atorkor did not voice the concerns of those who were kidnapped. They never saw their friends and neighbors again. In this oral tradition, we find no voices of the enslaved or even those of their descendants. Rather, what we have is a community remembering the enslavement of its own. It was a loss followed by shock, anger, and then retribution against those who were considered complicit in the kidnapping. It tells of an experience not from the perspective of the enslaved but from those who were left behind. By including it here, we can better understand that enslavement was not simply an individual or family experience but one that so affected communities that the experience could become embedded in their collective memory of themselves.[24]

*   *   *

The format of this book is fairly straightforward. It consists of four parts organized by genre. The first part focuses on a life history. The second explores two biographies. The third part focuses on a diary, while the fourth examines an oral tradition. Each section begins with an analytical essay that focuses on a range of issues and questions that I believe are important to consider when reading the narrative(s) that follow. For example, in part 1--which focuses on the life history of Aaron Kuku—I begin by outlining the basic story line of the narrative. I then explore a number of questions that have been of particular concern to scholars of slavery. Who was Aaron Kuku, really, this former slave who dictated his life history to another, and how did his background and interests later in life influence what he shared with his amanuensis, Samuel Quist, forty years after he was enslaved? Who was Samuel Quist? And how did Quist's background influence the way he structured Kuku's narrative? To what extent can we disentangle Kuku's voice from Quist's? Or should we also consider the possibility that they actually shared a set of common concerns and perspectives that negate the necessity to totally distinguish one voice from the other? I address these questions, but I do not end there. I also explore a set of issues that are of concern to historians of slavery in particular. How should we understand Kuku's escape from slavery, his six experiences with suicide or suicidal ideation, his efforts to free his mother, how he remembered his captors? Can his life story tell us something about the more general experience of enslavement in West Africa? I argue that it can, that through this narrative we obtain a much better understanding of how enslaved West Africans who never left West Africa remembered, talked about, and experienced life in slavery.

In part 2, I address a different set of questions. In exploring the biographies of Lydia Yawo and Yosef Famfantor, I discuss the challenges and opportunities associated with the task of unearthing the thoughts and feelings of subjects whose life stories have already been filtered through the particular prisms of their biographers. I then focus more specifically on the question of why Famfantor opted to remain in the area where he was enslaved, only choosing many years later to return to his natal home. I explore as well why Lydia Yawo opted to stay with her husband/master until she died even though she had been freed by him. Critical to the analyses of these two narratives is an exploration of gender dynamics and the role that both past and more recent experiences with family, friends, and the local political and economic environment played in influencing their decisions (and no doubt the decisions of others who were enslaved) about whether to stay or to return to their natal homes after they obtained their freedom. These narratives, I argue, help us understand how truly individual were the decisions made by the formerly enslaved when they were faced with a variety of choices and opportunities.

Part 3, which focuses on the diary of Paul Sands, begins with an analysis of the role diaries played in late nineteenth-century and early twentieth-century West Africa. After situating Paul Sands's journal within this local literary tradition, I move on to explore the social, political, religious, and cultural events that influenced his life as well as his family and community. I demonstrate that the chronicle of events detailed in Sands's diary allows us to see how his spoken and written command of both English and the Ewe language allowed him to simultaneously position himself among the social, political, and economic elite within his hometown while managing the stigma of his slave origins. That the content of his diary has continued to be a source of embarrassment for his late twentieth-century descendants is indicative, I argue, of the continuing legacy of slavery in West Africa.

In part 4, I begin my discussion of an oral tradition from the southeastern Anlo community of Atorkor by describing the c. 1850 kidnapping of a number

of its citizens by the crew of a passing slave ship. I then question why this particular incident was remembered when other kidnappings (described in a
number of European accounts from this same period and in individual family
histories) have been forgotten in the communities where they occurred. I argue
that a number of factors facilitated the retention of this incident in the collective memory of the residents of Atorkor and its neighboring villages. Among
the factors discussed are the recentness of the event and, more importantly, the
usefulness of this oral history to local ministers associated with the U.S.-based,
Negro-organized African Methodist Episcopal (AME) Zion Church. I describe
how local African AME Zion ministers—struggling to compete with the Bremen Mission and the Catholic Church, both of which had already established
churches and schools in the area well before the AME Zion denomination
moved into the area—appropriated and disseminated a modified version of the
Atorkor tradition when they discovered that the race rhetoric they had previously deployed as part of their evangelical campaign failed to win followers. In
arguing that the kidnapped Atorkor residents didn't just disappear but rather
gave birth to the Negroes who later founded the AME Zion Church, the African ministers affiliated with this denomination popularized and disseminated
an oral history account that would later transform the very identity of many
rural Anlos. Instead of understanding themselves solely as members of a particular village or town, those exposed to the tradition came to see themselves
as part of a larger worldwide African Diaspora.

The five narratives of slavery featured in this study are among the few texts
that highlight the lives of those in West Africa who both experienced and
talked about the institution of slavery and its afterlife. For unlike North American slave narratives—which number more than six thousand as autobiographical texts alone—West African narratives are rare. Most of the formerly enslaved remained illiterate their entire lives and never had the opportunity to
pen their own autobiographies, and only a few encountered others interested
enough to record their stories. No doubt many more shared their experiences
with family and friends, but the lingering traces of such memories have been
difficult to access. After abolition, many of the formerly enslaved, and perhaps
more critically their descendants, opted to forget what they considered to be an
ignoble past. With each passing generation, memories faded. This situation has
made the few existing West African slave narratives all the more precious as
texts that should be made available to others for study. In keeping with this
concern, I have included after each analytical essay the texts of the slave narratives that are the subject of each section. Each slave narrative, in turn, is preceded by a preface that places the events discussed in the text in chronological
order or describes issues associated with the editing of the texts.

By placing the various chapters within each section in this order—an introductory analytical essay, followed by a preface to the slave narrative, and then the narrative itself—I hope to provide the reader with the tools necessary to engage in an informed reading of the five different West African narratives of slavery presented here. As texts, they allow us an unprecedented opportunity to understand how those who were directly affected by the institution of slavery in West Africa remembered, thought about, talked about, and remained silent about slavery and the slave trade.

Part 1

Aaron Kuku:
The Life History
of a Former Slave

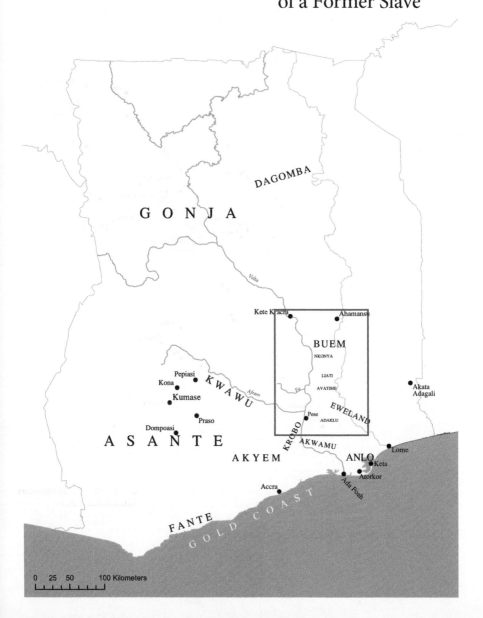

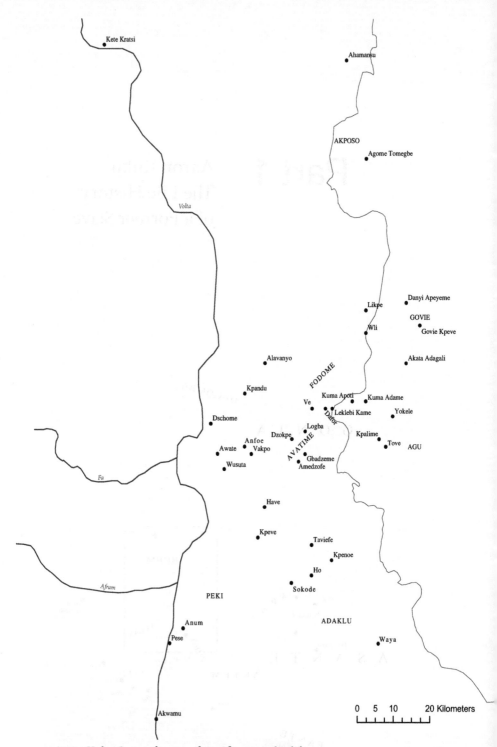

Aaron Kuku: Some of towns of significance in his life

1. Enslavement Remembered

In 1929, the Ewe Evangelical Church minister Samuel Quist recorded the life history of Aaron Kuku, an evangelist who had been enslaved by the Asante more than fifty years earlier, in 1870.[1] Captured as a child, Kuku related to Quist memories of his enslavement, his relocation to Asante, where he had two different masters, and his eventual escape and return to his hometown of Petewu some sixteen years later. Kuku's experience was far from unique, however. Thousands had been captured during the Asante's 1869 to 1871 campaign east of the Volta.[2] This group included the Basel missionaries Ramseyer and Kühne as well as the French trader M. Bonnat, all of whom wrote vivid accounts of their experiences.[3] Kuku's narrative—while of little literary value—is, however, quite unusual. It is one of the few life histories recorded in West Africa that documents the experiences of someone who was enslaved but not exported to the Americas. Like the East and Central African slave narratives collected and published by Marcia Wright and Edward Alpers, Kuku's account tells us a great deal about the enslavement experience: who was captured, when and how; the fear and terror that accompanied not only one's capture but also the suffering and humiliation endured during the transfer to a new home; the uncertainty and unpredictability of life for first-generation slaves that could have significant psychological impacts on the enslaved.[4] But Kuku's narrative does more than this. It raises fascinating questions about the discursive terrain that shaped both the content and the character of the narrative. Why would a former slave want to share his life history with a missionary? Why did Kuku's amanuensis, Samuel Quist, have an interest in recording this life history, and what purposes did the narrative serve?

AARON KUKU AND THE REVEREND SAMUEL QUIST: A GUIDED COLLABORATION

Aaron Kuku first came to the attention of the Bremen Mission c. 1900 when he converted to Christianity after hearing two local traveling missionaries preach in the area. In responding to the Christian message he heard, Kuku was not unlike many Ewe-speaking individuals during this period. As the historian H. Debrunner and anthropologist Birgit Meyer have noted, "after the Asante wars, confidence in the tribal guardian spirits was a good deal shaken. . . . The new religion provided new ideal orientations and material prospects in a situation of crisis."[5] What was unusual was that Kuku also agreed to relate in remarkable detail his life history to Rev. Quist. Why he did so and why his amanuensis was interested in recording the narrative probably had to do with their close friendship, Kuku's deep interest in education, and Quist's role in deciding, as a leader of the Ewe Evangelical Church and its schools, what materials should be adopted. Texts such as local Ewe fables and proverbs had long been used in the local schools run first by the North German Missionary Society (the Bremen Mission), and then later from 1922 by its African-run successor, the Ewe Evangelical Church with which Quist was affiliated. But the autobiographical statements that the Bremen Mission and then the Ewe church encouraged its members to write about their own spiritual development had never been incorporated into the curriculum. The Bremen Mission had published spiritual biographies of its Christian

Evangelist Aaron Kuku, 1929.
Courtesy of Norddeutsche
Mission.

Aaron Kuku's amanuensis, Samuel Quist (center), with fellow ministers Robert Baeta and Isaak Kwadzo sometime after 1917. Courtesy of Norddeutsche Mission.

African converts and associates in the 1860s. These, however, were written in German and printed in the Bremen Mission's publications largely to enlighten their supporters in Germany. Little of this kind of material had been produced in the Ewe language for a local audience.[6] Yet if biographies, autobiographies, and life histories were developed, they could serve as models for the kind of life church members were expected to lead. Thus in 1929 and 1930, the Ewe Evangelical Church began to produce Ewe-language studies of notable Ewe-speaking Christians that could be used to encourage others to lead an exemplary Christian life. Quist's work with Kuku was part of this initiative.

The production of Kuku's life history was clearly a collaborative effort. Without Kuku's cooperation, there would have been no narrative at all. Still, it was Quist who structured the interviews and who then recorded and edited Kuku's life history. Using as one of his templates the autobiographical conversion narratives that both the Bremen Mission and the Ewe Evangelical Church required of its church leaders, Quist organized Kuku's life story along lines commonly found in this centuries-old genre. At the heart of such narratives are "the progress of the protagonist from an original situation through a moral transformation to a final situation."[7] In Kuku's narrative, we see him as a child in his home village of Petewu, from which he was torn to suffer all manner of hardships: war, capture, enslavement, starvation, re-enslavement, social ostracism, and family loss. Only at the end does he convert to Christianity, for at this point Kuku has reached his goal, "the recovery of [the] right relationship with God." Conversion and captivity narratives (genres that had been popular in Europe and America for centuries and to which Quist may have been exposed while a student either in the Bremen schools in West Africa or in the Westheim School in Germany) appear to have been only one of the influences on how Quist opted to structure the narrative. Local West African tales about narrow escapes may have been equally influential.[8] Whatever the influences, Quist's editorial hand is clear. This is perhaps most evident from the dates that appear in the narrative.

Throughout the narrative, Kuku is said to have provided dates and time periods for the major events in his life. He estimated 1861 as his birth date. He speculated that he was about eight or nine years of age when he was captured and that he spent three years after his escape from slavery wandering about with his father before finally crossing the Volta to be enslaved for another nine years in the Ewe-speaking town of Anfoe. He recalled assuming the office of "chief" in his home village of Petewu five years after his uncle's death. He converted to Christianity three years after assuming the chieftancy.

This effort at dating raises a number of questions because accounts of Kuku describe him as largely illiterate in 1929, the time he narrated his life history. He could read the Ewe Bible, but he could not write in Ewe or German. He had had only sixteen days of classroom instruction. And while he certainly operated in a colonial world in which dates were important, he like most other illiterate Ewes would not have known, without some assistance, what month or year they were born. What then are we to make of this dating?

Certainly the Ewe did have a variety of means of keeping track of time. Kuku mentioned his mother recalling he was born about a year or two after the 1862 earthquake that shook the region. In 1894, the Bremen missionary Carl Spiess described additional means by which the Ewe calculated time. He noted that although the Ewe lived without calendars or clocks, they knew "exactly how many days they have spent [at a particular] place . . . the borrower knows exactly when to pay back [a loan] . . . arrival time[s] were always fairly exact." Using notches on a stick, marks on a wall, or corn kernels placed in a basket, individuals calculated the days that elapsed while resident in a particular location or when to return to collect a sick relative from a local healer, and they regularly calculated what time of day it was by the height of the sun in the sky.[9] Months were calculated according to the cycles of the moon; the passage of time in years was noted according to the agricultural calendar: "When [we] have cut the bush and then cut it a second time, [we] know that one year has turned around."[10] Kuku remembers that he and his father used one of these very counting systems, in this case sticks, to calculate how much time had elapsed since their escape. Unfortunately, when crossing the Afram River to return home, these were lost. Presumably he and his father started their time counting anew, for Kuku continues to indicate how many days were spent in one place or another after their river crossing. But would he have remembered these calculations so many years after the event? Kuku was captured by the Asante in their 1870 campaign in the Kpandu/Fodome area, and he did not relate his life history to Quist until 1929, almost sixty years after he was captured. Particular traumatic events would have certainly been easily recalled, but would he remember lengths of time spent in one place or another when the calendar system used for a portion of that time had been lost? How was Kuku able to know that he had spent exactly 108 months (nine years) enslaved in Anfoe when the Ewe simply did not calculate time according to Western notions of solar months and years? In the discussions that elicited the information Kuku included in his narrative, did Quist work with Kuku to make these particular calculations? Probably. For, as noted, Kuku attended school late in life for only sixteen days, and although he acquired in that time enough basic reading skills to read the Ewe Bible, he never learned any of the other skills associated with literacy: writing or the recording of dates according to the Western calendar. Thus it is unlikely he would have been able to provide the dates included in his narrative even if he had a particularly remarkable memory. That "The Life History of Aaron Kuku" was a collaborative effort is clear. The extensive use of Western dates is a testament to that fact. But as the narrator of his own life, Kuku made sure it also reflected his own interests and perspectives.

AARON KUKU AS LIFE HISTORY NARRATOR

ON HIS CHRISTIANITY AND SELF-CREATIVITY

According to the noted literary scholar of autobiography James Olney, a person who engages in an autobiographical act does so not as "a neutral or passive recorder, but rather [as] a creative and active shaper. . . . [That person's] memory creates the *significance* of events . . . [that is], events are lifted out of time to be re-situated not in mere chronological sequence but in patterned significance."[11] In drawing upon Olney's insights, we might ask of Aaron Kuku's life history what patterns of significance exist in this particular autobiography and what do those patterns suggest as to Kuku's own rationale for narrating his life history to Samuel Quist? In providing some preliminary answers, my purpose is not to sit Kuku on the proverbial couch to probe his inner psyche. Rather, I would suggest that by exploring the patterns that exist in Kuku's life history, we can get a better understanding of how a West African former slave in the early twentieth century remembered his enslavement and what significance he attributed to that experience as he looked retrospectively over his life.

Perhaps one of the most obvious patterns evident in Kuku's life history is his frequent use of biblical passages and comments about the power of the Christian God. According to Kuku, it was because of God's mercy that he was not killed when as a child he jumped into a pile of thorny branches. This same divine mercy spared him when he attempted suicide while captive in Asante and when as an adult he managed to escape the flames of an out-of-control bush fire. Recollections of being reunited (if only briefly) with his family as they fled the Asante military, of escaping execution while enslaved in Asante, and in managing to survive the perilous journey back to his hometown were all attributed to God's power to influence even the lives of people like himself, who at that time had yet to turn to "the true God." Even when he could not understand why he had experienced certain difficulties in life—being enslaved among the Anfoe Ewe for a period even longer than his time in captivity in Asante and being shunned as a leader in his hometown—he was prepared to accept the Christian adage that sometimes God's ways are simply too mysterious to understand. By interpreting his life through a Christian prism, by quoting liberally from the Bible,[12] Kuku used his life history to continue the work he had begun when he became an evangelist. He sought to encourage the Ewe to follow his path by seeing their difficulties as obstacles that could be overcome by converting to Christianity.

That he felt his perspective could be of benefit to others was certainly reinforced by the conditions and concerns felt by many Ewe from 1869, the time of the Asante invasion, to the time of his death in 1930. This was a period of tremendous change for those who lived in what is known today as Ghana's central Volta Region. Between 1869 and 1871, Asante and its allies ravaged the area, stripping the land of food, goods, and people. The aftereffects of the war were just as devastating and lingered for decades. As noted by Lynne Brydon:

> Apart from the immediate loss of life, enslavement and destruction, the socioeconomic networks underpinning the former development of the area were destroyed. Although big commercial centers such as Kpandu on the Volta began to be re-built fairly quickly, it took longer for the survivors of others groups to come back, to rebuild and re-establish the settlements, to plant and harvest, to begin to live and reproduce, let alone re-establish the trade and networks of the pre-war era. When missionaries from the Bremen Mission returned to Ho in 1875 to resume their work [four years after the end of the war] ... the Bremen Ho station, or what remained of it, was on land devoid of people ... [In fact] the people of Ho had begun to rebuild three of their villages only by the end of 1877 [a full six years after

the end of formal hostilities, because of the] anarchy, confusion and insecurity [in the area].[13]

Even after 1877, when resumed trade ties and new economic opportunities brought by the European colonial demand for cotton, rubber, and palm oil began to reconnect the towns and villages in the central Volta Region to the major trade centers on the Volta River and to trade towns to the west, south, southeast, and northeast, daily life continued to be affected by powerful yet seemingly uncontrollable forces. In 1883, a drought struck the region, causing massive inflation and accompanying hardship for those still struggling to recover from the effects of the 1869–71 war. In 1888, a smallpox epidemic erupted with devastating consequences for many, including Kuku, who lost his father, a brother, an uncle, and an aunt. In 1900, many in the region heard that 186 of their friends and relatives had been killed in Asante when residents of that state used warfare with Britain as a pretext to eliminate the many non-Asante migrants (Ewe, Fante, Gonja, Dagomba) who had flooded into Asante after 1896 to compete with the local residents for the profits from the rubber, gold, and kola industries.[14] Colonial rule brought its own difficulties. In 1895, a German military assault against the town of Tove—some thirty kilometers from Kuku's village of Petewu—resulted in the death of more than seventy-eight Tove citizens and the destruction of all the town's stored harvest.[15] Work conditions, heavy taxation, and limited economic opportunities encouraged Africans like Kuku who were resident in German colonial territory to conduct much of their business activities in Britain's Gold Coast Colony, if not to emigrate altogether.

Even if none of these issues was of particular concern to many in the Liati district where Kuku worked as an evangelist, most residents still had to deal with the social tensions that had begun to emerge after 1877 as the opportunities for wealth accumulation generated a growing gap between the haves and have nots in the area. Kuku experienced these tensions directly. Having prospered from his involvement in trading on the Volta River after his escape from Asante, he was not only able eventually to buy the freedom of his still enslaved mother and her child, but he also (as indicated in a biography by missionary Paul Wiegrëbe) engaged in a public display of his wealth by building himself a new, more modern house in his hometown. Such displays are known to have generated jealousy and, in the most extreme cases, accusations of witchcraft.[16] That Kuku became the object of such feelings is evident in his life history. He notes, for example, that in his hometown he was often brought to court for real and imagined wrongs, which cost him a great deal in fines. His unwillingness to use his assets for a sacrifice to those spirits that others in his community believed had spared him from harm when he fell into a hole was also probably interpreted as a form of tight-fistedness that could potentially bring harm to the entire community. Thus, when he dictated his life history to his amanuensis, he did so not only to continue his work as an evangelist but also to speak directly to those individuals like himself, who found the social bonds of community at times too restrictive on individual entrepreneurship and potentially threatening to one's financial and material well-being. In choosing the biblical passages to illustrate the power of Christianity, he focused on those that emphasized thanksgiving for being delivered from the kinds of hardship (war, enslavement, and disease) he and so many others in his area had experienced. But he also highlighted those passages, as found in Psalms 118, that emphasized the desire for protection from the dangers posed by those close at hand: With the lord on my side to help me, I shall look in triumph on those who hated me; with the Lord on my side, I do not fear; what can mortals do to me?

Kuku used his life history to give voice to an approach to Christianity widely held by other illiterate or minimally Western-educated Ewe Christians in the late nineteenth and early twentieth centuries.[17] In recounting his life as a slave in Asante, for example, Kuku described an incident in which he became stricken with chills and fever after throwing a stone at another boy. The usual home remedies failed to alleviate his illness, so he was transferred to the care of a local priest. It was this transfer that then became a source of speculation about the power of the local gods. According to Kuku, the deity of the priest in whose care he was entrusted had actually caused his illness and had done so after being alerted to his existence by the boy at whom Kuku had thrown the rock. The illness was supposedly a way for the god to obtain the slave it had been promised but which had not yet been delivered by the chief of the village. In recounting this episode long after he had converted to Christianity, Kuku indicated that he still believed, as did most Ewe Christians, that spiritual forces other than the Christian God existed not as metaphor but in reality and that these forces had the power to influence one's life. Thus, when indicating what lessons he felt others should draw from this particular experience, he offered the following adage: "he who does not believe that the devil exists, will not believe that God exists either." In other words, the world should be understood to contain a variety of spiritual forces. Some, termed the devil and his demons, could cause great harm, but it was belief in the true Christian God that protected one from these forces. Such a perspective certainly marked Kuku as a Christian since belief in spiritual entities that were defined as either all good (God) or all bad (the devil) were counter to Ewe and traditional African beliefs. As noted by Birgit Meyer,

> The Ewe like many other African peoples, did not oppose good and evil in dualistic terms, but rather understood both *nyuie* [good] and *vɔ* [evil/something bad] as potentials of all things . . . a *trɔ* [or god, for example, was] ambivalent in nature . . .

[and] supported his worshippers as long as they observed his rules and taboos. [But] anyone failing to do so would trigger the anger of the *trɔ* upon him or herself; sickness and other misfortune would result.[18]

At the same time, Kuku's concern about the power of the devil came directly from his conversion to the type of Christianity promoted in its early evangelical years by the Bremen Mission. According to Meyer:

> missionaries constructed [their brand of Christianity], Pietism and Ewe [and more generally, African traditional] religion in terms of oppositions. While they served God, the Ewe worshipped the Devil and his demons; while they emphasized belief, the Ewe relied on ritual; while God revealed himself through the Bible, the Ewe communicated with Satan's agents through dance and possession . . .
>
> Ewe Christians adopted the diabolization of the Ewe religion continuously preached to them by the missionaries . . . [even though] the majority . . . were people who had played no special role in the framework of Ewe religion. . . . [They nevertheless] converted because they were tired of serving a *trɔ* [god] without profiting from it [that is, gaining the wanted protection from illness, death and misfortune].[19]

Conversion to the Pietist way of understanding the spiritual world did not mean, however, that Kuku completely abandoned his own approach to living in the world. For most Ewe Christians, avoidance of evil and refraining from doing bad things (*nuvɔ*) did not so much involve—as it did for the missionaries and the local ministers—an examination of and a wrestling with one's inner demons. Rather it required—as indicated by Kuku—that one recognize the ability of *others* to inflict spiritual harm. Most evil existed external to the self, often in the form of witchcraft, and if one understood this, one also had to believe in the power of the Christian God, for it was that God that could overcome such threats and guarantee one's well-being. In sharing this perspective on his experiences in Asante, Kuku was doing more than working with his amanuensis to promote their common faith. He was also giving voice to his own understanding of the world.

A second pattern evident in Kuku's life history is the narrated memories of his role as leader. At the very beginning of his narrative, Kuku is at pains to emphasize to his amanuensis that it was his birthright to lead. He indicated he was connected to all the major extended families in his hometown and thus was regarded as someone who would naturally be impartial, favoring no one person over another on the basis of family connections when decisions had to be made. Accordingly, Quist described him as "a free child in all respects and was regarded as such. . . . He became a kind of leader among his peers." This self-described leadership ability also influenced his recollection of his escape from Asante with his father as a boy of eleven or twelve. Kuku asserts, for example, that it was he who insisted when they first made their getaway to return not once, not twice, but three times to try to rescue his mother. During their escape it was Kuku who directed his father to follow him in search of water; it was Kuku, who in eating from their cache of dried snails, led by example and was thus able to alleviate his father's concerns about the danger of eating too much of this food, the only sustenance they had during one period of their escape; it was Kuku who led his father in a fight with a farmer from whose fields they were collecting food. When they reached a deep river, seemingly impassable given their lack of swimming skills, it was Kuku who suddenly became a swimmer, giving his father, by example, new energy to complete the crossing.[20]

This concern to prove that he had both the family background and the demonstrated skills to provide leadership appears to have been driven by his seeming inability to command the respect he needed to retain comfortably the leadership position he assumed in Petewu years after his return from Asante. Even before he succeeded his uncle as Petewu chief, he commented with puzzlement on his lack of popularity. He was continually sued in court; when he suffered severe burns after narrowly escaping a bush fire, few offered him any sympathy or support. Only after he became the chief of his village, according to Kuku, did he "begin to have some peace," but that statement is belied by the fact that just three years after assuming the position, he abandoned it all to become a Christian. Did Kuku become reconciled with the residents of his hometown only because of his position as chief? Perhaps, having been recognized by the German colonial government, he was then in a position to be protected by the power of the state. But the authority granted to him, while buying him some relief from the disdain of his Petewu neighbors, may have only enhanced his unpopularity. As noted by Arthur Knoll in his study of German colonial rule in Togo, the colonial administration sought to run its colony on a fiscally sound basis by commandeering labor for road and railway construction. "Each village had to furnish a certain number of laborers to keep paths and roads clear, . . . [but no] remuneration was given to village laborers who worked in their [own] districts."[21] Kuku indicates that after he left his leadership position in Petewu, he was subject to these same exactions. Such highly unpopular demands led many to leave German Togo for the less exacting Gold Coast Colony, just as it probably encouraged Kuku to abandon the Christian village he had founded when his labor was demanded by the Leklebi chief on whose land he had established his Christian village.[22] When he was still chief of Petewu, however, it was he who had to furnish such labor. Finding his position as leader of Petewu made even more untenable by the demands of the German colonial government, it is likely that these were the reasons he jumped at the opportunity to abandon the position. Converting to Christianity, he reinvented himself by assuming a different leadership position: that of the founder of a new Christian village and an evangelist attached to the Bremen Mission (seen by many local residents as just another segment of the German colonial government).

But this emphasis on his continued activities as leader, albeit a Christian one, neither alleviated Kuku's bewilderment about his unpopularity nor ameliorated the resulting defensiveness. To address the lingering questions about his abilities, to prove to others and perhaps most importantly to prove to himself that he was indeed a leader, Kuku remembered himself as a child of eleven or twelve years who initiated the attempts to rescue his mother and who took the lead in bringing his father out of slavery. He recalled in detail how he brought others to Christ in his work as an evangelist, how he founded a new Christian village and successfully encouraged others to join him. Such self-invention, as noted by the literary scholar Paul Eakin, is integral to the autobiographical act. "The materials of the past are shaped by memory and imagination to serve the needs of the present consciousness." In narrating his life to his amanuensis, Kuku used these details to encourage others to convert to Christianity, to understand that faith in terms that were most meaningful to him and many other Ewes, and to engage in an act of "self-discovery and self-creation" that allowed him to understand his past life according to more present needs.[23]

One can no doubt find additional patterns of significance in Kuku's life history that reveal even more reasons why he decided to narrative his life history to Quist. But it seems appropriate at this point to turn to the concerns that more centrally inform this study: an examination of Kuku's narrative for what it can tell us about enslavement in West Africa, how it is remembered, and how it is talked about (or not) in the context of the discursive norms that informed public discussions of slavery in West Africa during the late nineteenth and early twentieth centuries. It is to this that we now turn.

ON MEMORIES OF FAMILY: HONESTY AND ANGUISH, LOVE AND OBLIGATION

Memories of family constitute the fundamental framework around which Kuku remembered both his early childhood and his enslavement. After a brief description of his natal village, for example, Kuku recounts a playful encounter gone awry that occurred between himself and his sister, Adanuvor, one and a half years before their capture by Asante military personnel in 1870. Adanuvor was cooking rice when Kuku threw a lump of clay at her, presumably in jest. Her response made Kuku realize immediately that his efforts at attention were quite unwelcome. She cried out in pain. This in turn put in motion a string of incidents that became the basis for one of the more important memories of his sister and mother, both of whom he would later lose as a result of the Asante invasion. Afraid of the punishment he knew he would receive, Kuku tried to ameliorate the situation by being the first to comfort his sibling. His mother, however, was not pleased. The next day she ground pepper and ordered him to come to her so she could put it in his nose as punishment for his actions the previous day. Kuku refused to budge, however, and instead slipped some cotton up his nose to blunt the effect of the pepper. Remembered most fondly was the fact that after his mother inserted the pepper with no effect and then discovered his ruse, instead of raging at him she only expressed exasperated amusement at his cleverness. This is only one of several stories about life with his relatives that he shared with his amanuensis. Elsewhere in his narrative, he emphasizes the role his father played in planning their escape from Asante and saving his life on various occasions during their perilous flight. He recounts with sorrow the later deaths from a smallpox epidemic of his father and other relatives with whom he was quite close. He recalls the shock and anger he experienced when his wife died before giving birth to their first child.

Most telling, however, is that he does not idealize his family life and family relations. Kuku portrays his younger self not as the dutiful child, ever respectful of his elders. Rather he admits to being at times both mischievous and manipulative. He remembers refusing to go to work with his father in their agricultural fields despite his father's insistence. He recounts manipulating his parents' emotions when they thought he had been severely injured after jumping inadvertently into a pile of thorny branches. He portrays his marriage and relations among his extended family as complex affairs. Tensions developed between himself and his wife when she insisted on accompanying him on his trip to the riverine trading port of Bator and then insisted again that they attend a dance immediately after their arrival. He recalls his disappointment with his uncle when the latter, swayed by public opinion, refused to lend him money so he could marry without having to leave town and work for a stranger to obtain the money he needed to pay the bridewealth.

Still, family was clearly a central feature of his identity. It structured his sense of self and his ethical obligations. When his father made his way to the village where Kuku was enslaved, Kuku immediately supported him during his confinement. He cooked for him and in time eventually agreed to escape with his father. The decision to leave, however, was not easy. Kuku had already begun to think of himself as a member of his master's household. More than fifty years later, he remembered his second master, the chief of Nsuta, not as a taskmaster but as someone who took the time to exhibit fatherly concern for his welfare. The chief explained to Kuku what had happened when he narrowly avoided becoming a victim of ritual sacrifice. He reassured Kuku that he need not worry about such things happening again. And when the chief needed someone to accompany his new wife on a trip to her hometown, he selected Kuku as someone he knew would be helpful to her while she was away. His memories of the other members of his master's household were similarly warm. After accompanying his master's wife to her hometown, he helped her as expected on her farm, but he remembers as well that he was allowed to rest even while she continued to work. When he fell ill, the chief's mother-in-law cared enough about him that she had her daughter (the chief's wife) accompany him back to his master's home, and it was the chief himself, according to Kuku, who provided the goods needed to pay for his care. The fondness with which he remembers this treatment may explain why eleven-year-old Kuku continually overslept and thus disrupted his father's numerous plans to escape. He had become accustomed to and comfortable in his adopted home. Natal ties eventually prevailed, however. Kuku and his father escaped from slavery and were pleased to do so. But he was also not prepared to forget the familial bonds that had begun to develop between himself and his master. When he remembered his experiences with the Asante, he recounted in vivid terms the horrid treatment that the Asantes meted out to their captives, but he was also not prepared to condemn those individual Asantes who had treated him as an adopted member of their own household.

The defining role family played in Kuku's life also explains Kuku's recollections of how he dealt with the enslavement of his mother and siblings. Just as he was told about his father's supposed execution in Kumase, Kuku also heard rumors about the location of his mother and brother. Thus, he told his amanuensis that when he and his father managed to make their escape from Kuku's adopted village, it was he who insisted that they attempt to rescue their still enslaved relatives. Thrice they tried, thrice they failed. In the second attempt they almost lost their own freedom and health. Undeterred by the passage of more than twenty years, Kuku continued to make inquiries about his lost relatives. Finally, he located his still enslaved mother and her child in the trade town of Krachi sometime between 1890 and 1894.[24] After spending two years accumulating the funds, he was able to purchase the freedom of both.

Such devotion and expenditure of energy to reunite with a lost family member was not unique to Kuku.[25] Even during the height of the Atlantic slave trade, families regularly attempted to ransom those relatives kidnapped or captured in war if they had not yet been sold into the Atlantic slave trade and were still being held by known individuals. Many times the attempts at reunification proved futile, but efforts were made nevertheless.[26] These attempts appear to have become far more common after 1874. In that year, Britain invaded and conquered Asante, an event that also loosened the centralized grip Asante had exercised over trade, travel, and political activity in much of what is now Ghana. In that same year, Britain also abolished slavery. The result was an unprecedented opening of opportunities to reconnect with lost family members, especially by those who lived in the communities east of the Volta that had only recently suffered family loss due to the Asante invasion of 1869–71. It was this upheaval, created by Britain's 1874 defeat of Asante, that may have allowed Kuku and his father to make their own escape from Asante in the first place. The subsequent loosening of Asante's control over the trade along the Volta River brought a tremendous upsurge in commerce along the river. And it was Kuku's participation in this trade that provided him with the opportunity to inquire about his mother's whereabouts and to make the money he needed to purchase her freedom.

But precisely how common was it for individuals to make an effort to reconnect with their home communities? How active was the average search for lost relatives, and for how long? Were certain familial relations, parent/child, brother/sister, husband/wife, uncle/nephew, given priority over others? If so, what factors influenced this priority? Studies that document the efforts of ex-slaves in West Africa to reconnect with lost family members are very few indeed, and thus we know very little about the phenomenon.[27] Should we assume that people would naturally want to return to their home communities or reunite with their families if possible? Perhaps, but accounts of the same still bear investigation. Why, for example, more than twenty years after he redeemed his mother, did Kuku find it necessary to emphasize in his life history the number of times he and his father sought to free his mother and the efforts he made to search for and redeem her? Answers can be found, in part, in the bond that is said to have characterized mother-child relations among the Ewe in the nineteenth century. In 1889 the Bremen missionary J. Spieth commented on these bonds:

> The mother takes care of almost everything regarding the child; she is almost exclusively responsible for the child's care . . . [and] although it is the father who continues this kind of education [and care] from the seventh or eight year [of the child's life] . . . the children [still] show a lot of thankfulness towards their old mother. . . . Do the children themselves acknowledge the mothers even when they become bigger and do not rely on their mothers any longer? Observations over a period of several years have proved to me that this question is definitely to be answered in the affirmative. . . .
>
> [B]oth daughter and son have unlimited faith in the old mother. When the daughter has left her parents' home to live with her husband, she'll keep her beautiful clothes and jewelry not in the husband's room; him she cannot trust entirely. The mother's house is the location [where such valuables are stored] . . . the son's trust of his mother manifests itself in a different way. If [an adult son] has had an accident or has fallen victim to a particularly difficult illness, his wife is not allowed to care for him. If the mother is still alive, she has to be around him permanently. It is she who cooks for him and does other services for him. Why? Because the mother's love [is considered] more genuine than the love of one's spouse. His

mother won't poison him; he can completely trust her [literally: he can receive every bit of yam and every gulp of water from her hand], but [this is not true] for his wife.

When the Asantes flooded the land of the Ewes in 1869, the inhabitants of the flatlands fled to the nearby mountains. These reach an altitude of 2–3000 feet and are entirely covered with forest in such a way that one cannot pass through them in places. At that time, the Ewe carried their old mothers along the steep slopes, through the thick bushy forests to keep them safe on the mountains . . .

Even in Africa, love is as strong as death.[28]

Spieth's observations—published in the Bremen Mission's quarterly publication—were written in large part to counter prevailing German stereotypes about the lack of motherly feeling among African women. His hyperbolic claim that an extraordinary amount of love characterized the Ewe mother-child bond is indicative of just how common this stereotype was.[29] More important for our purposes is his observation that the affective bonds between a child and his or her mother may have been socially reinforced by concerns about placing all one's trust in the bonds of marriage. A spouse—chosen by one's family—could prove in time, according to local thought, to be a productive helpmate, a faithful companion and trusted friend. Or that spouse could also act in ways that undermined one's own interests. One couldn't always tell for sure. Did these kinds of concerns act as an additional motivator for Kuku to locate and free his mother? Maybe. But based on his account, a more immediate concern was that he had already lost not only his wife and unborn child but also his father, his siblings, and at least two uncles to death or enslavement. It is in this context that Kuku made the extraordinary effort, more than twenty years after their separation—to locate and free his mother.

Equally important in understanding Kuku's account is that the narrative—dictated at the end of his life—was willingly presented to another. By participating in these sessions, he was able to use his amanuensis to present an image of the person he wanted others to remember. He emphasized the many efforts he made to rescue his mother; he explained the time it took for him to obtain the money needed to redeem both her and her child. In so doing, he was able to prove to others (and perhaps to himself as well) that he was not the selfish, self-centered, misanthrope imagined by his fellow citizens of Petewu, nor was he that mischievous, manipulative child who cared more about punishing his parents for some perceived slight than about their ultimate well-being. He was a dutiful son who risked his life and expended great financial resources to rescue his family from slavery.

ON REMEMBERING FEAR

If it was love and devotion that propelled Kuku to seek out and redeem his mother, fear was the pervasive emotion he recorded in recollections of his capture and enslavement. When he recalled the Asante military assault on his home village, he remembered the hurried preparations for war and fleeing in terror. Pervasive and continuous fear was also recounted as his state of mind when he was enslaved in Asante, and fear remained with him on his escape. Such vivid memories conveyed so many years after the events speak both to the indelible impression and the terrifying nature that the attack, his capture, and enslavement had on his young mind. It is also likely that the vividness of the memories were continually reinforced by the recollections of many others who suffered as well. Hundreds of villagers and townspeople in the region who escaped enslavement also saw their friends and relatives killed, carried away, or die at home from starvation because of the devastation of field and farm wrought by the Asantes. There were also the individuals who were enslaved but who like Kuku managed to return home and were thus in a position like Kuku to share and keep alive the memories of their fear.

That fear was the predominant feeling at the time is also clear from the writings of the Europeans who were operating east of the Volta. The Bremen missionary Weyhe recounted in 1870 at the height of the war the terror that the Asante engendered even among their own Ewe friends (in this case the Adaklu people of Waya, among whom Weyhe was living at the time):

> No writing instrument can describe how the Ashanti people plague the people here. First, they took everything that the earth had produced so that we already suffer here from dire hunger. . . . The city was looted just as the land had been. During the night the Ashanti made holes in the houses and stole everything. One is forced to suffer the harshest penalty for every little thing. A man sneezed; this sneeze cost him eight heads [of cowries]; finally he was forced to flee. Four Ashanti beat up a Waya. When he protected himself, this cost him forty-six heads [of cowries]. If he does not pay in two days, the fine will be doubled.[30]

> A[nother] example: an Ashanti took from a Wayan his mat and slept on it. Afterwards, the Wayan took it back from him. Then the Ashanti claimed that he had left tobacco lying on the mat. In spite of searching actively for it, it was not found. They then bought triple the amount [of tobacco to replace that which was lost], however the Ashanti said that the tobacco was stolen and then tied up the Wayan and said he would not accept tobacco as compensation, but instead wanted to send the Wayan as a slave to his camp. Only after much back and forth could the Wayan extract himself [from the threat of enslavement] by offering a sum of money.

> The situation is not much better for the . . . Angula [the Anlo, one of Asante's military allies]. . . . [The Asante] captured one of the Angula who entered a courtyard full of Ashanti and tied him up under the pretext that he wanted to steal from them. They let him go only when he had bought his way free with rum.

All courtyards are bolted; all doors are shut and usually someone sits before them and keeps watch. In the evenings, one does not see [the Wayans] sitting together and eating as is usually their custom. Instead everything takes place in secret because the Ashanti steal even from their pots.[31]

Writing shortly after their own capture by the Asante, Basel missionaries Ramseyer and Kuhne also wrote of the precarious, life-threatening position in which they found themselves (even though in many instances they were treated after their capture with far greater care than the African captives with whom they often crossed paths, all of whom were forcibly conveyed to Kumase, the Asante capital). Of their forced march, they wrote:

we often encountered the extremely sad traces of the battle that had taken place the day before: the wounded, the dead, heads separated from torsos, corpses without heads: what a sight! . . .

[W]e marched as slaves, daily enduring a fresh torrent of abuse; the old leader himself taking special delight in trying to extinguish our hopes while he drew lively pictures of the state of things in Coomasie and assured us that "our heads would be cut off there."

Ageana [the military person given specific charge of them] . . . seemed to look on the bad weather as a fault of ours. . . .

[Frequently] famished with hunger, we expected [at different times] a respite and refreshment, but to my intense and bitter indignation, this was contemptuously refused. . . . Our depression was often great.[32]

Of the Africans who were also being marched to Asante, fear for their lives would have clearly characterized their reaction to what they experienced. Ramseyer and Kuhne were particularly aware of the Asante's treatment of the many children who, like Kuku, had also been captured. In one village outside Kumase, they observed:

[I]n a yard [were] more than a hundred prisoners from Krepe [the name by which the Ewe-speaking area east of the Volta was known], men, women and children, all living skeletons, and infants on their mothers' backs, starving for want of their natural nourishment . . . my wife noticed a poor, weak child, who was commanded in angry tones to stand straight. The little fellow tried to obey, and painfully drew himself up, showing the shrunken frame in which every bone was visible . . .

After this, prisoners continued to arrive, just living skeletons. The sight of one poor boy touched us deeply; the thin neck was unable to support the head, which drooped almost to the knees. I spoke to him repeatedly, and offered him food; at length he gave me a look I shall never forget, and just said, "I have eaten," and the head hung down helpless as before; all hope seemed gone.[33]

Fear was thus warranted and pervasive. But it didn't begin or end with capture and the forced march to Asante.

If the African prisoners captured by the Asante survived the trek to Kumase (and many did not, as Kuku as well as Ramseyer and Kuhne remembered), they then had to face the completely foreign (and linguistically unintelligible) legal practices of the Asante, in which mutilation and public execution were used not only to punish criminals, but also to intimidate and cow the population, both free and slave. One such legal proceeding was recounted by Kuku in terms that reveal the fear engendered when one is subjected to the power of a judicial proceeding that is completely incomprehensible. Kuku remembers one day when "just after I started eating, there was a knock at the gate, 'Agoo.' . . . Before I was aware of what was happening, one of the visitors grabbed my hand. The food fell. . . . They handcuffed me to a weaving loom. . . . I had been condemned to death." No one told him why. From this account alone it is apparent that many of Kuku's memories of Asante were ones saturated with fear, an emotion made legitimate in his own mind by the experiences he certainly suffered on being captured as a child, separated from his family, and marched to Asante, while also witnessing death, destruction, and (according to his account) the physical mutilation of those who dared to defy their enslavement.

In emphasizing dread and anxiety, Kuku was doing more than remembering his own emotional state, however. What he recalled and was prepared to share with others was very much influenced by the local discursive terrain that deemed it acceptable, even expected, that when one was captured in war, fear was the emotion that could and should be expressed in public discussions of the experience. Evidence of this comes from a public performance that took place thirteen years after the end of the war.

In 1884, efforts were made on the part of the people of Anlo and Taviefe (both allies of the Asante in the 1869 war) to reconcile their differences with the people of Ho so as to normalize trade relations. Prior to this period, any trader from Anlo, Taviefe, Asante, or Akwamu who was found in Ho or in the other Ewe-speaking towns that had fought against Asante faced the prospect of being killed. Only in 1884 did the Anlo and Taviefe finally persuade many of their former Ewe-speaking enemies to allow them to resume trade activities in the area. It was at one of these meetings to normalize relations that a performance was staged to commemorate the events that brought them all together. All roles considered essential for an accurate re-enactment of the war were performed as indicated in the following description recorded by the Bremen missionary Zurlinden, who witnessed the performance:

> [As] we were waiting . . . several hundred Ho warriors appeared, from *dekakpui* (young men) to *amehoho* (old men), everybody who could carry a sword or a flint-lock gun.

They were decorated with white, red and black earth, draped with jaw-bones of dead Asante and with cords of cowries [while] the drums were ornamented with human skulls. . . . Everything that takes place in an African war except for robbery and fire was demonstrated. . . . We saw two enemies creeping over the grass like snakes . . . somebody climbed a palm tree in monkey-like speed to reconnoiter . . . a blood-thirsty seemingly giant figure holds a skull with his teeth and imitates the gesture of drinking. On the other side they seem to cut off somebody's head and tear his heart out of his body. . . . Someone pretends to be dead, [but] as soon as the enemy has left, he jumps tall as a man to tell of his adventure.

There somebody stands with mortal fear on his face; he has fallen into enemy hands and does not see a way out to save his life.

The women play roles, too. They circle the fighting with singing and make music to cheer them up.[34]

This re-enactment, in illustrating the acceptable forms of public speech about one's role in warfare (whether as fighter, spy, booster of one's military troops, or captive), indicates that expressions of fear by former captives were not something about which to be ashamed or silent. Fear—not indignation, and not complaints—was the expected, even the demanded, discursive form in which captives were to describe their experiences. That Kuku remembered his own enslavement in these terms, then, is not just a recounting of historical fact, but is evidence as well of how his recollection was deeply influenced by the local cultural norms that governed acceptable speech.

ON SUICIDE

If discursive norms dictated that it was acceptable, even appropriate, to remember one's captivity through the lens of fear, these same social norms also allowed Kuku to discuss with his amanuensis the many times he thought about taking his own life. Not once or twice, but five different times between 1870 and 1888, Kuku remembers having suicidal thoughts. The first occurred at the time of his capture. Pinned down by enemy fire next to a man from the allied town of Fodome, afraid of being captured or killed, he begged the man to give him a knife so that he could kill himself first. The next three instances occurred while Kuku was enslaved in Asante, while the fifth and final incident took place after his return to his home village, when he lost his father, a brother, and an uncle to the smallpox epidemic of 1888. How do we interpret these memories? Would a captured and enslaved child between the ages of eight and eleven really contemplate suicide? What does Kuku's narrative tell us about the circumstances that may have led him to consider taking his own life? And just as important, how were these acts viewed in his community such that he felt he could speak openly to his amanuensis about his repeated experiences with suicidal thoughts?

Answers to these questions are best informed, in part, by what we know already about Kuku. As argued earlier, Aaron—like other autobiographical narrators—was "a creator and active shaper" of his own remembered experiences. He willingly provided his amanuensis with details about his life that could be used to encourage others to embrace Christianity. At the same time, he constructed the narrative about his past that emphasized the role he played as an active leader of family and community. What does this have to do with understanding his suicide attempts? In many West African cultures, as noted by the historian John Illife, it was considered honorable (and even obligatory) in some cultures for military leaders who faced the prospect of capture or defeat in war to commit suicide.[35] This was the honorable response to humiliation. That this was the case historically for a long period of time in what is now Ghana is apparent from the numerous cases found in the documentary record. In 1792, for example, when the Anlo (the Ewe-speaking polity that would later align itself with Asante in the 1869 war) were engaged in a military conflict with the then separate polity of Keta, the military found itself surrounded on three sides by the enemy and the paths they could use to retreat virtually cut off by a fire. On seeing their dire situation, the rank-and-file soldiers fled in panic. Their right-wing military commander, however, chose to commit suicide rather than face capture or surrender.[36] More than fifteen instances of suicide threatened, ordered, or successfully carried out have also been documented involving the Asante between 1765 and 1886.[37] Every one of these cases, like that of the suicide in Anlo, concerned acts either by royals (male and a few females) or military commanders faced with the prospect of being humiliated by their enemies. Are Kuku's memories of having suicidal thoughts when he was about to be captured by the Asante part of his ongoing emphasis to portray himself as a family and community leader? Did he include this memory in his life history to underscore the notion that even as a child he demonstrated his willingness to act as any other leader would have to preserve his or her dignity? I believe so given what we know about the circumstances under which children have suicidal thoughts.

According to Cynthia Pfeffer, author of *The Suicidal Child*, children as young as two and a half and three years old can exhibit suicidal tendencies.

> Such young children talk about wanting to kill themselves and have attempted to jump from high places, ingest poisons and hang themselves.... [And] although suicide is relatively rare in children under 12 years of age, suicidal ideas, suicidal threats and attempts are relatively common.[38]

Kuku was about eight years of age when he remembers first threatening to kill himself. But Pfeffer also reports that specific factors are associated with the risks of childhood suicidal behavior. Among these are loss, separation, and particularly serious family stresses, as well as feelings of hopelessness.[39] In seeking to escape the Asante invaders, Kuku was certainly separated from his parents and faced tremendous stress. He had no idea where his mother, father, and siblings were, but he also had no time to even think about that. First and foremost, he had to elude capture. Yet it was during his efforts to flee for his life that he says he asked someone for a knife so that he could kill himself. Plausible? I don't think so. It appears instead that Kuku's memory of what happened just before he was captured had more to do with his desire to be perceived as a leader than with what was actually going through his mind at the time.

It is Pfeffer's findings about the circumstances under which children have suicidal thoughts and even attempt to kill themselves, however, that makes Kuku's accounts of his *other* suicide attempts so believable.[40] In all the subsequent instances, Kuku explains that he felt absolutely alone, abandoned, left to face particularly stressful conditions by himself at a time when he was also overwhelmed by feelings of hopelessness. He remembers attempting to hang himself shortly after hearing the distressing news that his father had been among those executed in 1871 and that his beloved sister, Adanuvor, had also died. Utter dismay appears to have overwhelmed the eight-year-old. The three other remembered instances of suicidal ideation also involved feelings of abandonment and hopelessness. Toward the end of 1874, Kuku's father managed to travel to the village where Kuku was enslaved. When Kuku realized that the chief of his village might separate them yet again by returning his father to his master, he remembered being unable to contemplate the possibility. He thought of killing himself. The same occurred when he thought his father was going to die and leave Kuku alone to find his way home through foreign territory. He considered taking his life yet again in 1888 when as a teenager he felt completely abandoned after everyone in Petewu had fled in the face of a smallpox epidemic and had left him alone to care for the sick and to bury his own father, brother, aunt, and uncle.

These instances of both suicidal thoughts and the one attempt Kuku made at taking his own life reveal the depth of the trauma that children, in particular, experienced as a result of their capture and enslavement. During the era of the Atlantic slave trade, there were many reports of enslaved Africans, male and female (especially those being shipped to the Americas), who attempted to or succeeded in taking their own lives. But in the vast majority of these cases, it was adults who were involved in this activity, not prepubescent children. Kuku's narrative is one of the few that reveals the despair experienced by children ripped from their homes.[41] Separated seemingly permanently from their parents and siblings, not yet acclimated to their new surroundings, feeling totally alone, overwhelmed by melancholy, many must have wondered, as did Kuku, whether life was really worth living.

Why would Kuku have shared these thoughts with his amanuensis? As an individual act that did not involve issues of honor, his suicidal thoughts and his one attempt at taking his own life would have found no support from the cultural communities in which he lived. As indicated in his account, he in fact experienced only admonishments. He remembers, for example, that after his master found him hanging from a rope and carried him home, "the people [in the village] said that he had done this to himself." No one else was to blame. He alone had to take responsibility for what they considered to be an illegal act.[42] When his father became ill from a snake bite during their escape and Kuku again spoke of suicide, his father ordered him not to kill himself. And when he finally left Petewu to live with an uncle to whom he told of having thoughts of suicide after burying his relatives, Kuku's uncle's response was to insist that he move into town.[43] Equally significant is that Pietist Christianity, the faith he professed at the time he dictated his life history, would have also taken a dim view of his suicidal thoughts and action. It would have been "considered a terrible religious offense . . . because [of its] interference with something given by God: human life."[44] Yet Kuku was prepared to discuss his suicidal thoughts and actions openly. Why? What allowed him to be so transparent about something that was clearly condemned in all the cultural communities in which he operated? The answer to this question can be found in the beliefs and practices introduced by the Bremen Mission and continued by the Ewe Evangelical Church. As noted by Birgit Meyer, one of the hallmarks of the Pietist approach to Christianity was its emphasis on introspection.

> [The] focus on the inside of a person was and still is a typical trait of Protestantism in general, and even more so, of Pietism in particular. In order to be accepted by God, it was not considered sufficient to perform particular rituals . . . or to behave properly in life (that is, to attend church, obey the authorities, follow the Ten Commandments, and love one's neighbor). What really counted was the individual state of mind that was only known to God and the believer. Pietism thus implied an individualistic concept of the self, a self that was always observed by God, whose all-seeing eye had to be paralleled by continual personal introspection.[45]

It was this emphasis on introspection that made the writing of autobiographical narratives a *rite of passage* for Christian workers in Germany and in the communities in West Africa where first the Bremen Mission and later the Ewe Evangelical Church operated. By detailing his own sins of suicidal thinking and the one attempt he made on his life, Kuku followed the autobiographical traditions established by his church. He outlined for the edification of the larger Ewe-speaking public the sins he had committed that they should try and could avoid if they embraced the calming faith of Christianity.[46] That he shared these perspectives while also deploying his wartime suicidal thoughts as a marker of his leadership abilities indicates the extent to which the late nine-teenth- and early twentieth-century discursive terrain that structured his life history drew elements from a number of different cultural sources. Local norms that defined suicide as honorable under specific circumstances but un-acceptable if carried out for reasons of melancholy were combined with Chris-tian notions about the need to air one's past sins. This combination made sui-cide, whatever its motivations, speakable for Kuku and his amanuensis.

On Memories of the Enslavers

In reconstructing his experience as an enslaved war captive, Kuku presented a negative portrayal of Asante military and ritual culture. He remembered with horror the punishment his father received after having been caught trying to es-cape during the Asante campaign. Not only was his ear brutally lopped off, he was also displayed in this bloody state to deter others from taking the same ac-tion. He recounts in excruciating detail the ritual execution he witnessed while enslaved in Asante and that almost cost him his own life. These memories would have resonated well with many in the areas east of the Volta. They had suffered terribly from the actions of the Asantes and their Akwamu and Anlo allies. Hos-tility toward Asante and its allies were rife well past the end of the war in 1871. In 1877, for example, Ewe-speaking residents in the towns on the Volta River har-bored such hatred of the Akwamu that traders from the town refused to travel on the Volta River further than the town of Pese for fear of retribution for their role in the war.[47] Similar feelings existed in Wusuta, which had hosted Asante troops for several years. When the Asantes realized that they simply did not have enough material and human booty to display as evidence of their self-declared victory, they turned on the Wusuta. They captured them and forcibly marched them to Kumase, where they were enslaved and dispersed to different masters.[48] In 1876, when the French trader M. Bonnat resumed his exploration of the trade opportu-nities east of the Volta that had been interrupted by his own capture and forced removal to Kumase, he observed that "the Wusuta were not so willing to forgive their enemies and had sworn implacable hatred to the Akwamus. They 'trembled with rage' at the sight of three Akwamus in [his] crew [of canoemen]."[49]

This anger also explains why the man who held Kuku and his father briefly as slaves in the Ewe-speaking town of Anfoe during their long journey home to Petewu were advised not to sell them, as he had wanted, to a friend in the As-ante-allied polity of Akyem. If such a sale came to be known in the region, he would have been attacked as the allies and friends of those who had caused so much death and destruction east of the Volta. Similar sentiments existed fur-ther south among the Ho. As noted above, this polity had decided in late 1884 to reconcile with the Anlo, who had also taken an active part in the war with

Asante against Ho. Prior to this, however, the political leader of Ho "did not tire of telling of old times. He never forgot what the Anlo [as Asante's allies in the war] had done, and he swore that no Anlo would come to Ho as long as he lived." This is why the reconciliation ceremony did not occur until 1884, after his death, and even then, during the ceremony itself, the young men of Ho argued against normalizing relations and threatened to kill any elder who signed the peace treaty.[50] This lingering hatred also explains why the people of Ho were so prepared as late as 1900 to defy the German colonial government that had extended its authority over much of the Ewe-speaking area east of the Volta. In that year, Britain had invaded Asante to bring it more firmly under its control. As part of the response to that invasion, the Asante citizens of Kumase massacred many foreign traders (including 186 citizens of Ho). In retaliation—and spurred on by memories of the 1869–71 atrocities committed against them when the Asante invaded their community—the people of Ho "tortured and killed [the Asantes in their midst] in a horrible fashion," even while knowing that the German government would likely prosecute them, as in fact it did.[51]

Unlike his Ewe friends and neighbors, however, Kuku's negative feelings about Asante military and ritual practices did not include a general antipathy toward its citizens. In addition to his memories of their bloody practices, he also recalled his first master's kindness immediately after he attempted to kill himself. He described the motherly attention he received from the chief's wife and his master's mother-in-law when he fell ill with chills and fever. He remembered the assurances of the chief of the village where he was enslaved that he need not be afraid any longer that he would be used as a ritual sacrifice. Why such mixed images of his enslavers, practitioners of brutal military and ritual practices but a people capable of treating even the enslaved with care? Certainly his Christian faith, with its injunction to love one's enemies, must have encouraged him to remember his enslavers in this way. But it is also likely that because he had spent quite some time in Asante he could not easily embrace the view held by so many of his neighbors that the Asante were simply the killers and enslavers of their relatives, the people who had burnt their homes, plundered their fields, and left them to starve. Not only were his memories more nuanced, he—like many others who eventually returned to their homes east of the Volta after the British abolition of slavery in 1874—had been exposed to a range of new ideas that brought them prestige after their return to their natal homes.[52] Kuku notes, for example, that some time after his return to Petewu, he was elected to head his village because his uncle had held the position before him. But he mentions as well that it was his "experience" that others considered an additional asset that could bring benefits to the office and the community. He gives no indication of what that "experience" was, but it probably had to do with the new knowledge he had acquired while enslaved.

According to Raymond Dumett and Kwame Arhin, the demand for rubber from what is now Ghana took off in the 1880s and 1890s, but prior to that, the Basel Mission had been buying for export as early as the 1860s rubber from villagers east of the Asante capital in Akyem. It was during this same period, according to the Bremen missionary Paul Wiegräbe, that Kuku (who was also enslaved east of Kumase) participated with his first master in the production of kola nuts.[53] For many, including perhaps Kuku's master, involvement in the sale of kola also meant participation in the collection and sale of rubber. Kola nuts collected from the forest, often by slaves like Kuku, were taken north and exchanged for slaves. These slaves were then brought back to Asante and either used in rubber production or exchanged for the rubber produced by others, which was then sold to merchants on the coast.[54] Was Kuku not only involved in collecting kola for his master, but also taught how to collect the rubber that Basel missionaries had begun to buy? It is certainly possible. He did make quite a bit of money from his involvement in the rubber trade after his return to Petewu, so much so that he was able in 1917 to give a total of three hundred marks to the North German Missionary Society in support of their work in both Germany and German Togo, and in support of the German kaiser's efforts during World War One.[55] If true, this would explain why Kuku expressed both negative and positive emotions about Asante. It was there that he may have learned to tap rubber, a skill that ultimately contributed to his recognition as someone of value to his own home community and to his later accumulation of wealth from rubber tapping.

CONCLUSION

Aaron Kuku's life history—like those of individuals enslaved elsewhere in Africa and in the Americas as first-generation slaves—speaks to the terror that accompanied the warfare that saw millions enslaved during the era of the Atlantic, the trans-Saharan and Indian Ocean slave trades. It provides an account of the horrors experienced by those who were forcibly marched to distant locations to be separated from family and friends and then sold to masters with unknown proclivities for kindness or inhumanity. It illustrates the particular insecurities and unpredictability of a life lived in enslavement. In Kuku's narrative we see the guiding hand of his amanuensis, but it does not exist as an "envelope," sealing within it Kuku's own voice. Rather, this analysis has emphasized that such narratives—especially those about the lives of first-generation enslaved Africans who never left the continent—as entangled as they are, can tell us a great deal about the enslavement experience within Africa. Their remembering was not dulled by the comparative horrors of the transatlantic slave trade or trans-Saharan trade. The enslavement recalled took place in sub-

Saharan Africa, and thus the narrators were spared the felt necessity to de-emphasize the terrors associated with capture, the coffle experience, and slavery since they did not have to respond to their identity being redefined and homogenized along racial lines. Kuku's memories instead were shaped by his experience as a child and a citizen of Petewu enslaved by a much more powerful and hierarchically organized state, and by the local discursive terrain that encouraged him to speak openly about his experiences according to known and accepted norms. Even as he structured his memories in response to both local discursive practices and his own contemporary concerns, his narrative illustrates as well the extent to which the trauma of enslavement continued to influence how he viewed himself and those who enslaved him. Nothing in Kuku's subsequent experiences seemed to have moderated his enmity toward Asante military and ritual practices. How much these long and deeply held feelings were peculiar to Kuku or were also typical of first-generation slaves is unclear. What we do know is that what he remembered and how he structured those memories are clearly evident in his life history despite the editorial hand of his amanuensis. Equally evident is that in sharing his life history, Kuku used this opportunity to both remember and forget, and to construct a past identity for himself for the present.

2. The Life History of Aaron Kuku

PREFACE

Aaron Kuku and his amanuensis, the Reverend Samuel Quist, offered a number of dates and elapsed time periods as a way to structure Kuku's life history according to Western norms. They gave the year 1860 as his likely birth date. They calculated that he spent about two years as a slave in Asante, that it took twenty-three months for him and his father to find their way home to Eweland, and that they spent another nine years in captivity in the Ewe-speaking area of Anfoe before they were able to return to their own hometown of Petewu. Verifying these dates and time periods, however, can be challenging. There are no local Asante records, oral or written, that record the names, ages, and origins of the individuals captured in war. And while both the Ewe and the Asante had their own ways of calculating time, these system cannot always be translated into our own Western methods of determining years and months. Still it is possible to date some of the events Kuku mentions in his life history. His capture certainly occurred in early 1870, the period when European documentary sources indicate that Asante attacked those in Fodome and Liati (where Kuku's home village of Petewu was located).[1] The smallpox epidemic that devastated his home village was probably the same one reported by the colonial German staff doctor, A. Wicke, who indicated that the disease made its appearance first in communities on the Volta River in 1888 and then spread from there to more distant communities connected to the riverine area by well-traveled trade routes.[2] We also know that Kuku and the others enslaved by the Asante were paraded in Kumase on 2 September 1871.[3] Combining these dates with the time frames offered by Kuku and Quist, the following timeline outlines the unfolding of his experiences of capture, enslavement, and escape, the return to his home village, and the eventual freeing of his still enslaved mother and his mother's child.

May 1869   Asante and its allies launch their first attacks against the Ewe and Guan-speaking communities of Peki, Sokode, Ho, Adaklu and Anum, located east of the Volta.

July 1869   By this date, some Ewe forces (along with the Akyem Kotoku leader, Dompre) escape and retreat north to Kpandu territory.

Early 1870   A small contingent of Asante troops that has been based in Wusuta (south and west of Kpandu, Fodome, and Petewu) since at least May 1869 are joined by Asante troops who have moved from the south to attack those Ewe forces that have retreated to the Kpandu and Fodome areas.

                Kuku is captured in fighting that also found the Petewu villages of the Liati district fighting alongside the men of Fodome.

                The Asante military commander, Adu Bofo, is ordered to return; he refuses.

Mid-1870   Adu Bofo starts to raid friends, foes, and neutral communities alike for captives.

                Kuku and other captives are marched to Kumase but are held at some distance from the capital.

Feb. 1871   The Asantehene sends reinforcements (food); Kuku is part of a group of slaves commandeered to deliver this food to Adu Bofo.

May 1871   Adu Bofo begins withdrawal from Wusuta.

2 Sept. 1871 Triumphal march by Adu Bofo with troops, slaves, and other booty through Kumase.

                Kuku is assigned to his master

c. 1874–77   Kuku and his father escape Asante and then return to get Kuku's mother.

c. 1877–86   Kuku and his father are enslaved in Anfoe.

c. 1886   Kuku and his father return to their hometown of Petewu.

                Kuku begins long-distance trading at approximately the age of twenty-three, traveling to Krachi and Keta among other places but largely confining his north-south movement to the Volta River and the trade routes that link Petewu to Agome Tomegbe and Lome.

c. 1888   Smallpox reportedly breaks out in villages on the Volta River and by this date has spread to the coastal communities east of the Volta.

c. 1890   By this date, smallpox has spread eastward from the Volta River into Kuku's home area; the outbreak kills many in his village, including his father, an uncle, a brother, and an aunt.

c. 1890–94   Kuku moves out of Petewu to live with another uncle until the epidemic subsides.

He then moves to Anfoe at the age of approximately thirty to obtain the bridewealth needed to marry.

Kuku's uncle, with whom he lived during the smallpox epidemic, dies.

Kuku travels to Krachi and buys the freedom of his mother's child and then of his mother.

Kuku returns with mother and mother's child to live in newly repopulated Petewu.

c. 1895   Kuku replaces an uncle as chief of Petewu five years after that uncle's death. According to German maps, the village at this time has only fifteen houses, down from the 100–170 dwellings that existed in 1890.[4]

c. 1898   Kuku is baptized as a Christian by Bremen missionary Mattäus Seeger, three years after being made chief.

1917   Kuku gives money to the German colonial government and to the Bremen Mission for their work in both German Togoland and in Germany prior to the missionary's expulsion from Togoland.

1928   Kuku narrates his life history to Ewe Evangelical Church minister Samuel Quist.

Dec. 1929   Kuku dies.

1930   Bremen missionary Paul Wiegräbe publishes extracts from Kuku's first-person narrative in the Bremen Mission's monthly periodical and as a short biography for popular distribution in Germany.

The Life History Of Evangelist Aaron Kuku

From his own oral account
written down by Rev. S. Quist in Palime
September 1929

Translated by Paul Agbedor
Edited by Sandra E. Greene and Kodjopa Attoh

Table of Contents

This man was born as Kuku. It is said that the name is associated with the name of one of his father's visitors, Kuma Tokpli. Others think that the name belongs to the category of names that is given to a newborn after the mother has lost earlier children. Apparently, the mother lost one child before Kuku was born. The father was called Ayisa, and the mother was Ahloefoe. [Kuku's] grandfather was a famous hunter of antelopes. On the day [Kuku's] mother's brother was born, the grandfather brought home some game (antelope). So, when he [the grandfather] returned home, they said to him "An antelope [that is, Kuku's mother's brother] has been born for you." Hence the mother's name Ahloefoe, which means "the antelope's younger sister." The father and mother both came from Petewu in Liati. Behind his uncle's house was a silk-cotton tree which was invaded by vultures (*pete*). So the tree was known as *petewu*,[5] meaning "vulture's silk-cotton tree." This became the name of the village. The parents were farmers, like all other people in the village. The father belonged to the royal family, and the mother came from a wealthy family. [Kuku's] paternal uncle was the chief of the village and was succeeded by another paternal uncle [his father's younger brother].

The village comprised three clans: Akpaxoe, Aposavi, and Asidovi clans. The father came from the Aposavi clan and the mother came from the Asidovi clan.

Kuku was born around 1860. As the mother recalled, he was eight at the time of the wars with the Asantes, which was around 1869–70. This information is also corroborated by the stories about the birth of Kuku's younger siblings— Adanuvor, Dalimedzrose, Mama—and the child that was born during the escape from the wars at Wlitodzi and who died two days after. This was one or two years prior to the great earthquake that preceded the Asante wars.

I. CHILDHOOD DAYS

He could not remember much, but the little narrative that follows is unique about him.

From his birth, he became the child of the three clans that made up the village. This is because his paternal grandmother, Agoe, from the Akpaxoe clan, married into the Aposavi clan and gave birth to his father Ayisa. The maternal grandmother, Nyador, also from the Akpaxoe clan, married into the Asidovi clan and gave birth to his mother, Ahloefoe. Hence, both the father and the mother were the nephew and niece of the Akpaxoe clan, and he became their grandson. He became a free child in all respects, and he was regarded as such. So he became a kind of leader among his peers whenever they played together. He became the love child of the village but has since become the unloved child today. God's ways are mysterious.

"Praise and gratitude to God" were his introductory words about the training and raising he had from his parents.

First is the story about his mother. It happened one day that while his sibling[6] Adanuvor was working on the rice, Kuku took a piece of hardened earth and threw it at her, hitting her hard. She cried, and being frightened by the cries, Kuku ran and took his sister in his arms before the mother came to their aid. Kuku admitted to the mother that he caused her to cry. The mother decided to apply a strong, hot spice into his nose as punishment for his behavior. She did not mete out the punishment that day. The next morning, after the father had left their small bedroom, the mother was indeed seen preparing the spice to be applied to his nostrils. Kuku realized, as a child, that the hour had come for his punishment. Since he could not run away, he only had to muster courage. What did he do? He craftily got some cotton wool from the room and inserted it into his two nostrils. Then he heard his mother calling him to come over. He responded and asked her to come and administer the punishment in the small room. She finally came and administered the concoction into the two nostrils, expecting young Kuku to start crying and wailing soon. He quickly ran out, removed the cotton wool from his nostrils, blew his nose, and exclaimed, "I didn't feel it! I didn't feel it." Realizing what young Kuku had done, the mother exclaimed, "See the cunning of a young child."

The second story reveals God's grace and mercy.

Though young Kuku usually accompanied his father to the farm, this particular day, he refused to go. His father did not like his attitude and wanted to force him to go to the farm. But his child ran away. The father ran after him as the boy ran into the bush. They reached a place where some people had cut palm branches and left the unwanted thorny parts in a pile. The boy jumped onto this pile. The father, fearing that the boy might be hurt, shouted, "I have lost him." The boy stood there visibly shaken, while the father also stood there watching and shaking feverishly. Passers-by hurried to the scene and took the boy. Surprisingly, he was not hurt at all, not even the slightest injury. It was all God's grace and mercy. They took him home, but for two days he refused to eat. He had discovered some ripe bananas in the bush and quietly went there to eat them. His refusal to eat made his poor parents even more worried. On the third day, thanks to a civet cat that ate the rest of the bananas that were in the bush, the young boy was forced to eat the food offered by the parents.

Now come Kuku's most dramatic experiences. They have to do with the Asante war that destroyed Wedome [inland Eweland].

II. STORIES OF THE ASANTE WAR

I was about eight years old when I heard about the Asante wars from my mother. The news at that time was that the Asantes were waging war on the area and had reached the Peki and Have areas. People were coming from those areas to our place, an indication that they were running away from war. Before, we only heard about the war; now it seemed to be very near.

One hot afternoon, we heard gunshots from the direction of Fodome. The Asantes had attacked them. This [particular Asante] division attacked from the Buem area. My father and his colleagues, wielding machetes, rushed from the farm to the battlefield. At that time, the whole village gathered and started running away from the war—mostly women and children. With my pregnant mother carrying Mama at the back, and my other sibling Adanuvor walking like me, we also joined those fleeing the war, moving toward Leklebi-Kame. My father and his colleagues who could not continue fighting retreated and joined us in the night. We had left our own village and become war refugees.

We headed toward Kuma Apoti. We met refugees from other towns and villages who joined us on our journey. Unknown to us, one division of the Asantes was approaching from Agu toward Yokele. There was serious fighting over there. Going forward was impossible. So we turned toward the Wli mountains. It was there that my mother delivered a baby boy, but due to the circumstances, fleeing from war, the baby died three days later without being named (this is because the names of the days of the week were not known in our area at the time).[7]

We had to leave the Wli mountains, go through Wli town, and then move toward Likpe. One of the Asante divisions had almost caught up with us in the mountains. A battle ensued that afternoon. The people of Fodome, returning from Likpe, fought them gallantly. My father was carrying my younger sibling, Mama, on his back; my mother was carrying the small boy, Dalimedzrase, on her back, and the rest of us were walking when the guns were being fired. We were all scattered. I lay down somewhere; some people dropped their straw bags (keviwo) where I lay. I selected some very good cloths, packed them in one straw bag and put it by my side. A man from Fodome also came to lie by my side. I asked him on several occasions to give me his knife so that I could take my own life, but he refused. Then another gun was fired at us. The man lying by my side got up and returned fire. Someone fell. I ran away and lay down at another place. Then an enemy came near the straw bag and wanted to take it. When he saw me, he left the bag and pursued me. I ran very fast and fell into a gully, sustaining an injury to my head. The man who followed me also fell into the gully near me and hurt his knee. Despite this injury, he caught me and took me up the mountain. On reaching the top, a quarrel ensued between him and the man who wanted to take my straw bag. The former hit the latter on the forehead, inflicting a cut that bled profusely. Their colleagues came and separated them.

My captors took me back to Wli and later to Kakpa. It was then that I saw my father and my siblings, Mama and Adanuvor, again. My father whispered to Adanuvor and then he hid at the outskirts of the town. His intention was to take us away. But the plot was uncovered and our captors watched us more closely. It was then that the Asante division that had gone to the Akposo area discovered that linguistically they [the Akposos] were not Ewes. They came back to join their colleagues [at Kakpa] and took us through Likpe and Boeme [Buem] to Ahamansu through Nkonya and Alavanyo. During those days, my father did not see me. My mother was separated from us right from the initial incident on the mountain when we were scattered by the gunfire. The only thing I could say was that "in joy or in sadness, we should wait on the Lord; that is the best thing." When my father had not seen me for some time, he decided to escape from his captors at all costs. He was shot at in the bush. There, by the grace of God, the Asantes split one of his ears with a knife and brought him to the town, where he chanced upon me and my captors.

1. LIVING IN ASANTE

We roamed through the forest before we came to Wusuta. There we crossed the Volta River to Kwawu. From Kwawu, we entered Asante territory at Konya [Kona]. At that time, word came that the [Asante] troops were running out of food, and they needed more fighters. We were made to hurriedly get food in the form of *kokonte* [dried cassava] to be sent to the troops. Another division of troops was also dispatched to the war. But after a short time, all the troops returned with the news that they had fought two battles at Agu and Amedzofe and that they had had to retreat mainly because of lack of food.

2. THE WAR BRIEFING TO THE CHIEF

After the troops had returned, they decided on a date to meet the king at Kumase and relate to him the story about the wars. On that day, they took all the captives to the king, whom they called Kekedi (the Ewes called him Krakani or Krakadi). My captor did not send me there, probably because I was young.

When they returned from Kumase, I asked about my father. I was told that he was coming. I asked a second and a third group and was told the same story. My fear was that we had heard that all the old people that were captured were all killed in Kumase.

My master asked me that afternoon to go and "fire" the palm trees[8] he was tapping. Because of what I had heard, I was weeping for fear that my father might have been killed. The torch I was using to fire the palm trees went out, and I threw it away and went into the bush. I found a hiding place. I took a rope and hanged myself. Incidentally, my master came into the bush looking for me and eventually found me hanging. He brought me down and took me home. It was long before I came to. All around my neck was sore. It was said that I intentionally scratched my neck. The sores were dressed with a mixture of chalk and other herbal medicines. Being alive today shows that God is truly great.

What caused me to hang myself that day was this: I heard that when they got to Kumase, my younger sibling Mama died. Word also came round that they had killed all the old captives, while my captors kept telling me that my father was coming. All this confused me and led to my action. Unbeknownst to me, my father's captor had given him to the king's relative in Kumase, and he became the carrier of the king's drum.

3. MY RELOCATION FROM KONYA TO SUTA [NSUTA]

One of the Suta chiefs was called Oseanewoa, meaning "he does whatever he says." It happened that the paramount chief of Suta, Kokoro, died. . . . He was the third chief that had attacked the Ewes in battle.[9] There was a dispute over the stool at that time between Oseanewoa and Yawokroma, and the case was taken [directly] to the king in Kumase [since presumably the person to whom the case should have been taken, Kokoro, had died]. Judgment was given in favor of Ose-anewoa. On his way back home, he heard that his chief military leader had died. He was called Epon. The chief [Oseanewoa] had to offer someone to be killed for the dead military commander instead of [just] a sheep. But then the commander [Epon] had no prisoners [of his own] because he was not a chief.[10] Konya was a place where chiefs spent the night on their way to Kumase. Oseanewoa spent the night there, and while he was lamenting about how he would get the sacrifice, he was told that one of his slaves was in the town. That was me. My master and I had just come home from gathering kola nuts. My master was eating; I was also eat-ing, sitting by the load I had brought from the bush. Just after I had started eating, there was a knock at the gate (*Agoo!*). Before I was aware [of what was happen-ing], one of the visitors grabbed my hand. The food fell from my hand. Before my master could ask what was the matter and why they would not allow me to finish eating, they had handcuffed me to a weaver's loom, hand and foot. I stayed there from twelve noon till eight o'clock the following morning before I was untied, after which they tied my waist with a rope made from grass. They made me carry a brass bowl called *sanaa* containing a big and heavy cannonball. I had been con-demned to death without knowing it. They took me to Asrame, which was about fifteen minutes' walk away. When we got there, we stopped in the street, where three gunshots were fired. Then the executioner asked the chief what he should do. The chief said everything was in his [the executioner's] hands. The execu-tioner stood up and was about to strike me with his knife when one of the warriors called Buatsi asked him to stop and look before him. There was in front of us a pregnant woman. She was carrying a large stem of the plantain tree, signifying that she had also been condemned to death. The captors narrated her story as follows: the woman had a quarrel with another woman, during which she swore an oath.[11] Upon investigation, it was discovered that she was rather the guilty one. She had thus become the chief's prisoner, and that is why they had brought her to the chief. Immediately, the chief, Oseanewoa, commanded that she should be taken away. Before he had finished, they pushed her down, broke her neck, tied her legs with a rope, and dragged her on the ground to the grave digger's. This was strange because the Asante never killed pregnant women. Meanwhile, the rope around my waist was removed. I was miraculously saved. I would have been killed. This realization dawned on me much later. It was God's greatness (Ps. 118). I was later sent back to Suta, where I became a servant in the house of the chief.

4. THE CHIEF'S BRIEFING

It was long after the last event. One day, the chief called me: Anyomimanboa. I responded loudly Nana. Then he asked me if I remembered the day we went to Asrame, and if I remembered the man who came to me after the firing of the mus-ketry. I responded "yes." He went on to say that I was to have been killed, but the pregnant woman took my place. I almost fainted when I heard these words, and I began to shake feverishly. The chief told me not to worry because those days were past. But even three days after, I had not fully recovered. I had become ill.

5. MY SOJOURN IN A FETISH HOUSE FOR THREE MONTHS

God's ways are not ours. I became seriously ill. What was the cause?

One day I was standing in front of my master's gate when a child my age was passing along the street by the house. I jokingly threw a small stone at the child. The stone hit him and he also replied, but his did not hit me. Soon after, I was called to the house and my master asked me to accompany his new wife to her hometown to go and help her colleagues on the farm. We set out immediately for the farm. The woman was working while I sat down and waited for her. Soon I became very feverish. It grew worse. The chief's mother-in-law immediately indicated I should be taken home. The chief's wife accompanied me back. When we got home, every effort was made to help me. The chief was informed. Finally, the chief provided some eggs and drink and asked that I should be taken to a fetish priest who could take care of me. The fetish was called Woadzifaye. I stayed there for three months. I was healed quickly, but I was not released early. The reason is as follows:

Before the chief Oseanewoa had gone to war in Eweland, he consulted two fetishes: one was Kunim and the other was this one, Woadzifaye, to whom I was taken. He promised that if they brought him back safely from the war, he would give them a person. After the war, he fulfilled the promise to the other fetish [Kunim] by handing over someone, but he denied the other fetish [its reward]. When I became ill, they consulted several oracles. The message they received was the same, that the fetish [Woadzifaye] was responsible for my illness. A messenger was sent to the fetish. Immediately after the messenger arrived, . . . [the] voice [of the god] asked what he wanted there. [It went on to state that the chief's] child had provoked him by throwing a stone at him in the street, but if he had wanted the stone that he threw back to hit him, [Kuku] would have been finished long ago. He was lucky. It was after this revelation that the chief gathered the items needed to pacify the god and asked me to be taken to the fetish house. That was why the fetish priest was not willing to release me after I was healed. But God took me away all the same.

This experience and others made me believe that someone who does not believe that the devil exists will not believe that God exists either. The following story confirms this assertion further.

6. REUNION WITH MY FATHER

Someone from the chief's house saw me at the fetish house and reported to the chief how well I had become. Three days after, the chief sent someone to bring me back. The fetish priest and his colleagues released me reluctantly to the chief. So I went back to the chief's house. It was then that my father was arrested and brought to the chief's house.

My father, who was before then the drum carrier for one of the relatives of the paramount chief of Kumase, had an opportunity to escape. He journeyed through the bush past his earlier captors and reached the outskirts of our village. For eight days, he hid near the path to the river, hoping that he would see me pass. On the ninth day, he saw a woman passing by and singing an Ewe song. My father came out to meet her, asked her where she came from and whether his son Kuku was in the village. After the woman had replied in the affirmative, he asked her to tell me that my father was around and that the woman and I should secretly come and escape with him. When the woman came back, she didn't tell me anything. Instead, she reported this to her husband, who also reported it to the chief. Immediately, the chief sent sixteen hunters to the bush to look for my father. They succeeded and brought my father to the village in the evening, by which time I had already gone to bed. The chief sent for me. When I got there, the elders and the military leaders had gathered. My father stood in the middle with a rope tied around his waist. I sat down. I was asked if I knew the person standing in the middle. I responded that he was my father. They asked my father, and he also confirmed that he was my father. They asked him where he came from and he replied that he came from Prasu [Praso]. They then asked him why he was hiding in the bush and why he wanted me to come to meet him in the bush. He replied that he was hiding there to see if I would pass to the river so that he could see me and greet me. They asked who his master was. He mentioned the name and said that he was in Kumase. He was handed over to the executioner who was to take custody of him for five days, after which he would be sent back to his master. Some suggested that he should be beheaded and only the head be sent to the master. But the chief did not agree. Thus, I had seen my father again, but he had become the prisoner of another.

7. EVERYTHING THAT GOD DOES IS GOOD

I asked permission to cook for my father while he was in custody, and the chief agreed. I cooked for him for two days. On the third day, when I took food to him, I lamented that if his hands had not been fastened to a heavy piece of wood but chained instead, he could have made an attempt to escape, just like someone did with chains a few days earlier. Unfortunately, his was the *apã*,[12] which was difficult to escape from. I told him that the day they were to take him away, I would go hang myself. It would be better for me to die than to see him suffering all the time. Then my father asked me what the chain looked like. He then proceeded to draw it on the ground and asked whether it looked like the one he had drawn. Immediately, I told the guard that my father said he had seen the chain with which the prisoner had escaped. The guard ran to my father and my father showed him the drawing of the chain. He took a close look at the drawing and said it was exactly the same chain and that he was going to tell the chief. I also set out to go tell the chief. I ran, while the guard walked because he was a respectable person and would not run. So, I got there before him. He also repeated what I had told the chief. The chief was very happy to hear the news. He asked the drums to be beaten to summon the elders and the military commanders to a meeting. The decision was that since it was already late, my father would lead them to the place the following day to bring back the chain. When day broke, the chief ordered the hunters to gather around my father, who took him to the bush and he showed them the chain, which they brought home with joy. The loss of the chain had been a great headache for the chief. For three months, they had looked for it in vain. At that time, the chief was even ready to offer a boy and a girl and forty pounds to anyone who found the chain. The chief then said that if my father was able to take me away, he would not mind. Only God deserves thanks.

8. PLANNING THE ESCAPE

Because of what the chief said, the guards did not pay much attention to my father anymore. The time had come for us to escape. But whenever my father wanted us to leave in the night, I overslept. One day, I devised a plan. I went to bed very early and warned my colleagues that they should not call me for dinner. When I woke up, everyone was asleep. I got up. But it was difficult to get out of the house. There was a door at the entrance with three locks.

How I managed to open the doors that were locked is a mystery to me to this day. I walked to the place where they had kept my father. Their door was firmly locked. I tried in vain to get it open. Then I went back, ran, and hurled myself at the door, and it split open. I ran to hide in a nearby bush. The sound had awakened some people, who got up to look for the person responsible. They did not find anybody. Some said it was a hyena that had come around. They made sure things were in order and went back to sleep. After a while, I went back. This time, I entered the room. My father was the first person, lying near the door. I raised his cloth to identify him. But to be sure, I inspected all the prisoners and came back to my father. I woke him up. He took a big knife lying against the wall and we took off. We walked for a while, stopped, looked at each other and shook hands. I called God and said "God will surely take us home." Yes, the day God redeems the prisoner, it will truly be like a dream.[13]

9. REPEATED JOURNEYS AND SUFFERING

Our escape had now begun. We went past a small town, but daylight soon came. So, we avoided the main road so as not to be seen and arrested. We reached Konyaland, where we had stayed earlier. We journeyed only at night, hid in the bush, and lay down like animals during the day. One of us at a time kept watch for people who might be coming around. Our hiding places were farms and between crossroads.

We then headed toward the Kwawu area. We had gone around for forty-one days before we reached a big silk-cotton tree. I climbed on the large root of the tree. Then the thought came to me that we should go back and get my mother and my sibling Dalimedzrose. So we went back toward Konya town. We hid at the outskirts of my mother's village Tsuafo, in a thick plantain grove. We stayed there for thirteen days, waiting for my mother to pass by so we could take her away. Unbeknownst to us, the people had heard about our escape, and my mother was transferred to another village. My mother later disclosed to me that she was taken to Dobuasu [Dompoasi], three days' walk from where she was before. We were tired of waiting, so we headed back to the Kwawu area. After walking for another forty-one days, we arrived at the big silk-cotton tree again. I again climbed the root and said that we should go back for my mother by all means. We went back and hid in the same plantain grove. This time, someone saw us and reported.

At dawn, the chief's drums, whistles, and horns could be heard from the distance. Then there was silence. The people were being summoned because of us; they were preparing for us. We remained in the plantain grove until it was getting dark. We decided to leave. We had barely walked twenty yards when we came face to face with people. They wanted to arrest us. My father plunged his big knife forward; the first person fell. We rushed through them. They followed us, firing at us until hunger took a toll on them and they retreated. By the grace of God, we did not get into their hands.

Meanwhile, I was terribly injured. While I was jumping, I had landed on a tree stump, part of which pierced my thigh. It was on the third day that my father removed the piece of wood from my flesh. I kept running even after that injury. Then I heard my father shout to me that I should come back. I jumped back. Behold, there was a trap, which was set there, and another step would have landed me in the trap.

We went into the bush again, entered someone's yam farm, uprooted and roasted some of the yam for food to be eaten at night. We remained there for three days before we left, passing through Tsuafuadua or Akukonumisio in the night. I went to open my mother's door to no avail. We left, and when we got to the outskirts of the town, I called out loudly to the people and said, "I have tried to get my mother out without success, I'm gone." Then we heard people shutting their doors, and we also took off. We again passed Konya, where we were caught earlier, and continued until we reached the silk-cotton tree. About four yards before we got under the tree, I suggested to my father that we should go by the right and he agreed. Soon it was daybreak and we hid ourselves again.

In the evening, we picked some leaves and prepared them to sleep on. My father had hardly lain down when he cried out that something had bitten him. Truly, he had been bitten by a snake on the shoulder. Immediately, he started vomiting. Our problems had multiplied. I broke into tears but later mustered courage and told my father that it was better that he was vomiting. But he said that when a snake bit someone and he or she began to vomit, it was a bad sign, and that he would surely die. I told him that if he died, I would also commit suicide. He told me not to attempt suicide if he should die.

Fortunately, my father survived the night; the only problem was that he could not eat. I looked around and found a tall pawpaw tree nearby with ripe pawpaws on it. I climbed it and picked some. Then I heard a voice that said "My spouse, pick some for me too." I was so shocked that I did not even know how I got down and how I carried two pawpaws to my father. The pawpaws served as the only food for my father. Thanks to God, the wonderful protector.

10. HEADING HOME AND STRUGGLING WITH DEATH ON LAND AND IN WATER

Now, we left and headed toward the Kwawu area at daybreak. We took the normal road during the night and avoided them during the day. One early morning, we found some mushrooms and we started to uproot them. Suddenly, a gigantic male slave appeared. He grabbed my father's knife and took off. My father picked the stick he was using to uproot the mushroom and followed him but we could not get him. We stopped the chase and continued our journey. Our main lighter and implement were gone. For twelve days, we ate nothing. We arrived at a village. There, my father forcibly entered someone's room in the night and picked up a knife and some fire [brands]. We were chased, but we escaped. But what we used to set fire had become wet and would not ignite. As a result, we stayed another eight days without food, making twenty days in all. We could have died during this period.

On the twentieth day, we were stuck virtually in the middle of the road. We were very weak and were writhing from hunger. We began to feel intensely thirsty. I begged my father to try to get to a nearby rock to see if he could find some water there to drink and to get some for me. He said he could not and that I should rather try. I also said I couldn't. Eventually, I managed to get up and tried to get to the rock. I found a broken pot and took it along. Unfortunately, there was no water around the rock. I came back and urged my father or both of us to move toward a thicket at the edge of the grassland. Behold, there was a small stream flowing by. We drank to our fill and were relieved a bit. We filled the broken pot; we set fire and cooked some dry snails we were carrying. My father refused to eat because he said those snails we ate earlier nearly resulted in death. I ate as much as I could and realized that it was agreeable to my system. When I told my father they were good, he agreed to eat them. I cooked some for him. We regained some strength and moved a little further, and we stayed there for three days to recuperate.

We continued our journey toward home, passing through more farms than before. One day, as it was getting dark, we spotted some pepper and decided to pick some. We did not expect anyone to be in the bush at that time, so we relaxed. Suddenly, my father spotted someone returning from his farm, putting his gun in a position to shoot. He shouted and we scattered. The man fired the gun. We reconvened in the evening. My father asked whether the shot was fired at me. I told him I had hidden, so it was fired at him. I asked if he was hit. He said he was safe, except for a stick that had pricked his heel. When we examined the heel, we realized that it was a bullet that had hit him and that it was lodged inside the heel. We remained there for three days during which we removed the bullet and planned our next move. We reached a territory that seemed familiar. We kept away from the main road as much as possible.

One day, as it was getting dark, we decided to go to the main road to find out where we could find something to eat. We reached the top of a rocky landscape. We found a farm hut. We saw a woman picking pepper, so we moved back quietly. Little did we know that the woman had seen us and had gone to report on us in the village. After waiting for some time, we climbed into the valley to find the main road. A man was walking stealthily along the edge of the valley toward us. All of a sudden we bumped into each other. My father shouted and we ran down [through] the valley. The man took his gun and cutlass and followed us. He jumped down and landed where we were. He got up, took his cutlass, and tried to strike my father. The cutlass landed in my father's palm, almost severing the thumb. I heard my father shout, "Don't kill me; you have already captured me." Then I ran back and hit the man with a club I was carrying. He turned toward me; I hit him a second and a third time. He fell and motioned for us to run away. He said we were not his people, so we should go. Then he turned and walked sluggishly back. At that time, my father was looking for a cutlass to kill him. I talked my father out of the idea and we ran through the valley until we reached a crossroad. We hid ourselves around that junction. At dawn, we heard women talking in the distance. Apparently, the man from the village had gone to the nearby town not quite long ago. When he was questioned, he said some escapees were passing by, and when he confronted them they beat him; he died later. The women were lamenting thus: "Oh! Some people's chief! Where is Antsui? We heard he has gone to Saraha [Salaga]."[14] We turned and looked into each other's face.

We hid there for two to three days, until the situation had cleared before we set off again one night, passing by the town, which was the last Kwawu town. (We were later informed that it was called Pepease). By then, my father's hand, which was bandaged earlier, had healed a little. Only God deserves praise and thanksgiving.

Now, we headed toward the big river known as River Afram. We reached at night a small village by the river. The people were asleep, lying against the boat, which we could have used to cross the river. We walked quietly to the river and went upstream. The river was full, and we could see crocodiles and hippopotamuses in the river in the distance. We came across some dried yams somewhere. I picked two and my father picked one, but we did not know in which direction to go. Finally, my father said that if he were alone, he would swim across. Enough was enough! We had spent almost a whole day by the riverbank. My father swam with one yam across to the other side. After a short rest, he swam back. He rested while we thought of what to do. I walked on a tree by the river, while my father waded in the river by my side. I fell and he took me back to the bank. My father prayed, calling on all the gods of our land. I also prayed that if it was the will of God, we would reach home. After waiting for some time, my father tied a rope [around his waist, knotted] at his back, with a loop at the end and asked me to put my hand in it. Then he stepped into the river. Now, all our belongings, which he was carrying on the head, fell into the deep river. He swam to midstream; he got tired. I jumped ahead of him, swinging my arms in an attempt to swim. I had become a swimmer. This effort encouraged my father and he followed, pushing me forward as I continued my swimming attempt. We were getting close to the other bank. But I became so weak that I could not make another move. Then my foot touched the floor of the river. I jumped up and continued swimming.

My father also had the same experience. We continued with the swimming until we got to the point where we could stand in the river. We then walked the remaining distance to the bank. We rested at the bank for some time before we climbed to a higher ground. We were thankful that nobody found us there; we would have been captured easily. All our belongings—knife, sticks we were using to count the days, the bullet, food, everything went into the river, except the clothes we had on. But thank God that we had crossed the river.

After some rest, we decided to go on. Then we came across another river, flowing over a vast area. What were we to do? It was a life or death situation. We stepped into the water to see how deep it was. We walked on until we reached the other side. God's ways are wonderful.

We had now left Asanteland behind. We give all the glory and thanks to God.

11. ARRIVAL IN EWELAND

We spent the night by the riverside and continued the next day, crossing the main road by which the Asantes took us to their land. We came across a hut, where we obtained a wooden torch and a pot, which we carried with us.

The path we were treading became bushy at a point, and we were not sure where to proceed. I asked my father where the sun rose and where it set: whether it was Asanteland or Eweland. He answered and said that it rose in

Eweland and set in Asanteland. Then I suggested that we should use the movement of the sun as a guide and move eastward to Eweland. So, we continued
the journey for another eighteen days before we reached a town.

After this long and tedious journey, we arrived at a place [and] stopped to
rest. We lit a fire and slept around it. We slept very deeply because of fatigue.
Then we heard a sound. We woke up suddenly with a shout. My father disclosed
that it was a lion. The animal had scattered the fire we had set and had run away.
I wanted us to reset the fire, but my father refused, saying that the animal did not
like fire [and would come again to scatter it]. Then we heard its cry in the distance.
The leaves of the trees fell on us. I was shocked; in fact I was unconscious. It took
some time before I regained consciousness and we continued the journey.

About seventeen days after we left the riverside, we reached what appeared
to be hunters' territory and a place where they grilled or smoked their game. We
breathed a sigh of relief. We had reached our own people's territory. The next day,
we saw a boatyard and the people who were carving the boats. We bypassed
them and rejoined the road, threw the wooden torches and the broken pot on the
refuse dump and entered the village. We met a woman in the village. She offered
us water to drink and called her husband, who was on the street fixing his weaving
loom. Soon, we were surrounded by people. After an exchange of greetings, we
were asked of our mission. We told them that the Asantes had captured us and
had taken us to Asanteland but we had been able to escape. "You have reached
home! You have reached home," exclaimed the people. Then my father asked of
the name of the village. They said it was called Awatoe [Awate]. We had not heard
of this name before, so my father asked if they knew the town of Nuita. They replied that it was to the north of their village and not far from there. My father asked
of the town Tsyome [Dschome]. They said it was to the south and not far. Then my
father asked of some people he knew at Vakpo. They said they knew them and
that they were relations. My father then asked them to send word to Vakpo for
those he knew to come and take us home. They agreed but said that when they
received escapees, they collected twenty cowries from the women and twenty-
five from the men. My father asked them to tell the messengers to inform our relatives to get the money when they were coming for us. But they never sent the
message and we remained with the woman and the husband.

12. BEING SLAVES A SECOND TIME IN OUR HOMELAND

The people took care of us for about three or more weeks. We were beginning
to put on weight. We accompanied our host to the Awatoe market. All this while
they were making plans to sell us.

One day, they called to inform us that the people who were coming from
Vakpo to take us away had arrived. But the people were rather from Anfoe.
They bargained with them and handed us over to them. We had become bought

slaves. When we reached Anfoe Bume, people gathered and our buyers narrated to them what had transpired. Meanwhile, they had cooked for us. Later when I overheard the amount for which we were bought, I cried. My father consoled me that at least we were in our home territory and we would hear news from home, and that it was not Asanteland. Our new master, who had apparently lived in our town before, also consoled us by mentioning the names of people known to us and pretended to be friendly to us.

We took twenty-three months to travel from Asante, the land of our captivity, to get to our homeland, only to become slaves in Anfoe Bume for nine years or one hundred and eight months. Oh! The depth of the riches of the wisdom and knowledge of God both! How unsearchable His judgments; how untraceable His paths (Romans 11:33).

If I should narrate our experiences during these nine years, it would take such a long time. But there is one thing I definitely have to talk about.

13. HOW WE MANAGED TO GET TO OUR HOMETOWN
After having deceived us into staying with him, our master by the name Koli, secretly sold my father to an Akyem, who was a very intimate friend of his. The Akyem man wanted me to be sold to him, too. Anfoe people heard the news. They were very angry with our master and asked what would happen if we were taken back to Akanland and we managed to escape and the Liati people (our people) heard that the Ewe people sold their own people to the Akans. So our master had to take back my father from the Akyem man. Those days they were trading in oil with Waya. Now our master sent word to our hometown Petewu. They came and summoned the Awatoe people to the court of Abram, Boso Nyaku's military leader (apparently charging them for trying to sell us back to the Asantes). After all attempts to settle the matter failed, he sent the case to the Hausa chief, Mamatsi (those days, the Hausas commanded a lot of respect). When the Awatoe people were not cooperating, Mamatsi sent a messenger to the fort at Adafo [Ada Foah]. Meanwhile, he had sent his own police to arrest the Awatoe man who sold us. Thus the Awatoe people gave in before the police from Adafo arrived. The Awatoe people paid back our ransom money to the Anfoe people, who in turn released us to our people. Thus, by God's mercy, my father and I entered our hometown Petewu again after many years.

Give thanks to the Lord for He is good; His love endures forever. Let the redeemed of the Lord say His kindness endures forever (Ps. 107).

III. SERIOUS EXPERIENCES AT HOME

My father became ill not long after our return from Asante. By God's grace, he recovered, and we continued our farming. Sometimes, I went on business (trading) trips to [Agome] Tomegbe or the Gold Coast and other places such as the Kratsi and Keta areas.

1. THE TERRIBLE SMALLPOX EPIDEMIC

About six years after our return, a dreadful smallpox epidemic hit our town. My mother's younger sister was attacked, and so was my uncle's house. I was fortunate to have suffered this dreadful disease earlier in Asante and I had now become the caretaker of the sick and even the one who buried the dead. It was a pity; the disease caused great devastation. Forty-seven people were killed within a month, and I buried them all. They included my father, my elder brother, my uncle, and my mother's elder sister. A lot of my other relations also died during the epidemic. The survivors ran away from the town to settle in their farm huts. The epidemic spread to the nearby town called Adafonu. I was the one who took care of the sick there, too.

Since most people had relocated to their farm huts, I was the only one left in the town. As a result, I became bored and often depressed. One day, I had a serious thought. In the night, I took my gun, made it ready for firing, and laid it down. I took my accordion, played it, and sang sorrowful songs, with the intention of committing suicide after the singing. I was about to get up and pick up the gun when I saw a bright light, like a big lantern, coming toward me. Suddenly and miraculously, I went into a deep sleep. When I woke up, the gun was lying by my side, and it was already daybreak. I got up and went to my paternal uncle in the farm hut. He advised that I should leave the town. I agreed and relocated to Soba. That place too was not agreeable to me, so I went and joined my uncle at Woti.

2. MY FIRST MARRIAGE AND THE DEATH OF MY UNCLE AND WIFE

During my sojourn at Woti, a relation of mine sent word to me from Liati that his daughter was seeking a divorce from the husband, so I should come and pay the bride price (to be returned to the husband) and take her as my wife. My uncle could have refunded this bride price easily, but because people's eyes were on me, and this affected him too, he preferred that I should go and borrow money from Anfoe Akukome. This would make me leave the town for a while because I would have to stay with my creditor until the loan was paid. Thus, I had to live in Anfoe a second time.

Two years into my living in Anfoe, I decided to go to Bator on a business trip. My new wife also expressed the desire to go with me. I did not agree initially, because of the miscarriage she had not long ago. But later, I agreed for her to go with me. We set off for Bator. We spent the night at Kpeve. Soon after we went to bed, we heard the drumming of "Gobe," a new dance in those days. My wife wanted to go there because the music sounded very good. I refused to allow her to go. But she persisted. Finally, I went with her to the drumming and dancing session. We came back after a short while. My wife could not sleep. She wanted to go back to the drumming spot. But I said to her: "I am tired. Why are you pestering me so much? Have you never gone to this drumming session in Anfoe before? Or are you being haunted by death?" She laughed hysterically and then suddenly exclaimed that she had a severe pain in the side (in the rib cage). The pain worsened. What a pity! My landlord came to help. A messenger was sent to Govie Kpeve that night to consult soothsayers. The message of the soothsayers was that she had taken money [cowries] from a man, and the man had cursed her in her absence. My wife said if the man cursed her in her absence, she would not contest. I obtained a white fowl to be sacrificed to the fetish that was invoked on her behalf. The fowl was slaughtered and put in a fire to be dressed. Suddenly, the supposedly dead fowl jumped from the fire and landed at a distance. Soon after, my wife put her two arms on me and breathed her last breath and died. The town mourned deeply with us. Messengers were sent to her parents and relatives. Before the messengers returned, a half-brother of my wife arrived from Accra. He decided to take charge of the funeral, saying that if they were in their hometown he would have to bury his sister anyway. So, before the parents came, she had been buried and the funeral performed. The next day, which was the ninth day after we had left home, I was taken back home.

3. LITIGATION WITH A MAN FROM AGOME TOMEGBE

About ten days after some Anfoe people came to visit me, I went to Agome Tomegbe to collect a debt from the man who was said to have cursed my late wife. His father had bought a slave from my father's elder brother and was left with fourteen cowries' debt to pay and they were both dead. I was angered by his connection with my wife's death, so I was determined to collect the money from him at all cost. Some people feared that I might rather incur more debt. I reached Agome Tomegbe safely. Incidentally, they were performing the funeral of a woman; she was one of the debtors I was coming to demand payment from. She was a concubine of the man who had cursed my wife. It was difficult for me to go and demand payment. I waited for some time. In the evening, I went to bathe; as soon as I put the towel into the water to wipe my feet, I heard a loud voice from the air saying: "Kuku, Kuku, get up! Get up!" I got up immediately, poured the water out, and went and sat by a fetish priestess, who was seated in front of her house. As soon as I sat down, two people came and greeted us. I asked them what their mission was. They said their relative was sick and they were coming to consult the oracles. It happened that the man I was coming to demand payment from was the one who had been ill for fourteen days, that is sixteen days after my wife's death. The fetish priestess consulted the oracles and said that two ghosts were trying to kill the man. The visitors said they understood the message concerning the ghost from their own town; what they did not understand was why the ghost from Liati, who rather owed the sick person, would try to kill him. I enquired about the name of the Liati woman. Another person mentioned the name and whispered to his colleague that the one who was making the enquiry was the husband of the woman. I overheard that too. When the man came back, I asked him to give me the name of the woman. But he refused, saying that it was too late in the night to mention the name of a dead person. I swore to him immediately that I would deal with him. The next day, the other party asked me to summon a traditional court. I told them they had to assemble the court members. They refused, so I told them that I had not reached the point where I could summon the court, and I left for home. They made me return, and we went to court. The youth were proving difficult, so I summoned them to Anfoe. The Anfoe people summoned them to meet at We, but they refused to go. They were then summoned to Kuma Apoti, which they accepted. They were found guilty and were made to pay my money to me.

4. BRINGING HOME MY MOTHER

After these events, I heard of my mother at Kratsi. So I took the little quantity of rubber I had to Krobo, sold it, and went to get her. On my first trip, I managed to bring back the child she was carrying at the time. It was in the following year that I was also able to bring my mother home. By then, the people who were scattered because of the dreadful epidemic, came back to rebuild the town of Petewu once again. I also left Anfoe and went back home.

5. A UNIQUE REDEMPTION BY GOD

I took to serious farming. One day, when I went to cut sticks for supporting yam, I fell into a pit at the bottom of a rotten trunk of a baobab tree. It took me a long time to get out of it. When I reported the incident at home, I was asked to provide a white fowl for purification, after which it would be thrown into the pit. I turned a deaf ear to the request. Instead, I went back the following day and tried to fill the pit with as many stones as I could find. Then I collected the sticks I had cut and took them home. Nothing happened to me.

6. PERSECUTION BY MY PEOPLE

Here is evidence of the unfair judgment meted out to me in court. I was unjustly asked to pay a fee for reversing an oath made by a dead person; I was also unjustly convicted in a case in which someone swore on the collapse of our house.

But the persecution I faced is clearly evident in what follows: One day, we agreed to go on a hunting expedition with the people of Soba. We designated a spot where the first person who reached that place would shout. The Soba people lay ambush. As soon as I arrived at the spot and shouted, they set fire all around me. I was surrounded by fire. It took great effort and the mercy of God for me to escape it. I had to crawl on both hands and feet, with a cartridge box around my waist, and a gun at the back. The first person who saw and recognized me even passed by; some other people passed by but later came to take me across the river home. I was burnt all over, my hands and feet being worse. I later suffered from painful urination for some months. I miraculously survived. The gunpowder in the cartridge box did not blow up, and the loaded gun did not fire by itself. This was all due to the abundant grace that God had bestowed on me, but which I had not realized. Father, forgive me.

Finally, let me tell you the story of an older person that confirms the plot to persecute me. One evening as I responded to nature's call, I met an elder of the town. Recognizing me, he called and told me that my wisdom was greater than the wisdom of the whole town put together, so I would never be found innocent in any court in Liati.

IV. MY BECOMING A CHRISTIAN

Five years after my paternal uncle died, I was installed by the new chief to succeed him. It was then that I began to have some peace. This continued for about three years.

1. HEARING GOD'S WORD THE FIRST TIME AND MY DECISION

One day, while I was handling a case at the palace, messengers of the gospel, Mr. Jacob Anku from Avatime and Mr. Cornelius Kodzo from Ho, came. They preached God's word to us. I am sorry I cannot remember all that they said, but the following words I remember very well: They have mouths but cannot speak; they have eyes . . . (Ps. 115:5ff). After the preaching, the people responded that they had heard them. But I stood up and said that what we had heard was not the words of our fetish Togbo and all those petty fetishes. These words were peculiar. That was the first time I had heard the words of God. We attended a big rally held at Abrenino-Dome, but I listened only to the organ and songs. Incidentally, I became interested in these preachers. I went with them to far away Dafonu [Dafor], where they preached. I came back with them and later saw them off to Soba.

After some time, I felled some oil palm trees, about eighty-six in number, to be tapped for palm wine. On the third day of firing the palm trees, my decision to become a Christian dawned on me. I was served palm wine, which I drank and poured the dregs on the ground. I was "congratulated."[15] I responded by saying that in three days I would go for God's word. We met another day again, and after drinking and pouring down the dregs of the palm wine, I said that whether we had closed or not I was going to work in the vineyard of God. They took it for a joke. As soon as I got home, I packed a few clothes and things and informed my household that I was accepting the word of God. I was gone.

My people feared I was going crazy. They followed me and took my luggage, trying to prevent me from leaving. I managed to slip away. My nephew told them that I was not crazy and that I had been talking about receiving the word of God for the past three days.

I went to Ve, and continued to Logba, where I stayed with Messrs. Anthony Binka and Joseph Aba. I attended church service at Dzokpe. The Dzokpe Christians wrote a letter to Mr. Seeger, the pastor then stationed at Amedzofe. He responded that I should rather go to Leklebi. Those days, Mr. Martin Asima Kwasi lived in Leklebi as their teacher. I started studying with him. Not long after that, he left his house and farms in my care, saying he was going to Agome Kpalime and would be back. Unknown to me, he was leaving the mission work and going into another employment. It was by God's grace that I was able to read. I bought a primer and asked Mr. Samuel Agboka to teach me. He did that for only sixteen days, after which I was able to read the Bible to some extent, a feat that surprised Mr. Seeger, who tested me and gave me a copy of one of the books of the Bible. I had become a reader. I was lucky because it took a long time for another teacher to be sent to Leklebi, in the person of Friedrik Barn, with whom I continued my studies.

We the learners were quite many. When Mr. Seeger visited us, only five of us were selected for baptism. Mr. Seeger himself chose the name Aaron for me. Oh! I had also become a son of the Almighty God who saved me from uncountable problems and even death; I had also become his at last. Praise and thanks to Him forever.

2. BEGINNING OF STUDIES TOWARD BAPTISM

I was surprised that Pastor Seeger gave me the name Aaron by himself. At first, my colleagues suggested the name Abraham. He refused when I mentioned it to him. Later they suggested the name Joseph. He turned down that one, too. It was during the baptism that he called me Aaron. Later, when I thought about it, I realized that he probably believed that I would be an assistant to a messenger of God, just like Aaron was to Moses. Before my baptism, when I had been studying for only three months, and I was able to read the scriptures, I was filled with a strong desire to share this valuable wealth with my poor relatives. I began to preach.

I took my preaching to Fodome. I took with me a student, who served as my bellboy. I usually based my preaching on a text in the Bible or by using real-life stories to show the people how to get through to God. I also traveled to Danyi. I brought one child from there to Leklebi. I brought one child also from Agome Tomegbe. I preached with the same zeal during my travels as I did in Leklebi, which had become my home. The people were surprised and wondered how I, who had recently joined them, was rather teaching them the word of God.

At that time, no Christian had put up a building at the station or Kpodzi. I became the first person to do so, and I brought Sam Fia (who was called Agboka),

Daniel Agama, Jonas Kuma, and Emmanuel Kwasi to stay with me. Because the building was becoming overcrowded, and because many people wanted to stay with us, I added two more rooms. My colleagues lived in these rooms while they put up their own houses. Other Christians and students who were preparing for baptism joined us at the station. Our number had increased considerably, and I became their leader. By the grace of God, I trained them to the best of my ability.

There was pressure on me to get a teacher from Amedzofe. The pressure was so great that traveling from Leklebi to Amedzofe became almost a daily routine. One day, when I went to Amedzofe on the usual mission, Mr. Dettmann saw me from the distance and exclaimed: Who are you? Where do you come from? What is your name? Were you not the one who came here the other day? And three days after you are here again? Don't you know that there is disease in Leklebi? You want us to also get the disease and die? These words almost made me faint, and I stood motionless and speechless. I was gripped by fear. But the man himself started to console me and slowly led me to a seat. Then he talked to me with explanation and encouragement before seeing me off. I must say that this was the strongest word I had heard from the priests that I have known; they were not evil words though.

Finally, we were given a teacher. He was Friedrick Barn from Keta. We were very happy with him. During his time, the leadership and welfare of the congregation was still my responsibility. As a result, I could not travel on crusade. However, the entire congregation of Leklebi went on crusades to neighboring towns and as far away as Wli. These are some of the stories of my learning period.

3. ACCEPTING BAPTISM AND AFTER

After my baptism, I went to the Gold Coast for some time. It was a self-examination period for me. I met a Wli citizen there, and during our free times, we read the Bible and discussed issues. He left before me. When I went back to Leklebi, I met him again. We continued our discussion as we did earlier. He became convinced and moved from his hometown of Wli and settled at Leklebi Dugã. He started studying for baptism. Before long, he brought his wife and two of his sisters to join him. Soon after, I moved back to my hometown and took to farming as before.

About a year later, there was a decree that everybody should go out for road construction. One could not refuse to go because it was a government directive. As a Christian, I was not pleased with the oath that accompanied the directive. That was the second time [I decided to leave Leklebi]. After the construction, I went to the bush, cleared a portion of land and settled there. I resumed farming again. The place was the farming area of the Woti people. We used to meet often. One of them asked me for some oil palm trees to be tapped for palm wine. I allowed him to fell a few trees for tapping. Soon, the place became a haven for drinkers. Thus, I had the opportunity to preach to the people who came around. One day, when I was returning from Leklebi Dugã, where I went to church every Sunday, I met the spokesperson of the Woti chief. I started talking to him about the word of God. I asked him why he did not accept the word of God, and I invited him to church the following Sunday. He received the invitation with joy. On Sunday, he came to me, and we went to church together. He accepted the word and began studies. He became Jacob Dzomeku. I laid a foundation in the palm wine tapper also, and indeed the entire town. Eventually, he and eleven others (including their wives and children) agreed to go to church with me in Dugã. So, we had become a group of co-travelers.

The pastor S. Newell later discovered that our number was quite appreciable and that the routine walking to church was also problematic. He brought a student, Herman Xevi, from Ve to come and assist me in taking care of the congregation at Woti. Thus, I moved to Woti.

The hatred that some of my people had for me and the consequent persecution visited on me earlier was revived, and they started planning fresh cases against me. They thought that I had moved a whole town to join Leklebi (because the people attended church at Leklebi). Three meetings were held with regard to this issue. At last, one of the citizens, Anthony Adzome (whose name Anthony was taken from the man he stayed with in Keta) came out boldly to defend me. He said to them: You were harassing this man till he went and gave himself to the pastors, but you still want to pursue him. He is now a royalty and if you dare harass him again you will have to face the royalty. Thus Anthony managed to discourage them from any further persecution.

When Mathias, who was a citizen of Wli, heard that I was now settled at Woti, he moved with his family to join me. It was a pity that our teacher, Herman Xevi, fell in his faith. Henry Kwadzokuma was brought in to replace him.

Because our number was increasing and the number of pagans was decreasing, it was decided that we should build a chapel. I offered a plot of land for it. But the building of the chapel was rather slow due the controversy about where to site it. The Christians said the site was too marshy and also at the foot of a hill. Because of these comments, the builders were discouraged and abandoned the project. Later, we were shown another place where we finally built the church. Our teacher was transferred and was replaced by Simon Agbogidi.

Not all the people joined us at the mission. At that time Pastor Newell was transferred from Leklebi to Ve. Because of the refusal of some people to join us at the mission and its attendant problems, our teacher was taken away. I also went back to Soba. Mathias and the family also moved back home. We were scattered.

I soon established a village at Soba and my people started coming to me. My village became present-day Petewu.

V. MY LEAVING HOME FINALLY

During the Great War, my people resumed their persecution of me, especially when there was a change of government and a family from the coast came to settle in our town. I therefore decided to make way and went to Kusuntu, where I lived for quite some time.

1. BECOMING A FULL-TIME CHRISTIAN WORKER

Though I lost many earthly things by leaving home, I came across what I considered God's gift, which I had been yearning for all this while. I became a full-time worker in God's vineyard. I became an evangelist. The pastor at Palime [Kpalime], who knew me earlier, talked with me and employed me as an out-station evangelist to serve the neighboring congregations. The demands of the time made it imperative for me to make stopover visits to the various places.

At first I was sent to Kuma Adame, where the teacher had to leave but where we had very prominent citizens studying to become Christians. I helped them till they were baptized before I was sent to Danyi. I stayed in Danyi Afeyeyeame. Later, I moved to Kpeto, which became my permanent station. I visited home occasionally. Illness sometimes disrupted my work, but I made the best out of the situation. I was later sent to Akata Adagali to prepare a small group of catechumen that had been formed there.

2. MY WORKS

I was sorry that I could not do much. I could not teach because I did not go to school myself, and I could not write. But I taught the catechumen and prepared them for baptism; I also conducted church services for the congregations to the best of my ability. I would like to conclude this write-up with my encounter with some individuals.

i. Encounter with Tsifokpo

One of the prominent people I met was called Tsifokpo. During a conversation with this man, I put a question to him: If a man's wife does not respect him and does not love him, but his mother-in-law loves him and does everything that he wants for him, could she be a substitute for the wife? He said I should continue. I went on to say that the world is like the situation I was trying to paint. All the pleasures of this world are like a mother-in-law's love; they do not come close to the love of a spouse. The world is like cassava *fufu*;[16] no matter how fine it is you still find some lumps in it.

ii. Encounter with Gbawodome
Gbawodome was a very rich man from Danyi Kpeto. One day I put the following question to him: If there is a nearby hunting ground where you go, but you do not get any game, and there is another hunting area, which is far away, but which usually yields game, which of these two places would you like to go? He replied that he would go to the more distant place. I went on to tell him that the distant place represents heaven, where one would never lack anything; the nearby place is the world. The things of this earth pass away; they are vanity. This man became a Christian later.

iii. Encounter with a Christian from Govie [Govi]
I went to the house of a Christian at Govie. While exchanging greetings, I observed some food mixture on a mound on which pots of drinking water were placed. I asked him about the food, and he replied that it was for his small deities. I asked him whether the deities ate the food. He said they did. I further inquired when they would eat the remaining food. He smiled. I continued my interrogation and asked him why his bed clothes were scattered on the floor. He said some ants had stung him in the night. I told him the ants were the small deities that ate the food he put there. I told him that most people have been deceiving themselves with these practices. He thought deeply and said that he had been convinced and that he would not practice that again.

iv. Encounter with a man returning from the farm
On one of my journeys, I sat down near a stream to rest. Soon, a man also came there. He asked me if we would ever rest from the evangelism work. I asked him where he was coming from. He said the farm. I further asked him if he had finished supporting the yams on the farm. He said "yes." I told him then he had already finished eating them. He said he did not understand. I explained to him that just as he made the farm small so that he could have more free time, so would the harvest get finished in a short time. I told him that what we were doing was something that would last forever. Then another man appeared, greeted us, and introduced a joke, which disrupted our conversation. We then went our various ways.

v. Encounter with the chief of Akata Dagali
My new station was Akata Dagali. Their chief was a pagan. One day I visited him. He offered me a seat, and we had a conversation. Soon I changed the topic and told him that our life in this world is like that of a slave who had been bought. Some of them enjoy their enslavement to the extent that even if they are to be redeemed they refuse to go back home. There are others who are ready to leave if a redeemer comes around. There are yet others who attempt to run away. They are

caught and beaten severely, but when they get the opportunity they run away. This is a sign that they do not want to remain there. That is exactly how our lives are. We are all free children of God. But the devil has made some of us slaves to sin. Some like to remain slaves to the devil. But those who stand up and follow their redeemer are the Christians. Christians are people who have refused to remain under the power of the devil. These words inspired the chief, and he accepted the word of God and joined the catechumen.

3. CONCLUSION

These are a few instances of my life. I must confess that the most critical aspects of my life history are yet to be told. Of all the things I have had recorded here, there is only that which is personally important to me and which I would like my friends who have heard these stories to do something with them for me. That is what Ps. 106, verses 1–5 and 47–48 say. So I am saying to myself just like the Psalmist:

> Praise the Lord, O my soul;
> Everything that is in me praise his holy name.
> Praise the Lord, O my soul;
> And forget not all his benefits;
> Who forgives all your sins,
> And heals all your diseases;
> Who redeems your life from the pit;
> And crowns you with love and compassion;
> Who satisfies your desires with good things;
> So that your youth is renewed like the eagle's.

Permit me to conclude my story with the last verses of Psalm 103 (whose first verses I have made my own) from verse 19 to the end: The Lord has established his throne in heaven . . . Praise the Lord O my soul.

THE DEATH OF MY PATERNAL UNCLE

A few weeks after I had come to Anfoe, I went back home to visit my uncle and did some work for him. Unfortunately, he was also attacked by the dreadful smallpox epidemic, and he did not survive. My uncle had died.

Part 2 The Biographies of Lydia Yawo and Yosef Famfantor: Life in Slavery/Life after Abolition

MOSSI

KUSASI

GRUSI

LOBI

●Wa

DAGOMBA

GONJA

Salaga ▣

GYAMAN

▣Bonduku

▣Kintampo

Volta

Kete Krachi ▣

▣Takyiman

BUEM

▣Nsuta

KWAWU

Afram

Eu

AVATIME

▣Dwaben

AGOTIME

Kumase

ADAKLU

ASANTE

KROBO

AKWAMU

AKYEM

ANLO

Lome

▣Praso

●Keta

ASSIN

Accra ▣

Abakrampa ▣ ▣ Salt Pond

FANTE ▣Cape Coast

GOLD COAST

0 25 50   100 Kilometers

Legend
▣ Sites Associated with Yosef Famfantor's Life History
▲ Sites Associated with Lydia Yawo's Life History

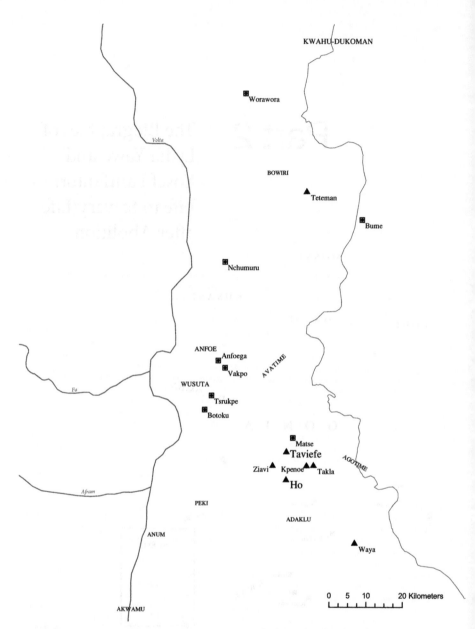

Lydia Yawo and Yosef Famfantor: Some towns that figured in their lives

3. To Stay or Go:
Exploring the Decisions of the Formerly Enslaved

Individuals enslaved in Africa responded to their plight in myriad ways. Some, like Kuku and his father, escaped when the opportunity presented itself. Of those who fled, many attempted to return home; others joined maroon communities or sought asylum, while still others offered their services to rival political communities. Escape was difficult, however. Revolt was even less common. Much more frequent were efforts at accommodation punctuated by more subtle acts of protest, resistance, and the manipulation of cultural values.[1] With the abolition of slavery came even more options. In areas where the lives of slaves were particularly harsh, massive exoduses occurred. Martin Klein has estimated that more than a million slaves left their masters in the West African sudanic areas colonized by France. According to Hogendorn and Lovejoy, thirty thousand fled from the northern Nigerian polity of Nupe between 1897 and 1901.[2] Most, however, remained in the districts where they had been enslaved. They may have moved to the nearby areas where they could obtain land or employment; they may have negotiated new relations with their masters. They did not return home, however, at least not immediately. This was certainly true for the elderly and for those who had been born into slavery or raised as slaves from a young age. The aged who knew their origins often found the possibility of return too daunting given the still hazardous travel conditions they might face; the others simply knew no other home. But what of those who did remember their natal communities, who were physically capable of making the journey, but still remained where they had been enslaved? Why did they not return? Raymond Dumett and Marion Johnson have noted that:

> Everything rested on individual choice and on such criteria as the degree of oppression that had existed under a particular slave holder, the extent to which information about emancipation was circulated, and most important, the chance for refuge and for material support once the step towards independence had been taken.[3]

In some areas, such as Guinea, many former slaves remained on the land they had always worked, but did so only after they were able to insist that they were working for themselves rather than for their masters.[4] For those who were treated with respect despite their slave origins because of their association with royal households, the idea of returning to homes that lacked such prestigious positions made little sense. This was also true for those who had managed to accumulate wealth through trading while enslaved. After gaining the trust of their masters, they used this goodwill to establish for their own benefit valuable business contacts. Many opted to remain where they had been enslaved rather than return home to an area where they had no such connections and where trade opportunities were simply not that lucrative. Others, especially recently enslaved women—who constituted the majority of the enslaved and who may have wanted to return home—found their ability to leave hindered even more so than their like-minded fellow male slaves. Masters (whether male or female) were particularly reluctant to allow their women slaves to depart. Viewed as productive and reproductive assets, many were discouraged if not outright cowed by their master's use of intimidation and physical violence. Some were simply not prepared to leave if they could not take their children with them.[5] In summary, former slaves who opted to remain in or near their masters appear to have founded their decisions on issues of opportunity and security, whether physical, economic, or social. Were these the only considerations? Did other concerns also factor into their decisions?

Could someone who already knew that her mother, father, and all her siblings had been captured and sold away feel that she could seriously consider leaving her master/husband and her children to return to her hometown? Would someone who had as a child been orphaned and then sent away by an uncle to live in another community as a pawn (debt slave) be eager to give up the stability he had finally obtained as a slave to return to a home where most of the inhabitants had been carried off into slavery? Efforts to answer these questions have heretofore been difficult because scholars have had to rely largely on European colonial records maintained by district administrators and colonial courts that provide precious little detail about the lives of individual Africans. Records by missionary societies offer more. Although many European missionaries were never fluent in the languages of the communities in which they worked, they nevertheless came to know quite well the histories and personalities of those individuals who converted to Christianity. As pastors, they served as counselors and guides to formerly enslaved Christians and often worked closely with them to convert others. Africans trained to work in their home areas as ministers were in an even better position to gain access to the personal concerns of their parishioners. Language and cultural barriers were minimal.

It is these biographical sketches, collected by European missionaries and African ministers, that provide scholars with the opportunity to get beyond the useful but nevertheless homogenizing and impersonal categories that most have had to use in their studies about the lives of the enslaved after abolition. Who were these individuals, these former slaves? And what factors, both the obvious and the more personal, influenced the choices they made when deciding whether or not to return to their natal homes?

To answer these questions, I examine two biographies. The first, written in 1877 by the Bremen missionary Johannes Merz, details the life of Lydia Yawo. He describes her birth in the village of Taviefe, how her parents and siblings were enslaved during the 1869–71 Asante invasion of the areas east of the Volta, and her own capture and enslavement as a result of the internecine conflicts that developed in the region after the Asante withdrawal. Perhaps most intriguing is her decision to remain with her master/husband in her adopted community of Ho. What role did that relationship have on her decision? Ho was only about eight kilometers from Taviefe. Did the proximity of her natal village to her new home operate as an incentive to remain where she had been enslaved? Or did it make her situation even more difficult given the deep hostilities that characterized relations between the two towns? What circumstances, common to most enslaved women but also peculiar to her particular situation, made Lydia decide to remain in her adopted home? Equally interesting are questions about the life of Yosef Famfantor. His biography was written in the Ewe language by his neighbor, good friend, and minister the Reverend G. K. Tsekpo of the Ewe Evangelical Church sometime after Famfantor's death in 1933 and was eventually published by Longman in 1948. As indicated in this text, Famfantor was a citizen of Wusuta, a town allied with the Asantes during their 1869–71 war in the region. In 1871, however, Famfantor and the majority of citizens of Wusuta found themselves forcibly enslaved by the very allies they had hosted for four years when the Asantes discovered they did not have enough booty to display as a sign of their supposed victory in their long and difficult war east of the Volta. Unable to capture enough of the enemy, they attacked and captured their allies. Enslaved as a teenager, Famfantor was certainly old enough to remember where he came from. Nevertheless he opted to remain in his adopted community in the Fante-speaking area of south central Ghana for quite a few years before returning home. Why did he decide to do so? How did his identity as a male but also as an individual with his own peculiar experiences before, during, and after his enslavement influence his decision to remain (at least for a while) in his new home? By answering these questions, I hope to demonstrate how an analysis of such biographies can enliven our understanding of how truly individual were the decisions that the formerly enslaved made as they confronted the opportunities and challenges created by abolition.

Analysis of these rare, detailed biographical sketches to better understand the actions of the formerly enslaved presents it own set of challenges, however. As indicated by a number of scholars, the writers of biographies do more than simply assemble the facts. They also interpret. They sort through all the known experiences of the person about whom they are writing. They then select and organize into a coherent narrative those life events that appear to have been most important to the subject and for understanding that life. The amanuensis who records, composes, and publishes the life history of another does the same, but in a biography, one never hears the actual voice of the person whose life is being presented. Instead we must rely on the biographer to tell us what the profiled person did, what he or she thought or imagined. It is the biographer who organizes the elements of that life to explain the person's inner life, the person's thoughts and dreams, hopes, desires, and fears. To present a convincing analysis of things unseen and unstated, the biographer must use his or her imagination; he or she interprets. That interpretation, in turn, is profoundly shaped by the factors that influenced why and how the biographer chose to write in the first place.[6] One sees this clearly in the two biographies analyzed here, Johannes Merz's biography of Lydia Yawo and Kwaku Tsekpo's biography of Yosef Famfantor.

Johannes Merz, a missionary affiliated with the Bremen Mission, worked in the Ewe-speaking area beginning in 1870 during and after the Asante invasion. He witnessed the death and the destruction that accompanied the war. He saw the toll it took on the population, including members of his own Christian community, as so many fled in terror, only to return to ruined homes and fields. He was also an eyewitness to the horrible suffering that resulted from the famines and the retaliatory conflicts that erupted between former foes within the local area long after the Asante had retreated from the region. While deeply sympathetic to those whose lives had been so severely disrupted, he nevertheless maintained his sense of superiority as a European and a Christian. It was these sentiments that deeply influenced his approach to writing Lydia Yawo's biography. For example, in discussing what he viewed as the lamentable "heathen" culture from which Lydia came, he characterized the farming practices of the Ewe as mere hackings of the land. Their houses were described as "lowly," and the practices of bridewealth and child betrothal were depicted as another form of slavery. The series of attacks and reprisals that beset the area after the Asante invasion were attributed not to the war's destruction of the institutions and norms that usually supported law and order in the region,[7] but instead to the supposed fact that "the Negro knows no limits to vengeance and will not desist from it, even if he is to ruin himself through it." In other words, his analysis of the social context into which Lydia was born and the potential that he attributed to her as a human being was deeply influenced by the prevailing imagery of Africa and Africans that circulated in nineteenth-century Europe and Germany, even as Merz's attitudes were tempered a bit by his direct exposure to the Ewe-speaking Africans among whom he worked. His depictions reinforced already existing images that associated Africa with primitivism (lowly houses) and a lack of culture (farming as hackings of the land) and that depicted Africans as hypersexual (as imaginatively attributed to the institution of polygyny) and unintelligent. Yet he also believed that Africans were capable of being "civilized," enticed from their "primitive" and overly violent ways if they could be converted to Christianity. Incapable of reaching the enlightened level attained by Europeans, Africans, according to Merz, were nevertheless to be encouraged to rise above their lowly state through conversion to the true faith.[8]

This attitude of superiority alone, however, does not fully explain why Merz wrote as he did. Equally important, Merz chose to structure his biography according to the conventions of the nineteenth-century Pietist conversion narrative. As a missionary, Merz was certainly familiar with the format. It was the same one he would have been required to use when describing his own life in his application to serve as a Bremen missionary. One began by describing the time and place of one's birth and giving a few details about one's parents and early childhood. This was then followed by the description of all the evil influences and sinful acts that one engaged in as a young adult and that engendered in the person a sense of nervousness, unease, fear, and unhappiness. The narrative came to an end only when the narrator detailed how he or she had "exchanged [his or her] sins for the narrow path and the cross of Christ. . . . [preferring] to be with the little number of people carrying Jesus' cross along the narrow path and endure mockery and ridicule, instead of tumbling into eternal damnation with the great mass."[9] Such a format emphasized verifiability, that the information and perspective provided could be trusted because it was obtained through eyewitness experience or from reliable sources. It was also to be organized chronologically, emphasizing movement in the person's life, "from sin to forgiveness, from misery to bliss, from a world wicked, damned and meaningless, to a world redeemed."[10]

That Merz followed these conventions is clear. In his biography, he gives what information he can about Lydia's birth, the place, date, and day, and then speculates about her early childhood, based on his knowledge of the culture into which she was born and raised. He then describes the conditions under which Lydia began to lead a sinful life. Her home area was described as racked with endemic violence, where "revenge and a thirst for booty ensure that war and bloodshed never come to an end." Africa as a whole was described as "deeply ill." In addition, according to Merz, Adzoba, as she was named at birth, "understood nothing of that which makes humans truly happy" because she did not know Jesus Christ. Although he describes her life as a slave as "not so bad," he indicates nevertheless that she had suffered greatly. She lost her mother, father, brothers, and sisters to war; her husband died before she gave birth to their (and her first) child; she had great difficulty adjusting to life in the Christian community where she and her second husband had moved. Merz indicates, however, that after much struggle and the necessary introspection about her own life, Adzoba decided to convert to Christianity, taking the name Lydia. From that point on, even though she was often physically ill, Merz asserts that her spirit "assumed a very joyful and pleasing form." And although illness eventually took her life, Merz indicates that when he last saw her, "she was [still] so devoted to the will of the Lord that I had to say to myself: Lydia is [indeed] a dear child of God."

Given Merz's obvious use of the conversion narrative (as well as elements of the captivity narrative[11]) as a template for selecting and organizing Lydia's biographical information, how useful is this narrative in actually getting at how Lydia herself understood her own life? This question becomes even more relevant when one realizes that the structural organization of the nineteenth-century Pietist conversion narrative was not the only factor influencing the way he wrote Lydia's biography. In his portrayal of her life, Merz was determined to keep his audience engaged by allowing them to view her life as a drama to be observed from a satisfying distance. When discussing Lydia's spiritual life, for example, he documents the opportunity she narrowly missed on being exposed to Christianity when missionaries came to her first master/husband's hometown. He also describes the many opportunities to convert to Christianity that Lydia subsequently ignored before she finally decided to embrace the new religion. By structuring his narrative in this way, Merz made sure his German readers "experience[d] the thrills of watching [his] protagonist stumble, in [her] ignorance, first away from [the faith], and then toward it." He gave his readers the opportunity to "look down upon [Lydia] . . . hoping that [she] will finally make it home, but also enjoying the spectacle of [her] mistakes and sins." Merz employs this literary tactic for a reason. While Lydia's biography was designed to be read by his German audience as a comfortingly familiar conversion narrative, it was also penned to celebrate the triumphs of the mission's evangelical work in Africa and to recruit others to join in that effort.

We know, for example, that by the time Merz published his biography, the Bremen Mission had been operating in the Ewe-speaking areas of West Africa for some thirty years. In all that time, however, it had largely failed to convert anyone except a small group of Euro-Africans, a number of workers who were employed by the mission and several children, most of whom had been purchased from the slave markets in the region. Only in the late 1870s did significant numbers of local residents, both men and women, begin to express a genuine interest in converting to Christianity.[12] This increasing receptivity to Christianity, especially on the part of women, contrasted sharply with the situation prior to the late 1870s and was of great interest to the Bremen missionaries, who believed that women, in their role as the principal educators of their young children, could play an especially critical role in bringing many more boys and girls into the faith.[13] Yet there were simply not enough European or local African women affiliated with the mission to meet the increased interest on the part of Ewe women to learn about this new religion. Up to the late nineteenth century, the few European women who worked in West Africa as part of the Bremen Mission had come as wives. In this role they were expected to serve their husbands as silent helpmates as dictated by norms in mid-nineteenth-century Germany. They were to provide for the home-based social, physical, and psychological needs of their spouses so the latter could carry out their duties in the larger world. But as missionary wives, they were also expected to work simultaneously as nurses to the Christian community, as well as lay teachers, providing the education and religious instruction of the African girls and women affiliated with the mission. By the 1870s, those in the field and at home in Germany realized that the few wives associated with the mission were simply unable to handle all these different tasks. Help was needed. It was in this context that Merz penned Lydia Yawo's biography.[14] He structured it not only to replicate the conversion narratives that were so central to and popular with his Bremen Mission audience, he also penned it to celebrate the valuable, successful, and rewarding work that awaited any Pietist German woman (or man) willing to serve God by working in Africa to bring African women to the faith.

Even with these overarching structurations (the larger cultural perspectives and discursive norms that Merz used to organize the narrative and the particular concerns that prompted Merz to pen the narrative in the first place), I argue that it is still possible to hear Lydia herself.[15]

*   *   *

Similar issues must be taken into consideration when reading the biography of Yosef Famfantor. Written in the Ewe language in 1939 by Rev. G. K. Tsekpo, an Ewe-speaking minister affiliated with the Ewe Evangelical Church (EEC),[16] the biography clearly portrays Famfantor in terms that served Tsekpo's desire to highlight the life of an Ewe Christian that others in his community should seek to emulate. Despite being pawned by his maternal family after the death of his mother, despite being forcibly enslaved in the Asante, despite only narrowly escaping death by ritual sacrifice, and despite being forcibly sold from one master to another, Famfantor is presented as ever-cheerful, ever-respectful, whether toward his slave masters or toward the elders in the different communities where he lived. He is described as honest, hardworking, enterprising, loyal, willing to listen to others, prepared to forgive, but also unafraid to defy custom and personal comfort if necessary to do what he thinks is right as a good Christian. According to his biographer, he was loved by everyone who knew him because of his pleasant, accommodating personality. He had all the positive traits respected by both the Christian community and the local Ewe culture and none of the negative features that one would normally find in the average person. Yosef is said to have never harbored an unkind thought. He never acted out of anger. He never expressed feelings of resentment or frustration. The biography, one can assume, is a fairly sanitized version of Famfantor's life.

What prompted Tsekpo to construct his biography as he did? That Famfantor was not only a fellow Christian but was also a friend and neighbor was certainly important for understanding his praise of Famfantor. Equally important, however, were the circumstances under which he constructed his text. Tsekpo published his biography in 1948, fifteen years after Famfantor's death. But it is likely that he had already begun composing elements of the text some fifteen years earlier, which he had read at Famfantor's funeral in 1933. Such biographical readings were typical in early twentieth-century funerals among the Christian Ewe community. At such a forum, Tsekpo would have been expected to remember the deceased with words of praise and celebration, for the discursive norms that structured early twentieth-century Christian Ewe funerary practices—norms that had their origins, in part, in Christian European funerary practices brought to the Ewe in West Africa by the Bremen Mission[17]—would have demanded as much. But another influence on Tsekpo's approach probably emanated from the norms that governed the funerary practices of non-Christians, those Ewe who continued to believe in and live according to their older traditional polytheistic beliefs but who also attended Famfantor's funeral because he was someone of such local importance. Here as well the emphasis was on praise and celebration. We know, for example, that in traditional nineteenth- and early twentieth-century Ewe funerals, music, poetry, and dance were routinely offered as part of a funeral celebration to facilitate the passage of the deceased person's soul from the world of the living into the company of his or her fellow dead in the spiritual world (Tsiefe). This was in sharp contrast to the Ewe Christian funerals, in which only solemn Christian hymns were to be sung and where any displays of grief were to be kept resolutely under control.[18] Still there were similarities in terms of how the deceased were to be remembered. According to Kofi Anyidoho, among the most elaborate of the traditional funerals were those accorded to hunters. Descriptions of the dances typically performed at such a funeral illustrate that at the center of such actions was the importance of praising and celebrating those elements in the deceased person's life that were worthy of emulation:

> In the event of a hunter's death . . . his family will arrange that his colleagues in the hunter's association can give him such a farewell as would make his soul depart in peace and be welcomed into the association of hunters in Tsiefe.
>
> The dance of hunters is extremely brisk and dramatic, full of symbolic gestures and movements. It sometimes develops into a brief dramatic sketch in which the performer reenacts a confrontation with and the overpowering of big game. . . . As [A. Manure] Opoku points out, '. . . hunters' dances are mimed versions of the actual . . . achievements of [the] dead.'
>
> If the dance sequence provides occasion for dramatic embellishment and symbolic movement, the hunter's song often defines the scope of the heroic life of hunters.[19]

By following the norms that structured both Christian and non-Christian funerary discursive practices, Tsekpo shaped his biography in response to both. Each demanded praise and celebration. Each demanded that the life of the deceased be remembered in terms that others would find worthy of emulation.

At the same time, Tsekpo firmly situated his narrative within the parameters of Pietist discourse by eschewing any emphasis, as found in traditional Ewe funerary narratives, on the admirable acts, physical or intellectual, performed by Famfantor. He offered no praise for his friend's ability to survive his forced march to Asante as an enslaved prisoner of war. He refused to attribute any acts of cunning to Famfantor when he managed to evade while enslaved in Asante a group of men who were bent on killing him as a ritual sacrifice. Instead, Tsekpo emphasized Famfantor's inner qualities, his kindness, his humility, his gentleness. These were the very qualities that the Bremen Mission, as a Pietist Christian organization, emphasized their converts should cultivate. Success as a Christian was possible only through serious introspection and by using one's inner strength to live the life of a committed Christian. In embracing this approach, Tsekpo incorporated only those aspects of traditional Ewe funerary discourse that overlapped with Pietist ones, and then used his text to promote the ideals and attitudes he had embraced as a student of the Bremen Mission and which he sought to encourage others to accept.

Given all this, is it still possible to hear Famfantor himself? If we only have access to his life and his words through his biographer, can we still use this source as a means to understand why Famfantor delayed a return to his hometown for so many years? What did he consider when deciding whether to remain where he was enslaved? How were these considerations similar to or different from those contemplated by Lydia Yawo? I believe we can answer all these questions, but when reading Famfantor's biography—as with Lydia's—we must assume that the basic information provided is accurate, that among the reasons he remained in the Fante area was because of its trade opportunities and because of its Christian community. By accepting these details as fact, we can then ask more probing questions. Why were these realities so important to him, more important than returning to his hometown, where there were also great economic opportunities because of the booming trade that emerged on the Volta River with the defeat of Asante by the British in 1874? Reading Lydia's biography requires the same approach. Let us assume that Merz's details about her life are factually accurate, that she did indeed refuse to return and that her parents and siblings were lost to her. If we take these as given, we can then ask why she didn't return to live with her uncle. Why did she find it necessary to take the side of her husband's hometown in conflicts between that place and her own village? How much did her identity as a citizen of Taviefe influence her actions and decisions? By engaging in an informed reading of the sources that were clearly written to serve a Pietist Christian agenda, by accepting as fact certain unverifiable details about the life of Lydia Yawo and Yosef Famfantor, this chapter seeks to understand why these two individuals, former slaves in late nineteenth-century West Africa, made the decisions they did on whether to return home or to remain in their adopted communities.

LYDIA ADZOBA YAWO:
ON THE PERSONAL AND THE POLITICAL

The polity of Taviefe, Adzoba's hometown, consisted in the nineteenth century of four villages located in a valley and the surrounding hills north of Ho (some one hundred kilometers from the Atlantic coast). After Taviefe was established by coastal Anlo refugees in the late eighteenth century, its early founders found themselves in constant conflict with the earlier inhabitants, who refused to give them land on which to settle. Only through constant warfare were they able to hold onto the high hills and valley that ultimately became their final place of settlement. In time, however, an uneasy peace emerged. Trade relations developed. Marital ties were forged in recognition of ongoing economic and social relations. Still the people of Taviefe maintained their political independence. When the other Ewe-speaking polities joined together in the 1830s to free themselves of the tyrannical rule of Akwamu, the people of Taviefe declined to join them. They refused to recognize the right of any polity—whether

Akwamu or Peki (which led the Ewe alliance)—to exercise authority over their community. Instead, they insisted on maintaining their independence and their historic ties to the coastal polity of Anlo (a trade partner and ally of both Akwamu and Asante).

In 1869, however, when Asante invaded the area, the Taviefe changed their political position. Instead of remaining neutral, they threw their support behind Asante, Anlo, and Akwamu. When Asante attacked the neighboring town of Ho in late June of 1869, for example, Taviefe participated. They sent troops to assist in the assault, and when Ho launched a counteroffensive a month later, Taviefe and its Anlo ally helped the Asantes defend themselves. Several months later, when Asante troops began moving north in pursuit of their enemies, Taviefe agreed to serve as their hosts, escorting them through the area and providing them with food.[20] And when those who had been defeated and driven out earlier by Asante began filtering back to their home areas, the Taviefe worked yet again with the Asantes to force them out once more.[21]

Because of their actions in the war, the Taviefe found themselves deeply disliked by their neighbors. The anger felt by the people of Ho was especially acute. When Asante first entered the area, not only did the Taviefes agree to provide them with military assistance to destroy the town, they had also insisted that those women from Taviefe who had married men from Ho return home. And then, when some of the children from these marriages decided to join their mothers instead of remaining with their fathers, the Taviefe handed them to the Asantes for enslavement.[22] By the end of the war in 1871, the people of Ho had seen countless friends and family members die in battle or be betrayed and enslaved. Starvation and disease dogged the remaining population at every turn. Fleeing to friendly allied territory was often no help. There they were taken advantage of, forced to pay higher prices for food than others paid, fined for every minor or imagined infraction. It was after experiencing such suffering that many in Ho, including the chief of the town, Howusu, swore revenge. They vowed to kill every one of Asante's local allies, including all Taviefe citizens. They refused to countenance normal trade relations of any sort with their former enemies. Thus, when anyone from Taviefe traveled to Ho, he or she found himself or herself roundly jeered and taunted. Others were simply attacked.[23] This was the context that led to Adzoba's enslavement.

In middle to late 1871, Taviefe itself was engulfed by famine. Some months earlier, a number of Asante troops, desperate for food, had passed through the area and consumed virtually everything. Food was so scarce that no one was able to eat more than one meal a day.[24] Since the Ho market had yet to be reestablished and the Taviefes would have been unwelcome there anyway, the town organized a large caravan to travel south to the market in Adaklu (which

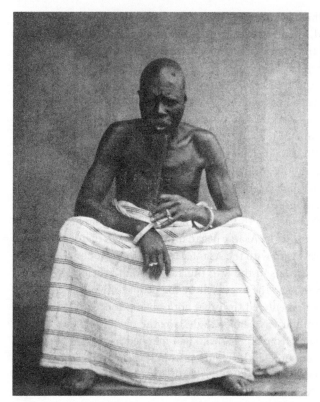

King Kofi (Howusu)
of Ho. Courtesy of
Norddeutsche
Mission.

had also aligned itself with Asante during the war). Adzoba joined that caravan. To avoid trouble, they passed around the unpopulated ruins that were once Ho. But this in the end did not protect them from those who were hot with the desire for revenge. Somewhere along the route to Adaklu, the caravan was attacked, and Adzoba and sixteen others were kidnapped. All were sold away from the area except Adzoba. She was purchased by Gamo of Ho Gbenoe [Kpenoe], a man to whom she was related. Was Adzoba's uncle or husband (Merz was uncertain with whom Adzoba was residing before her capture) unaware of her fate? If they knew of her whereabouts, had the war so impoverished them they were simply unable to raise the money needed to ransom her? We simply don't know. Whatever the case, Gamo bought Adzoba and quickly thereafter initiated sexual relations with her. By doing so, he established his rights to her as both his slave and his third wife. And because she conceived almost immediately, he probably would have been unwilling to release her anyway.

What of her status as a slave? In his biography of Adzoba, Merz compares her situation favorably with the fate of female slaves in Anlo:

although she was a slave, as the wife of her husband she did not have it so bad. For in the interior the lot of a slave who has been taken by her master to be his wife is not as harsh as on the coast, where mother and children remain slaves. In the interior of the country children receive rights and even the mother is considered a full member of the family.

Merz may have genuinely believed this to be the case, but his understanding was based on a misreading of the situation both on the coast and in the interior. In Anlo, it is true, commercial opportunities had generated the kind of wealth that allowed individual entrepreneurs to accumulate large numbers of enslaved men, women, and children. These slaves were placed on farms, where their marriages to each other ensured that their slave status continued to define their social status well beyond the first generation within the extended families of which they had become a part. But it was also the case that many enslaved women were married and accepted as the spouses of their masters. This was as true on the coast as it was in the interior. These marriages, however, did not mean that the slave spouses and their children were "free." Because the women had no relatives to protect their interests vis-à-vis their master/husbands or their free co-wives (if they had them), the husbands were in a particularly strong position to do with them and their children as they liked. If a master needed to borrow money, it would be the enslaved wife's children who would be pawned to the lender as a guarantee that the principal would be eventually paid by their master/father. The absence of relatives to whom an enslaved woman could turn also deeply influenced how she related to her master/husband. Such a woman worked harder. She was always present since she had no relatives to visit or use as an excuse to spend time away from her marital home. She was more vocal in expressing loyalty to her husband/ master since he could do what he wanted with her. If she displeased him, he could sell her. If she disobeyed, she could be physically disciplined without incurring the wrath of her relatives.[25] Merz understood none of this, yet it explains in part why Adzoba was so willing to accept Gamo's decision that she marry his brother, Yawo, after his death. She was in no position to refuse. How could she, with no relatives to support her decision and with nowhere else to turn? Her vulnerability as an enslaved woman also goes far in explaining why she, unlike her new husband's other wives, was prepared to consider converting to Christianity. Completely under the authority of her husband, she had little choice. Unlike her co-wives, she agreed to attend prayer services. She willingly accompanied him when he decided to make the dangerous journey to Waya to receive baptismal lessons. Even enslaved women could resist in their own way, however. When ultimately faced with the real prospect of having to adjust to a different culture and a foreign dialect while also abandoning her traditional faith for one that was really of little interest to her, she balked. She diverged from the path laid before her

The Old Mission House in Waya where Lydia studied to become a Christian.
Courtesy of Norddeutsche Mission.

by her husband/master by focusing on her child, playing with him, soothing
him, and refusing to be parted from him during her lessons. Only when faced
with the prospect of being abandoned by her master/husband did she relent.

Her vulnerability as a slave is evident as well in how she responded to the
deep hostilities that existed between her natal home of Taviefe and her adopted
home of Ho. According to Merz, Adzoba "took the side of her husband and the
people of Ho rather than that of her former home, Taviefe, in regard to political
questions concerning the country." Merz explains this by suggesting that her relationship with her husband was so happy, he being "a very industrious, influential and highly regarded Negro," that she considered herself at home in Ho. But
this seems implausible. Yes, her marriage to a wealthy man gave her prestige by
association. And yes, the fact that her husband had two other wives as well as a
number of slaves considerably lessened the amount of work she had to perform.
Still, she was a slave with all the liabilities that came therewith. Just as important,
she was from Taviefe, a town that had not only hosted the Asante during their
assault on Ho, but had participated in the killing of Ho citizens on the battlefield
and had handed over the sons of Ho men married to Taviefe women when these
sons sought refuge with their Taviefe mothers. To avoid suspicions of being the
"enemy within," Adzoba had to express her loyalty to her adopted home, vocifer-
ously and frequently. To do otherwise would have brought the possibility of expulsion from Ho and the loss of her only child. With her father dead, her mother

Church Elder Noah
(?Lydia Yawo's husband),
c. 1926. Courtesy of
Norddeutsche Mission.

and her siblings enslaved in Anlo, and with no contact whatsoever with the uncle or husband with whom she had lived before her own capture, this child was essentially all Adzoba had in terms of natal family.

Her joy at seeing her brother (with whom she was reunited briefly in Waya) must have been tremendous. As indicated by a number of missionary observers, such reunions were normally greeted with "a jubilation bordering on insanity... because [the returnee]... who had been shipped off... had finally succeeded in making it back to his home village."[26] Their meeting must have raised for Lydia the desperately hoped for possibility of reconstituting her family, one that could provide her with the kind of familial support so different in kind from that available from her husband/master or her recently accepted Christian community. But those hopes were quickly dashed. Her brother preferred to return to the coast and remain as a slave to his master even though the

British had extended their colonial control over Anlo and had abolished slavery. Lydia had no such choice. She lived not on the coast but in Ho and Waya. Neither place had been colonized by Britain, and slavery was still legal. To return home meant traveling on roads that were terribly unsafe, through territory that was exceedingly hostile to all Taviefe citizens.[27] Even if she had made it to Taviefe, how would she have been received? Her parents and siblings were gone. She had thrown in her lot with the hated home of her husband/master, a fact that if known to the missionaries must have also been known to the residents of her natal village. Lydia remained with her master/husband. He was wealthy and respected, and, according to Merz, he treated her well. Living only about eight kilometers from her natal village, Lydia Adzoba never made it home. The distance was simply too great, made so not by geography but by her personal history, her gender, and the local politics of the time.

YOSEF KWAKU FAMFANTOR: ON FAMILY MATTERS

Yosef Kwaku Famfantor was yet another who found himself enslaved as a direct result of the 1869–71 Asante invasion of the areas east of the Volta. Captured as a young adult, he, like Aaron Kuku, experienced while enslaved a number of frightening incidents directed explicitly at his person. He narrowly missed being offered as a ritual sacrifice sometime in 1873 when Asante resorted to this practice as a means of coping with an impending invasion by the British.[28] Shortly thereafter, he experienced the humiliating ordeal of being sold unwittingly to another master in the Fante district of Assin and then being designated as that person's *ǫkra,* the individual who would be killed to accompany his new master into the spiritual world upon the master's death.[29] Most intriguing of all, however, is Famfantor's insistence on viewing his life as a slave—despite these experiences—in quite positive terms. According to his biographer, Famfantor remembered his two masters as particularly kind and considerate. Nyameadesie, his Asante owner, is said to have "worried about him like his own son." He sent Famfantor to his sister's farm, according to Famfantor, to shield him from the food shortages that had become so acute in Kumase in 1873. Relocating him outside of Kumase also protected him from the possibility of being killed by palace servants who sought victims, in September of that year, to accompany into the spiritual world the Asantehene's recently deceased sixteen-year-old brother.[30] When he was abruptly sold, probably in 1874 after the roads between Kumase and the coast reopened, he did not blame his master, but simply expressed surprise. Memories of his owner in Assin were also quite positive. As noted in his biography, Famfantor remembered that "this new master . . . loved him even more than the Kumase one. [Famfantor] ate with him like his own children." When Famfantor was old enough to marry, it was his master who gave his own daughter to him as a wife. The success he achieved as a businessman Famfantor attributed to his owner, who gave him his first capital with which to trade. These positive feelings, recounted to his amanuensis, Rev. G. K. Tsekpo, some thirty years after he returned to the land of his birth, speak not only of the way he chose to remember his years in Asante and Assin but also how he remembered Akan culture in general.

Throughout the late nineteenth and early twentieth centuries, British colonial officials and missionary societies working in West Africa regularly decried the practice of ritual sacrifice in Asante (even after it had been abolished voluntarily). They did so, as indicated by a number of scholars, to justify the expansion of colonial rule and to prove the superiority of European culture and the Christian faith.[31] In late 1894, for example, Governor Griffith of the British Gold Coast used an erroneous report about the ritual sacrifice of four hundred individuals at the time of the new Asantehene's installation to discourage an Asante delegation from proceeding to Britain for direct negotiations with the Colonial Office in London. He told the Asante ambassadors that the British government refused "to receive a mission from a ruler who is accused . . . of allowing human sacrifice." This refusal came at a time when the British were attempting to negotiate a peaceful expansion of their rule over the Asante state.[32] Missionaries regularly included in their accounts of the lives of slaves who had escaped their Asante masters incidents of narrow escapes from being killed as a ritual sacrifice. Famfantor's biography is not substantially different in this regard. Of all the experiences he had as a slave that he recounted to his amanuensis, it was his escaping two threats on his life by ritual sacrifice that figure prominently in his biography. Did his biographer, G. K. Tsekpo, a minister, focus on these particular incidents while ignoring others to vilify these non-Christian practices? Or was he motivated to highlight the practice of human sacrifice because of the experiences of his own hometown friends and relatives? Perhaps. Tsekpo was from the village of Alavanyo, which itself had suffered considerable devastation from the Asante invasion. But Tsekpo did not simply use Famfantor's life for his own purposes. Instead, he tried to be faithful to the person whom he had come to know during the many years they lived, worked, and worshipped together. Thus, even in this biography—written specifically to memorialize its subject, one that was also designed to encourage others to follow in the path forged by Famfantor—we can still hear Famfantor's voice. It was he who praised the kindness of his slave masters. And it was Famfantor, like Aaron Kuku, who was not prepared to see the culture in which he had spent a significant portion of his adult life portrayed in purely negative terms. In sharing his experiences with Tsekpo, for example, it was probably Famfantor who indicated that it was not just slaves who were vulnerable to such killings. Others too could suffer a similar fate. In 1869 and 1873, for example, the rush to obtain sacrificial victims to accompany deceased royals actually masked a wider political campaign to eliminate political enemies that ended up engulfing quite a few innocent bystanders. Rumors of such impending killings obtained through social connections were one of the few means by which individuals could shield themselves from such unpredictable events.[33] In Famfantor's case, it was his Asante master's position as an *ahenkwaa*, his concern for the well-being of his recently acquired slave, and Famfantor's fortuitous absence at the time of his Assin master's death that protected him from harm. In remembering these incidents, however, Famfantor chose to use them not to condemn the practice of ritual sacrifice or to illustrate the way in which he may have been viewed primarily as a valued working asset. Instead, he interpreted the protection and care he received as illustrative of the close personal relationships he had with his masters.

Why did he make this choice? Why did Famfantor opt to focus on such positive memories of his days in enslavement given the obviously precarious nature of his life as a slave among the Akan? Not only did he twice narrowly miss being killed as a ritual sacrifice, the status he had achieved under his Assin master, of being "almost free," disappeared immediately on his master's death. Inherited by another, he found himself suspected of dishonesty and scorned as a slave with too much money to spend. Such a turn in status was hardly unique to Famfantor. As noted by Thomas McCaskie and A. Norman Klein,

> A foreign-born slave was in essence a good. No matter how long such slaves survived, or how trusted or favoured they were, their status as disposable property was always [a possibility] . . .
>
> The real price paid by these people was more private, personal and psychological. These were people who, in the inner sanctum of the lineage, were always threatened with being exposed for the inadequacy of their credentials, even though they could depend on lineage support in the outside world . . .
>
> [T]he ' . . . stigma of slavery' . . . was one from which they could not escape so long as they remained in a traditional Akan, that is, lineage setting.[34]

That Famfantor felt this disability quite deeply is evident from the fact that he attributes his interest in Christianity in part to its wholehearted acceptance of slave and free alike, that it was not prepared to recognize any differences between the two. Still Famfantor stayed. He may have moved from his master's town of Assin Praso to Abakrampa, about eighty kilometers away, but he continued to see himself as part of his master's family. When he did move to Abakrampa, he stayed with his deceased master's uncle. He made no attempt to seek his freedom by contacting the British government at Cape Coast, where he regularly traveled for trade purposes, even though the abolition of slavery had been in effect since 1874, the same year Famfantor had been sold as a slave to his Assin master. He also did not, at that point, think about returning home. He opted to remain near his slave master's family until c. 1889 and remembered how well he was treated almost fifty years after his initial enslavement. Why?

Famfantor's biographer suggests he was simply a positive person, having "no animus toward anyone." Other explanations are also possible. Scholars who have studied the decisions of first-generation former slaves (those like Famfantor who remembered their origins but who chose to remain with or in close proximity to their former masters) emphasize the calculus many must have used to make their decisions. What was more important, the social connections and economic opportunities that existed in their adopted communities or the ones that awaited them in their natal homes? What would they gain and what would they lose in staying? In leaving? Famfantor's biography suggests that he believed he had a lot to lose by leaving. Although life as a slave could be precarious and humiliating, Famfantor was still able to prosper economically. He remembered making numerous profitable trips as a trader between Cape Coast and the market towns of Bonduku and Kintampo. Both markets emerged or grew considerably as major centers of trade after 1874. In that year, Britain invaded Asante and marched into Kumase. And even though the occupation of the Asante capital lasted only one day, it set off a series of events that had repercussions throughout the entire region. Territories both northwest and northeast of Asante asserted their independence. In c. 1876, the polity of Gyaman, tributary to Asante since 1751, broke with Asante by offering refuge to rebels from Takyiman. In late 1875 or early 1876, the eastern Brong areas of Buem and Nchumuru rebelled, declaring their support for the earlier 1874 break from Asante by Dwaben (long a central member of the Asante confederation). They blockaded the northwest trade routes that linked Kumase with the massive market town of Salaga and then invaded it, with the acquiescence of its ruler, killing "many hundreds of Kumase people, who were [there] . . . as officials, weavers and traders."[35] The response in the Fante districts at the coast where Famfantor lived was equally swift. In 1876, several Cape Coast chiefs sent messengers to the Gyaman market town of Bonduku (a place to which they had formerly had no direct access) to open trade connections with the coast.[36] Famfantor's master must have been among those who took advantage of this opening. Famfantor remembers selling in Bonduku the kinds of coastal and European commodities (salt, gunpowder, and guns, for example) that the Asante had formerly prohibited for sale.[37] By the early 1880s, travel to Bondoku was made virtually impossible by civil conflicts that continually disrupted the trade routes. In response, Famfantor, operating by this time both for himself and his master, shifted his operations eastward to the newly emergent market of Kintampo.[38] It was here that Famfantor remembers—by being given the opportunity to trade far and wide in ways rarely offered to female slaves—making massive profits with his second wife. He exchanged European manufactured goods obtained at Cape Coast for the slaves that were now brought to Kintampo rather than to Salaga or Bonduku. He did so in response to the great demand for unfree labor in both Asante and Fante, as more and more people sought additional household help, porters for carrying trade goods to market, and laborers to expand production both for the local and (in the case of kola) regional markets as well as for the European market (where palm oil was in demand).[39] With this kind of success, economic considerations must certainly have played a major role in encouraging Famfantor to remain in the Fante area. But there were also more personal reasons.

Perhaps even more important than economic security was that Famfantor believed, at least for a time, that he had achieved a much-sought-after goal: a family and community supportive of him and his individual interests. After working for his Assin master, for example, he found himself, as he remembered it, treated with the kind of love and respect that he had not experienced since perhaps his mother's death. He was allowed to eat with his master and his master's own children. In time, he was trusted enough to be given not only money to trade on his master's behalf but also his master's daughter in marriage. Famfantor also recalled the welcome fatherly advice he received from the man who claimed him as property: that he should not hesitate to take what little money he had to trade on his own behalf when he was also working for his master; that he should take care not to engage in sexual relations with women who might transmit to him a disease that would only shorten his life. As Famfantor remembered it, his master "loved him more than his own children."

In a matrilineal society where a man's children after the age of about seven often spent more time with their uncle than with their father, it is certainly plausible that Famfantor's master treated him as if he were his own son.[40] But this does not explain why Famfantor was so eager to believe that his master's actions were not also informed by the numerous Akan proverbs that reminded slave owners that good treatment was the best policy if one wanted to get the most out of one's dependents. As these late nineteenth- and early twentieth-century aphorisms advised:

A servant is like . . . corn ground into flour; when a little water is sprinkled on it, it becomes soft.

Even if your mother's son is 'Kobuobi' [i.e., an ɔdɔnkɔ, a slave] would you tell him that the big drum was a fit thing for him to carry?

When a servant (akoa) knows how to serve (his master well), he is permitted to take his own earnings.

A good master becomes rich.[41]

Famfantor also remembers his friends in Assin Praso being particularly supportive of him during the period when his first marriage was failing, even though that support seems to have eluded him when his second marriage also failed. These positive experiences figured prominently in his recollections of his time as a slave, especially in Assin, not only because of the seemingly kind treatment he received but also because he so longed for a stable, supportive family, something that apparently eluded him during his most impressionable years as a youth in his natal home of Wusuta.

As noted by his biographer, Famfantor's father was remembered as the brother of the chief of Wusuta Hoto. He died, however, when Famfantor was still young. This in itself was not unusual. During the early nineteenth century disease and accidents regularly claimed the lives of the young and the old as well as those in the prime of their lives. More interesting is that Famfantor seems to have had such limited contact with his father's relatives even though they all lived in the same village and all observed patrilineal descent. It is true that when a father died, very young children most often stayed with their mothers—as Famfantor did—until they were a bit older. On reaching the age of six or seven, however, fatherless boys were often taken under the wing of a paternal uncle who would assume responsibility for their socialization and training.[42] Famfantor's life followed a different path, one it seems initially forged by his mother.[43] When Famfantor's father died, his mother would have been faced with a major decision concerning her own marital future. Would she marry another member of her husband's family, as was common in her community at the time, to reinforce the alliance that the marriage had forged between her family and her husband's, or would she assert her recognized right to sever those ties?[44] Famfantor's mother chose the second option. She declined to marry one of her deceased husband's relatives and instead married a man from the polity of Anfoe. That marriage, however, did not last. When she left to return to Wusuta Hoto, she and Famfantor probably went to live with her own family, as again was customary.[45] Famfantor remembers being especially close to his mother during this period. He helped her with her farming and was the object of her strong, perhaps even overly protective instincts. During the earthquake of July 1862, she ran over to him while he was playing with his friends and tied him on her back as if he were still an infant, even though others would have deemed him too old to be handled in such a manner. On her death, he remembers being so emotionally attached to her that he refused his maternal relative's advice to participate in a ritual that was designed to protect him from his mother's spirit.[46] He would have none of it. It was because of this deep attachment that he probably never went to live with his paternal family. Instead, he lived with his mother's relatives. He did so first as a youth, and then many years later as an adult, when he decided to return to Wusuta after years of enslavement among the Akan. It was his close relationship with his mother that is especially important for understanding what he refused to say about the years he spent in Wusuta between the time of his mother's death and his capture by the Asante. This relationship also explains why he commented so on the love he experienced when enslaved there.

Living with his maternal relatives allowed Famfantor to continue to associate with that branch of his family with whom he felt most attached after the death of his mother. But it is also likely that no one could really replace the one individual from whom he had received the greatest support. His sense of loss and emotional abandonment was only compounded when he was selected from among all the members of his maternal household to help his family repay a debt they had incurred when the Asantes moved into the area. As noted in his biography, Asante sent a delegation to Wusuta in c. 1867 or 1868 ostensibly to help commemorate the life of the recently deceased Wusuta chief. This was at the same time, however, that Asante was also sending delegations to other communities east of the Volta in preparation for their 1869 invasion.[47] According to Famfantor, Wusuta suspected nothing. During their stay, however, the Asantes behaved with extreme arrogance. They uprooted his maternal grandfather's oil palm trees even though they were explicitly shown others they could have used for the extraction of palm wine. They made clearly fallacious allegations of wrongdoing against the local population and demanded unreasonable punishments for crimes they were unable to prove had even taken place.[48] When Famfantor's maternal uncle attempted to protect his trees from further Asante depredations, he was taken to court. In an effort to save their lives in the face of Asante demands for their deaths, the Wusuta Hoto chief and his elders were finally able to broker a compromise that required Famfantor's maternal family to pay a particularly heavy fine. Unable to produce the total amount, they were forced to borrow the money and send a member of the family to work for the lender as payment on the loan's interest while they worked simultaneously to repay the principal. Famfantor was the one chosen to go into debt bondage. With his mother deceased and because of his limited contact with his father's family, he had no one who was in a position to argue that someone else should be the one offered as a pawn to their lender. Years later, he seems to have understood that his maternal family did all they could to select a lender from their own home village so that he would not be so distant from his immediate relatives in Wusuta Hoto, but this probably meant little to a young man who had only recently lost his mother and was now placed in pawn to live away from the very family with which he felt most attached.

Life as a pawn for Famfantor only heightened his sense of emotional abandonment. The individual to whom he was pawned was evidently quite wealthy and had other youngsters under his authority as either pawns or slaves. In such a situation, as noted by a number of observers during this period, the one pawned "must unconditionally work for the lender and do everything that is demanded of him, whether it is field-work, house work or weaving; he must obey." The lender would also "punish [the person] who seems to avoid work without adequate reasons . . . [he] may imprison him, beat him, have pepper strewn in his eyes, [or] take away his food." He does this not only to impress upon the individual being punished the importance of doing everything the lender asks of him, but also "so that [the] second and third [pawn] doesn't start avoiding work as well."[49] Was this what Famfantor experienced? He says little about his time as a pawn, although it lasted well over two years. Hints of how he remembered this time do surface throughout his biography, however. When he explained what he found so attractive about Christianity, for example, he emphasized that it made no distinction between slave and free. This lack of differentiation reminded him of his time as a pawn in Wusuta and when he was a slave in Asante. In each of these situations, he evidently felt deeply the stigma of being under the complete control of another. But it was not just the issue of control. Everyone in both Asante and Wusuta was under the authority of others, whether they be family elders or the political leaders. And everyone in these communities, including pawns and slaves, had rights that they could exercise and successfully defend.[50] Rather it was the absence on the part of his Wusuta and Asante masters of any concern about him as an individual (despite his protestations to the contrary about his Asante master) that appears to have prompted him to equate those particular experiences with such negative feelings. By asserting in contrast how he was so loved by his Assin master, how he was treated like a son, how his master taught him how to trade, encouraged him to refrain from sexual excess, and even provided him his own daughter as a wife, he signaled how deeply he had a felt need for the kind of affection that had eluded him since his mother's death. Not only had he lost a mother, but his maternal family to whom he had turned selected him for service in debt bondage on their behalf. In recognition of this painful event, he chose—on his conversion to Christianity—to assume the biblical name of Yosef, a man who like himself had been deeply loved by one of his parents but who suffered at the hands of other members of the family by being sent into bondage. In time, as mentioned, Famfantor came to have a better understanding of the circumstances that forced his maternal relatives to take this action, but the experience so remained a part of his remembered past that it significantly colored his memories of his time as a slave. It was these memories of home, where his maternal family that had sold him into debt slavery, that encouraged him in part to remain in Assin as long as he did.

Famfantor did eventually return home, however. After spending more than fifteen years among the Akan, he used his association with the Christian community in Assin Abakrampa to make his way back to Wusuta. Motivating him were the same factors that had earlier encouraged him to remain: the desire for a stable and supportive family. As indicated in his biography, Famfantor felt deeply the betrayals he remembered experiencing throughout his life. When recounting the details of his marriages, for example, he indicated that both failed because he could no longer trust his wives. His first wife developed a reputation as a thief. In matrilineal Assin, it would have been her own family who bore the brunt of community opprobrium. It was they who would have been held responsible for teaching her to behave in such a manner.[51] But Famfantor was affected as well. If the victim of the theft cursed the goods that were stolen, in this case the yams that his wife was fond of pilfering, that curse could injure those who unwittingly consumed them. It was for this reason Famfantor felt he could no longer trust his first wife. If she prepared the stolen yams for his meal, she endangered his own life. Relations with his second wife were made difficult by disagreements with his wife's sister about their joint business ventures. After incurring a number of fines from being judged guilty in what appears to have been several slander cases, she used the money she and Famfantor had made together from engaging in the domestic slave trade to liquidate her debts. No doubt other incidents must have occurred that Famfantor chose not to share with his biographer. All, however, seem to have made him mistrust not only his sister-in-law but also his wife. In the end, they too divorced. And even though his wife left Famfantor with their children, presumably in accordance with concerns common at the time among the matrilineal Akan that his spirit (*sunsum*) might take out his anger at his wife on the children, Famfantor did not feel prepared to take responsibility for their upbringing.[52] In the end he lost not only his second wife but also his children. On realizing that the love and respect he thought he had found in Assin had slowly disintegrated into nothingness, he felt intensely unsettled. His first wife engaged in behavior that he could only interpret as a betrayal of his trust in her as the person responsible for ensuring his dietary safety. His second wife and her family took advantage of his trust in them and undermined his economic well-being, while his new master accused him of being untrustworthy with his former master's money.

So deeply did Famfantor feel these betrayals that he even remembered this same phenomenon as the cause of his own captivity and that of a large segment of the Wusuta population by Asante forces. In recounting this history, for example, he emphasized the close friendship that had previously characterized relations between his hometown and Asante (most particularly the Asante polity of Nsuta). According to Famfantor, hunters from both areas shared the same hunting grounds, presumably without incident, and when a delegation of Asantes came to Wusuta in 1867 or 1868 ostensibly to help mourn the death of the Wusuta chief, they never suspected ulterior motives. This is what he remembered despite the long history of conflict that characterized Asante-Wusuta relations. He mentioned, for example, the Wusutas telling their Asante guests that they had moved from Matse to their current location, but he failed to also note that this move was caused by the annual raids the Asante launched against the residents east of the Volta, raids the Wusuta were finally able to evade because they were no longer so near the river. In discussing the particularly close ties that existed between Wusuta and the Asante polity of Nsuta, he also ignored the fact that in 1818 the Wusutas refused a request by the Asantes that they accompany them to war in Gyaman.[53] In 1823, the Wusutas and the Asantes—under the leadership of the Nsutahene—were actually at war with each other. In this conflict, the Asantes managed to capture some 130 prisoners of war from the many different Ewe-speaking polities they attacked, but in the end they lost far more men than they could afford and even failed to obtain the booty needed to pay for the war, in part because of Wusuta's military opposition to the invasion.[54] In 1826, when Asante faced a massive uprising by its conquered provinces and then suffered defeat in the Katamanso war, Wusuta was not among those who assisted its so-called friend.[55] In 1836, they went beyond this position of neutrality to actually join with the polity of Peki to attack Asante's ally east of the Volta, Akwamu.[56] Given this history, one could hardly characterize Wusuta and Asante as "the closest of friends." Why then did Famfantor describe the relationship in these terms? Why would he persist in making this claim when according to his own account the behavior of the Asantes during their stay to help celebrate the death of the Wusuta chief was tolerated only because the Wusutas were afraid any opposition would create even more difficulties for them? Answers to these questions can be found in how Famfantor came to see the history of his own relationships. Having felt personally betrayed by those closest to him, his two wives and his master's successor, Famfantor mapped his own experiences onto the remembered history of Wusuta. In so doing, he gave new priority to that which connected him to his own hometown. Not only was this the place where he was born and raised, where his maternal relatives lived, and where his mother was buried, it was also a place that had suffered, as he had, a betrayal of trust. It was this understanding that seems to have propelled him to follow in the footsteps of his biblical namesake. Like Yosef, he decided to forgive his family. Only then did he resolve to leave his adopted home and to settle not in Cape Coast or Kintampo, where he had such strong business connections, but rather in his own hometown of Wusuta. It was, in part, because he felt so betrayed by his Wusuta family that he opted to remain in Assin. But it was because he also felt so betrayed in Assin that he decided to return to his own hometown of Wusuta.

CONCLUSION

In many ways, the biographies of Lydia Adzoba Yawo and Yosef Kwaku Fam-fantor confirm much of what we already know about postemancipation West Africa: that the enslaved made decisions about whether to remain with their masters or to return to their natal homes on the basis of how well they were treated, whether or not they remembered where they came from, what oppor-tunities (economic and social) existed locally and at home, whether or not it was safe to travel, and what arrangements were possible for their children. All these factors clearly influenced the decisions made by Lydia and Famfantor. But their biographies tell us more than this. They provide us with an opportu-nity to see how these factors played out in the lives of specific individuals. By analyzing their biographies—as mediated as they are—we can get at the more personal and the emotional. Lydia, for example, may well have wanted to leave her husband/master. That option, however, simply didn't exist for her as far as she was concerned. She was alone. Her mother had been enslaved. Her brother expressed little interest in remaining in the area to be near her. Since her en-slavement, she had heard nothing from her father and uncle in Taviefe, travel to which was too dangerous anyway given the unsettled state of the region and the widespread hostility toward all Taviefe citizens in the area. She had no one but her children (who by local law belonged to her husband) and her spouse. Not only did she stay with her master/husband, she was desperate to do so. Famfantor's decisions were equally informed by his own particular concerns. Issues of loyalty and betrayal were especially important to him. Famfantor, for example, chose to remain with his Assin master's family because he felt such loyalty to his deceased owner. When, however, those relations accused Fam-fantor of being untrustworthy, of hiding his master's profits from them, he moved. He opted not to return to his hometown of Wusuta, however. He had yet to forgive his maternal relatives for what he considered their betrayal of his own trust in them after they sent him into debt peonage. Instead, he moved to Abakrampa to be part of the Christian community. Only later when he felt betrayed yet again by his second wife and sister-in-law did he decide to forgive his maternal relatives and return to his natal home. Both Lydia and Famfantor, like so many others in postemancipation West Africa, made decisions on whether to stay or go based on their individual situations. It is only by critically reading their biographies, however, that their dilemmas can truly come alive.

4. Come Over and Help Us!
The Life Journey of Lydia Yawo, a Freed Slave:
Preface and Text

As a citizen of Taviefe, Lydia Adzoba's life was significantly affected by both the past and more contemporary decisions made by the political and military leaders of her hometown. Taviefe was founded sometime in the eighteenth century. But as Taviefe elders explained in 1915 about their own history, "We found many nations had come before us and settled in this land. . . . No one would give us land [on which] to settle so we fought them and eventually settled where we now are."[1] In the early nineteenth century, this period of initial hostility had given way to an uneasy peace. Taviefe refused to align itself with any of the other Ewe-speaking groups that had united to fight against Akwamu and Asante, but they also established marital ties with their neighbors. The political leader of Ho, Howusu, who vowed after the end of the 1869–71 war to exterminate all Taviefes because of their alliance with the Asantes, was married to a Taviefe woman. So were many other men from Ho. Still, the recent war and Taviefe's past political decisions did not endear the community to its neighbors. It is this context, dated and described below, that should be taken into consideration when reading Lydia's biography.

1820	Akwamu breaks with the regional power of Asante.
1823	Many of the towns and villages north of Taviefe also refuse to recognize Asante authority, in which they were expected to provide troops for Asante's expansionary and punitive wars. Asante troops are sent to crush the rebellion. These troops are defeated. Taviefe remains neutral.
1826	Akwamu, formerly an Asante ally, leads a number of its subordinate Ewe-speaking polities in war against Asante at the Battle of

Katamanso, in which the British provide troops who also fight to defeat the Asante forces.

Taviefe remains neutral.

c. 1829–33   A number of Ewe-speaking polities under Akwamu rule rebel.

Taviefe remains neutral

1833–69   Between these years Akwamu launches three different attacks on the Ewe-speaking polities that had successfully asserted their independence. Akwamu forces are defeated.

Taviefe remains neutral.

Early 1850s   Adzoba is born in Taviefe.

1859   The Bremen missionaries Steinemann and Knecht make their first visit to Taviefe.

1862   An earthquake felt in Taviefe and Ho is used by the Bremen Mission to win recognition for the power of its God, to reinforce their activities in the area, and to win converts.

26 June 1869   Asante invades Ho; the residents of the constituent towns of this polity retreat to Takla.

Taviefe aligns itself with Asante and its war allies Akwamu and Anlo.

Yawo, Adzoba's future second husband, escapes the war at Ho and takes refuge in Taviefe, his mother's village. He is sheltered there even though many other Taviefes who, like Yawo, had a father from Ho and a mother from Taviefe were handed over to the Asantes.

8 July 1869   The Ho military, with support from troops from Agotime, launches a counterattack on the Asantes and Anlos stationed at Ho.

Troops from Taviefe assist the Asantes in countering the Ho/Agotime attack.

Sept. 1869–   While one contingent of Asante troops pursue the people of Ho
early 1870   as they retreat first east and then to the north, the remaining Asantes in the area relocate their camp to Taviefe, which they deem more defensible. They billet there briefly before moving on to the Asante base camp in Wusuta.

c. Feb. 1870   A few people from Ho begin to return to their villages although life is still quite unsafe. Skirmishes take place between those from Ho who have returned home and some Anlos troops passing through the area.

c. Apr. 1870   The political leader of Ho and most of his people move back into their farm villages.

June 1870   Asante and Anlo troops that had engaged in battles north of Ho begin to return south in five different groups; in their retreat, the Asantes begin to pillage and attack friend and foe alike, including the Taviefes.

Anlo troops aligned with the Asantes agree to protect a group of Taviefe women and children by taking them to Anlo away from the war zone; Adzoba's mother and brother are among this group. All are either enslaved in Anlo or sold away from the area.

c. 1871   Asante troops leave the field of battle; retaliatory raids and reprisals between Ho and Taviefe begin.

Adzoba is kidnapped in one of these raids.

c. early 1872 Adzoba's master/husband, Gamo, from the Ho village of Kpenoe, dies. Adzoba is taken as a second or third wife by Gamo's brother, Yawo. She gives birth to Gamo's child, Kutame.

May 1872   Mission assistant Aaron Onipayede is sent by Bremen missionary Merz to survey the situation at the mission station at Ho. He reports the Christian community there is intact and awaiting the return of the Bremen missionaries.

April–   Onipayede makes two more trips to Ho on behalf of the Bremen
Nov. 1872   Mission.

Dec. 1872   Adzoba's husband, Yawo, travels with a local Christian from Ho to Waya (a town that had aligned itself with Asante and Anlo against Ho during the war) to learn about the new faith. He remains for fourteen days before returning home to the Ho village of Kpenoe.

July 1873   Yawo returns to Waya to receive Christian religious instruction for three months.

28 Sept. 1873 Yawo is baptized with the Christian name of Noah. He divorces two of his wives but remains married to Adzoba only on the condition that she convert. He also frees her and all his other slaves.

Early 1874   Adzoba's child, Kutame, dies.

17 Oct. 1875 Adzoba is baptized with the Christian name of Lydia.

18 Oct. 1875 Lydia and Noah are married in a Christian ceremony.

13 March 1875 The long-standing hostilities between Taviefe and its neighbors that have been simmering since 1869 in the form of kidnappings and robberies erupt into open warfare when the political leaders of Ho and Peki stage an attack on the Taviefe with the intent of "waging a war of extermination." In this attack, the Taviefe lose forty-four men, but the Ho and Peki militaries are eventually

forced to retreat when Madse, a Taviefe ally, attacks the Ho and
Peki forces at their rear.

5 March 1877   Lydia dies.

Come Over and Help Us! The Life Journey
of Lydia Yawo, a Freed Slave

Told by Johannes Merz, Missionary, Bremen, 1877

Translation from German by Anna Parkinson
Edited by Sandra E. Greene

I. THEY DO NOT KNOW THE WAY OF PEACE

During my youth I was already deeply touched by the Word that I read in The Acts
of the Apostles 16:9: "Come over and help us."[2] I saw that Word in many a missionary paper or tract. There, the poor heathens stand with their hands out-
stretched toward us in Europe, and they want to receive from us the blessing of
the Word of God. The Lord granted me my dearest wish and sent me to Africa, to
a land in need of help before all other lands. Here, on the slave coast of West Africa, the call: "Come over and help us!" touches our hearts and reaches our ears
every single day. Even if it is only a few who articulate this plea to us, we nonetheless sense the call loudly enough in all that we are forced to look upon daily.

This Africa is a great and immense continent; nevertheless, it is estimated
that there are only 191 million inhabitants. Why is this abundant land so sparsely
populated? It is said that the export of slaves has taken her children to foreign
parts of the world. Indeed, this appalling trafficking in human beings has for the
most part robbed this land of its inhabitants. Yet that is not the only cause. Millions of Negroes were brought into slavery, but here in the West this trade has
stopped and, wherever it once again surfaces, attempts are made to repress it.
And nonetheless the situation has not yet improved, for the damage lies at a
deeper level. That which is written in Romans 3:15–18: "Their feet are swift to
shed blood; destruction and misery are in their ways and the way of peace have
they not known. There is no fear of God before their eyes,"[3]—is valid for this
country. Revenge and a thirst for booty ensure that war and bloodshed never
come to an end. If prisoners of war or other abducted enemies can no longer be
sold on ships, they are butchered or brought to the coast, where they become
porters for the indigenous traders and, in particular, will be used to carry the
pernicious spirits [i.e., liquor] into the interior. Many children are given names
that constantly recall the injustice they have suffered. For example, *Nyasogbo,*

i.e., many words. When the Ashanti came inland, many tribes of the Ewe believed that they could secure the interior through an alliance with them, which certainly was to their detriment; for as soon as they had billeted with them, they made their allies into their slaves. However, the king of Ho had not forgotten about their breaking with his people; rather, he recorded the injustice toward him at that time by the neighboring tribes in the name of his son. He called him *Gbadewo,* which means, "it has collapsed on top of them." This thirst for vengeance and the fact that everyone dispenses their own justice makes all journeys unsafe. Almost every day an unsuspecting traveler is attacked by highwaymen, bound, and dragged off by a circuitous route to a remote village. On account of such dangers the Negro is always armed with a knife and a shotgun, and only seldom does one come away without being wounded or killed.

Africa is still deeply ill and bleeds from innumerable wounds. The compassionate love of the Good Samaritan must rise up, and the soothing oil, the Gospel, must be brought to the slaves of sin and death. If we should come to their aid, then we would experience that God is devoted also to this people and can make them into seekers of peace. How often have we been privy to witness how he turns that which people thought of as evildoing into good, and that his ways, however obscure they appear to be, nonetheless reveal themselves to be the ways of peace and serenity. This will also be demonstrated to us through the following life story.

II. HOME AND YOUTH

The Ewe tribe of the Tafiewe [Taviefe] lives on the slave coast of West Africa, approximately thirty hours inland from the sea. The tribe lives in a variety of smaller and larger cities, perhaps eight in number, on a mountain range, which makes of the land a natural fortress. This factor certainly contributed to how the Tafiewe had cut themselves off from the other surrounding tribes and had, for some time now, joined up with the Anlo and the Ashanti. This is also how it was during the war in 1869 waged by the Ashanti and the Anlo against the Ewe tribes in the interior. When these enemies had returned home from their military expedition there, the Tafiewe found themselves in a difficult situation, and if their land had not been shaped like a fortress, then the surrounding tribes certainly would have annihilated them a long time ago.

In this land at the beginning of the fifties, a girl was born, whose story we want to tell. The year and, further, the month of her birth cannot be accurately determined, for Negroes do not retain these things in their memory. We are, however, all the more certain that we know the day on which she was born, for she was named Adsoba [Adzoba], and the Ewe give this name to girls who are born on a Monday: Dsoda [Dzoda]. As was the case with other heathen children, her youth did not consist of all that many days of merriment. Even though the beautiful homeland, the tall banana and plantain farms with their sweet fruits, the large yam fields, the harvest of which even a Negro child would not spurn, have a beneficial effect on a young soul. And how lovely it is to look upon the universe of stars and the shining full moon! This splendor and this radiance must be seen in the world of the tropics. But the Negro child is blind to this. Where would one find the heathen mother who instructs her child: Do you know how many little stars there are in this blue canopy of heavens! Adsoba may indeed have delighted with the other heathens when the full moon rendered the night as day, then, when cool breezes alleviate the day's heat, when one and all gather together to dance and sing until deep into the night. But it was also there where she saw and learned the sins of the parents. Yet even the Negro child does not lack the love of its mother. In accordance with the custom of the Negro, the mother would have bound her to her back and carried her around this way until her fourth year of life. When the child is eight days old it already has found its place on the mother's back. She carries out all of her work with the child: she fetches water, chops up wood for cooking, cooks her food, spins cotton, goes to market in distant places, hacks her land and plants maize, yams, beans, cabbages as vegetables, cotton, etc.; or she even dances around with the others in the evening by the light of the moon with the child always tied onto her back by a piece of material of one or two meters in length. Only seldom does she put her naked child down, and usually on the material in which she carries it, and sometimes even on the bare earth. As she then learned to walk properly and became strong, she would have helped her parents, who were simple country folk, assisting her mother with the daily domestic duties. There was the low house, covered with grass, and with a fence around it forming an enclosed courtyard, where there is a hearth, washing chamber, and loom all to be swept; water and wood had to be brought in, maize roasted and ground; dishes and clothing were to be cleaned, cotton to be spun, local soap to be prepared, the fruits of the field to be sold, and the younger brothers and sisters to be taken care of. When the child reaches eight to ten years of age, she or he begins to cultivate her or his own plot of land. At this time it also all too frequently happens that the child begins to refuse to obey the parents. Should the mother cook something that the child finds unpalatable, then the child will cook something from its own provisions for her- or himself and also gets tidbits from an aunt and uncle. The grandmother on the mother's side couldn't let a day pass by without slipping something to the grandchild. Otherwise the future husband must contribute, for most girls are already engaged at an early age, and from time to time the groom gives presents to his young bride and her parents. When she reaches fourteen, fifteen, sixteen years of age, the poor girl discovers that she has practically become a slave through the few presents. And no exception was made in Adsoba's case.

III. IN FOREIGN PARTS AND IN CAPTIVITY

Thus Adsoba grew up. She understood nothing of that which makes human beings truly happy. For although two messengers of the Gospel, Steinemann and Knecht, had already briefly visited the Tafiewe in 1859, it appears that she had heard nothing at all about this. God wanted to use other means to draw her to him. Earlier on she had already lost her father, about whom we only know that his name, Oklu, meant that already before his birth he had been dedicated to the *trọ* (fetish), for that is what his name means. Even her mother, Sa, was not allowed to close his eyes. When the Ashanti came to their country, they wreaked the most dreadful havoc. Their sole thought was to capture slaves, and they did not even spare their friends; rather, they found it all the more easier to succeed in this respect, as the latter believed themselves to be safe from their allies, and they noticed their betrayal only too late. The Ashanti feared only the Anlo; for that reason, many people joined up with the Anlo, who also promised to bring them home again after the withdrawal of the enemy, which certainly rarely happened. However, it was always the lesser of two evils to be a slave in Anlo, for at least they had no human sacrifices there, as was the case in Ashanti. This way Sa also went as the woman of an Anlo with her children to the coast; only Adsoba remained at home. The mother, whom Adsoba spoke of with love for a long time, is supposed to have been snatched away by smallpox and her children sold off as slaves. In Tafiewe Adsoba stayed with her husband or uncle. It was such a dreadful time, even though the Ashanti had withdrawn for a while from the area of Tafiewe. For a great famine was upon the land, particularly there, wherever the Ashanti had landed like locusts. It looked awful; for miles around there were no longer any yam fields to be seen, even all of the grain crops were exhausted. This drove the people to visit distant marketplaces, even if the roads they took were unsafe; for people-hunters who carried off anyone they could get hold of lay in wait everywhere in the high grass and bush. The war had already sown enough evil seed to spread vindictiveness and greed, and the Tafiewe, who had been treated badly through their neighbors' treachery during the war, would have done well to incite no further provocation. But the Negro knows no limits to vengeance and will not desist from it, even if he is to ruin himself through it. A man from Ho, whom the Tafiewe had captured, had his head cut off, and Ho soon repaid like with like. Women who were married to men from Ho, even those who had descended from the Tafiewe, were snatched away from their men, etc.

This also happened to Kukeha from Ho. He himself was related to the Tafiewe and had a wife who had been born there. When the Ho had to leave their villages during the war years, he provided for his wife as well as he could under the circumstances. Scarcely had he returned with his wife to Ho when his relatives took his wife away from the very same man and gave her to another man in Tafiewe. This was also wrong in the eyes of the Negro, for as Kukeha himself was related to the Tafiewe he should not have been treated like an enemy. Kukeha meditated revenge and soon he found an opportunity. It must have been around the time when the Ashanti had retreated from the area when the entire caravan of Tafiewe went to the Adaglu [Adaklu] market to buy corn— or, more likely rather, to exchange it for palm oil. They could do this because the Tafiewe were friendly with the Anlo and the Adaglu. Their journey took them past Ho, but this city was still devastated, and the Ho still lived mostly out of town. Kukeha took advantage of this opportunity and, with his helpers, constantly lay in wait close by the road. One day Adsoba was sent along to the market. Kukeha's people held up those mature enough for the market, kidnapped sixteen people, almost solely virgins, and Adsoba was also among them. They were all sold on the Gold Coast. Adsoba would have shared the same fate if a certain man, Gamo from Gbenoe [Kpenoe], had not heard of her. Gamo came from the same family that Adsoba belonged to; his mother was a native of Tafiewe and also lived there. For this reason he did not want Adsoba to be sold to a foreign country; instead he bought her for himself for 110 marks and took her to be his wife.

The Lord took pity on Adsoba when he led her to Gbenoe. She had certainly lived through hard times. Father, mother, brothers, and sisters had been stolen from her; she herself was in foreign parts. But she was, however, among a people whose language she understood. Although she was a slave, as the wife of her husband she did not have it so bad. For in the interior the lot of a slave who has been taken by her master to be his wife is not as harsh as on the coast, where mother and children remain slaves; in the interior of the country children receive rights and even the mother is considered to be a full member of the family. The good fortune of being a mother and, through this, a family member befell Adsoba. Thus she lived in a happy relationship with her husband, who was a very industrious, influential, and highly regarded Negro and a "god fearing heathen." She had become so settled in her new homeland that she took the side of her husband and the people of Ho rather than that of her former home, Tafiewe, with regard to political questions concerning the country.

Did she perhaps receive even more from Gbenoe, her new homeland, than from Gamo that helped her get over the loss of her former home? This could very well be the case, for Gbenoe is part of Ho, where missionaries had been preaching the Gospel for a total of ten years. By then they had certainly been driven away by the war, but is it likely that Gamo had told her nothing about these men? In the year 1862 the Ho people were frightened by an event that was completely new to them. A small earthquake stirred up the population. The missionaries found this to be a convenient occasion on which to propagate the Word of the immovable Kingdom. In Gbenoe too the earthquake had moved souls. A law was established there that from then onwards Sunday was to be honored and they asked the missionaries from Ho to come and preach. For a time, the preachers delivered the Good News on Sunday, often accompanied by a crowd of followers, and in Gamo's house there was prayer, singing, and the name of Jesus was propagated, just as if the entire situation had been initiated at his request. One would like to believe that the memory of this did not completely die out in Gamo's house. But before the disseminated seed could come to fruition, a series of even more serious disruptions would have to take place.

Only a brief period of married bliss was granted to Adsoba. Her husband Gamo died even before her first child was born. After the widow had given birth to a daughter, she named the child Kutame, which means: "Death hates human beings."

IV. ADSOBA BECOMES THE WIFE OF A CHRISTIAN

According to the law of the Ewe, a wife is never again free from the family into which she marries. If her husband dies, then the widow must marry another member of the family after a year. Brothers [of the deceased husband] have first claim on her. Incidentally, it is the *trọ* (fetish) that signals (of course in all truth only really confirms) the choice through a fetish priestess or priest. However, sometimes the woman does not wish to marry the man, and she professes that the *nunu* of the man, i.e., the spirit that accompanies him, is harmful to her. Gamo did not follow this custom; his faith in the spirits may well have wavered because no one could make him healthy. Before he died, he called his brother Yawo to him and asked him to marry his wife, Adsoba, after his death. Of course, Yawo was already married, but that was no obstacle. For the more women a Negro possesses, the richer he is considered to be. In this way Adsoba became Yawo's wife.

Yawo had, like his brother Gamo, already heard the missionaries speak, but he had not heeded their word. However, the Lord did not allow this to pass. Since that earthquake, which the missionaries had spoken of as the miraculous sign sent by God, the illness of smallpox had arrived; then in 1869 the war broke out, and even Yawo had suffered greatly from it. One sign after the other had ensued: earthquake, pestilence, and war, and the fetish had proven to be completely useless. His [Yawo's] brother had been sick for a long time and there was no fetish priest whom they neglected to consult in their search for help. Each one of them promised help and believed to have a stronger spirit at their disposal than the spirit of the illness; it had to do with the sacrificial offering brought before their spirits, like the priests of Bel, whom Daniel unmasked. Gamo died in spite of the sacrificial offering. All of the Ho had worn fetish cords in battle in order to protect themselves against the perils of war. One Christian man, who lived in Yawo's village, and three men who had applied for baptism and had undertaken their baptismal training before the missionaries had to leave Ho, had done without the magical charms and nonetheless remained safe. Indeed, a certain Christian man, Samuel Kwami by name, had experienced something exceptional. Once, during an attack after nightfall, the Ashanti captured Samuel's child, and the next day the child came bounding toward its father. Much to everyone's amazement it [the child] had escaped.

These experiences weakened Yawo's faith in the fetish and made him eager to hear the Gospel that he had once held in such low regard. He consulted Samuel, who had himself been a fetish priest earlier on and who would surely be able to tell him even more about the deception of the fetish practice. But he had even better news to share with him; he knew how to tell him of the love of Jesus, who goes after those who are lost and makes them into the children of God. Yawo quickly made a decision; it was his firm resolution to break off immediately with the old ways and to become a Christian, whatever it might cost him. He learned from Samuel the Ten Commandments and the Lord's Prayer, as well as all else that remained in Samuel's memory. In their simplicity, both of them conducted evening prayers every day in Yawo's house. Actually, one should rather say courtyard, for the Negro's house is too small; except for the door opening, it has no light. It is also usually only there to protect the things and to sleep in. Meals are usually taken in the courtyard or on the veranda. There, too, one usually carries out any work that needs to be done and also receives guests. Yawo had inherited many slaves from his brother; he now brought them together daily for evening prayers and some of the village inhabitants also joined them. They learned together there the Ten Commandments and the Lord's Prayer. In this way they attempted to edify themselves, but Yawo was not satisfied with this. He wanted more; he yearned to be baptized so that he might become the property of Jesus.

Everything that Yawo once held dear had now become foreign to him. In July 1869 the missionaries had had to leave Ho; after much courageous resistance even the Ho themselves had had to give up their homeland and were wandering about the country. At that time Waya, the closest station—at a nine-hour distance from Ho—was still occupied [by the missionaries], and one could only hope that the work there remained undisturbed. For during the war, the individual campaigns that can certainly never be able to be fully recounted, the Ashanti, in battle with the Ewe tribes, had retreated from the region. It is most likely that at this time too the capture of Adsoba took place, which led her to Gbenoe. But in the summer of the following year the Ashanti moved again toward the south and attacked the Adaglu. Suddenly in Waya we also saw ourselves surrounded by them and on October 18, 1870, I, along with Missionary Müller, had to rescue myself from them by traveling to the coast. Waya stood empty for almost a year, and it was only in July 1871 that I was able to move to Waya once more. However, the conditions were not by any means such that we could plan to go to Ho. It was thanks to special circumstances that our Negro helper, Aaron Onipayede, was able to make the first visit to Ho in May 1872. He first told us of how those who had applied to be baptized in Ho had remained faithful and that the Ho longed for the missionaries. This was confirmed when I succeeded in going to Ho in August. However, it was still not the right time to do anything more for the [believers in] Ho than to send Aaron to them from time to time. It was during a visit later in October that Aaron got to know our Yawo in Gbenoe and heard his story and his desire to become a Christian. This desire was now great enough to overcome all obstacles. On December 19, 1872, Samuel Kwami appeared in Waya with three heathens from Gbenoe. Among them was Yawo; he had been warned of how dangerous it would be to go to Waya at this troubled time, but he was prepared to take everything from the hand of God. He remained for fourteen days in Waya and received lessons in God's Word. But all agreed that his baptism should be postponed until he had received more extensive and thorough teaching.

In July 1873 Yawo once more met up in Waya with another man from Gbenoe, Dake. When Yawo had expressed his desire to become a Christian to his three wives, Lydia who was the one among them who expressed the most friendliness toward his wish, also attended the prayer services, which neither of the other two did. This cast of mind and the fact that she brought along with her Kutame, the brother's child, who was much loved by Yawo, made him decide after consultation with the missionaries to allow her to accompany him to Waya so that she might participate in the lessons, a wish with which Adsoba gladly complied. With her first appearance in Waya she immediately gave the impression of having a childlike disposition and a modest, delightful nature, so that we all had hopes for her. She also immediately joined with the Christian women, the girls, and Mrs. Illg, and let herself be told the holy stories by way of biblical images, with which she was very taken. However, it was all very alien to her; it was a completely different world. The white man was foreign to her; the European-built house was in her eyes odder than an elephant is in the eyes of children. She crawled, rather than walked, up the staircase, and when she had finally reached the top, she was overcome by an enormous fear of the floor collapsing beneath her. When she took a few steps, she tread so softly that she scarcely would have been able to break an egg. When the wall clock chimed, she would have liked best to hide herself away. Even the language was foreign and difficult for her. Yawo too spoke a dialect different from that which was common in Waya, but within a few days he had accustomed himself to it for his heart was open. Thus, it became difficult for Adsoba to follow the baptismal lessons with interest and concentration. Little Kutame, whom she always carried with her and whom could only seldom be taken from her, also hindered and disturbed her. She would often be admonished by us or, in particular, by her husband and told to demonstrate more attentiveness and seriousness, which she gladly heard said to her, but without this altering the situation in any significant manner. The following holds true for her: The child of nature knows nothing of the spirit of God. However difficult it was for Yawo, he had to reconcile himself to the fact that on September 28 he alone along with Dake, the other man from Gbenoe, and a Waya were baptized. After a three-month long sojourn with her husband, now named Noah, Adsoba returned a heathen to Gbenoe.

V. THROUGH THE NIGHT TOWARD THE LIGHT

Noah went back home delighted in his Lord like a chamberlain from Cush.[4] Indeed, he knew very well that he was about to confront a bitter battle; therefore even on the day of his baptism he had expressed the wish to be with his Savior both now and forever. But he also knew that now he had to demonstrate that he had become a Christian by way of his actions in his homeland. To have three wives, as did Noah, was not in accordance with the spirit of the divine Word. The dilemma was soon resolved. When he had told the women that from now on he wanted to have only one wife and to live with her according to the Christian order, two of them refused him, whereas Lydia consented to this. Yawo was therefore determined to keep her; however, he became hesitant once again when he observed that Lydia would not convert to Christianity as quickly as he might wish her to. Thus he arrived at the conclusion that it would be better for him to live completely alone, and one day he explained to Adsoba that she was free and could go wherever she wanted to. That was a heavy blow to the woman; for she was then homeless. To return home was impossible for her; even at the borders of Noah's land she would be captured and taken away; her future looked very dark indeed. Adsoba wept and urgently begged Noah not to cast her out.

That was the impetus for change. That which was contained already within her now came to expression. Her experience with the strange ways of Christian life in Waya had not been in vain. Already on September 29, when she saw her husband receiving the holy christening, there awoke in her heart for the first time a serious desire to partake of the same grace; and, before leaving Waya, she had expressed her regret that she had not taken things more seriously and now had to leave as a heathen; she had agreed that she would return [to Waya] soon. The danger of losing her husband led to this sense of gravity taking command of her once again. From then on she increasingly obeyed and came to love the Word of God. She took part in the prayer services held by those who had been baptized. What the Christians were able to give was, however, somewhat limited; they drew upon the modest capital that they had accumulated in Waya. However, we may add to this: the Spirit of God was with them and this compensated for their lack. They had to make do with this kind of care for even longer. For in the autumn of 1873 war once more came upon the land; Waya was once again surrounded by the dangers of war and the road to Ho was closed to the missionaries for quite some time.

However, God himself took care of furthering Adsoba's education at the beginning of 1874. The much-loved Kutame was torn away from her. The little child was, like his mother, not baptized. However, Noah wanted his child to be laid to rest just as a Christian child would be. No shots were fired, as is usually the custom of the heathens. He made a path through the grass to the grave, beside which they sang a song and prayed. This defection from tradition provoked the wrath of the heathens. They said, when one accords death so much honor, even clearing a path to the place of burial and neglecting the traditions of the ancestors, what will the consequences be? Death will rejoice and take many victims. That will not be difficult for him; he now knows exactly how to find the way; indeed, the Christians have cleared a path for him. Namely, Negroes believe that death as well as the most varied spirits of illness linger in the bush; thus they place objects on all paths that are intended to frighten death and keep him outside of the town or the village. Most frequently these are clumps of earth in the form of sugar loaves that have chicken feathers stuck into them. This protection had been ignored by Noah and now he and the Yesutowo—the people of Jesus, by which the small circle of people who had gathered around the Christians was known—had to suffer some oppression. They, too, were led along the road so often ordained for those who wish to enter into the Kingdom of God. This certainly intimidated some; however, many remained steadfast, and among these was also Adsoba, who now wished to add herself through baptism to those who belonged to Jesus.

This wish remained unfulfilled for some time. Only in September 1874 was Missionary Illg able to visit Ho, and to his great joy he found in the villages of the Ho tribes a group of twenty-two adults gathered around the small Christian community who wished to be designated by the name of Christ. It was necessary to administer counsel to them. So, even if a white missionary was still unable to go to Ho, a gifted Negro assistant arrived there before the year was out and, in the meantime, he took over the guidance of those desiring salvation. However, another year passed before October 17, 1875, on which day Adsoba underwent holy baptism. She was given the name Lydia, for now one could say of her as of the seller of purple fabrics in Philippi: The Lord opened her heart.[5] On this day twenty-two souls along with Lydia were incorporated through baptism into the communion of the Lord. May their new names all be found in the Book of Life in days to come.

VI. THE CHRISTIAN HOUSE AND THE BETTER HOME

After the day of celebration on October 17 there followed another day of festivities on October 18. Noah and Lydia had become of one faith; both of them had sworn to be faithful to the Lord; now they also had to remain loyal to one another. On October 18 they wanted to take this vow before the Lord and receive his blessing of their Christian matrimony. Noah had built himself a new house, and the ceremony, in which three other Christian married couples in addition to Noah and Lydia had participated, was celebrated there in Gbenoe. Now, even at home, they were all to give credence to the passage that Missionary Illg had enjoined on them in his marriage speech: As ye have therefore received Christ Jesus the Lord, so walk ye in him![6]

After the lengthy period of affliction, this change assumed a very joyful and pleasing form. Lydia went on to enjoy several happy months during which she was able to live unhampered with the Christians in Gbenoe. However, soon the Lord deemed it appropriate to grant Lydia a particular education. It was the first Christmas that she was able to celebrate in communion with the Christians, as well as the first that had been celebrated here since the destruction of Ho. The assistant had come from Waya furnished with all kinds of things for the Christmas tree and the small group of Christians from Gbenoe, Achlicha, and Wegbe united around the Christmas tree on Christmas Eve, joyously sang their songs, and listened to the story of the incarnation of God's son. Lydia was also among those rejoicing. It had become rather late by the time the people from Gbenoe had come out of the hot meeting place and into the cool night air and started out on their one-and-a-half hour long journey home. Lydia contracted a cold that immediately expressed itself as a pernicious cough and as the beginning of a long process of suffering. The seed had already been sown much earlier on. Along with her Gamo, she had experienced the afflictions of war, and it is impossible to imagine what people had endured in those years of war. Often, and for weeks at a time, they were forced to stay in the midst of high grass and out in the open, oppressed by the singeing heat by day and without protection at night; they were soaked by the piteous blanket of the dew that falls so plentifully here that it substitutes for rain for the flora for months on end. Add to this the tropical rainstorms and a hungry stomach that often had to go without for days on end and we should not be surprised when even robust constitutions are susceptible to the seeds of disease. Lydia was in poor health from this time onward. Noah, of course, ensured that she did not lack for food; he stressed that she should not neglect herself according to the Negro way of doing things. But it is difficult to break with old habits. Negroes do not know how to prepare hearty dishes. Although yams may indeed offer more substantial nutrition than do potatoes, they are not sufficient for such invalids. Meat is a rarity; eggs, raw or half cooked, are horrifying to them, and milk, even were they to have this, would be something they would disdain to touch.

At this time there was, unfortunately, not yet any missionary in Ho who might have been able to take better care of her. Thus the disease was progressively able to take hold of her. Furthermore, she along with the other Christians had to suffer through a period of trouble. When around Christmas time the misfortune of shooting another man befell the Christian Isaac, this brought hard times to Noah's house, in which Lydia's delicate health suffered further damage. When Missionary Illg went to see her in January, he was shocked by her condition. He asked her if she would like to go to Waya and remain there for a while as a visitor. At this her eyes sparkled with joy, and she requested that Noah should be asked; she had long harbored this wish, but Noah had had misgivings and believed that she was too inept and would not know how to conduct herself properly there. On hearing Illg's offer, however, Noah was very grateful, for there in Waya Lydia would be able to receive better treatment and soon everything was arranged so that she could travel with Illg.

In the first week of her stay Waya appeared to be doing some good for her health; the remedies applied to her took effect. Otherwise, she used the time with much zeal and skill to learn how to sew, something with which she, as with other Negro women, was unfamiliar, as the men usually carry out this task. How very happy she was when she had completed the first dress of European cloth for herself and was able to put it on! She was not homesick, however; she always looked forward with longing for news from Ho and was happy when the many messengers traveling to and fro would bring her greetings and gifts from her husband. Once when she was surprised by the difficult news that Noah's house had been attacked and plundered by the hostile portion of the inhabitants, she was very worried and full of concern for Noah and cried a lot; however, she always let herself be comforted when one spoke of God, who protected him, and would not allow anything to happen that he did not deem good. When her condition was tolerable, she could be very cheerful and well disposed and then she would tell of her experiences of the last war. She was a good storyteller and could entertain the girls admirably as they worked, for which reason she was also most popular. Once she even had the joy of seeing one of her relatives from Tafiewe. He had come to Anlo through the passage of slavery, as was described above, and was transporting freight to Waya. Lydia was of the opinion that he was now free, according to the law of the British and that he should return to his homeland. He, however, found his life with the Anlo to be to his taste, and he wished to remain there, something which Lydia could in no way condone.

Lydia remained for over two months in Waya; however, her condition did not improve. During the afternoons, she would often fall asleep from exhaustion in the room of the missionary family, and one had to anticipate with concern the time in the future when she would not have this care at her disposal, whereas she herself was longing to have Noah come and visit her. When she heard that he would be coming to Waya—the new chapel there was to be consecrated—she was completely delighted and did not attempt to hide this. When one could finally say: *Noah gbo na,* i.e., Noah is approaching, she rushed to greet him in the most friendly and heartfelt manner, something which is otherwise uncommon among Negro women. Everyone present was able to see with what bliss and joy Lydia celebrated with her husband the ensuing days of celebration, the consecration of the chapel, baptism and marriage, and she herself could not find sufficient words in which to express this. She had become particularly close to one of the three brides who were celebrating their betrothal, and it was precisely this woman who also went with her husband to Ho. In this way the day of departure arrived quickly; her gratitude was moving and this separation unforgettable, also for the missionary Illg and his wife, who did not dare to hope that they might see her again, for they were also intending to return to their homeland soon.

Thus Lydia was once again in Gbenoe and tried to go about her business. She was a diligent Negro, and the household duties of her husband gave her more than enough to do.

Noah is a great farmer, owning expansive yam fields and oil palm forests. Lydia could not stop herself from going to the fields. What a magnificent sight is indeed afforded by such a yam plantation! Its cultivation may best be compared to that of hops. The soil must be thoroughly broken and piled up. The seeds are planted just like potato seeds, but only an eye with shoots is planted. The tuber, weighing ten to twenty pounds, develops in the earth; the runner with its dark green, taut foliage winds its way upward along its stake; the darker the leaves, the greater the joy of the farmer, for it then promises to yield an abundant harvest. When the tuber is ripe, it is dug up in order to wander in the ground once again, laid out one beside the next, until months later, they will be hung up in the airy yam house. The yam house is very simple; it is made of palm branches with a roof of the same material. When the tuber is taken out, the roots of the runner are carefully covered with earth, and then it again produces three to four small tubers, which are then used as seed fruit. The general harvest is linked to a celebration; before the yams may be eaten this celebration must be held. This means that the fetish is the first person to taste the yams.—Lydia was not able to see the yam fields for any length of time; she was once so exhausted by a walk that she took that she fell to the ground and had to be carried home. Now she remained in her little house all the time. Every Negro woman has her own house, which also contains her kitchen if the clay oven, which is built in the form of a horseshoe, does not stand in the open air. Lydia could be found there the whole day long, sitting beside a small fire and spinning cotton. At this time Noah also had to endure much from the side of the heathens. No one could understand his calmness, for although Lydia was so ill he would not get her a magic necklace. To be sure, the blind heathens did not know that Noah and Lydia had placed their hope in the living God and therefore did not want any help from evil spirits. Among the heathens it was soon said: Noah is tired of Lydia and wants to marry another woman. Even as Noah had to endure much from the heathens, Lydia's childlike faith brought him comfort. When heathens are sick and fear that they could die, they fall into a state of monstrous fear and give anything to find help. Should they see no improvement in their state, they then give in to an ominous brooding so that it is no longer possible to exchange even a word with them. Lydia was peaceful; she knew the eternal home. And when her coughing prevented her from sleeping a wink at night, she would pray to her Savior. On October 1, 1876, she experienced a particularly joyful occasion once again. Communion was being given in Ho. Lydia herself could no longer travel the one and a half hour journey from Gbenoe to Ho, thus Noah gladly accepted our offer to use our hammock. On Sunday morning she was carried to Ho in it. She sat there with a radiant face and appeared to devour every word of the sermon. Our hearts were all beating with joy, for the group that accepted Communion had grown to forty-one black people including those who had been baptized eight days earlier. The Lord had done this without us missionaries being able to contribute much at all! When I saw her for the last time, she was so devoted to the will of the Lord that I had to say to myself: Lydia is a dear child of God. On the third Advent she enjoyed the banquet of the Lord for the last time in this life; her days were numbered and the Lord found his disciple to be ready. The final days were difficult; her lungs could no longer breathe in enough air, and this drove her increasingly to her Lord in prayer. When the constriction often became great, then she would begin to sigh: *"Jesu cho nam,* Help me, Jesus, *Jesu chom yi gbo wo,* Jesus, take me to you!" As long as she still had strength enough she would pray kneeling; later she was only able to do it sitting. Noah recounted how whenever he slept or watched over her he always heard how she was occupied with her Savior. In dreams she spoke of the missionary or their stay in Waya. On March 5, 1877, the time of her deliverance arrived; she lay there in the night peaceful but also very weak. Her husband, who was watching over her, was at that moment overcome by sleep and fell asleep and dreamed that six men came from Ho and wanted to carry Lydia away. Lydia called for Noah, which caused him to wake up, and as he bent over Lydia her spirit had already flown. Yes, "Blessed are the dead who die in the Lord!"[7] On the following day her worldly remains were given over to the earth. Christians and heathens listened to the speech of the missionary; neither shooting nor noise, rather prayer and song accompanied the ceremony, as is the custom of the Christians. The heathens were silent—perhaps they may have been thinking: He who dies in this way, dies well?

Should the Lord continue to give to us many souls such as that of Lydia, then we might soon establish his kingdom all over the world. For the vision is yet for an appointed time, but at the end it shall speak and not lie: though it tarry, wait for it; because it will surely come, it will not tarry. Hab. 2, 3.[8]

5. Yosef Famfantor: Preface and Text

Because Famfantor's association with the Bremen Mission, and because the war in which Famfantor was captured and enslaved was of such concern to a number of Europeans (who felt their own evangelical and business interest threatened), we can date many of the events described in the narrative by using a variety of German-, English-, and French-language reports.

c. 1855	Date of birth in Wusuta Hoto.
1862	An earthquake is felt in Famfantor's home village of Wusuta.
c. 1867	Asante (from Nsuta) enter Wusuta, ostensibly to mourn Wusuta's recently deceased chief.
c. 1868	Famfantor's family offers him as a debt slave in Wusuta Anyigbe to pay for fines incurred by his maternal family as the result of a dispute with some of the visiting Asantes.
1869	Asante troops establish a base camp in Wusuta from which they launch military operations against a number of polities to the east.
1871	Famfantor and many other Wusuta citizens are taken captive by the Asante military and marched to Kumase.
09/1873	Famfantor witnesses famine in Kumase. He is sent by his Asante master to the master's farm village. This protects him as well from the ritual killings that followed the death of the Asantehene's younger brother and which were taking place at the same time.
c. 1874	By this date, Famfantor has been sold by his Asante master to a new master in the Fante coastal district.
c. 1876–1880	Famfantor travels to Bonduku to engage in trade.
c. 1881–1888	Famfantor moves to and lives in the Fante town of Abakrampa, where he is exposed to Christianity by converts associated with the Wesleyan Methodist Mission.

c. 1888	Famfantor returns to Wusuta.
1889	Famfantor is visited by the Basel missionary Peter Hall.
1890	Famfantor is baptized after studying the previous year with the Basel Mission Catechist Cornelius Otu in Botoku.
c. 1892	Famfantor receives a hand bell from the Basel missionary Gottfried Martin, which he uses to call the people of Wusuta to worship.
c. 1903	The Basel Mission opens a school to serve both Botoku and Wusuta.
1903–1906	The Basel Mission churches and schools, including those in Wusuta, are transferred for administrative purposes to the Bremen Mission.
1927	Famfantor meets the inspector or head of the Bremen Mission, Gottfried Stoevesandt.
13 Dec. 1933	Famfantor dies.

Yosef Famfantor

G. K. Tsekpo

Translation by Kodjopa Attoh with Kenneth Krieger
Edited by Sandra E. Greene

I: THE STORY OF FAMFANTOR'S CHILDHOOD

Kwaku Famfantor was born in Wusuta Hoto in about 1851.[1] His father, Akrofi, was the brother of the chief of Hoto who could also become the chief. Famfantor was a slightly built person and had no animus toward anyone since the time he was born. This is why he was named Famfantor, which is Twi, meaning in Ewe, Kpakpaluwui [butterfly]. He was really named Kwaku, since he was born on Wednesday. His father, Akrofi, died when he was young, so he was left with his mother, Gbeklo, who was from Wusuta Anyigbe. The mother did not stay at home; a man married her and she moved to an Anfoega village called Denui on the Tafi road. So Famfantor became the stepson of the Anfoega man. Not long after that, the mother received a message about a death and she returned to Wusuta, never to return to Denui. He [Famfantor] helped her with her farming.

One day, he [Famfantor] and his age group were playing in the sand. It was about 1858[2] when he was around seven years old, and the land was shaking. The mother ran over, picked him up and strapped him on her back. Famfantor was a wonderful man with a sharp wit, so he remembered everything about his childhood.

Around 1863, when he was about twelve years old, the mother also died and he became a complete orphan. According to the old traditions of the Wusuta people, when a child's mother died, he was given a rock to stone the dead body so that the dead person would leave the living alone and would not be following the child to kill him or her. They gave the rock to Famfantor to hit the mother, but he refused saying, "My mother is dead; she didn't do me any harm. How can I hit her? I will not stone her ever because I never hit her when she was alive, nor will it happen at her death." They pressed him, but he refused.

His maternal uncle, Dodotse, came for him after his mother's death to raise him. He took him to farm regularly. In those days, the paramount chief of Wusuta, Dzaba, died. The Asante chief, Kakari, sent a delegation of about forty to the chief's funeral. Kakari's delegation brought a lot of chiefly regalia, including gold objects and many other things. They brought two bottles (*abodiabo*) and two people instead of sheep, and presented them to the new chief, Kwasikuma. The people of Wusuta also presented three bowls (*gbonu*) of yams, two sheep, two bottles of drink, two pots of palm wine, and they bought a person for thirty *hotu* and presented this to the Asantes to welcome them. They sacrificed all three people immediately. Nyrabasefia Noanyidzro, who was the Gyasehene and subchief of the Wusuta chief, hosted the Asantes.

Where they were staying, the Wusutas and Asantes were socializing (*noha dem enye*), and they were saying that the Wusuta people came from Matse to where they were not on the Volta. They and the Asantes met frequently in the hunting grounds on the Volta [Afram] plains. The Wusuta people are hunters, and there existed great plains from their area to Kwawu, all the way to Asante without any settlements. The Wusuta chief and the Asante Nsuta chief were the closest of friends among them all.[3] Wusuta was not aware that the Asante were of two minds with regard to the Ewes. They were also not aware that this friendship would become deadly for themselves and their Ewe brothers. If they knew, they would not have had friendly relations with them. "An untested friendship is like a valley" (*Xolo matekpo awli wonye vava*).

II: FAMFANTOR'S ENSLAVEMENT IN WUSUTA

During the Asante's stay in Wusuta, they asked Nyrabasefia Noanyidzro to give them some oil palms to make palm wine. It was surprising that although they came for a funeral, they stayed so long; they must have had another plan. Their host gave them some palms just as they requested. In uprooting the palms, they provocatively uprooted someone else's, although they had been shown clearly the boundary. They uprooted some of the palms belonging to the grandfather of Famfantor, Kwaside, in addition to the ones they were given. Kwaside's son, Dodotse, who was caring for the oil palms, saw what they had done. He went and told his father. The father told him that he should mark his own using dried grass (*bedze*) so that no one would tap them. This was the traditional way of notifying someone that they had felled someone else's palms. When the Asantes saw this, they exploded. "The person who did this is trying to kill us using spiritual means [ɖu dzo] so that if we should have a drink, we will die. The chief should bring the person who did this to us to be executed." The case became very difficult. Fiaga Kwasikuma passed judgment that in their area, that was the way the people did it. It was not meant to be an evil spell. Rather it was just a mark, indicating that the palms did not belong to the feller, but to someone else. The Asantes were insistent that they had to execute the person. They forcefully grabbed Dodotse and placed him in fetters (de gae) and insisted that they had to execute him. The paramount chief and the elders negotiated before the Asantes agreed not to carry out the execution. Rather, they fined him [Dodotse] one hundred hotu,[4] which was a lot of money to fine anyone in those days. If someone were to have such a debt, that person would have to be sold because at that time, a healthy young man went for thirty hotu as you have seen already. Gbeklo, who was the brother of Dodotse, sold twenty-one pieces of cloth, which left only one piece for Famfantor, so he could pay the fine. He earned seventy hotu from selling the twenty-one pieces. This left the remaining thirty hotu, which was the price for one person. The plan was that they could sell Famfantor into slavery in Tsrukpe, for the thirty. We can say that was the selling price (dzradzra xoxo).

The linguist, Adatsi, did not agree that they should sell his maternal nephew into debt slavery (awɔba) in another town. Instead, they should send him to their hometown. Amega Sanda from Wusuta Anyigbe took in Famfantor as a slave for the price. The Asantes who came to Wusuta stayed there for a long time, traveling around the Ewe towns paying attention to details. They stayed for more than one year, so that when the Asante war started, they were the leaders.

III: THE MOVE TO ASANTE

When the Asantes declared war on the Ewes in 1869, one of the war leaders passed through Wusuta where they had sent their people in the past. They gathered there and didn't advance immediately. They pledged not to declare war on them because they were brothers. Having stayed there for such a long time, they consumed all the crops from the Wusuta farms.

So that they wouldn't be hungry and die, some [Wusutas] moved to the other side of the river to the big forest where they could gather wild mushrooms and wild yams for food. The elder, Sanda, also brought his young people, among whom was Famfantor. At that time, Famfantor was about eighteen to nineteen years old,[5] but he was not big. He looked like a young person. When he was in the bush one day, the Asante came to say to them, "Paramount chief Kwasikuma has sworn that every young male Wusutan should follow them to Kumase, and anyone who refused to go, they would all pay the price when he returned.

The reason the chief swore this was because the war against the Ewes waged by Adubofuo [Adu Bofo],[6] the commander of the Asante military forces, had not gone as planned, so he wanted to take them as prisoners of war (*aboyome*) without having had any war with them. Adubofuo decided to take all of them there [to Kumase] because the predator does not return home without prey, and any Ewe was an Ewe. First, he would kill the chief and all the elders before taking the youth and the women. Fia Kwasikuma heard of his plans before he [Adu Bofo] came to him. In thinking how to outwit [the Asantes] Kwasikuma swore an Asante oath that if Adubofuo wanted to kill him or any of his young people, it would have to be settled before Karikari; and if they were to kill them that is where it would be settled. Then he composed this [cynical] proverb: If the hyena (*amegaxi*) grabs you and the lion comes to save you, don't celebrate, because the lion wants to eat you as well." All the Wusuta people set off for Asante. Only a few remained at home. Famfantor and his master were among the people who went. He didn't see his uncle, Dodotse, except once in Kumase. After this, they were separated because they were divided up among different people.

The Wusutas and Asantes traveled for seven days without passing through any town. They went through great plains and forests and crossed great rivers. Hunger worried them before they reached Kumase. The largest rivers they crossed were the Amu [Volta], Fa, and Afram. They traveled another fourteen days from Kwawu to Kumase, so the whole journey took about twenty-one days or three weeks to one month. Many died on the way from fatigue and hunger. On arrival in Kumase, Karikari showed the Wusutas where they would stay, in a placed called Asratowase. They lived there under hardship.

IV: SLAVERY IN ASANTE

A few days later the Wusuta chief, Kwasikuma, was summoned before the Asante chief, Karikari. He asked him to deliver three hundred men to be *ahenkua* (servants of the chief[7]): *Amesi wu ame nu lae ɖea ga toa ame ƒe alɔkpa*: the person who is stubborn allows metal (*ga*) to pass through the palm of his hand. Kwasikuma should make the men useful. What Adubofuo wanted to do in Wusuta, he accomplished in Kumase. Famfantor was among the three hundred. Karikari didn't assign these people to himself, but divided them amongst his military commanders (*asafohenewo*), like something cheap picked up and brought back from Eweland (*wode Eweme ɖasi ame legbɔe ene*). Those who were sent to the small towns were "free" and survived. Those who stayed in Kumase became victims of the sword. If a chief or an elder died, they had to sacrifice one of them for the burial. They did it also to other strangers from elsewhere.

Famfantor was given to Karikari's *ahenkua* whose name was Nyameadesie. The meaning of his name was God's treasure. This man liked Famfantor a great deal. He worried about him like his own son. Because of the years of hardships caused by food shortages in Kumase, his master gave him to his servant to be taken to his sister, Akua, to stay with her in the village, so he wouldn't be hungry, and also so that he would not be sacrificed if something should happen. The week after Famfantor went there, a lady sent Famfantor to take some beans to his master, Nyameadesi in Kumase. He was to stay and get some salt and fish to bring back. On his way, he encountered a man on the road. The man told him, "Hey, *gyina ho!*" which means stop there. When he did so, the man approached him and asked him to put his load down. When he obeyed, the man stripped him of his cloth. His plan was to kill him, because Karikari was conducting a religious ritual and the ritual required that anyone who was traveling alone was to be killed.[8] He took him to the bush to the fetish ground (*busuyife*). They dug a hole there so the killed person could be buried in it. The sacrificed animals were all by the hole. When they arrived, they asked him to take off his loincloth (*godui*). There was nothing he could do to save himself. After he took off his loincloth, they realized he was circumcised and they immediately allowed him to go, because they didn't sacrifice circumcised people in Asante. "The word of god and his signs are deep, so his ways are truly unknown." The fetish people (*busuyilawo*) instructed the person who brought him to take him on to Kumase before he returned because there were others on the road who might kill him without removing his loincloth. In this way, Famfantor's life was saved. The man was from Subritosisi, which is near Kumase, and they were close to his town before he let him [Famfantor] go [on to Kumase]. He went into town, delivered the fried cakes[9] (*akla*) to his master's servant, Kofi, and told them what happened to him on the way. Kofi also delivered the things to his master, Nyameadesie. The master told him to spend the night in town and to wait for daybreak before setting off. He didn't tell his master himself how they wanted to kill him. His master did not want him to travel at dawn (*ǫufoke*) alone; rather, he was told to wait and go with others traveling there after they finished buying what they needed. On arrival, he didn't tell of his encounters to his mistress, Akua, either.

After eight days, the master sent Kofi to meet with Famfantor to travel to Praso to buy an oil palm forest. They traveled for five days before arriving. When they arrived, Kofi looked around for a long time before returning and brought some people with him. After a little discussion, he stripped him [Famfantor] of his cloth and told him to follow them because he had become theirs. So this is how he was sold. Famfantor became a slave for a second time. The man bought three people: Famfantor, Tadikan, who was a Mossi, and Lemanhia, who was Grushi.[10] He took them to his father where he told him how much he had paid for them. Famfantor cost £7; the Mossi cost £8, and the Grushi girl cost £10. Eight days after they were bought, he decided to name them. He liked Famfantor very much. He reviewed his ancestral history and decided to name him Kra-Kofi, because he was bought on Friday; in addition, his master's name was Kofi Gyakare and he was wearing a flat golden necklace. Because he was named Kra, it meant the day he died, he [Famfantor] would be the one who would be sacrificed. This new master also loved him even more than the Kumase one. He ate with him like his own children. Famfantor was almost like a free man. When Famfantor had grown up, at about twenty years of age, in 1871,[11] they gave him anywhere from £5 to 20 to go and trade. He would go to Saltpond and Cape Coast and buy things to sell. He would buy cloth, gunpowder, guns, salt, tobacco, a lot of other things, and sell them in Bonduku. If the things were not bought, he would barter them for an Ewe cloth[12] and then sell the cloth so as not to incur a loss (*etọnẹ dọa li Eẉevọ va dzrana be woagaxọ ga la de etefe ko*).

One day, he was on a trading journey, and on return, he encountered his master's brother and was told his master had died and that they had already held the funeral. This was good luck for Famfantor, for he was not sacrificed for his master's burial because he was not at home. Famfantor walked for fifteen days to Gua (Cape Coast), and he bought one demijohn[13] (*adzafi*) of hard liquor and a box of gunpowder to do his own funeral for his master who died in his absence. The death of his master really saddened him because he [Famfantor's master] loved him more than his own children. Whenever he took £20 to the market, he took his own £5, which he used to buy things and made a lot of profit. This was also the advice from his master himself anyway, because he said: "An intelligent slave makes a profit off his foolish and naïve master" (*Kluvi nyonu dua afeto de vi tsi bome dzi*). He also told him that he should buy good food to eat so he could be strong, because the monkey says: "The one in the stomach is yours; the one in the mouth is for the hunter." He should take care not to engage in fornication (*ahasi*) or fool around and catch a disease, because a whoring man hurts himself and cuts his life short. Famfantor held these things in his heart and acted on them his entire life.

Asefia Otibu and his *asafohenega*,[14] Mensa, brought a case against Kofi Gyakare after his death. Otibu gave his *asafohenega* the £6 cost of taking a lawyer (*nyaxọdakọla*). They assigned £6 to the stool of Famfantor's master, which meant that anyone who was to sit on it would have to pay that amount. Since no one was on it at that time, they decided to pawn a daughter. When the mother saw that Famfantor was back, she cried to him. Famfantor consoled her by paying the fine, not taking any money for the favor, and in that way this would also make her free, just as his master had made him a "free" man.

Famfantor made a big funeral celebration for the master to the surprise and annoyance of the whole town. The person who inherited his master's property, who now owned Famfantor, gave him a lot of trouble, because he thought he [Famfantor] was hiding his deceased master's money and that he hadn't returned all that he had brought from trading to him. But it was not like that. All these troubles caused by this person made Famfantor leave the house and go to live in Abakrampa. He stayed there by himself thereafter.

It is said that the young lady for whom he had paid the fine should stay with him and go to the market for him. But Famfantor said he didn't want to make her a slave because she was his master's granddaughter. His master didn't make him a slave so he wouldn't make his [master's] granddaughter a slave.

During his business trips from Abakrampa, he heard the word of God, which left something in his mind to become a Christian. So when his master's inheritor was worrying him, that is why he moved to Abakrampa. Famfantor loved calling the name of God, and since most people in Assin were heathens, they were not pleased with him calling the word of God.

V: MARRIAGE IN ASSIN

When he was mature, his master gave him one of his daughters to marry. He married according to the traditions and carried out all the customs appropriate to the area. The woman's name was Akuwa. She gave birth to a male son after one year. After three years, she gave birth to a second male child whose name was Yawo Tebi.

Famfantor didn't spend time at home even during this marriage; going to market was his business. When he returned from trading, people complained to him about his wife. "She is stealing." Stealing was something people hated very much in that area. The thing she liked stealing most was *kɔkɔlimakɔe,* which is a type of yam. When someone was caught stealing in that area, they would disgrace the person so much that the person would want to kill him- or herself or move out of town. Thieving made one very filthy, to themselves, to the family, and the descendants.

Famfantor's business partners loved him and respected him because of his character and the way he carried himself. When he returned from Gua (Cape Coast), his friends advised him to divorce his thieving wife, even if it meant he would remain unmarried. So be it. But because of his character, it was unlikely that he would remain unmarried. Famfantor agreed, but said it was not only because of their words that he had agreed but also because where he came from, one does not marry a thief because they will kill you. If she steals [something] and cooks [it] for him and his children, they could all die, so he couldn't stay married to her any longer. After the divorce, the people of the town loved him just as before; he too was satisfied with himself (*ame lǫa edokui*). It was not obvious at all that he was unmarried. He went on trading and stayed away for three months before returning, during which time his older son, Kwaku Gyakari, died. They did the funeral and assessed him £1-5 to pay on his return. He stayed that way for a whole year. Then his mistress, Ama Nyakowa, approached him and asked him to marry her. Because of Famfantor's character, he did not agree, but his friends also encouraged him to marry her and this prompted him to agree. After the marriage, he and his sister-in-law began to trade. Famfantor bought her fifty animal skins to export to Europe because she could read. They received in return a quantity of silk (*sedaku*), sufficient for three strong people to carry. The two of them went and sold them in Kintampo. They [their customers] bought them with cowrie shells, enough to fill two big rooms. Because they couldn't carry all this money, and it wasn't wise for them to leave it, they stayed for two years and used it to buy seven slaves, which they would sell later. When they were bringing the slaves home, they encountered the son of Adubofuo. His name was Mayore Opoku. He was a bully (*ŋkukledo-amela*). He told them sternly that white people had abolished the slave trade[15] so why were they still buying people? He was going to arrest him [Famfantor] and take him to Accra to be imprisoned. Famfantor became frightened, begged him, and he [Mayore] took £7 from him before he let him go with the slaves.

The wife had another male child while they were in Kintampo. He was also born on Wednesday, and so it was said he was the return of Kwaku Gyakare[16] and he was given exactly the same name.

The sister-in-law with whom he was trading was a very bad person, very selfish, and liked to belittle people. Famfantor's business suffered because she incurred a lot of fines. Of the more than £70 they received from the sale of the seven people they sold, all went to pay the fine; as a result, the profit which they should have made became a problem. Ama Nyakowa, Famfantor's wife, and the rest of the family were all untrustworthy, and the latter took his wife away but left him with the children. Famfantor asked, "What will I do with the children? Once you take the wife you might as well take the children too." And so they left with the children.

Since he no longer had a wife, he was very unhappy, and he planned to leave.

VI: HIS BECOMING A CHRISTIAN IN ABAKRAMPA

During his trading, he heard the word of God from the uncle of his master, James Kwaku Behwie, who was a Christian with whom he stayed. These words had such an effect on him that he wanted to become a Christian. The name of God and the words of God were on his lips, something his household did not like because they were traditional believers (*trǫsubǫsubǫ*).

Because he wanted to become a Christian, he moved to Abakrampa in Assin. He stayed with James Kwaku Behwie. He got there on Saturday and on Sunday his host asked him to go to church with him. He agreed, and they went together.

The words that were preached that day were centered around the gospel of Christ. He [the minister] said: When he was nailed on the cross, the land shook, the curtain in the temple split into two so that everyone could easily see the holy of holies where God himself had his seat (*be woayi kɔkɔefe fe kɔkɔefe la me faa, afisi amea ɖeka mekpɔ mɔ, dena tsã o, negbe nunɔlagã ko zi ɖeka le fe ɖeka me, afisi Mawu ɔutɔ le la*). The Jesus who was nailed on the cross opened his arms and invited everyone in; he would take everyone regardless of how much sin, whether a free person or a slave.

These words had a strong effect on Famfantor in two ways. First, it reminded him of the earthquake in Wusuta in 1858[17] when he was a youth. So he understood the message more than anyone else who attended. Famfantor said, "When I heard these words, I felt as if I could see Jesus directly, his hand being nailed." Secondly, that slaves and free people could come, demonstrating that there was no difference between them, reminded him of his indentured days at home and his enslavement in Asante, and he wanted to be a totally free person by becoming a follower of Jesus.

The words that day had such an effect that he told his host, James, after the service that if being a Christian was like that, then he would become a Christian immediately. His host was also pleased, so he took him to the teacher to sign him up for baptismal lessons. When they got there, Famfantor asked the teacher to write his name so he would become the Christ that he talked about. The teacher asked him to talk about his life. He told him about the whole of his existence, from his childhood hardships, to Asante, up to that day. The teacher said it was good, so he signed him up, and his Christian name would be Yosef, because Famfantor's life story was similar to Yosef, the son of Jacob, who suffered just like Famfantor.

God had blessed his [the biblical Yosef's] work and the works of his host [the Egyptian pharaoh], and it was hoped he [Famfantor] would become a redeemer, just as [the biblical] Yosef was for others. And so Yosef became his name from that day. That was the name used to baptize him. He started his lessons immediately.

VII: THE RETURN HOME

Famfantor went to the lessons with enthusiasm. The word of God made him very happy. He liked to ask many questions so as to understand the teacher completely. When his studies had advanced, he had a dream at night in which he saw a man holding a lamp who came to stand by him. The man asked him to take the lamp.

He asked why the man was giving him the lamp. The man told him to take the lamp and to go wherever he wanted with it. Then the dream ended and he awoke, but he had difficulty going back to sleep. He thought about the dream the entire night. Finally, he realized that the lamp was the word of God, given to him, which he could take to his home area where traditional worship (*trɔsubɔ-subɔ*) was intense, for the light to shine for them also. He recalled God's words he had heard one day in church: "Your word is the lamp for my feet and a light for my path." Because of this, from that day on, he began preparing to go home. A few days later he announced to his host that he would take the word of God to his home. James told him to wait to be baptized before he went. But he said, when he went home he would have it done there. As God had called him and assigned him a duty, he could not delay. He would become the disciple of God; otherwise he would not be able to give an account later on [to God] if he did not. This commitment impressed James very much. He told him to go in peace, and the task given to him by God, he should do it to His glory. He should be careful that the light not go out before he reaches home. When he arrives, he should not put it in a bowl made from the silk-cotton tree (*fianu*) and hide it. Rather, he should put it on a lamp stand so it would shine for everyone, not just for the people of his hometown but for the entire neighborhood so that the darkness would disappear. He [Famfantor] thanked him for this very good advice. Before he left, he told his teacher and the entire congregation, all of whom gave him advice. The teacher gave him a certificate so that whenever he reached a Christian community, they would accept him as a member to ignite the word of God among them. His departure brought sadness to the congregation in Abakrampa, because his character was good for the church. He was a good listener, enthusiastic in church attendance and church worship, and every assignment that came his way, he did it better than even the older Christians.

When he left, he passed through Ge [Accra], staying for a couple of days before continuing. During the whole of his trip, he was a guest of the Christian community and he showed them his certificate. After a few days, he reached home and saw some of his relatives.

VIII: THE LIGHTING OF GOD'S WORD IN WUSUTA

There was no Christian life in Wusuta before Famfantor returned, although the Basel Mission was active in Botoku, Vakpo, and Anfoe, which were towns surrounding Wusuta.[18] Traditional worship was very strong there. Just before Famfantor returned, the Wusuta towns, which used to be large, had been reduced in size because most people went to Asante and had not returned.

Famfantor went to live with his maternal uncle who was the linguist of the chief of Wusuta Anyigbe. His name was Adatsi. He was talking about God's words to them, but they didn't understand. It seemed to them sometimes that he [Famfantor] was not mentally well, because what he said was different from what they thought, and his lifestyle was very different as well.

One day his uncle, Adatsi, called him before Chief Adom, telling him, "Look, my nephew, Famfantor, I am old. I cannot travel much anymore, so I would like you to take the linguist stick [i.e., take over the position of linguist] and gain something from it and bring some to me as well. Famfantor did not agree with his uncle's suggestion. He said he could not do it. The uncle asked, "Why can't you do it?" He answered, "I bring you God's words in order to be the linguist of the world. So I will do it [only] for God who is the king of kings, because to spread the word about Christ is why I returned. God sent me; otherwise I would not have returned. Because of this I will not abandon God's work and substitute worldly work."

These words annoyed the old linguist and the chief because he had said God is king of kings, which indicated a lack of respect for them as chiefs. For this reason, they hated him even more. They told him that from that day onward, he was not one of them.

One day Famfantor bought three bundles (ati) each of yam and water yam for planting. Before he could get to the barn, someone had taken all the water yam, leaving only seven out of sixty-six, which was the number for three rows of plantings. When he returned, he told his uncle. He [the uncle] advised him to curse the person who stole the water yam. If the person did not return it, he would die, and that was the way he would do it. But he [Famfantor] refused, saying he was a Christian. Christians don't curse others. The person who stole it could go. He didn't care. So he [Famfantor] went ahead and planted the yam.

He regularly went for Bible lessons in Botoku,[19] which did not endear him to the traditional believers among whom he lived; because they didn't like the prospects of him becoming a Christian; they worried him. If there was an accident in the town, they would confront him and state that it was his Christianity or his new taboos that annoyed their gods. That way they were being punished. One day the missionary (mawunonola) Peter Hall came from Worawora on his way to Botoku.[20] He told Famfantor that he realized his living among traditional believers was worrisome for him, so he should move to live among the Christians in Botoku instead. He did not agree; rather he told him, "If I move to Botoku, how will the people of Wusuta get converted? I have to be the light in the darkness, to shine for the people in the gloom, because you don't take a light to where it is already bright. That would not be useful. There are Christians in Botoku; because there is light there already, I will stay at home and go for my lessons there." This impressed the missionary. He gave him encouraging words before he left.

Fortunately, Famfantor's light started shining in the darkness. People's eyes were beginning to open to look for the light. God blessed his words. A gentleman by the name of Kwadzo Mensa from Wusuta Anyigbe also decided to take lessons, so he could be baptized. The two of them went to Botoku on Sunday. Unfortunately, Kwadzo Mensa suffered from a serious illness called *baba*,[21] so the journey from Wusuta to Botoku, which usually took one hour, took five hours. The teacher, Otu, who was in Botoku was very pleased and asked him a variety of questions; later he signed him up for classes.[22] According to Kwadzo Mensa, the first miracle occurred as soon as he began the lessons: his *baba* illness disappeared completely. No medication was involved. It was an old type of *baba* and not easily cured. This then surprised everyone in the town, and people started turning to the word of God. Before Kwadzo Mensa began his lessons, Famfantor was baptized with the name he had chosen in Fante Abakrampa, Yosef, on September 3, 1900; so his name became Yosef Famfantor. With Kwadzo Mensa's conversion, other people started to convert, especially because he was one of those who was strongly against Famfantor breaking [town] taboos before he himself changed his mind and started following him.

The miraculous cure of his *baba* made people call on him. It wasn't long after Kwadzo Mensa's conversion that Mr. Kofikuma, who was a relative [of Mensa] from Botoku, also converted. They baptized the two after two years of lessons. Kwadzo Mensa took the name of Petro, and Kofikuma was called Noa. These baptized did not take the European names for nothing. Rather, they were the names of people they heard about in their lessons. Petro Mensa's recovery was such that the number of young men and young women who cried out for Christianity in Wusuta was beyond their imagination. When Wusuta people were going to services in Botoku every two weeks, the teacher would come to Wusuta on the third Sunday, so they built a shed under which they held services. Even the elders came to church when Otu visited from Botoku.

IX: WORKS AFTER BEING BAPTIZED

When Missionary Martin[23] came from Anum one day, he brought a hand bell for Yosef to use to call the people to attend church. He gave him instructions on how to teach about baptism to the Wusuta people who wanted to learn. The students became more than they expected. Within two years, they baptized several people at the same time. The Wusuta people accepted the word even more than the Botoku people where the teacher lived. Yosef did not forget the town of his birth, Hoto. Every now and then, he would travel through the Wusuta towns preaching. They listened to him in some places, but were hostile in other places. Of the eleven Wusuta towns, Anyigbe was his residence; [the others were] Tsikoe; Anyirabase; Dzigbe where the paramount chief (*fiaga*) lived; Hoeme; Anyafoe, Wa, Tokpeta, Hoto, and Hotonyigbe, which were not far from each other. Yosef's enthusiasm surprised the teacher and the missionary. The church, which he led, expanded, so the leadership was so pleased early on with Wusuta that they moved the teacher from Botoku to Wusuta. The first Basel Mission teacher who lived there was Otu,[24] who taught in Twi. The arrival of this teacher energized the town for church attendance. Yosef was encouraged and very pleased as he remembered the suffering meted out to him by his people in the beginning.

Although the teacher arrived, Yosef did not neglect the tasks at hand. He even took over [some of] the tasks of the teacher. On Sunday afternoons, he would go to preach to the traditional believers. Yosef didn't marry early at home, but there was still no blemish on his character with regard to other people. Finally he married a widow from Hoeme, who delivered him a boy called Beautis Kwasi and one girl called Mariana Kwasifoe. Yosef established an area for the church at Anyigbedu down the hill from Anyigbe. He showed great energy for church work in recruiting with the elders, students, and in everything else the leadership asked of him. It wasn't only for the good of the church that he was excited but the good of the town, the [town] government, and all that he could do to raise the status of Wusuta. If there was a conflict between the towns, he tried to straighten it out so the entire community came to realize the goodness of God's words. Yosef's history in Anyige was such that nearly all Anyigbe people were converted before he died. The successor of Fiadom, who tried to force him to abandon his new faith, submitted himself to the words of God, and he took lessons and was baptized. He was called James Dzandu Kofi Adom. His [Famfantor's] uncle, the linguist Adatsi, who wanted him to become a linguist and then liked him less than before after Famfantor refused, was also succeeded by someone who converted to Christianity, Johnson Govu. Before Yosef died in 1933, all the people he baptized numbered up to seven hundred. As for Anyigbe itself, only two males who lived on their farms were not baptized . . .

X: THE LAST DAYS OF YOSEF AND HIS DEATH

Yosef was healthy up to the day of his death. When the Wusuta people were moving, especially the Christians, from their [old] location to a new place called Wa, which was about a one-half hour walk from the Christian settlement in Anyigbe, Yosef didn't want to go with them. It was obvious why since he was not able to participate in the new construction. One of the teachers understood and offered him one of his rooms, but he refused, saying that he was no longer strong enough to walk the long distance from that place to his farm, and he was aware that his time was approaching. He and several others stayed. Leaving him did not please the teacher, but since he didn't agree, Teacher Tsekpo left him with much concern; but from time to time, he went in the afternoon after classes and on Sundays as well to visit him.

Yosef was well until his last moments. On December 13, 1933, about 9 AM a very important person, indeed an upright person, the apostle of Wusuta, gave up his ghost quietly and without struggle to his maker who he worshipped for many years just as the Bremen missionary G. Stoevesandt honored him in one of his missionary writings.[25] The entire town of Wusuta, all the chiefs, all the households, the congregations in Botoku, Bume, Anfoega Akukome, Tsrukpe, and Vakpo all gathered. The chiefs brought all their regalia. They took his body into the church. Catechist Tsekpo preached briefly and read Yosef's life story, from his childhood to his death, just as he heard it from Yosef himself and saw with his own eyes during the last days of his life. After the service, they took his body and buried it with a lot of celebration.

Part 3

Paul Sands's Diary:
Living with the
Past/Constructing
the Present and the
Future

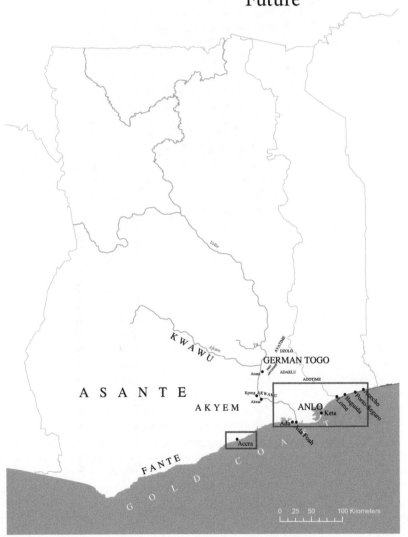

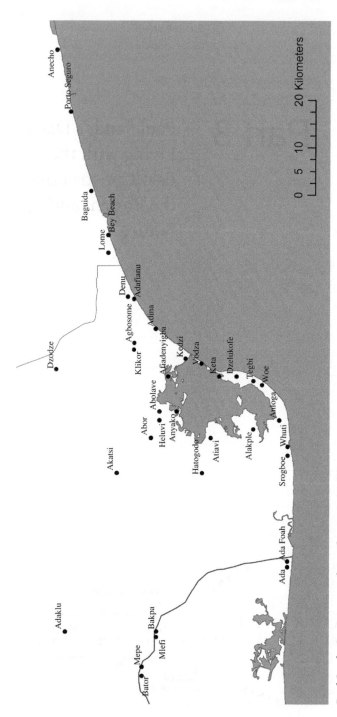

Paul Sands: Some towns of significance in his life

6. Open Secrets and Sequestered Stories: A Diary about Family, Slavery, and Self in Southeastern Ghana

African family histories that openly and fully acknowledge the slave origins of specific individuals are notoriously difficult to obtain. Why this is the case throughout much of West Africa has been discussed perhaps most thoroughly by the anthropologist Bayo Holsey.[1] In her study of memories of slavery in Ghana, she indicates that even at the turn of the twenty-first century, the historical reality of domestic slavery exists largely as a "public secret."

> Everyone not only knows that it existed, but often can identify people in the community if not in their own families who are descendants of slaves. But despite this knowledge the topic is strictly sequestered from discourse.[2]

Holsey pays particular attention to the open secrets maintained today by the elderly descendants of slave owners because it is often only they who know the origins of individual members within the family.[3] Making public a person's slave origins, as Holsey indicates, would not only "violate 'traditional' legal and social codes of behavior, it would insult those individuals [identified]." Accordingly, such knowledge is consciously withheld so as to maintain family unity.

But what was the situation in the late nineteenth century, when slavery had only recently been abolished? What did the children and grandchildren of the once enslaved know of their social origins? What did they do with that knowledge? How did it affect their life choices, their social positions within their families, their status as citizens in their home communities, their understandings of themselves, and their future possibilities? Tentative answers to these questions can be found in the diaries maintained by those of slave descent who used their Western education in missionary schools in the late nineteenth and early twentieth centuries to record their thoughts and experiences.

Scholarly studies of the diaries kept by nineteenth- and early twentieth-century Africans—whether free or of slave descent—have emphasized the extent to which the writers—who were introduced to this form by European missionaries—used the genre for their own purposes. Among European Pietists, for example, diary keeping was traditionally "a way to recognize and acknowledge Providence" [i.e., the hand of God] in their lives. By recording events they considered notable, they constructed an understanding of themselves and their experiences that conformed to their own notions about the self and the world in which they lived. It might be written most as a document for personal use or one to be shared with others; it often served to facilitate spiritual enquiry, but it could also be used as a forum for complaint or commentary.[4] Most individuals in West Africa who adopted this form for themselves used the diary (like many in Europe) to reinforce ideas about their own identities and place in society. But in colonial Africa, in particular, diarists—especially those from the middle and lower ranks of the educated elite: teachers, clerks, and artisans—often also revealed great "cultural insecurity" about the positions they held within their communities.[5] Their limited educational backgrounds provided them with fewer opportunities than lawyers and doctors had to obtain the wealth they needed to secure a place among their more elite fellow Africans. At the same time, opportunities for success in business were few. Those of slave descent found even more challenging circumstances. In her biography of the Nigerian Akinpelu Obisesan, for example, Ruth Watson noted that Obisesan's father obtained an Ibaden chieftancy in 1893. This, in turn, placed Obisesan in the position of being identified as his father's potential successor. But Akinpelu's mother was a slave.[6] It was this additional social fact that pushed Obisesan to focus his energies and his self-identity on becoming a "modern man of means" within the British colonial system in early twentieth-century Nigeria, rather than trying to succeed his father. He enrolled in and obtained an education from a school run by the Church Missionary Society. There he learned English and accounting, among other subjects, and thereafter worked as the family secretary, managing their land holdings and serving as his family's principal liaison with the colonial government. In his own mind, however, Obisesan never achieved the success he had hoped for himself. He failed to make the kind of money that would have elevated him into the ranks of the most prestigious educated Africans. Even more interesting is that he blamed his lack of social and economic success not on his social origins or the colonial racism that limited African access to government positions and bank financing, but on his language abilities. He fretted, unnecessarily so according to his biographer, about his English-language skills and even came to express ambivalence about the very value of literacy. His mastery of the English language, in his mind, was supposed to open to him unlimited opportunities. When it did not, he blamed himself and wondered if his lack of success was due to a degree of laziness and indolence in his past and present life.[7]

Others of similar social and educational background also used their diaries to work through their own concerns about their status. One such individual was the Gold Coast citizen Paul Sands.[8] Born in the coastal town of Keta in
1849 to a Euro-African father (Elijah Sands of Danish Accra) and a local Keta
woman (Ama) of Danish-African descent, Paul Sands—unlike Obisesan—
spent little or no time fretting about his status as "a modern man."[9] By descent,
he understood himself to be a "mulatto,"[10] an identity based on his family's
historic connections to Europeans. But he was also of slave descent. His maternal grandfather—pawned to a Danish officer based in Accra in exchange for a
loan—became a slave to his European master after his family failed to repay
the loan. His great-grandmother came to Anlo as an enslaved war captive.
These were facts that many of his fellow Keta residents refused to forget. They
were facts of which Sands was also well aware and which seem to have influenced his diary writing. Throughout his journal, one finds a surprising number
of references to slave status. He identified numerous individuals either as purchased, *fle*, or as war captives. He produced detailed lists that documented the
slaves owned by particular relatives, where they came from, whether or not
they had children, and, if they did, how many and who they were by name.
Why did Sands feel compelled to record such information? Equally significant,
these entries were all written in the Ewe language, while the rest of the diary
was written in English. Why the change in language? What do these entries
reveal about Sands's views on the institution of slavery as it operated within his
own hometown and family? What was the relationship between these views
and how he managed his own identity given the fact that he himself was of
slave origin? I attempt to answer these questions by analyzing how one individual sought to define himself in a society in which slavery was officially condemned and outlawed by both his Christian faith and the colonial state but
which continued to operate as an important institution, regulating social, economic, and political relations and identities.

*　*　*

Although we know little about Sands's early years, we do know that he was
born into a community in which slavery was an accepted institution. States
that sought political and military support often gifted the political elite of Anlo
(the polity of which the town of Keta was a part) with slaves to seal their alliances.[11] Those who went to war had long measured their success in battle, in
part, by the number of individuals they were able to capture and retain as
slaves. Economic status in Anlo and in Sands's hometown of Keta was measured partly by the number of cowries—representing slaves owned—the wealthy

would string around the central pillar of what was called a wealth stool (*hozik-pui*). Thus when British colonial efforts to abolish slavery were extended to the area in 1874, the potential for conflict between the Anlo and their colonizers was great. Massive discontent on the part of some of the slave owners, most particularly chiefly officeholders, was largely avoided, however, as it was elsewhere on the Gold Coast, by the way the antislavery policy was implemented. As noted by the then British colonial governor of the Gold Coast, George Strahan, "no forcible disruption of domestic arrangements was intended."[12] The chiefs at the Cape Coast and Accra meetings appear to have accepted this. So did the majority of political leaders at Keta when they were informed of the new law.

Adjustments in the managements of their households and businesses followed as the passage of the colonial law making slavery illegal brought to Keta a number of high-profile prosecutions of those accused of holding slaves and pawns.[13] Some, like Chief Nyaxo Tamakloe—an important political and military figure in Anlo, a wealthy businessman, a major slaveholder, and someone with whom Paul Sands had close ties[14]—decided, for example, to defy local norms governing chieftancy positions. Those norms stated that "it was not natural for [slaves] to hold political or religious posts."[15] By the 1890s, however, Tamakloe had successfully persuaded the traditional authorities in the Anlo capital to recognize his former slaves as free and independent, with their own community leaders who deserved official recognition. Chief Tamakloe's son, Christian Nani Tamakloe, explained:

> At Sonuto, the chief was Tamakloe Tupa. Tupa is not an Anlo name. It was the name of the town where he came from. Agbeve was made a chief at Adzato over all the slaves; so Agbeve was chief of Adzato. He was also a slave, but installed as a chief [over the other slaves]. Tamakloe was about to install Lekete at Hatogodo but it couldn't come on. He sent a petition for this to come on in 1915, but it wasn't completed when in 1918 he died.[16]

Tamakloe did even more than this, however. He and others in Anlo began to send their intellectually most promising slave children to the schools established by the European Christian missionary societies operating in the area. They did so to produce their own English-language-educated political advisors and accountants. This, in turn, allowed them to better manage their affairs as British colonialism came to have more and more influence on the political and economic life in the region.

Was Paul Sands selected by his family to be educated because he was a slave descendant? Probably not. As noted, Sands's father was a Euro-African or "mulatto" from Danish Accra, but Sands himself was born in Keta and raised in the household of his maternal uncle, Yao Mensah.[17] As a respected local community leader, Mensah was defined by the citizens of Keta as a resident stranger, but one who served as an important political and economic intermediary between the Anlo and the different Europeans who operated in the area. When serious disagreements arose between the Danes and the Anlo in the 1840s, for example, it was Yao Mensah who helped calm the situation.[18] When the Danes sold their trading rights in the area to the British in 1850, it was Yao Mensah who served as interpreter for the British and who advocated that the Anlo not militarily resist when Britain decided in 1874 to extend its colonial rule over Anlo. Thus, when Mensah enrolled Sands in the Bremen Mission primary school in Keta, he did so in large part to maintain their identity as Euro-Africans and their involvement with the European world. Sands's education meant the family had continued access to the language of their European trade partners, a relationship that had brought them political prestige and wealth and ensured their ongoing membership in the still prestigious "mulatto" community on the Gold Coast.

Sands's experiences as a student at the Bremen Mission—given his identity not only as a "mulatto" but also as someone of slave descent—tells a very different story, however. Begun in the mid-1800s, the Keta school drew its nine pupils initially from "one [Euro-African] family that had settled in the coastal towns of Dzelukofe and Denu,"[19] a few kilometers west and east of Keta, respectively. In time, other Euro-African families also sent their children to Keta's Bremen school,[20] but the numbers enrolled remained small, much to the dissatisfaction of the missionaries. As a result, between 1857 and 1867, "the mission purchased the freedom of 109 'slave children,' in order to give them a Christian upbringing . . . , but also to gain them as workers, and as teachers, interpreters, preachers and catechists."[21] It was this group of early students— composed of "mulattoes," the enslaved children purchased by the mission, and a few sent by their parents to the mission in exchange for loans—that constituted the community into which Sands entered as a student himself c. 1860. While the school maintained its own separate educational facilities where students studied, ate, and slept, none was socially or physically segregated from Keta town. For those of slave descent, this meant they could not escape the social stigma of their origins. As noted by a number of Bremen missionaries, many in Keta believed that "the white man was simply the slave trader,"[22] and anyone purchased by the white man was necessarily a slave, the white man's slave. This belief had a profound effect upon those of slave origin, including the children attached to the Bremen Mission. They lived, worked, and interacted with others in a community in which knowledge of another person's identity was considered essential for guiding how one should interact with that person.

Social etiquette demanded particular terms of address (depending on one's own social status and identity) for elderly women and men, maternal and paternal relations, older and younger siblings, strangers, and slaves.

The abolition of the slave trade did bring changes. The existence of the British fort in the middle of the town, for example, meant that the enslaved who felt aggrieved about their condition could (and did) flee there to seek their freedom.[23] This in turn prompted residents of Keta to see the British presence as a potential threat to the integrity of their households. One local leader responded by denouncing the abolition and relocating his slaves to a village located on the periphery of British colonial jurisdiction. A few, like Chief Tamakloe, as mentioned, eliminated any distinctions they had previously made between free and slave. Others opted to maintain the distinctions but to moderate them by using euphemisms when referring to those of slave origin. Instead of calling the individual men, women, and children whom they had purchased "bought slaves," *ame fe flewo,* the lowest on the scale of slaves,[24] they used such terms as *alọmeviwo* (a person acquired through working with the hands) or *ndọkutsu* (someone for whom you worked hard in the sun to get),[25] so as to blunt the assault on their slaves' self-esteem and to further reinforce the ideology that encouraged slaves, even first-generation slaves, to see themselves as integral and valued members of their master's household.[26] In time the political authorities in the Anlo capital of Anloga made it illegal to refer to the slave origins of another. But in the 1870s and 1880s, it was still common to use terms designed to remind an individual of their low social status. Common as well was the response of the enslaved when their origins were used to humiliate them. In 1875, for example, the Bremen missionary Johannes Merz noted that "the mere mention of the term *"ame fe fle,"* bought person, make slave children pull back. They sink . . . into quiet brooding for they cannot change their situation."[27]

The Anlo did not identify Sands as an *"ame fe fle."* His ancestors had never suffered the humiliation of being sold with other commodities in the markets of West Africa, but it was an open secret in Keta that his mother's grandmother had been a war captive. Obtained by a prominent military figure during the 1769–70 war with Ada,[28] she bore her husband and master six children before she and her children were finally redeemed from her Anlo captors by her Ada relatives. Sands went into great detail about this history in his diary. He recounted how his great-grandmother's relatives sought to ransom her shortly after the conflict had ended, but her master had refused to accept the payment because she had already borne him a child. Only after her master/husband died, when his relatives decided to sell the slave wife and the children, did the relatives of Sands's great-grandmother finally arrange to borrow the money to buy their freedom. As Sands noted with great relief, "had [the money not been

Slave children who had been purchased by the Norddeutsche Mission, c. 1860s. Courtesy of Norddeutsche Mission.

paid] we would have been slaves to the inheritors [of our great-grandmother's master]. . . . I thank God!" In recounting this history, Sands used his diary to prove to himself and to his family that they were not slaves. They were never sold; they were never bought. Yes, their maternal great-grandmother had been a war captive, but she and all her children, according to Sands, had been re-deemed long ago. Still, this history haunted him. In his diary, he noted with obvious despair that "in some instances they [still] insult us as *da aŵa li ɸe ma-mayɔviwo*," grandchildren of a war captive.[29]

*   *   *

Sands did more than use his diary to defend himself and his family from ac-cusations of slave origins, however. He also used it to elevate their status far beyond even that of the free Anlo citizenry. According to Sands, he and his family had not only been free before their ancestor was enslaved, and then fully redeemed, they were also connected to royalty. His mother's family, he claimed, was linked to the ruling family in Ada, while his maternal grandmother's husband had ties to the royals of Agotime. Whether or not these claims were true is less important than the fact that Sands used these supposed connections to establish an identity that provided him with connections to powerful families that his fellow Keta citizens were bound to respect.[30] Led by its royal family, Ada had proven to be a formidable military opponent throughout the eighteenth and nineteenth century. By the 1880s, when Sands first began his diary, Ada was also a major center of economic activity. It operated as a port through which significant quantities of palm oil were traded. It was also still an important source of enslaved domestic labor for the booming coastal towns of Accra and Keta.[31] Agotime had an equally glorious military history. It had successfully defended itself while inflicting heavy casualties on its enemies in the Asante invasion of 1869–71 before the town's residents were forced to flee before the combined armies of Asante and Anlo. It had also been an important trade partner for Keta since the mid-eighteenth century.[32] To claim connections to the royals of both these towns reinforced Sands's identity as a member of a family with extensive political and economic influence at a time when the status of Euro-Africans or "mulattoes" was being undermined by the increasing British colonial preference for handling local affairs through the chieftancy system.[33] That was not all, however. Sands also made a conscious effort to document seemingly every social connection that linked himself and his family to the politically and economically prestigious in the area. He recorded the names of the political leaders whose funerals he attended. He indicated who married whom within the Keta "mulatto" community and the weddings he attended.[34] He explained in detail how his relationship with one of the most prominent political leaders in Keta, Chief Ephraim Lotsu,[35] allowed him to travel to ports all along the West African littoral and into the interior to establish his own business ties while simultaneously maintaining a profitable relationship with the British colonial government in Keta. Social connections and the right genealogical pedigree were clearly important to Sands. In documenting his ties to a range of individuals, Sands used his diary—as did the Nigerian Akinpelu Obisesan—to reinforce his sense of himself, in this case, as an educated Keta "native merchant" of "mulatto" and "native" descent whose family was large, prosperous, and both politically and economically influential.

Sands's diary also served to elevate in his own eyes his status within his uncle's family. When Sands completed his education at the Bremen Mission in 1872, he could count himself among the most educated individuals in his family, with an enviable range of employment opportunities. He could have worked

The Bremen Factory (trade post) in Keta where Paul Sands worked for a number of years. Courtesy of Norddeutsche Mission.

with the Bremen Mission as a catechist or teacher. Or he could have entered business on his own, with his uncle or by working with any of the many other African or European firms operating in the area. In 1872, the opportunities in business were especially attractive. By that date, the use of steamships on the Gold Coast to convey cargo between West Africa and Europe had generated so much competition with the older sailing ships that freight rates had dropped enough to bring significantly higher profits to enterprising individuals engaged in the import/export trade. Credit was also easier to obtain (at least for a while) and interest rates were significantly lower than they had been in the early 1860s. Demand for African products in Europe (palm oil, palm kernels, and to a lesser extent cotton) was met by an equally strong demand locally for imported to-bacco, liquor, and firearms. In the end, Sands opted to pursue business, like so many of his fellow students.

After teaching briefly for the mission, he obtained employment with the Bremen Trading Post, a company organized by the same Bremen business family, Friedr. M. Vietor Söhne, that was deeply involved in supporting the Bremen Mission's missionary activities in Keta. Six years working as an agent for the Bremen Trading Post provided him with the experience he needed to estab-lish his own business. In 1879, he submitted his resignation and joined with another entrepreneur from Bremen, Frederick Bellois,[36] to establish his own firm. If Sands had difficulty making ends meet, as so many small entrepreneurs did once the boom years of the 1870s gave way to more difficult times in the

1880s and 1890s,[37] he did not dwell on this fact. Instead he maintained an image (to himself and to family members who may have read his diary) of a successful "mulatto," a "native merchant," and an advocate for moderniza-tion. In 1880, he opened a "native school." Between c. 1881 and c. 1897 he worked for Chief Lotsu, handling some of his business affairs and managing his political relations with the British government. Business interests saw him live for periods of time in Ada (1886–1890) and Akuse (where he worked for the Akim Trading Company in the 1890s). He traveled as well for briefer peri-ods of time to Accra and Germany.

Businessmen like Sands, who engaged in the import and export of a range of commodities, faced tremendous difficulties during this period. Most suf-fered from unpredictable swings in global demand for the commodities they offered to their overseas buyers. This in turn led to low profit margins. Some-times suppliers failed or refused to provide contracted goods; other times they had difficulty obtaining the credit they needed to underwrite their operations. Challenging at all times was the issue of labor. Once the British colonial gov-ernment abolished slavery in 1874, individuals like Sands had to decide how best to proceed given the prior widespread use of slave labor, especially for the transport of goods from one locale to another. It is true that the colonial gov-ernment did little to encourage masters to free their slaves or slaves to leave their masters, but the policies of the Bremen Mission—with which Sands was closely associated for much of his life (as a student, as a teacher, as a business employee, and as a member of the Bremen Mission church)—strongly encour-aged the individual congregant "to commit himself if possible to . . . freeing [his slaves]."[38] How did Sands—a committed church member and a descendant of a slave himself—handle this situation?

Whenever he mentioned his own workers in his diary, Sands referred to them individually by the term "boy." In an entry dated 18 November 1878, for example, he recorded the following: "[an] attack [was made] on my two boys, Gavi and Amedor [at] Abolove by the natives when I sent them to buy corn to feed the criminal prisoners in Quittah gaol, [I] being then the contractor [for] the prison." Although it is unclear exactly when he recorded this entry, "boy" was a term regularly used along the coast of West Africa to refer to those who were employed as paid skilled laborers, the majority of whom were from east-ern Liberia and western Ivory Coast and were known as "Kruboys."[39] His use of the term "boy" also contrasted with the terms he frequently used for enslaved laborers: "confidential servant," "slave," "bought slave," "servant," "purchased confidential servant." This, of course, does not mean that he did not use slave labor. Most traders during this period found it particularly difficult to obtain the workers they needed for their businesses. Coopers (who constructed the barrels used to transport palm oil down the Volta River) and longshoremen (skilled in the use of canoes to transport goods between the littoral and European ships waiting offshore) were scarce. Carriers to convey goods between the coast and the interior were also difficult to hire on a reliable and regular basis. As the Bremen missionaries operating in the area noted, "African bearers were *still not proletarians,* but chose with complete freedom in favor of [transporting] goods, [engaging in] trade or even [cultivating] agricultural products, depending on what they could earn in each case."[40] Even with the availability of Kru labor, problems remained.[41] Thus, while Sands may have avoided buying slave labor, he undoubtedly had to find some way to overcome the wage labor shortages that were common during this period. Perhaps he relied on the numerous slaves associated with his own extended family. Whatever the case, it appears he opted to tread that fine line that had previously been mapped out by the Bremen Mission. He acted in accordance with British law by not purchasing the many slaves that were still available on the market in the 1870s and 1880s, but practical considerations required that he also accommodate himself to the reality of living, working, and, in Sands's case, being part of a family and society in which slavery was an accepted institution. He defined those his uncle and grandmother had bought as part and parcel of his own family. He acknowledged their importance to the family by recording their births and deaths. He expressed shock and regret when relations between slave and free within the community and within his own family deteriorated into violence.[42]

Sands was not prepared, however, to erase the social distinction that separated him and other free members of his family from their slaves. He meticulously recorded the genealogies of all family members, distinguishing those who were the descendants of free parents from those who were the children of a free father and an enslaved mother, and those who were to be understood purely as slaves based on both the origins and the social statuses of their parents. Why such detail? He was at pains, for example, to explain that Kwami, a family member whom he defined as a confidential servant of his uncle, was in fact a purchased slave. He documented this in his diary even though after the uncle's death, the other surviving members of the family accorded Kwami the status of a family head because of his age, wisdom, and his close association with Sands's uncle. Why did Sands still refuse to accept Kwami as a leading member of his family? Was it because of sensitivity about his own slave origins? Did it also have to do with other insecurities?[43] We may never know, but maintaining such detailed records about his family's slaves appears to have allowed him to reinforce in his own mind his status as a free citizen of Keta in the face of continued taunts about the enslaved status of his great-grandmother. Even more certain is the way his assumed role of family historian and protector of the family's reputation influenced how he managed his and his family's identity as they sought political power despite the stigma of their social origins.

*   *   *

When Britain extended its authority over Keta, first in 1850 and again after a period of noninvolvement[44] in 1874, they brought with them an administrative system that had already been implemented in their claimed territories west of the Volta. Chiefs who agreed to work with the government were offered stipends in recognition of their status. In return the chiefs were to acknowledge British authority and administer their courts as part of the larger British colonial judicial system.[45] One of the difficulties the British authorities faced, however, was determining exactly who qualified as a chief in the town of Keta. Having been virtually abandoned by most of its inhabitants in 1847, Keta included quite a mix of people among its residents when the British returned in 1874: native "mulattoes," local religious leaders, and several wealthy local traders from other Anlo towns had moved to Keta because of its increasing importance as a trade port. Who should be given the authority to manage their own courts, to hear appeals from lower courts, to determine punishments for those convicted of crimes? Implementation of the 1883 Native Jurisdiction Ordinance required colonial officials in Keta to obtain answers so they could put in place a system of native administration that could be relied upon to assist in the governance of the town.[46] Answers were not easy to obtain, however. Recognition by the government, for those who were interested, could bring numerous benefits: a regular stipend at a time when profit margins from business were declining; opportunities to influence policies that could have a direct impact on the community's as well as one's own economic interests; insider knowledge about government actions from which one could benefit. By this date, however, the British government was not prepared to recognize just anyone who was prepared to work with them. They sought leaders who were also considered by their own communities to be legitimate political figures. The names of individuals recognized as chiefs one year might disappear from the government list of approved chiefs the next year if they were deemed incompetent or corrupt, if they engaged in criminal activity, or were considered illegitimate as political leaders by the local community.

Of concern here is how the Anlo community itself determined whom they would support as having a right to chieftancy positions in Keta. Because it was a town only recently reoccupied, having a long history of residential leadership was not a concern. Virtually everyone in Keta was a stranger. Having military leadership skills was certainly prestigious, but of little practical importance.

Warfare between regional polities had virtually come to an end with the expansion of British colonial rule. Wealth was important but not critical. Of greatest concern was familiarity with European ways. As one local resident recalled in the early 1930s, "prior to the [1907] installation of Fia Sri II [in the 1880s and 1890s], the nation was itching for educated and civilized chieftancy."[47] Sands's maternal family certainly met a number of the criteria now considered important by many Anlo leaders for the chieftancy positions in Keta. They had been resident in Keta since at least the early nineteenth century. Their long associations, first with the Danes and then the British, meant they were intimately familiar with European ways. Having educated their sons at the Bremen Mission school where English was taught, they were able to communicate easily with the British so as to influence colonial policy. And just as important, they had the backing of two of the most wealthy and powerful chiefs in Anlo, Chiefs Tamakloe and Acolatse, both of whom were also close associates of the British. Not surprisingly, then, the British recognized Sands's maternal cousin, the son of his maternal uncle, as a chief of Keta in 1885.

Did it matter that their maternal ancestor had once been enslaved in Anlo? Clearly not. Did it matter that this new Keta chief was by origin also a stranger? Evidently not. Others who gained and retained the position of chief or head chief in Keta had also established only relatively recent residency in the town. Sands's family suffered taunts about their origins well into the 1880s, but this too does not seem to have bothered the Anlo political leadership. Other matters were more important: competence, commitment to upholding the interests of the community when working with the colonial government, the ability to contribute to Anlo's modernization. Despite the vote of confidence he and his family received from the Anlo political establishment, however, Sands remained acutely aware of the stigma attached to his family's history. His insecurities remained. Most telling is that when writing about his family history, he did so not in English, the language of the vast majority of his diary, but rather in Ewe. Was this Sands's attempt to sequester the stories about his family, to signal that this was private information that had nothing to do with how he would like to be perceived in his public role as "mulatto" and "native merchant," as an educated citizen of Keta and political advisor to one of the most prominent chiefs in Keta? Perhaps the best answer to this question can be found by examining his relationship with the Bremen Mission.

As noted, Sands was educated by the mission. In fact, he performed well enough to be accepted in 1867 at the mission's seminary for more instruction and was then employed briefly as a teacher. In 1872, however, he resigned, ostensibly because of his low salary. As a teacher, he was expected to perform a dizzying array of tasks: teach twenty to twenty-two hours a week, produce his own teach-

ing materials by translating the scriptures and other texts into Ewe, conduct de-
votions and prayer sessions with members of the congregation with which he was
affiliated, visit and console the sick, deliver the Sunday sermon, teach Sunday
school if the European missionaries were unable to do so, and preach the gospel
in the markets and streets of the towns in which he lived and in its associated villages. Sands and his fellow teachers were expected to do all this on a salary that
was fixed with the idea of "keeping salary expenditure to a minimum." Earning
extra money from secondary occupations was also strongly discouraged. Rather,
African teachers were to devote themselves full time "not 'for temporal gain' but
in order 'to serve God.'"[48] Such work demands for the wages offered brought continuous conflicts between the missionaries and the African teachers. Some pro-
tested. Many simply resigned, as did Sands.[49]

Salaries were not the only issue of concern to Sands and his fellow teach-
ers, however. A second concern had to do with the attitudes that many of the
Bremen missionaries brought to the relationship with their African assistants.
Too often, Africans—even those educated by the mission—were assessed as
inferior, both spiritually and culturally. The inspector or head of the Bremen
Mission in Germany, Michael Zahn, believed, for example, that:

> Africans—even as colleagues in the mission—[are] . . . wholly *incapable* of reach-
> ing the very highest level of [spiritual] attainment . . . [due to] a lack of capacity to
> distinguish properly between good and evil . . .
>
> The black simply [tends] to impropriety and excess . . . in contrast to us who
> have been in instructed in the truth from our youth upwards and measured by the
> unalterable criteria of a Christian life. . . . The African worker still has a good
> many heathen attitudes—and hence the European has a duty to lead.[50]

Of course, not all Europeans affiliated with the mission subscribed to these
views. Many who actually worked with African teachers in Keta and elsewhere
deeply respected their African colleagues and often advocated, in their communications with the Bremen Mission officials in Germany, for the African
teachers to receive better salaries and working conditions. One such individual
was Louis Birkmaier. It was he who requested permission to ordain the mission's very first African minister, Rudolph Mallet. When mission authorities in
Germany denied him permission because of Mallet's supposed moral defects
and lack of spiritual maturity, Birkmaier defied the committee and ordained
Mallet anyway.[51] Was it simply a coincidence that it was Birkmaier whom Sands
arranged to baptize his son, in November of 1881, one month before he also ordained Mallet?[52] Perhaps. But it is also possible that Sands, as someone deeply
connected to the mission, asked Birkmaier to conduct the ceremony out of respect for a man he knew was prepared to challenge the mission authorities'

negative attitudes about the abilities of Africans to be the cultural and spiritual equals of Europeans.

Yet another issue that brought differences between Sands and the Bremen Mission was the question of language training in the mission's schools. Since its beginnings in Keta in the mid-1800s, the Bremen Mission sought to bring its Christian message to the Ewe in their own language. To do so they relied on the assistance of African assistants, early converts who remained with the mission to teach the Ewe language to the European missionaries and who produced alone or in collaboration with their European colleagues the Ewe-language materials needed in the schools. With the assistance of the Keta resident Christian Quist, for example, the Bremen missionary Bernhard Schlegel was able to produce in 1857 his *Key to the Ewe Language* that included a number of Ewe proverbs and fables.[53] By 1858, Schlegel had also translated a number of Bible stories into Ewe from a German collection produced by Christian G. Barth. These efforts, in turn, became the basis for mission language policy, formulated between 1864 and 1867. According to these policies, the Anlo dialect of Ewe (the one spoken in Keta) was to be the basis for all teaching resources in the Ewe language. The rationale: "only . . . an education conveyed in the language of the country was healthy and able to touch people in their hearts."[54] Even today this makes sense. But the Bremen Mission's insistence on limiting the teaching of English to only the upper classes in its seminary at Ho (where only 7 percent or 35 students out of a total of 507 were enrolled in 1893), and then their refusal to use English as the medium of instruction even in their English foreign-language class, raised the ire of many. As noted by Hans Debrunner in his history of the Bremen Mission, the "small stratum of up-and-coming" businessmen in Keta was adamant about the need for more educated English speakers. "All the trade was conducted in English," not only at Keta, and in the other ports on the Gold Coast (Ada and Accra) where many Keta businesses maintained branches, but also in Anecho and Lomé, where "even the German merchants and officials used English . . . with their subordinates."[55] This failure to produce enough graduates fluent in English meant that local African merchants were unable to obtain associates capable of engaging in meaningful political intercourse with the British colonial government and with the European merchants who operated in West Africa and in Europe. Sands was certainly among this "indigenous bourgeoisie."[56] When the Bremen Mission refused to yield to the demands for more and earlier instruction in English, he took matters into his own hands. In January of 1880, Sands opened his own "native [primary] school." Information about the curriculum and the founding principles that shaped Sands's school are currently unavailable, but much can be deduced from the names of the children he listed in his diary as enrolled in the school in 1883. All came from Keta's "mulatto" community or from the house-

holds of those influential traditional political leaders in Keta who were committed users of "modern" business practices. It was this group of families that was
most interested in English instruction. This was the case not only in Keta but was
also the dominant sentiment among the "mulattoes" and "native merchant" families in the Fante speaking town of Cape Coast. There, the Wesleyan Mission met
the demand for English-language instruction.[57] In Keta, it was Sands who organized his own school to provide English-language instruction at a much earlier
age than was available in the Bremen Mission school.

By the 1890s Sands had distanced himself from the Bremen Mission. Following the lead of another Keta Christian, Hermann Yoyo, he used his own
interpretation of the Bible to denounce the Bremen Mission's ban on polygyny
as a European cultural interpretation of the holy scriptures.[58] In 1892 or 1893,
Sands took a second wife without dissolving his first marriage. More important for our purposes, he also sought during this same period to expand the
religious and educational opportunities available to Keta residents. He did so
by traveling to Cape Coast with two other colleagues in 1898 to invite the
founder of the African Methodist Episcopal (AME) Zion Church in Cape
Coast, Rev. Thomas Freeman Jr., to extend the work of his new church to Keta.
Sands's interest in this new organization was probably sparked by an article
that appeared in the *Gold Coast Aborigines* newspaper in November of that
year. According to this article:

> [The AME Zion] church thus composed of Africans and entirely governed and
> worked by Africans was indeed "bone of our bones and flesh of our flesh," which
> would naturally take a much greater interest in their missions in the Motherland
> than can be possible with Missionary Boards and Missionaries of an alien race
> who are *not above the colour question.*[59]

On reading this report, Sands must have been particularly excited. Here was a
new Christian community that, unlike the Bremen Mission, not only believed
that Africans were the spiritual and cultural equals of their European Christian
counterparts but was also—unlike the Bremen Mission, which had severely limited the number of ministers it was prepared to train and ordain—dedicated to
support the development of an educated leadership from the indigenous population.[60] As emphasized at the AME Zion's inaugural meeting in Keta in 1899:

> [The AME Zion Church] is, indeed, an entirely negro church; organized by ne-
> groes for negroes, manned, governed, controlled and supported by negro energy,
> intellect, liberality and contributions. In fact, it is the sentiment of the church that
> however great may be the friendship, intellect or interest of any white man in their
> well being, Christianization and enlightenment of the negro race, be he European,

American or Asiatic, he cannot successfully reach the emotional feelings of the masses of our people.[61]

Equally important for Sands was that the new church's founder was intimately linked to the Methodist church that was so well-known on the Gold Coast for producing the vast majority of the English-speaking clerks who worked for the British colonial government.[62]

As indicated earlier, Sands and some of his fellow elites in Keta shared with their counterparts in Cape Coast and Accra a particularly strong interest in English-language education. It was "the language of government [and] of overseas trade."[63] For Sands and his colleagues, however, English [was] "more than mimicry of western culture designed to bolster trading relationships." As noted by Stephanie Newell, "locals were interpreting and utilizing 'western' education, English literacy, mission Christianity and colonial power structures for their own ends."[64] For Sands, these ends involved, among other purposes, using English as a language to be deployed in both public and private (for example in his diary) to reinforce his social status as an "educated mulatto," "a native merchant." It was in English that he wrote the dated entries of his diary, recording the business and political affairs in which he was involved, the day, month, and year of such publicly celebrated events as the births, deaths, and marriages of family and friends, and the significant local political and legal decisions of the day. As an avid reader of English-language travelers' accounts and histories of the Gold Coast, he dutifully copied segments of these texts into his three-volume record book. It was his ability to read, write, and speak English that allowed him to work for the Bremen factory after he resigned from his teaching post. It was this same language facility that provided him with the opportunity to work as Chief Lotsu's intermediary with the British government, to travel to Britain and Germany for business, and to read about the African Methodist Episcopal Zion Church in the *Gold Coast Aborigines*. For Sands, like his Nigerian counterpart Akinpelu Obisesan, his command of English defined a particular public identity. But English did more than this. It also influenced how Sands deployed his own mother tongue, the Ewe language, in his diary.

Sands certainly considered Ewe—used regularly in daily conversations with family, friends, and the vast majority of the Keta public as well as at church and with business associates such as Chief Lotsu—a public language. As a spoken form of communication, it was the predominant means of discourse not only in Keta but also in the larger Ewe-speaking region where so many Keta businessmen, including Sands, sought to expand their trading enterprises.[65] As a written language, however, it had a more limited reach. Most Ewe speakers were illiterate in their own language during Sands's lifetime, yet it was the only means by which the vast majority of those who were literate only in Ewe could access the Bible for their own personal and private contemplation. It seems this is why Sands chose Ewe as the language in which to write the histories of his maternal family and their origins and social statuses. For Sands, this was knowledge he considered private and personal, to be shared with family members alone, to be sequestered from public view, to be written *not* in English, a language that was reserved for the recording of events of broad public interest, but rather in Ewe. Using his mother tongue for these particular passages was also a way for Sands both to acknowledge his family's history while simultaneously signaling his continued acute sensitivity about the enslavement of his maternal ancestor more than one hundred years earlier. Such knowledge was to be hidden from public view and its distribution limited because of its potential to destroy the family's claim to high social status and the Keta chieftancy position it had only recently acquired.

CONCLUSION

At the beginning of this chapter, I posed a number of questions about the descendants of the enslaved who lived in the late nineteenth century on the Gold Coast. What did the children and grandchildren of the once enslaved know of their social origins? If they knew, what did they do with that knowledge? How did it affect their life choices, their social positions within their families, their status as citizens in their home communities? Definitive answers to these questions must await the study of a statistically significant number of individuals and families in Ghana. But this study of the diary of one man and his family suggests that those of slave descent not only knew of their social origins, but that the larger society in late nineteenth-century Gold Coast was also not prepared to allow them to forget them. This was the case especially if they were in a position to compete for prestigious positions within their communities from which their social origins would have previously excluded them. Sands certainly experienced this. Although he indicates in his diary that his great-grandmother and her children, captured in 1769 and enslaved in Anlo, had been ransomed and freed, he still experienced the taunts of his neighbors in the late nineteenth century, more than one hundred years after his ancestor's enslavement. During this same period, however, past practices began to change. Under the influence of British colonial rule, Anlo society adjusted to the times. Strangers and individuals of known slave descent were seen increasingly as integral members of their families and communities with a right to respectful treatment. Their ability to contribute to their families and communities was no longer taken for granted as the abolition of slavery tested the bonds that had once held slave to master, captive or bought wife to husband. Older prohibitions that had barred individuals of slave origin from leadership positions began to fade. Sands himself operated as a respected leader of the educated Keta community; his maternal uncle—also of slave origins—obtained with the support of the larger traditional political community a prestigious chieftancy position. But changing times and the opportunities they presented did not necessarily assuage the insecurities felt by individuals like Sands. For that, diaries became a useful means for privately managing their own identities. Sands traced his family's ancestry to a war captive but one who had been redeemed. He established their ties to royalty. He insisted on distinguishing his status from that of the slaves in his own extended family.

In using his diary in this way, though, Sands did more than reveal his insecurities and concerns. He also sought to actively manage the stigma of his family's slave origins. He did so not by confronting his tormentors, which would have simply kept in the public eye questions that he would have preferred to disappear completely. Instead he used his diary to prepare his family for the possibility of information he could not control being used against them. That his efforts were taken to heart by his heirs became clear when I interviewed his descendants in 1988. None were prepared to discuss their family's history. Fear that the information I sought would be used by others to challenge their right to the chieftancy position they still held prevented them from revealing anything about their origins. This was the case even though the use of such information had been banned by the traditional Anlo political authorities one hundred years earlier. Such ongoing concerns, as reflected in the diary of Paul Sands, illustrate the staying power of certain social stigmas, especially slave origins. They can live on, as they have in West Africa, affecting the lives of individuals and families for more than two hundred years.

7. The Diary of Paul Sands: Preface and Text

Paul Sands's diary is a multivolume work that contains many details about the major and minor events affecting his own life and his home district of Anlo. Instead of reproducing the diary in its entirety, however, I have opted to present a number of extracts. The two sections presented here, the family histories and the dated entries, reflect the essential character of the diary, but they have also been edited with particular concerns in mind. The family histories, for example—written in nonstandard Ewe—were translated with great care and patience by Jasper Ackumey with minimal editing. But a number of the names have been changed to pseudonyms to respect the sensitivities of Paul Sands's descendants about their origins. The other major segment of his diary presented here consists of dated entries. Sands listed many of these entries in chronological order, but not consistently so. On occasion, he inserted later dated material between earlier entries, as he used his text to document what he understood to be the relationship between earlier and later events. In reorganizing the diary to be more uniformly chronological, I have obviously obscured Sands's own historical sensibilities. I do so, however, to better illustrate what events he found worth recording, when the events occurred, and how he used his diary to understand the historical trajectory of his own life and the history of the community in which he lived. In editing this section, I have also eliminated duplicate entries, of which there were many. In a few instances different dates were assigned to an event that had been recorded a number of times in different locations. Where this has occurred, I have included the event once and indicated in italics that two different dates were assigned to this same entry. In a number of other instances, Sands provided incorrect dates. When I can determine this, I have provided the correct date in brackets. I have also standardized the form in which the dates appear.

Evident in the section of dated entries are Sands's interests not only in slavery, the slave trade, and its interdiction (see entries for 1784, 1839–40, 1842, and 1844 for example) but also in Anlo foreign relations. He listed the conflicts that erupted between Anlo and Ada in the eighteenth century, the very ones that led to his great-grandmother's enslavement. He documented as well Anlo's long association with European traders, whether Danish, Dutch, Portuguese, or British, and the role his maternal uncle, Yao Mensah, played in facilitating these trade ties (see entries for 1865 and 1866). He recorded the coming of British colonial rule (see the 1850 and 1852 entries) and the many conflicts that erupted after 1874 when Britain as the colonizing power used Hausa troops to interdict the smuggling of liquor, firearms, and ammunition into the Gold Coast (of which Anlo was a part) from the areas that were outside British control to the east (see entries for 1878, 1883, and 1885). He also described—as someone deeply interested in business—those events (man-made disasters, disputes, and wars) that disrupted trade relations.

Sands was particularly meticulous in identifying by name the majority of the places and peoples that were significant to him. Many, as noted earlier, were Euro-Africans like himself, but another important group included the major local political, religious, and economic leaders of Anlo. These individuals have been identified below by name and position. Equally important to him were the social origins of particular individuals. In recognition of the sensitive nature of this topic in Ghana to this day, I have provided pseudonyms for a number of individuals whose identities, if revealed, could be used to identify Paul Sands and his descendants, themselves descendants of slaves and strangers. Many actual names, however, have been retained. To distinguish the actual names from pseudonyms, the latter appear in italics.

Certain names of peoples and places are also repeated throughout the diary using different spellings. No effort has been made to standardize the spellings in the diary itself. Instead, I list here the names of the places with more recent and a generally accepted English-language orthography.

PEOPLES/POLITY NAMES

Abolove = Abolave
Addah Foah = Ada Foah
Addahs = Addas
Addafia = Adafianu
Affiadenyigba = Afiadenyigba
Akati = Akatsi
Akim = Akyem
Angulas = Anlos
Awoonahgah = Anloga
Atokor = Atorkor
Awoonah = Anlos

Awunahs = Anlos
Awunas = Anlos
Bato = Bator
Bey Beach = a section of the coast now part of Lome, Togo
Blappa = Bakpa
Creppy = Krepi, the term used to refer to the Ewe-speaking areas of the
　　central Volta Region
Danoe = Denu
Djogee = Dzodze
Grushie = the generic term applied to decentralized areas in northern
　　Ghana that were subject to slave raiding by their often centralized
　　neighbors
Jellah Coffee/ Jellacowe = Dzelukofe
Kedgee = Kedzi
Krikor = Klikor
Kwahu = Kwawu
Kwittah = Keta
Kwitta = Keta
Jolo = Dzolo
Little Popo = Anecho
Merpe = Mepe
Osu-Christiansborg = district around the Danish fort in Accra
Tonyigbe = Tanyigbe
Taviewe = Taviefe
Tegbey = Tegbi
Tshis = Twi-speakers (or Akans)
Voji = Vodza
Wei = Woe
Wutey/Wuti = Whuti

LOCAL LEADERS

Ahorloo [Axorlu I]	*Awadada,* head of the Anlo military, c. 1844–1883
Akolatse [Acolatse]	A chief of Kedzi, businessman, advocate of "modernization," long-time resident of Keta
Akrobotu	Military leader from Srogboe; friend of the African trader Geraldo de Lima; linguist (spokesperson) for the *awǫamefia,* the Anlo political and religious leader, c. 1890s
Amenya Awhalavi	Military leader from Atorkor, with family connections to Ada
Amegashie	A priest of the god Nyigbla, assigned to oversee trade ties with Europeans conducting business in Keta on

	behalf of the Anlo's political and religious leader, the *awǫamefia*; a major figure in business
Anthonio	A chief of Woe, whose father was from Ada and whose most well-known name, Antonio, was given to him by a European trader; great-grandfather of Togbi Gbordzor
Azalekor	A businessman involved in the slave trade, with ties to Anloga and Atiavi
Borgor [Gbordzor]	The major chief of Woe; leader of the right wing of the Anlo army; a prominent businessman and supporter of "modernization"
Chichi [Tsitsi]	A chief of Anyako; ally and friend of Tenge, both of whom were harassed by the British because of their opposition to British trade restrictions
Djokoto [Dzokoto]	A chief from Anyako; left wing leader, *miafiaga,* of the Anlo military; father of Tenge
Katsriku [Katsriku II]	Head, *Awadada,* of the Anlo military after Axolu; held this position from 1899 to 1924
Tamakloe	Chief of Whuti; successor to Dzokoto as left-wing leader, *miafiaga,* of the Anlo military; businessman; major advocate of "modernization"
Tenge	A chief of Anyako, a businessman; deeply hostile to British efforts to control the area through the imposition of taxes on trade in the region; involved in military conflicts with the British and Tamakloe in 1885; the British attempted to arrest him and his friend and ally, Tsitsi, in 1889, but he escaped and went into exile in German Togo; returned from exile in 1899 to be arrested in May of 1899 but was released in August that same year after guarantees were offered to the government by other chiefs in Anlo

EURO-AFRICAN FAMILIES

The majority of these families had members resident in cities and towns located on the Atlantic coast, from the Fante-speaking areas of Cape Coast, through the Ga-speaking town of Accra and the Adangbe-speaking village of Ada, to the communities of Anecho/Little Popo and Porto Seguro in present-day Benin. Some—like the Williams and Johnson families—also had branches in the British colony of Sierra Leone. Many had adopted European names in recognition of past (and sometimes present) close association with Danish, Dutch, Portuguese, and British traders who had taken up residence for periods of time in the region. I list them here to distinguish them from the many Europeans whose names Sands also mentions in his diary.

Augustt/August	*Mensah, Yao*
Bischoff/Bischoff	Olympio
Cole	Quist
Hansen	Randolf/Reindorf
Heyman	Renner
Holm	*Sands*
Johnson	Sistrop
Lassey	Van Lare
Lawson	Tay
Lima	Tettey
Lykke	Vander Puye
	Welbeck
	Williams

The Diary of *Paul Sands*: Excerpts

Edited by Sandra Greene

1750   The first war between the Awunahs and the Addahs; the Awuna were defeated, but two of the royal blood of the Addahs were taken prisoners.

A *different entry on the same event:* The first war between the Angulas on the eastern and the Adas on the western side of the Volta—in which Tsum Ampoforo, the King of Akim and Sakiame Tendeng, the King of Akuapem, assisted the Adas in conjunction with these Tshi warriors. The Angulas defeated, but two of the royal blood of the Tshis =, viz, the two sovereigns themselves were taken prisoner.

1767   Peace was made and the Awunas traded to Addah: the royal captives were ransomed with a large quantity of cam wood.[1]

1776   The Awunahs attacked the Addahs by surprise having made an alliance with several tribes; the contest was frightful, nearly one half of the population was slain, great numbers were taken prisoners. The remnant of the Addahs became free . . .

1784   June 22: The Danes built Quittah fort known as Fort Prindsenstein.

1807   Jan. 3: The vessel Dahomey first arrived at Kwitta.

1828   Feb. 13: Tuesday, Abraham Augustt of Jella Coffee was born and died Sept. 12, 1881 at 53 years.

1838	June: *Mensah Agbodzi* of Jellah Coffee and Quittah was born before the bombardment of Quittah and died at Keta.
1839	Feb. 7: The Danish government stipend[ed] the kings and chiefs of Awoonah.
1839–40	Governor Hans Angel Gide was informed that one Don Jose Mora (Ado hose), a Portuguese slave dealer, had established a depot at Bato on the bank of the River Volta. The Governor at the head of about 60 soldiers and some armed men, the chaplain Mr. Toroloff, and Mr. W. Lutterodt marched to Bato to apprehend Don Jose Mora. He tried to fire a pistol at the Governor, but failed and was captured with his weapon. His goods and a few slaves he had bought were confiscated. After promising never to carry on slave-trade in the jurisdiction of the Danish Government, he was set free. He shortly after opened the slave trade at Wei in Angula.
1842	The Danish governor Wilkens with Mr. W. Lutterodt, the Secretary and Treasurer, and 150 soldiers set sail in an American trading vessel to apprehend the malefactor. They landed at night, and marched to attack Don Jose, who managed, however, to jump through a window of his house and escaped. His property and slaves were captured and brought to Christiansborg.
	Christiana Ablewovi August was born at Popo.
1844	Sargent J. C. Hesse was appointed commandant of Keta to relieve H. Meyer. Mr. Hesse one night saw Mr. Don Jose Mora passing by the fort with a gang of slaves. Ordering out the few soldiers under his command, and joined by Mr. Walter Hansen, and some young men from the town, he overtook the gang and ordered them to halt; upon which Don Jose Mora pointed his pistol at Mr. Hesse and three times attempted to fire, but without effect. He was then caught, and the pistol taken from him. The slaves were brought to the fort, but the dealers were suffered to depart.
	The Awoonahs were prepared to break open the doors of the prison. The king held himself responsible in case the Governor should claim them back from him. Thus, by the advice of *Mr. Andreas Lykke* and *Mr. C. Lykke,* Sargeant Hesse and Mr. Hansen agreed and gave the slaves back to the king, who had promised to keep them til the Governor's arrival. Governor Carstensen arrived Kwittta with soldiers under Lieutenant Swedstrup.

1847   June 21. The revolution between the Danes and the natives of
              Quittah took place; several of the Natives were killed as well as
              the Soldiers under the Command of Mr. Sistrop.[2]
              June 21: Houses at Quittah after the bombardment[3]
                  1. The Fort (Mogã la)
                  2. *Abui*'s house (Awegame)
                  3. Kpomifeme (F & A Swanzy) now Yaovi's premises
                  4. Mission house (Sofowefeme) or Lagbo House
                  5. Bremen factory at the beach
                  6. Amegashie's house at the lagoon
                  7. Atsui's house at the lagoon
                  8. Yoluga's house
                  9. Koklo's house
              Gardens (Abowo)
                  1. Lotsu's *dsrawe*'s garden (now Blavo's house)
                  2. Hlogbe garden (now Dugbatse's house)
                  3. BiSawu garden (now Mrs. P. Renner's house)
                  4. Kluvifofo (father) garden (now Madam Tolo's house)
                  5. Hododee (father) garden (now Markham's house)
                  6. Sogbato garden (now T. D. William's house)
                  7. Ahovis garden (now Garkpo's house)
                  8. Tronuas's garden (now C. J. Quist's house)
                  9. Amenohu's garden (now Ado's house at the lagoon)
                  10. Koshi's father's garden (now Nugbloloh's house at the
                      lagoon)
                  11. Avonus garden (now Chief James Ocloo's house at the
                      lagoon)
                  12. Owusu's garden (now Amutse Tamakloe's garden)
1849   March 31: *Walter Sands* (alias *Paul Sands*), the first son of *Jack-
              son Sands,* born today.
1850   March 12: the English took possession of Quittah by Governor Sir
              Wm. Hinek of Cape Coast Castle, accompanied by Rev. J. B.
              Freeman of the Wesleyan Society. The English soldiers occupied
              the fort of Quittah.
1852   April 19: the Proclamation of the poll-tax by his Excellency J. J.
              Hill, Major in the Army, Governor and Commander in Chief of the
              Forts and the Settlements.
              July 2: His Excellency J. John Hill, Governor-in-Chief accompa-
              nied by Captain Bird visited the King of Awoonah.[4]

1853	Jan. 6, Thursday: Simon August was born at 4 o'clock, died January 1874 at Cape of Good Hope, aged 21 years.
1854	July 24: William S. August was born Tuesday, 8 o'clock, August town.
1855	July 8: Sunday, H.M.S. Dutch steam sloop of war, Amsterdam arrived at Quittah on her way to India and China.
1856	29 [no month given]: Monday, Charles August was born.

Feb. 20: Aye was murdered by Asamyamer, a domestic of Abr. August by a stroke on the head; he was delivered up to be killed.[5]

June 8: Wednesday, C. August the beloved daughter of Mr. A. August died at 6 o'clock in the evening.

June 9, Thursday: Amega, the beloved nephew of *Yao Mensah* died 4 o'clock.

July 25: Death of John August, Sunday at 4 o'clock.

1859	June 3: The death of the dearest mother of *Yao Mensah,* Thursday, morning.

Nov. 8: Maria Bischofs, the beloved sister of Ino Bischof departed this life; she delivered a child and died few days afterwards from pain in the side.

1860	A serious [civil] war broke between Agwey people and Pedro Quadro and caboceer Coome between them. Pedro Quadro was obliged to send for General Ahorloo and the Awoonah people for assistance. The General lose [*sic*] no time to go there in company with his brother Abofrakumah and other officer [*sic*] by names, Moni, Zewu and Aboflakumah and Tsee, Kudolo, Date, Kpodugbe, Quashie Klue, Kuimakie Akue Akpafloo, Ayao, Venawo dede, Kpable dzi. 11 men from Wutey and 5 men from Anlo.[6]

June 3: G. L. Lawson, Esqr. of Popo died.[7]

July 2: Susana, the wife of Mr. Abraham August died at Popo.

1862	Dec. 1: Mr. C. C. Lima died on Monday afternoon.
1863	Sept. 20: Revd. F. Plessing died Sunday evening.[8]

Nov. 14: Capt. Joaquim da Costa Leemos married to Caroline the niece of Abrahim Quist.

Dec. 6: H.M.S. Rattlesnake commodore J. P. S. Wilmot, C.B. senior officer of the W.C. of Africa, arrived at Jellah Coffee, permission was granted to the officers and seamen in the afternoon Sunday, in order to have pleasure trip here. On their returning to the ship some of the seamen were quite drunken, and the canoe capsized outside the surf, and the men nearly drowned. The Commodore was very much annoyed, as he gave a previous warning to the people of Jellah Coffee not to give them any rum then imposed a fine of $100 on the chief of Jellah Coffee as punishment, the said money was paid by the whole merchants on Tuesday morning, 8 December at 6pm. The said canoe belonged to Mr. John Tay.

Dec. 6: Jellacowe was bombarded, a fine of $100 (gaalafa) paid by John Tay.

1864   Jan. 14: Mrs. Theodor Catherina Quist died on Thursday morning, 6 AM.

April 12: A confidential servant of Mr. A. August died.

May 19: Mr. John Bischoff died.

May 24: Sarchie of Jellah Coffee was put into room to Mr. A. August.[9]

July 10: The old mother of Mr. Abraham August died, 1 PM.

In 1855, first school was opened with 19 home boys mostly from Accra and Dselukowe.

In 1864, Rev. Boatshin [Brutschin] and his wife opened it again with eleven enfranchised girls and nine boys . . .

1865   March 7: 11 o'clock AM. A Hamburg brig ran ashore at Jellah Coffee. Assistance was rendered to her by the officers and men of the H.M.S. Vindictive and also by *Yao Mensah* and A. August in sending their canoes with cowries from the brig to the Vindictive at a rate of $100 for 100 bags, which was agreed upon and all their canoes were sent for the same. Five minutes afterwards, the Captain of the Hamburg brig discharged a quantity of cowries overboard, so the natives rushed on with canoes to take some of the cowries. Those on board were driven [off], many of the natives wounded; one man by name Dsimisah was killed; 4 days afterwards the ship got away. The next day, H.M.S. Vindictive bombarded the town and 7 men were killed by the shots of cannon.

April 20 to May 24: A serious war took place between the Awoonahs and the Addahs in consequence of that the people of Addah were indebted to Mr. Geraldo de Lima and they refused to pay him. He seized some of the people of Addah, their oil. The parties were enraged and burnt Mr. Geraldo's house as well as some fishing houses [that] belonged to some Atokor men on the other side of the Volta. On account of this, the whole of Awoonahs rose up for assistance. The senior officer of H.M.S. Ranger tried to settle the palaver, which was disagreed by the Awoonhas, for this reason the Commander sent 8 boats with men armed with guns, rockets, and opened fire on the natives. The natives were defeated and returned back to their homes. The natives also went with their 6 canoes and them [they] and, the captain [were] killed, and several [were] wounded. 10 of the natives [were] killed and 16 wounded. The name of the Captain of the Ranger was William E. Gordon; he was made Commander on 20th August 1861.

Dsidee Tamakloe, a confidential servant of *Yao Mensah* died in that action.

June: Removal of H.M.S. Vindictive from Jellah Coffee to Fernando Po; towed by H.M.S. Rattlesnake, Commodore A.P.E. Wilmot, C.B.

1866   The Awoonahs under the command of one Geraldo, a notorious slave dealer for some trifling misunderstanding . . .[10]

July 16: Friday, the chiefs of Awoonah received from the Cape Coast Governor the stipend of £156 for the year 1885.

Oct. 6: Letter regarding the re-establishment of peace between the Accras and Awuna and Geraldo [de lima] to be delivered up for guarantee for peace to Chiefs Borgor [Gbordzor] and *Yao Mensah.*

1867   Sept. 6: Schooner Ondinement ashore between J. Coffe and Quittah, Friday

Sept. 25: Jellah Coffee was burned up with fire accidentally by cooking of a woman on Wednesday, noon . . . a great conflagration . . .

1868   Nov. 19: Treaty of Peace: Addah and Awoonahs on board the colonial steamer, Eyo, in the presence of His Excellency Sir Arthur Kennedy, C.B.

[Note: This treaty was actually signed not in 1868 but in 1869. Two separate entries cite different dates as well: one dates the signing on 11 November, the other on 30 November as indicated here, neither one of which is correct.][11]

1874   Jan 26: Glover war at Anyako.[12]

Feb. 26: At Addafia on Thursday, 3–4 PM, my second sister, *Heloise,* died. The body was conveyed to Keta for burial.

March 8: Doh, the mother of Dedevi; mother died at Affiadenyigba and buried there.

April 16: Chief *Yao Mensah* died at Affiadenyigba. It was reported that he was killed by his own slave by name Labidey, (who was also killed at Agortimey in May) and buried at Kwitta.

Nov 3: Slavery was abolished on the Gold Coast.

1875 June 8: Ikoy of Accra died at Jellah Coffee.

Sept. 12: Marriage with my first wife *Martha, Mrs. M. Sands*, on Sunday.

Sept. 16: J. F. Smith of C. Coast was drowned at Keta.

Sept. 27: Old Elias Quist (Nukpese) died at Awoonahgah and was buried at Augustt town.

[Note: A second entry for this same information adds that he was buried at his house.]

1876 J. A. *Lykke* and Peter Nubakpui left to Lagos.

1877 Sept. 12: *Cleotus Kwame Mensah* died this day suddenly.

1878 Jan. 14: *Desiree Mensah* of Desuwoo died at Jellah Coffee.

Feb. 4: Monday, the Brig Evans chartered by Mr. G. B. Williams arrived this day.

March 5: Chief Amenya (Awlavi or Awalavi) died at Atokor on Tuesday.

March 6: Mansa, the daughter of Nunekpoku, died at Afiadenyigba.

March 6: Wednesday, S.S. Africa arrived homeward, Mr. G. B. Williams from Danoe and S. B. Cole from Little Popo.

March 7: Quami, a domestic of Chief Amegashie enticed the younger messenger who brought the death news of Mansah to take refuge in the fort.[13]

March 15: Death of Larsey, King John Mensah's brother, Porto Seguro.

March 29: Dadi Renner and Mr. Peter Renner embarked S.S. Ethiopia to Sierra Leone and England.

Oct. 23: Abolove war by Captain Ellis; Lo was killed.[14]

[Note: Sands included a second entry about this under the incorrect date of 17 November. That entry included more information: "The attack upon the D.C. Captain A. B. Ellis and Capt. Laver at Abolove; one Lo had been killed by the D.C. and two others wounded."]

Nov. 13: Tegbey was on fire.

Nov. 29: Kedgee was burned down by the Hausas of which six persons killed and nine wounded, and great quantity of property lost.[15]

[No date given] Mr. *J. A. Lykke* returned from the Bight.

[No date given] Geraldo de Lima, whose real name was Geraldo de Vasconcellos was a servant of Cosar Cerquira, slave dealer, who lived at Voji, a village about three miles to the east of Keta, and who died in 1862, leaving a large fortune.

1879   Jan. 3: Friday. Akolatse's wife was killed at Anloga by Nyiko.[16]

Jan. 7: Tuesday, Market Day. S.S. Africa arrived; Mr. and Mrs. Johnson Dundas per same to S. Leone.

Jan. 13: Sunday . . . A crew boy of G. B. Williams died.

Feb. 3: Gadese, the brother of Dsatugbui, Chief Akolatse's wife, was killed at Anloga by Nyiko.

March 14: Philipa Mago, the daughter of Mr. J. J. Johnson and Madame Sotemety, was born at Little Popo.

June 9: Monday, John Heymann, my beloved cousin, died at J. Coffee; the coffin was made by Mr. *J. A. Lykke* and myself, whilst Chief Amegashie, the uncle refused to do so.

June 11: Wednesday, resigned from the Bremen Mission factory work (*Paul Sands*).

June 24: Agbomadokponu, the brother of *Jonas A. Lykke* died on Tuesday at Jella Coffee.

Aug. 17: Sunday, the wife, Djatubui, of Mr. J. B. Cole died.

Nov. 11: The first time landed 25 barrels of rum (bale bags—325 gbs.), 1 scale (spring balance) ?bor liquor and 1 demijohn molasses for the firm Bellions and *Sands*.

Nov. 18: Arrival of Capt. Wilson with 40 Hausas [from] Accra; attack made on my two boys, Gavi and Ameoord [at] Abolove by the natives when I sent them to buy corn to feed the Criminal Prisoners in Quittah gaol, being then the contractor [for] the prison.[17]

Dec. 10: Mr. G. B. Williams, in company with people from J. Coffee, Vodza, Keta and Kedgee attended the funeral customs of the late Chief Quadjo of Adina (one of the grandest funerals).

1880*   Jan. 19th: *Paul Sands*'s school (native) was established Monday of the above date under the management of Mr. Layeh Amanarh (teacher from Osu Christiansborg).

Aug. 4: Mr. J. Sistrop established J. Coffee Infant School at his own premises.

Dec. 29: Dọmanu of Kedzi, wife of Chief Tamaklo, born a female child by name Afayode (mother of Godwin Tamakloe, police).

1881   Jan. 11: Chiefs Tamakloe and Akolatse and people at fetish today.

Jan. 17: *Paul Sands* was sent by Chief Akolatse to Bey Beach per Barque Diverty, Captain Marks and Weeds, to land goods.

April 20: Mr. T. D. Williams, brother of G. B. Williams, died and entered into the Old North German Mission cemetery.

[Note: Two different entries exist for this; one announces the deceased as T. D. Williams; the other lists the deceased as J. D. Williams].

July 31: Abraham August of Jellah Coffee died on Sunday morning.

Oct. 4: *Richard David Sands (Richie)* was born this day and baptized, 28th Nov 1881 by Rev. Birkmaier.

1882

Feb. 7: Great fire in Little Popo, 90 persons killed.

March 17: Andrew C. Holm (of Accra) died and his corpse interred into the North German Mission Cemetery on the 20th, Sunday, 8 o'clock.

Nov. 14: Bey Beach took fire.

Names of *Sands*'s Schools boys at Quittah, 1882

> I-Class
> 1. Edmund Augustt
> 2. Edward Tamakloe
> 3. John Tamakloe
> (These [last] two are no more at the school)
> II-Class
> 1. Joseph Vanderpueye
> 2. Alfred Randolf
> 3. R. D. Lassey
> 4. *Albert Mensah* (gone home; he has sore on his feet)
> III-Class
> 1. William V. Lassey
> 2. Frederick Christian (gone with Sands to Addah)
> 3. Samuel Tamakloe
> 4. Hennes Welbeck
> 5. Old man (Mr. L. Markham-late)
> IV-Class
> 1. Laway Tay Simeon
> 2. Lawetey Simeon
> 3. Jonas Atipoe
> 4. John D. Cole
> 5. George Augustt
> V-Class
> 1. Tetey Akpabi (now V. J. Parbey)
> 2. Kọmla Defor

3. Henry Tamakloe

4. Kwashi Bakari

5. Toshu Bakari

6. Kudjo Renner

? 1887[18]   Sept. 11: Agudawo, [my] native clerk . . . died at Bey Beach
Nov. 17: Bey Beach took fire.

1883   June 8: Hunebezo, the wife of the *late Yao Mensah* died at Ba-
guida, the corpse brought up to J. Coffee this day.

Aug. 15: Wednesday, the outrage of the Hausas at the house of
Chief Nyaho Tamakloe. Chief J. Akolatse and others received se-
vere wounds, which brought many of the neighboring towns to
Quittah on the 16th instant.[19]

[Note: This incident occurred not on 15 August but on 15
September.]

Aug 22: A meeting held today, Wednesday by the natives of
Awoonah at the residence of Chief Akolatse that the Quittah market shall [not] open till they get a redress from the government on
the outrage committed by the Hausas.[20]

[Note: This entry was mistakenly listed under the date 1879.]

Sept. 18: Tuesday, Chief Akolatse introduced me this day to Capt.
Firminger to be his representative in political matters.

Nov. 9: Adudawu, my clerk at Bey Beach, died Tuesday at
Hejeranawo.

1884   Feb. 10: Governor Rowe and suite; Chief Akolatse, *Sands,* Hanu-
aga *Mensah,* Akroch and 30 other boys (men) embarked on S.S.
Ekuro to Little Popo at 4 PM.

Feb. 12: Arrived at Little Popo, 10 AM; grand salute to Governor
with guns, cannons and drums; King Lawson in Asante-hammock
to meet the Governor.

Feb. 15: A large meeting, comprised of King, chiefs, townspeople
and scholars with His Excellency the Governor and suite. His Excellency distributed among the women at Popo the sum of £150
from 1/-5—a head. The Governor reminded them that the country
belonged to the English by treaty of 1852.

Feb. 18: William Alesander Blavo died at the Hospital at Quittah,
buried at the cemetery of the Roman Catholic Mission.

Feb.18: A Present from Governor Rowe:

1. Chief Akolatse		£1500
2. *Paul Sands*		200
3. 8 Attendants		400

4. Messenger to Porto Seguro   1100
5. King John Mensah, Porto Seguro   500
                                    £ 27100

Feb. 22: Messrs. Williams of Swanzy, and Darke and C. C. Lokko and a crewboy were bailed out today from custody. Mr. G. B. Williams and Chief Akolatse for Mr. W. H. Williams, Messrs. C. Rottman and G. Zurlinden for Daacke. Mr. G. B. Williams and Prince Ashiabour for C. C. Lokko, for £100. Mr. Olympio for the crewboy, £10.0.0.[21]

Feb. 23: H.M.S. Forward arrived from Accra with instructions to proceed down to Little Popo. Capt. Dudley and Mr. *J.A. Lykke* embarked thereto.

Feb. 26: Monday:

A special meeting was held to abolish the Nyikor custom;

(2) road to interior to be opened;

(3) the promised stipend of the late Governor Ussher was delivered to the chiefs and others (£600);

(4) distribution: 1) King Amevor £100; 2) Chief Ahorloo, £100; 3) Chief Tamakloe, £140; 4) Chief Anthonio, £80; Chief Akolatse, £130 = £600;

[Note: although these numbers do not total £600, these are the numbers cited in the diary.]

(5) Chief Akolatse was this day appointed chief of Quittah.

[No date given]: Mr. W. A. G. Young: Renewed disturbances in Awuna district-Disturbances in Awuna due to suppression of smuggling.

Oct. 28: Nudsro alias Mabua, the sister of Chief Attippoe died at Anyako.

Captain Campbell's Journey to Ho (with Chief Akolatse and others)[22]

Nov. 14: Started from Quittah, 3 PM; arrived Anyako 6 PM. Chiefs Atikpo and Azalekor came to welcome; Tenge and Chichi did not make their appearances.

Nov. 15: Started from Anyako 5 AM; arrived at Heluvi in morning; started from Heluvi [then to] Weme to Abor; Abor to Jerakatei, Jerakatei to Akati. Chief Sakpaku and his army surrounded us. Permission was granted us to pass on; breakfasted; it rained and thundered; Akati to Wowoenu/Werlab; Wowoenu to Adeota or Ahogbo; Adeota to Wute; overnighted.

Nov. 16: Wute to Tetemaleh or Atikpo's village. Tetemaleh to Kpevemahe (headman: Zodanu). A drunken man insulted *P. Sands*. Kpevemeh to Doda (market place); Doda to Hahekpo; Hahekpo to River Tojee; arrived Waya 7 PM at the mission station.

Nov. 18: Started 6 AM from Waya to Miaho (breakfasted). Arrived at Ho, 6 PM.

Dec. 23: C. Fr. Tettey, beloved friend of *Paul Sands* died Tuesday at 6 o'clock.

1885   Jan 17: Wuti war (Captain Campbell wounded).

. . . sometime on the 17th Jan 1885, the people of Awoonah, about 3000 in number, attacked Captain Campbell, the D.C then of this place on his way from Wutey to Kwitta. In that attack, Chiefs Ahorloo, Tamakloe, Antonio, Akolatse and Kukubor and some native scholars assisted Captain Campbell and rescued his life from the enemies. In this attack, the stool and sword of Awoonah was taken away by General Ahorloo to J. Coffee. From that time, the people of Awoonah divided into two parts: the above mentioned chiefs with their people on the part of the government and the other party independently of themselves. After the disturbance was over, the people of Awoonahga demanded the stool [and] sword from the late general Ahorloo, who refused to give same up. General Ahorloo did not return to Awoonagah, but died at Jellah Coffee, and the Stool and sword are now in possession of his son, Ahorloo Mega.[23]

Jan 31: Anyako was burned by commander Parr of H.M.S. Folie with a small party of Seamen and about 100 Hausas under inspector C. Dudley.

Feb. 2: Awunagah was similarly destroyed without any resistance met with.[24]

Feb. 5: Captain Firminger went to Atiavi; some people insulted him.

June 25: Old Chief Amegashie died at Afiadenyigba and buried at Atiavi.

Oct. 5: Captain Firminger and Capt. Freeman and 42 Hausas left for Moduikpota (Anyako): 4 small huts were burned down.[25]

1886   July 16: Friday, the chiefs of Awoonah received from the C.C. Governor the Stipend of £150 for the year 1885.

Aug. 2: Land and Plantation bought at Djogee (Kave) from Chief Azalekǫ; value: £12-10-0.

Sept. 4: Treaty between Mr. C. Riby Wiliams and the chiefs of
Bator, Merpe, Mlefi and Blappa.[26]

1887　Sir W. B. Griffith: Krikor country taken over by British government
to prevent German annexation. Krepi and Akwamu formally brought
into Protectorate.

Jonas Abraham Lykke born at Keta, 27th [month not
indicated]

April 22: My aunt Juanita died at Keta on my arrival from Cape
Coast to Addah; and buried her at J. Coffee before proceeding to
Addah on the 23rd instant.

June 5: Manu, the beloved daughter of my sister Denise and
Masah the beloved daughter of Latey Agboh, died on the 5th June
of the same day.

Aug. 11: Chief N. Tamakloe has a claim of £500 from the British
government for destruction of his house in the Wuti war
[1885–86].[27]

[Note: In a second entry, this date is indicated as the time
when "Chief N. Tamakloe received money of £500 from the
Colonial chest for destruction which took place in his proper-
ties at Wutey"].

Sept. 2: Friday, my cousin, A. Lykke, died at Addah . . . and buried
there. Born 27 January 1834 (53 years).

Sept. 14: My son R. D. Sands was vacinated [sic].

Sept. 16: Mr. Charles Francisco Van Lare born this day.

Sept. 29: Chief and General Ahorloo at Jellacoffe was buried at
Anloga.

Sept. 29: A ball party the Mulattoes called on the occasion for the
wives of the late J. A. Lykke.

[Note: A second entry about this event indicates it was followed by a thanksgiving to the public on the 30th instant.]

Sept. 29: The wives of the late J. A. Lykke entered into widow-
hood, and on the 30th instant, a general Thanksgiving day. I sent
20 heads of cowries to be distributed among the widows.

Sept. 30: Chief and General Ahorloo died at J. Coffee. [According
to the stool history of the office of the Awadada, the correct date
for his death is 1883.]

1888　Jan. 6: Adoahs of Wutey seized 6 puncheons of rum with a canoe
belonging to Mr. Theophilus Tamakloe at Affiadenyigba.

July 3: Acknowledgment of fealty by the chiefs and people of
Adaklu, Taviewe, Tonyigbe, Avatime, Waya, Jolo and Krepi and

people of Agotime and Anum and head Chief of Buem for himself and the people of Buem; Agreement by the kings and head chief of Krepi to keep open the roads.[28]

July 17: Mr. Christopher Holm died at Lagos and buried on the 18th, of illness of 8 days. The sad news reached me here on the 14th August.

1888–89   Sir W. B. Griffith: Kwahu brought into Protectorate. [The actual date for Kwawu's incorporation to the Protectorate is 1888; in another entry, the date 1889–90 is listed]

1889   May 4: William Augustt died at Anloga; also *Deborah Mensah* [my wife and cousin] at Addah Foah, the same day.

> [Note: Either the date of his wife's death, above, or the date she gave birth, below, is incorrect.]

June 29: My beloved wife and cousin *Deborah* brought forth a daughter at Ada, 11:30 AM.

1890   Sir. W. B. Griffith: convention with Germany [on] boundary between Gold Coast and Togo Protectorate.

June 9: Land donated to the Catholic Mission by Chief N. Tamakloe.

1891–94   Sir W. B. Griffith: First international conference to restrict sale of liquor in West Africa.

1891   August 10: Engagement of Madam *Amalia*. . . . as my wife

> [Note: A different date for his engagement is below under 1892, Aug. 9.]

1892   March 28: A great conflagration at Quittah. Providentially the factory of Regis Aine had been spared. There were 200 puncheons of rum and other goods and about 100 kegs of powder which the fire did not touch.

Augt. 9: Engaged Madam *Amalia* as my wife.

> [Note: See earlier date indicated for this engagement under 1891: Aug. 10.]

Aug. 30: *P. Sands* with seven others were arrested by Capt. Mitchell as conspirators against the government.[29]

1893   Jan. 10: Tuesday, Sewoyi, the wife of John D. Williams, put to bed of a male child by name Kobla.

15 [no month given]: Monday, Mr. J. Payne the agent of C. Goedelt died at Kwitta.

25 [no month given]: Mawuga, the daughter of the late *Yao Mensah* lost her daughter this day.

May 4: Sunday. A visit paid to J. Coffee to attend funeral of Mr. William Theodor, the beloved nephew and last survivor of late Mr. Abraham Augustt of Jellah Coffee, died this day. Mr. W. Theodor was blind from his middle age till his death.

June 3: Johann Quist died at Quittah.

August 5: *Paul Sands,* Quittah to the District Commissioner, Quittah, 5th August 1893.

Sir,

I have the honour to bring the following facts before your notice, which I think is the preliminary [*sic*] cause of Chief Atikpo and others calling over to see you yesterday, that some time on the 17th January 1885, the people of Awoonah, about 3000 in number attacked Captain Campbell, the D,C, then of the place on his way from Wutey to Kwitta. In that attack chiefs Ahorloo, Tamakloe, Anthonio, Akolatse and Kukubor and some native scholars assisted Capt. Campbell and rescued his life from the enemies, although he received seven wounds on the body from the enemies and also lost two Hausa soldiers. In this attack, the stool and sword of Awoonah were taken away by general Ahorloo to J. Coffee. From that time the people of Awoonah divided into two parts, the above mentioned chiefs and their people, on the part of the government and the other party, independently of themselves. After the disturbances was over the people of Awoonahgah demanded the stool and sword from the late general Ahorloo, who refused to give same up. The matter was brought before Capt. Firminger, who confirmed that the stool and sword should not be returned to Awoonahgah.

General Ahorloo did not return to Awunahgah but died at Jellah Coffee and the stool and sword are now in possession of his son Ahorlu Mega. Now the object of my writing you this is that the people of Awoonahgah are still demanding the said stool and sword which in proper speaking are prizes to the people on the part of the government. In the opinion of the public including myself, I do not think it is fair to have these prizes returned and that in my humble opinion a new man can be selected from the people on the part of the government in the room of General Ahorloo, and also Chief Tamakloe, who was great sufferer in that attack made on Capt. Campbell to be reinstated to his former position as Chief of Wutey. Then peace be insured.[30]

Aug. 25: The Awoonah people demanded the stool and sword of the late Chief and General Ahorloo to be removed from Jellah Coffee to Awunagah, which was refused but afterwards agreed to.[31]

Sept. 27: My father-in-law, the father of my wife *Amalia,* died at Accra (by name *Amattah*).

1894   Jan. 10: Atsuwui, the beloved wife of Mr. W. A. Blavo, died this day.

April 17: My second son, *Albert,* died this day and buried at J. Coffee.

June 28 [no year given]: My wife, *Amalia* (now Mrs. *Amalia Sands*) was summoned contra . . . 127, No. 12 of 1892 by causing a fouling water flowing to a well situate in the complainant's yard at Quittah and sentenced to 3 months imprisonment with hard labour.

June 30: Mr. J. D. Williams, alias Tomi, died at Sierra Leone, Fourah Bay . . . ; he was born in 1862 . . . Married 17th Nov. 1887 to Martha daughter of the late W. J. Donley.

1895   April: *Martha Lykke,* born 30th May 1858, Sunday (alias Mrs. *Paul Sands*) at J. Coffee. Married 12th Sept. 1875, died April 1895, aged 37 years.

June 25: Old Amegashie died at Affiandeyigba; buried at Atiavi.

1896   April 28: Marriage between Fred Bischop and Miss Mary *Lykke.*

July 6: Mr. Geo. J. Johnson died this day, 5 PM.

1897   May 8: *Paul Sands* first paid visit to King Mensah, Porto Seguro.

Nov: My mother-in-law, *Mrs. Elizabeth Lykke,* died at Accra this day.

[Note: This same event is listed below under 1898, Nov. 3.]

1898   Feb. 1: Solimedy, the beloved wife of Mr. J. G. Johnson died at Vodja.

Feb. 10: Wednesday. Today we the heads of the Family of *Yao Mensah* have transferred a piece of land at Alata Rose Street . . . to Mr. E. N. Tamakloe of Keta in consideration of the sum of £155 sterling, being an interest for two years and three months on £100 at 5% per month be borrowed [i.e., lent] to *Paul Sands.* . . .

July 27: Accra arrangement with Rev. Thos. Freemann to bring the new Zion Mission from America to Quittah.

Nov. 3: My beloved mother-in-law [my second wife's mother], *Mrs. Elizabeth Lykke,* died at Accra.

[Note: This same event is listed as having occurred in November of 1897 above.]

Dec. 4: Old Ameku, the beloved cousin of Chief N. Tamakloe died this day, buried on the 5th. Catholic Mission Cemetery.

Dec. 22: Marriage between Mr. Nyamadi Anthonio and Miss Zok-pleame Akolatse.

3rd Tuesday [no month]: A. M. E. Zion Church inaugurated.

1899   Jan. 7: Aɟedo of Chief Amegashie died.

Jan. 8: Boko[32] Klu of Augusttown died.

Feb: Zion Mission to Keta.

Feb. 15: Benjamin Domprey Atipoe died at Adidome and the body conveyed to Anyako for burial on the 17th instant.

1900   June 24: A large, handsome church could be consecrated. Pastor Mallet, formerly a slave boy and now a preacher of the Gospel among his countrymen, gave the sermon; thirteen white and black men besides him addressing the congregation . . .

1902   May 1: Asinu Akolatse, the wife of Mr. John Lykke, died.

1903   Oct. 28: Monday, A.M.E. Zion Church organized.

In 1876, Rev. Hornberger counted in the continually growing town [of Keta] 886 souls, including 77 Christians; communicant there were indeed . . . 28. One year later, when the Sierra Leone Christians were added, the number had risen to 70. But these strangers were not all of them true Christians and soon complaints were heard of their pernicious influences as well as that of brandy, yet the community steadily increased through the baptism of adult heathens. In 1886, the town increased to 1,700 . . . At the end of 1902 . . . little insignificant Keta has within fifty years grown to be a large town of about four thousand inhabitants.

1904   Feb. 18: William Alesander Blavo died at the hospital at Quittah, buried at the cemetery of the Roman Catholic Mission.

June 23: J. F. Quist died at Quittah, 6 PM.

Sept. 10: Mr. G. B. Williams died in S. Leone.

1905   Aug. 27: Sewenya Akolatse, the wife of Mr. G. M. Lawson, died at Addah, and body conveyed to Quittah for burial.

Oct. 28: Wednesday, foundation stone [AME Zion].

Dec. 14: Mr. E. M. B. Atippoe died [in] Keta,.. and buried at Anyako.

1908   April 26: Jonah Quist died at Lome.

April 26: Chief Akrobotu died at Aboatia; the corpse conveyed to Srogboe for interment. [The year (?) 1908 written 108.]

1909   Saturday: My daughter, *Alexis Rose Abena Abui* was Christianized this day.

Feb. 5: Mr. Douglas Yovu died this day at Akuse and buried on the 6th instant.

1911	June 18: Chief Tenge, alias Agbemadu, died at Anyako. Grandfather Gligui . . . father, Djokoto died 1869. Chief Tamakloe made him [Tenge] chief in the room of his late father, Djokoto, at Nyitui in 1873; mother Adage.
1914	July 19: Kofiga . . . of Geraldo de Lima died today and buried at Vodje.
1916	Sept. 21: *Paul Sands* left here today for Accra via Anloga and Akuse.
	Kwami *fle,* servant of *Yao Mensah,* died at J. Copwe this day.
	Nov. 8: The mother of Rev. Peter Quist died today.
	Dec. 16: Mr. W. L. Van Lare resigned the business of Messrs. F. and A. Swanzy and now under pension, about £100 a year.
1917	Nov. 26: Our dear Mr. W. H. Chapman died today.
1919	March 1: *Donald Sands,* Esq (the Independent) agent of Calabary, half brother to the late S. Bannerman lived continuously in Calabar 17 years as a Merchant. Mr. W. Bannerman B/L and S. Bannerman of the S. Coast were nephews and Mr. Samuel Bannerman Sands of Swanzy Produce and Mr. T. W. *Sands,* were his sons and Mr. *Paul Sands* of Quittah his cousin.
1924	Sept. 13: The demise of Awadada Katsriku on the 13th September. His funeral custom was observed on Sunday, the 21st 1924.
1925	Sept. 23: *Sands,* Mamattah, Khartey, Kupeta and Quist left for Awunaga on National Affairs.
1926	April 28: Marriage between Fred Bischop and Miss *Mary Lykke.*

Family Histories

Translated from the Ewe language by Jasper Ackumey

(p. 125–127) Chief *Yao Mensah*'s Family in Anlo

Our great-grandmother who gave birth to *Abui* (who is [a] *Mensah*) was from Ada. Her name was *Ama Tetteh.* She came from the family of the chief of Ada (Osei Tsuiewo). She was a real daughter of the chief ([a] real princess). In the past, a war was fought between the Anlos and the Adas after the Sagbadre War. The people of Anlo declared a retaliatory war on the people of Ada because the people of Ada had helped the people of Akyem plunder the Anlo towns. The Akyems took away the Anlos' wives, children, and women. The people of Akyem also burnt their towns. Because of this, the people of Anlo retaliated by declaring war on the Adas. The Anlos took away the women of Ada.

One of the women who was captured by the Anlos was *Ama Tetteh,* our great-grandmother. *Amega Fui . . .* who was Amega in Anlo proper was the person who captured *Ama Tetteh* and married her. Members of *Ama*'s family at Ada later came to take her back to Ada, but *Fui* refused because she had borne him children already.

Another Version

(p. 301) Once a war broke out with Ashanti. The people of Ada gathered their wives and children all into boats and instructed their slaves to paddle them to Kpong Glikpui. They inadvertently "went into the hands" of the Anlos. *Abui*'s mother, *Ama Tetteh . . .* was among them. She was a sister of Tunfo's mother. *Kwame* and *Abui*'s mother *Ama Tetteh* were paternal first cousins.

(p. 125–127) *Ama Tetteh*'s children are:

1. Kportufe's and Mawusi's mother
2. Afe, Dona's sibling
3. Vilovi/Kumakonu
4. Dra
5. Kpe
6. *Abui* (*Yao Mensah*'s mother)

The children of Mawusi's mother were:

1. Tonyi: Fui's father
2. Fiatu
3. Gbesika
4. Abui; born immediately after Mawusi. Abui was Wofexa's mother and the mother of twins Atsuwo and Atsufi (who were born after Wofexa). Atsufi is the mother of Dumenya of Alakple [who] died 12 July . . .
5. Mawusi
6. Kpotufe (Kportufe-godigbe's father)

Afe's children are:

1. Agbloh (Kumado's father) and [?father of Yewe member] Koshonshi

Kumakonu's children:

1. Kumako (Hayime's father)
2. Admah (Damali and Payena's father)
3. [no name mentioned]
4. Kponu

Dra's children: Dra did not have children before his death.

Kpe's children:

1. Kpoku (his children: 1) Desewu; 2) Gatsiko; 3) Sashi (?Seshi? Sawoshi? Zashi); 4) Yevu
2. Atsu
3. Afetogbo: Lotsu, Ocloo, Anipa
4. Dey
5. [no name mentioned]
6. Do (Atsu's twin sister and Dedwi's mother)
7. Folo: Awamako's and Kudzengo's mother
8. Notufe
9. Dofui (she is the eldest of them all)
10. Adabau
11. Adzanozi (mother of Toshi and Atsu Klokpe, who died at Afiade-nyigba 18th March 1887).
12. Kosonde (child: Dovi)
13. Agbodugbe (Sosu's mother)
14. Kukoxa
15. Kofi (Ewi and Amedome's father)
16. Noviaka (never had a child before death)
17. Kudayah (children: Kudoyo-Ramson's father)
18. Nudiko (Agbeadeyife's mother)
19. Letsa
20. Awagashi (Wotogbe's mother)
21. Kwadzo
22. Kokobu (Agbeadeyekpe's mother's junior sister/aunt)

Abui's (*Yao Mensah*'s mother) children:

1. Akofi
2. Gblu
3. Dede (the mother of *Ignatio* who[se father] was from Spain)
4. Koko (Hanyeaya's mother)
5. Sashikpe (Ja's mother)
6. *Yao Mensah* (or *Kpe*)
7. Nartey
8. Afe
9. Zuao
10. Ewi
11. Madui (*Paul Sands*'s mother)
12. miscarriage

(p. 127/p. 187) The Emancipation of *Abui* and her children in Anloland

After the death of *Amega Fui,* members of his family at ?Agu conspired to get hold of *Abui* and her children and to sell them because *Fui* captured *Abui*'s mother in war. When *Abui*'s family at Ada heard of this they . . . brought [the matter] to *Amega Kumako* at Alakple; and paid all the debts and bought them. And Mama *Abui* and her children became nobody's [?slave./word indistinct] in Anlo. Had this not been the case, we would have been slaves to *Fui*'s inheritors. But still, in some instances, they insult us as "*Da awa li ƒe mamayọviwo*" (Grand-children of war-captive). I thank God.

(p. 141) Mama *Abui*'s People [Slaves]

NAME	ORIGIN	GENEAOLOGY
Ablah	Akwamu	Ashantsi-Lodonu's mother
Ablah	Akwamu	Adoonu's mother
Ablayeye	Grushie	Ablewovi's and Dinah's mother
Abla Ashiagbui	Creppy	Ebu's mother
Laletor	Lagos, Nigeria-	Never had a child (the woman cared for *P. Sands*)
Zononya	Lagos, Nigeria	Never had a child
Koshiba	Grushie	Kudzodzi's mother
Akuwaoga	Grushie	Never had any children
Akuwoga	Grushie	Never had any children
Tekodi	Grushie?	at Afiadenyigba (Afevi's father)
Ametrokpe	Creppy	Ewi's [?and] Ashiportua's mother
Babanyra	Grushie	Gbadayikpe and Mansah's mother
Adinyrah	Grushie	*Mama Abui*'s stable-boy; never had a child
Isha (Issah)	Creppy	Never had a child.
Nyaletsegbo	Creppy	Never had a child.
Koshia	Creppy	Mr. A. Lykke's mother

(p. 325) The old *Yao Mensah* has only eight (8) children:

Arthur Mensah (Ayehu *Nyadroh*'s fathers)

Thomas Mensah (children: Ackumey and Kugbadzo)

Christopher (Chief *Charles Mensah*'s' brother)

Cletus

Christine (wife of old man Akwetey *Davidson,* [who] bore Selabu and others]

Korkor Toyi

Fia *Kwami* (child: Chief *Yao Mensah II*)
Terrance (goldsmith) died in Lome.

(p. 325) The old *Yao Mensah's* four nephews:

Paul Sands
George Parsons
Anderson Crest
[4th not listed]

Yao Mensah bought a slave who begat the following children:

Carl Mensah	*Cleotus Mensah*
Stanley Mensah	*Roger Mensah*
Everett Mensah	*Maximums Mensah*
David Mensah	*Frank Mensah*
Marilyn Mensah	*Alexandra Mensah*
George Mensah	
Arthur Mensah	

Janice Mensah . . . was born to an Agbosome man by the name of *Sowli* and not *Mensah*. She [was adopted by] *Yao Mensah* because the elder brother was born to Kwami, the purchased confidential servant of *Yao Mensah* . . .

(p. 127/p. 187) *Kofi Latebi*
Kofi Latebi (*Yao Mensah's* father) was *Mama Abui's* husband. His father was the chief of the people of Agotime from Begi at Atiate. He pawned his son to the Danes in Accra to be their slave. In Accra, elders and chiefs give their children to the whites and collect something from the whites just as the North German Mission also bought people to stay with [them] in Eweland.

Kofi was a blacksmith. The white man who got *Kofi* was Sikkini. This is a name given him by the Africans. I don't know his "white name"

When Siken was coming to govern the fort at Keta, he brought *Kofi* also with him. Here he continued with his forging. He was the one to whom the Danes gave *Vuime*. It was here that he, *Kofi*, married our *Mama Abui* and they had many children . . .

Another version of *Kofi Latebi's* Origins: Ada
(p. 301) The mother of *Kwami* (the elder) came from Tefle. *Kofi Latebi*, *Yao Mensah's* father, came from Kogbo in Ada Labia Wem (house). The Adas "found" the ancestors of the *Kwamis* and the Adas put a neckband of fan-palm strips around the necks of these people [?reference to the *Kwami's* having been in the area before the Adas' arrival and they were acknowledged as priests as was the case in Anlo and the insignia of this position is the raffia palm necklace as in Anlo] . . .

Part 4

A Kidnapping at Atorkor: The Making of a Community Memory

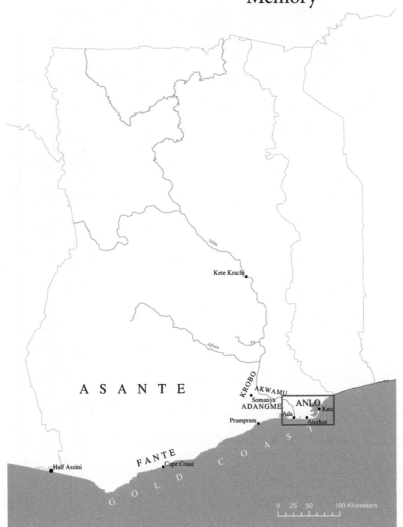

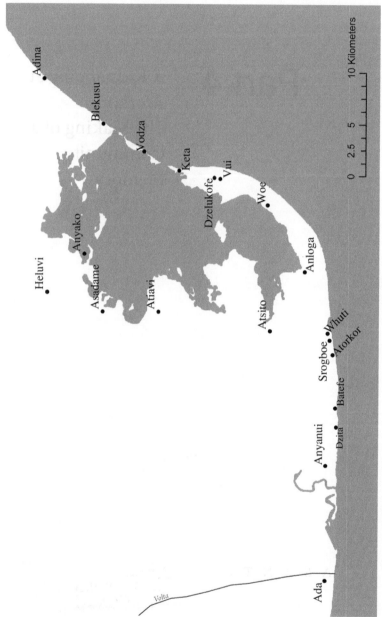

Some Gold Coast towns associated with the remembering of the Atorkor kidnappings

8. Our Citizens, Our Kin Enslaved

Life histories, biographies, and diaries, like the ones analyzed in the previous chapters, provide unprecedented insights into how individual men and women and their descendants in late nineteenth-century West Africa remembered the experience of enslavement and talked about its impact on their lives. Such detailed written accounts, however, are rare. In fact, we have access to these particular perspectives only because the enslaved themselves and their descendants decided for their own reasons to document their own experiences or to share their life histories with others who committed their memories to writing. Equally rare are African *oral* sources that identify specific individuals—men, women, or children—who were lost to their families and communities through enslavement. With each passing generation, memories fade; names are forgotten. In time, other individuals, other histories, become more important when oral narratives are marshaled to address the pressing concerns of the day.[1]

The forgetting that has characterized so many oral traditions about the loss of specific individuals to enslavement has been far from universal, however. Where the remembering of individuals is important for both personal and political reasons, memories persist. This is especially evident in a set of oral traditions I recorded in 1988 about individuals enslaved and transported to the Americas from the Anlo village of Atorkor. According to a number of local Anlo elders, there were three important ports for the export of slaves from the Ewe-speaking areas that stretched along the Atlantic Coast from the River Volta to the Mono River in present-day Benin: Atorkor, Vodza, and Cotonou.[2] At these ports, Africans met the European demand for slaves by traveling to a number of different markets in the interior where they purchased slaves and then brought them to the coast for sale. In the Anlo town of Atorkor, the individual most associated with this trade was a man by the name of Ndorkutsu. He not only sold slaves to European buyers, he was also implicated in a particular incident that was still vividly remembered more than one hundred years later. According to these elders, the crew of one of the European slave ships took a particular interest in the local music and invited a drumming ensemble

onboard to play for them. A group of male drummers, accompanied by an en-
tourage of women and children from Atorkor, boarded the ship, performed as
requested, and then mingled with the crew, who rewarded them by providing
them with alcoholic beverages. According to oral accounts, the adults became
so completely inebriated that they failed to realize that the ship had begun to
sail away. All on shore assumed they were then chained and reduced to the
status of slaves, for they were never seen again. Their relatives were obviously
deeply upset and vowed revenge. Instead of attacking Ndorkutsu as the individual with whom the Europeans were most closely associated, the citizens of
the town decided to retaliate by playing their own trick on the first European
slave trader who returned to their town. According to oral traditions, they did
so by having one of their own sell a group of so-called slaves (in reality complicit Atorkor citizens) to one such trader. Once the monies were received and
the "slaves" transferred to the custody of the buyer, the "slaves'" compatriots
followed their movements, located the site where they were being held, and
then returned at night to free them. In this way they at least received compen-
sation for the loss of those friends and relatives who had accepted the invitation
to entertain the crew of a European ship only to be imprisoned and carried off
to be enslaved in the Americas.

In 1992, some five years after I recorded these traditions, Anne Bailey collected additional oral accounts about the Atorkor incident and published her
analysis of the same in her book *African Voices of the Atlantic Slave Trade*. In
her study, she used European documentary sources to date the incident to 1856
and then analyzed the traditions in terms of what they told us about the trag-
edy of the transatlantic slave trade: the random violence and general disorder
of the trade that made everyone a possible victim; the limited effectiveness of
European abolition efforts; the corrosive effects of the trade on local social relations and political and religious institutions. But questions remain.[3]

We know, for example, that kidnapping and the sale of individuals into the
transatlantic slave trade was far from unusual in the polity of Anlo, of which
Atorkor was a part. In his study of the voyage of the ship *Diligent*, for example,
Robert Harms noted that in 1731, the captain of this ship was forced "to leave a
hostage on shore [in the Anlo town of Keta] before any African officials would
come out to the ship because six months earlier a French slave ship from Bor-
deaux had abducted several Africans who had come out to inspect a cargo."
Although this particular incident occurred some 125 years earlier than the one
at Atorkor, the kidnapping of men, women, and children—whether for sale
into the domestic slave trade or the transatlantic slave trade—was a constant
threat throughout the eighteenth and nineteenth century. In 1978, the Anlo
elder Alex Afatsao Awadzi described how a kidnapping that occurred around

the same time as the Atorkor incident (the mid-nineteenth century) affected his own family, then resident in the town of Anloga:

> In those days, slave traders formed large groups...they surrounded people, caught them and sold them. My own grandfather was almost caught. My mother's mother was caught and hidden in [a] ... cult house[4] in [the Anlo village of] Woe. It belonged to her brother. When this man saw my mother's mother, Mable, he asked her why she was there. She said she had been caught by slave traders. Her brother, Nudali, approached the capturers and she was released. Only she and another woman were released. If you hide something with them [i.e., in the "cult house"], they don't release it and they sell them to the Europeans.

In 1860, four years after the Atorkor incident, children were still being snatched and spirited away. One such child, living in Keta and affiliated with the North German Missionary Society (also known as the Bremen Mission), suffered such a fate. Unfortunately news about his situation arrived too late for him to be rescued, as indicated in the following Bremen Mission account:

> Since the English have abandoned their fort in Keta [in 1856], the slave trade is increasing in a frightening manner.... One evening, [the mission brothers] found missing a boy named Moritz who had recently been baptized.... All efforts to find at least a trace of him were in vain. Then, after a while they received a letter from a Portuguese slave trader informing them that the boy had been kidnapped and sold. At the place where he was said to be hidden, [the Missionary] Plessing called for an investigation and punishment of the guilty.... The Africans presumed, and it seems to be true, that the Brother's former horse groom in Keta who had left the brother and was roving about for some time near them, had conspired with the cook in Keta and three others who worked for the Bremen businessman Brother Rottman to kidnap and sell the boy. Undoubtedly, they had done the same with a girl who went missing earlier. The Africans have already punished [the kidnappers] by placing them in fetters and displaying them in public; and the money for which the poor Moritz had been sold, was also returned to the Brothers, although they had to spend half of it on court fees. Still there is no trace of the boy. Nine days ago [sometime in early November 1860], just as the criminals were being discovered, a transport of slaves was shipped to Bahia. Probably the poor child is among them.[5]

In both of these incidents, the one in Anloga and the one in Keta, the general public was made aware of the kidnappings. A general alarm was raised. In the Anloga incident, the kidnappers were forced to release at least one of their captives. In the Keta incident, the boy was lost to the Atlantic slave trade, but legal proceedings took place. The culprits were identified, captured, and punished.

Yet community memories about these two kidnappings today exist only as family recollections or not at all. Why then is the Atorkor incident so vividly and widely remembered? What factors made it worthy of discussion, recounted time and again in villages and towns well beyond Atorkor for another two hundred years? The answer to these questions can be found by exploring the history of Atorkor.

*   *   *

Atorkor is a village of relatively recent origin. It began as a temporary fishing hamlet in the early eighteenth century when local residents from some of the older towns in the area (Batefe and Anloga, for example) erected temporary shelters while working the ocean as well as the creeks and lagoons in the area. By the mid-eighteenth century, traders from Akwamu (to the north of Anlo on the Volta River) and Asante (to the northwest, well to the west of the Volta) had begun to travel regularly on foot to Atorkor to purchase the smoked and dried fish produced by those who had begun to erect for themselves more permanent homes. In time, the name of the new village became known not by any local Ewe-language name but rather by the phrase *Mẹ tọ, mẹ kọ* (I buy and go) from the Akwamu and Asante language of Twi (which was then truncated into Atorkor). As trade partners, the Akwamu and Asante were interested not only in the local salt and fish they could purchase at Atorkor but also in European goods, especially firearms. These they bought by offering in exchange the men, women, and children they had obtained as enslaved prisoners of war. Asante and Akwamu travel to Atorkor increased significantly after 1792, when the larger coastal trading town of Keta to the east was destroyed by war. Further increases occurred after 1807, when Britain's successful efforts at blocking the slave trade at the Gold Coast ports of Cape Coast and Accra forced many to move their export operations to a number of different towns and villages on the Atlantic littoral to the east of the Volta. The Portuguese trader Baeta, for example, settled in Atorkor in the 1820s or 1830s and proceeded to build the Anlo area's first well so he could provide his slaves with an adequate supply of water before he sold them for shipment to the Americas. Foreign sellers and buyers were not the only ones attracted to Atorkor, however. Neighboring towns and villages in the Anlo area also began to use Atorkor for their own purposes, in this case to dispose of their problematic citizens. Individuals from area towns convicted of minor and major crimes were regularly sent there to be sold. When local money lenders found it difficult to collect an outstanding loan, it was the citizens of Atorkor to whom they turned when they needed to hire someone to find the debtors, capture them, and sell them so they could recover at least a portion of the money they had lent to the defaulter. Only in the 1840s, when the Danes, who claimed exclusive rights to trade in Anlo, launched a number of raids to stop slave trading in the areas did this traffic in human beings begin to subside. Baeta abandoned the town and relocated to the east. Others, however, especially locals who could operate more inconspicuously, simply took their place. One such person was Ndorkutsu.[6] It was this individual who was remembered as the major slave trader in Atorkor when citizens from the town were kidnapped and carried as slaves to the Americas. Still, the days of the slave trade were coming to an end. By 1855 Ndorkutsu had died. With no one to take his place, all slave trading activity in the town gradually come to an end,[7] to be replaced by a new export commodity: palm oil. Oil sales brought some prosperity to the town, but it never replaced the slave trade in the minds of many Anlos as the business that really made Atorkor.

When I began conducting research in the 1980s on the slave trade in the Anlo area, it was Atorkor that many residents recalled as being an important place where the slave trade was conducted. In support of their assertions, they pointed to a number of physical sites in the town that acted as ready reminders of this history. There was Baeta's well, remembered as being constructed initially of barrels sunk into the sand to capture the fresh water that lay above the heavier salt water below. Even though it had been reconstructed with cement walls, it still stood as a reminder of the Portuguese trader who made his living from the sale of human beings. There was also the building in the center of town that had thick adobe walls and an unusually narrow, high window. This was a structure that was said to have been built by Ndorkutsu for use as a prison to hold his slaves until he could sell them to the passing European slave ships. Both the origins of the village's early prosperity and the physical reminders of the slave trade in the town itself kept intact the village's association with the slave trade. But what of those in Anlo who didn't know Atorkor, who had never visited the place, who didn't know of its history or the existence of any physical remains? Why would an incident that occurred in a small village in 1854 be remembered not only in Atorkor itself and its immediate neighboring villages but also in many other parts of the Anlo polity?

In answering this question, I suggest that the widespread dissemination of this oral tradition was primarily the result of efforts by a local minister, Rev. F. K. Fiawoo. Born in 1891, only some forty years after the Atorkor kidnapping, and raised in the village of Whuti, just 1.6 kilometers from Atorkor, he would have certainly heard about this history. More important, however, was that he came of age at a time when many in West Africa and the West were enthusiastically embracing and disseminating the tenets of African cultural nationalism and Pan-Africanism. Circulated and debated widely during Fiawoo's formative

years were notions about the importance of respecting black and African culture (including their rich oral cultures), the need to forge alliances among the
different West African countries colonized by Britain, and the importance of
building stronger links between blacks in Africa and in Africa's Diaspora. Race
rhetoric constituted a major theme in the publications of many educated urban
West African thinkers from the 1890s into the 1920s. Fiawoo was certainly influenced by these currents. He chose to further his studies in the United States
at the Negro institution of higher learning, Johnson C. Smith University in
North Carolina. And it was to a branch of the Negro-founded African Methodist Episcopal Zion Church that he returned as a minister in 1933.

Fully conversant with the oral traditions of his home district, Fiawoo appropriated the Atorkor oral tradition about the kidnapping and modified it so
that those who had been abducted were understood not just as lost but as the
ancestors of those who were now known as United States Negroes. It was also
Fiawoo who disseminated this modified history, making the Atorkor story
popular throughout the Anlo polity. Why did he do so? What prompted him to
encourage the rural residents of Anlo to understand themselves as they had
never done before: as part of a wider black Diaspora, as individuals connected—
through the village of Atorkor—to others across the Atlantic? Prior to Fiawoo's
efforts, race had meant virtually nothing to them. Although they lived under
British colonial rule, most had virtually no contact with others of a different
color. What motivated Fiawoo to pursue this effort? Equally important, why
were local elites on the Gold Coast interested in the AME Zion Church in the
first place? And why did a number of Anlo businessmen from the town of Keta
(just c. twenty-four kilometers from Fiawoo's village of Whuti), travel to Cape
Coast, where the church was first introduced, to bring this new missionary organization to their own community when there were already two such organizations in the area (the Bremen Mission and the Roman Catholic Church)?
Only by addressing these questions can one fully appreciate how the citizens of
this one small area in what is now southeastern Ghana came to understand
themselves as part of a worldwide black Diaspora, as do virtually no other rural
residents in much of West Africa even up to this day.

*   *   *

At the close of the nineteenth century, educated West Africans found themselves—whether entrepreneurs or civil servants, aspiring teachers or would-be
clergy—operating in a world in which opportunities for upward mobility, even
economic survival, were increasingly difficult. African businessmen and women
beginning in the 1880s "struggle[d] to survive downward fluctuations in world

prices for palm products [and] cutthroat competition from both African and European rivals."[8] Narrow profit margins and an increasingly racist business environment limited their access to European capital.[9] The situation was no better for those who worked as civil servants. By the 1880s, the British colonial government had begun to limit the number of Africans and blacks from the British colonial empire they were prepared to appoint to government positions. Those who already held some of the highest posts found themselves driven out by European superiors determined to reserve those positions for whites.[10] Attitudes toward Africans by the European missionaries who controlled the religious and educational institutions on the Gold Coast were no different.[11]

Local responses to these developments were far from uniform. Criticisms of the British colonial government in the locally run newspapers increased even as most of the educated coastal elite continued to believe in the overall uplifting potential of British colonial rule. The Wesleyan Mission came under particular criticism for not doing enough to encourage local-language education in the Fante area even though this very approach had earlier been (and in some instances, continued to be) praised by many local elites.[12] Those who had adopted European surnames and forms of dress were encouraged by local individuals and organizations (the Mfantsi Amanbuhu Fekuw, for example) to abandon both and assume instead African names and sartorial styles to reflect their pride in being African. The organizational encouragements often came, however, from groups whose members themselves refused to abandon their top hats and wool coats.[13] Nationalist sentiments were extensive enough, nevertheless, to generate considerable interest among the most educated local Gold Coast elite in working with others from around the world who were similarly interested in promoting the spiritual and material development of Africa.[14] It was in this context that they welcomed the coming of the African Methodist Episcopal (AME) Zion Church.

Officially established in 1801, the AME Zion Church was founded in New York City in response to the refusal of the white members of the John Street Methodist Church to recognize as their equals the African American members who had organized themselves since 1796 as a prayer community within the John Street Church. Black members of the white church "were not permitted to come to the sacrament until all the white members, even children, were communed. "Those who felt a call to preach and who sought advancement within the church hierarchy were denied opportunities at every turn. They "were not permitted to receive holy orders [i.e., to be ordained] nor to join the itinerancy [to preach to others]." In establishing their own denomination, the members of the new church decided that in the end, after much struggle, "the black man must go on his own plane, must climb his own ladder, [for] the white man will never step aside to make room from him."[15] More than sixty years after its founding, the AME Zion Church had responded so successfully to similar frustrations in other communities that by 1864 it had spread to nearly every state east of the Mississippi.[16] In 1876, the AME Zion Church also crossed the Atlantic to West Africa. This particular expansion, however, was not motivated by frustrations with white racism within the Methodist Church alone. More critical were developments within the United States as a whole. After the end of Reconstruction in 1877, African Americans faced a seemingly unstoppable surge of hostility: overt discrimination, disenfranchisement, a racialized judicial system, lynching and intentional efforts to hinder black economic opportunity. In response, members of the AME Zion Church began to listen far more attentively than before to the exhortations of such noted speakers as Henry McNeal Turner and Alexander Crummell. Both offered Christian evangelical expansion as a way for African Americans to obtain relief from the degradation of being black in America, while also working to improve the race. According to Turner, "to passively remain [in the United States] and occupy our present ignoble status, with the possibility of being shot, hung or burnt," was clearly unacceptable. He advocated for "the better class of colored men" to go to Africa, for "never will Africa's sons [in the United States] be honored until Africa herself sits among the civilized powers."[17] Crummell argued as well that "Afro-Americans [were] an elect group who had been exposed to Christian civilization, tested by the 'sorrow, pain and deepest anguish of slavery' and [were] freed so they could take civilization to Africa." Both were messages couched in the prevailing language and thought of nineteenth-century America: Africa was considered both primitive and uncivilized; its redemption could come only from outside the continent, brought by "civilized westerners," whether white or black. Educated African Americans were deemed especially suited to the task of evangelizing the continent either because of their tropical origins or because of their exposure, while enslaved, to the "truest of all religions," Christianity. Trumpeted by black and white ministers alike, it was a message that resonated especially well with one AME Zion minister, Andrew Cartwright. In 1876, he immigrated to Liberia and was the first to organize AME Zion congregations in West Africa.[18] Others were to follow. Critical for the establishment of the Zion Church in the Gold Coast/Ghana, for example, was another minister, the AME Zion bishop John Bryan Small.

Elected in 1896 to serve as a bishop of the AME Zion Church responsible for the church's West African mission field (which at that time included only Liberia), Small was the first member to visit the Gold Coast. As a missionary, he was motivated by the same concerns that caused other American missionaries, black and white, to travel to the continent. But as the bishop of a church "organized by negroes for negroes," as someone who already made many friends among the educated elite of Cape Coast[19] during his more than three years resident there during the 1860s as a member of the West India Regiment,[20] as someone already fluent in the local Fante language, and as a person who brought with him experience as a British colonial subject born and raised in Barbados,[21] Small was particularly adept at presenting himself and the church to the educated citizens of Cape Coast as a vehicle that could serve the interests and needs of its citizens as they sought to grapple with the racism they were encountering in the British-controlled religious, economic, and political institutions on the Gold Coast.

To address the lack of opportunities to advance within the British colonial civil service and the European missionary societies, for example, Small arranged for a number of young men to continue their studies at Livingstone College, the AME Zion educational institution in North Carolina, where he himself had studied and received his doctorate of divinity in 1887. He also used his acquaintance with another well-known West Indian missionary family, the Freemans, to gain their support for the establishment of AME Zion on the Gold Coast.[22] The patriarch of this family, Thomas Birch Freeman Sr., was widely lauded by many throughout British West Africa and in Cape Coast in particular for using the Wesleyan Methodist mission schools with which he was affiliated to support the expansion of Western education on the Gold Coast. It was Freeman's son, T. B. Freeman Jr., who distinguished the new church from the Wesleyan Methodist Mission by describing it as "bone of our bones and flesh of our flesh."[23] Equally important, if only for symbolic value, was that Small was "black as ebony" in color. This seemingly small detail was especially important for those Gold Coast citizens who felt aggrieved by a colonial system that not only discriminated against them because they were native Africans but had also generated a social pecking order that encouraged the local population "to esteem some because they are light [in color] and . . . [to] disagree with others because they are dark."[24]

Because the church was launched in Cape Coast at a time when many among the educated elite throughout the Gold Coast were particularly alienated by the lack of opportunities afforded them in the 1880s and 1890s, it is no wonder that the church was greeted with tremendous enthusiasm in the local newspapers. According to the *Gold Coast Aborigines,* it was this church alone, of all those currently operating in the Gold Coast, that was capable of "reach[ing] the emotional feelings of the masses of our people."[25] This was, of course, the perspective of those affiliated with the Aborigines Rights Protection Society (ARPS), for which the *Gold Coast Aborigines* was the official organ.[26] As an organization, the ARPS was principally concerned with challenging British legislation that threatened to transfer various lands on the Gold Coast to the colonial government for management and control. Their protests emphasized the existence of previous British legislation and statements that recognized limitations on British claims to Gold Coast lands. Their petitions invoked the notion that local Gold Coast citizens had a "natural right of absolute ownership" to Gold Coast lands whether held communally or by individuals and families.[27] This emphasis on natural law and custom was only part of the rhetoric employed by the ARPS in their battles against the British, however. They also deployed the language of race. The motto of their newspaper, the *Gold Coast Aborigines,* was "For the safety of the public and the welfare of the *race.*"[28] Published in its pages were many articles protesting the racist treatment meted out to educated Africans. In a 15 January 1898 article, for example, an ARPS writer commented on the refusal of Europeans resident in the coastal town of Saltpond to include Africans at their Christmas Eve dinner party. The author described the incident in the following terms: "There was a grand dinner at one of the European houses, attended of course by all the Europeans in the town, 'dogs and niggers' as usual were not admitted."

Such concerns about race and racial discrimination were not confined to ARPS members. As noted in the previous chapter, the Keta resident and local businessman Paul Sands felt a similar disquiet about the Bremen Mission's refusal to train large numbers of Africans for the ministry or to provide other opportunities for higher education. In the face of such affronts, it was no wonder that a broad spectrum of educated individuals on the Gold Coast sought support at the turn of the twentieth century for establishing in their own communities, a branch of the AME Zion Church. Here was a Christian organization that was founded to counter racism in the United States and was now ready to extend to the Gold Coast all the opportunities for leadership and educational advancement that had been denied them by the other missionary societies.

But what did such race rhetoric really mean for those on the Gold Coast? For the majority of whites in Europe and the United States, race referred to the notion that "there was a hierarchy of races with the Negro at or near the bottom: there were 'innate and permanent differences in the moral and mental endowments' of races; each race had its own 'talents', 'instincts' and 'energy'; race rather than environmental or circumstantial factors 'held the key to the history' of a people; there existed 'an instinctive antipathy among races', and the homogeneity of race was necessary for successful nation building."[29] Educated West Africans rejected the hierarchical aspects of this racial ideology, but the notion of race as an uncontestable way of categorizing the human race and the idea that certain races had certain distinct and inherent qualities was an idea that circulated widely in West Africa. The most outspoken and widely known advocate of the "fact" of racial characteristics was Edward Wilmot Blyden. A West Indian who immigrated to Liberia in 1851 and then to Sierra Leone in 1872, Blyden was extremely influential in the region. Described in an 1890 issue of the regional newspaper the *Lagos Weekly Record* as "an oracle" and "the highest intellectual representative and the greatest defender of the African race,"[30] Blyden rejected white European and American ideas about African inferiority but stressed nevertheless the reality of racial difference. In his speeches and in his publications, he emphasized the notion that Africans, whether in Africa or elsewhere, had particular characteristics, a specific personality. This "personality" was characterized by "cheerfulness, sympathy, [a] willingness to serve," and an innate spiritual orientation that made an African distinct from the "harsh, individualistic, competitive and combative" European. Using this same logic, he argued that because of their unique attributes, only educated Africans (a group that included black Americans and black West Indians) were capable of bringing development to their fellow Africans.[31]

A number of Blyden's views certainly found acceptance among educated Gold Coast residents. In 1911, J. E. Casely Hayford characterized Blyden, in his book *Ethiopia Unbound: Studies in Race Emancipation,* as a "leader among leaders of African aboriginal thought"[32] and then emphasized, as had Blyden, the notion that Africans may live in Africa or in the West or the East, scattered there by the slave trade, but they were still of one race. Casely Hayford, however, was also a cultural nationalist. For him, the solution to racial uplift was not simply the return of Africa's darker children to the continent, as advocated by Blyden. Rather, returnees also had to understand themselves "as *Africans* or *Ethiopian,*" as members of a people who "have our own statutes, [and] the customs and institutions of our fore-fathers, which we cannot neglect and [still] live."[33] Others among the educated elite of the Gold Coast were equally invested in race thinking, but they too departed from Blyden's ideas in important ways. This was especially the case for those who supported the establishment of the AME Zion Church on the Gold Coast.

J. E. K. Aggrey, for example, received his BA and MA from Zion's Livingstone College in 1902 and 1912, respectively, and later became widely known throughout Africa, the United States, and Europe as a leading educational thinker. He is remembered today for his famous speech in which he emphasized cross-racial cooperation: "you can play a tune of sorts on the white keys, and you can play a tune of sorts on the black keys, but for harmony, you must use both the black and the white."[34] Others affiliated with the denomination felt the same way. AME Zion's African ministers on the Gold Coast regularly invited the white missionaries associated with the European missions in the area to celebrate with the Zion Church the opening of their schools and various anniversaries.[35] Zion leaders also regularly sought financial assistance for its schools from the white British colonial government when it began to make grants in aid available to mission schools.[36] Still, embraced without reservation was the importance of Africans understanding themselves as a member of a particular race and the need for all Africans (whether from Africa or the Americas) to engage in racial self-help.

When the church first began in 1898, for example, T. B. Freeman Jr., the son of the English mixed-race pioneer of the Wesleyan Mission in West Africa, T. B. Freeman Sr., stated in Fante as well as English that the AME Zion Church "would *naturally* take a much greater interest in their missions in the Mother-land than can be possible with Missionary Board and Missionaries of an alien race."[37] In 1914, the Rev. Frank Arthur Osam-Pinanko, a graduate of Living-stone College and the first official head of the Gold Coast Zion Mission, ran an advertisement in the *Gold Coast Nation* describing its schools as "A Great Op-portunity for the Race."[38] In 1922, S. Athanasius Pomeyie, another graduate of Livingstone College and a leader of the Zion denomination in Anlo, gave prominence to the double meaning of race in a speech to a Keta Zion Mission audience as he urged them to support the mission's educational efforts. As re-ported in the newspaper the *Gold Coast Leader,* Pomeyie "compared the world to a large race course and life to a race which could be won by only the fittest. He said that the policy for the Negro race should be to train and render fit the children of to-day so that they may be able to survive the race tomorrow; that any race that will not consider the training of the rising generation as a pri-mary factor in the development work shall become inert and substantially go into extinction."[39]

Such rhetoric was common among the educated elite at this time, but how were such notions about race received by the local *non-Western-educated* pop-ulation? Did racial appeals work to galvanize communities that had already come to understand through centuries of interaction that all whites or Europe-ans were not the same?[40] How did local West Africans' own understandings of themselves—as members of particular kin groups (lineages and clans), as citi-zens of particular villages, as individuals who identified themselves with par-ticular economic occupations and social positions, as members of larger politi-cal communities with social, economic, and cultural ties to others within the region—resonate with the racial rhetoric of the AME Zion Church? If this lan-guage of race did not find immediate reception among the populations tar-geted by the educated elite of the AME Zion Church, how did they adjust their message to generate the enthusiasm they sought for this new missionary effort, especially in an area like the Anlo district, where there were at least some sur-viving traditions (like the memories of the Atorkor incident) that could be used to emphasize the existence of historic links between peoples of African descent around the Atlantic world? Answers can be found by examining the history of the AME Zion Church, particularly in the Anlo district.

*   *   *

As indicated in the previous chapter, the Zion Church came to Anlo by invitation. Impressed by news reports that it was "an entirely negro church; organized by negroes for negroes, manned, governed, controlled and supported by negro energy, intellect, liberality and contributions," the businessmen Paul Sands, E. Nelson Tamakloe, and a Keta resident from Sierra Leone, a Mr. Johnson,[41] contacted Thomas Birch Freeman Jr. and encouraged him to work with them to establish the church in Keta. Frustrated with the racial climate within the Bremen Mission and eager to expand educational opportunities in the Anlo area, they obtained support from Chiefs Nyaho Tamakloe and Joachim Acolatse to help house the church and school temporarily until more permanent accommodations could be built. Thomas Birch Freeman Jr. became their first minister and school headmaster but was soon followed by a series of ministers, both African and African American, all of whom were deeply committed to the concepts of racial uplift and self-help and regularly referred to the same in their efforts to recruit members.[42] Progress was slow, however. In the minds of most Anlos, it was the Norddeutsche Missions-Gesellschaft (the Bremen Mission) that deserved their support. In 1898, when the AME Zion Church organized its first church services and school in Keta, the Bremen Mission had already been working in the area for forty-five years. Its churches and schools had long operated with support from some of Anlo's wealthiest and most politically influential leaders in the towns of Keta, Anyako, and Woe. Many of the schools' graduates worked in the area for the Bremen Mission as teachers, evangelists, or catechists. Even in the far more numerous towns and villages that had not a single school or church, interested individuals welcomed visiting Bremen preachers. They organized their own study groups to teach each other to read and write. They held catechism classes for those interested in learning more about the new faith. They sent their children as boarders to be educated by the Bremen Mission in the towns where schools did exist. The Bremen Mission's business associate, the Bremen Trading Company, provided economic opportunities for the community that had allowed many to develop their own businesses. It was also the first to provide educational opportunities for local women.[43] The Bremen Mission was not the only competitor for the AME Zion Church, however. In 1890, eight years before the AME Zion Church expanded to Keta, the Roman Catholic Church posted two priests to the town and immediately opened an English-language school. By 1912, it had expanded its educational institutions to seven other communities in the area.[44]

In comparison with the Bremen Mission and the Catholic Church, the AME Zion Church had come late.[45] More significantly, its efforts to attract and retain members and ministers was greatly undermined by financial difficulties. As documented by Walter Yates in his history of AME Zion's missionary efforts in West Africa, local members of the church contributed in kind and in cash the land, materials, and labor on which to build the denomination's schools and churches, but these contributions were inadequate to cover the salaries of Zion's ministers and teachers.[46] Additional funds were promised and expected from the home church in the United States, but more often than not these monies never arrived. When support was provided, it often proved insufficient. As a result, quickly after its founding, the Zion Church began to lose not only ministers, members, and teachers, but it also faced ridicule in the community. In c. 1905, J. Drybauld Taylor resigned in protest over the lack of payment of his salary. His departure left the church and school without supervision for a year until the home church could transfer the African American missionary J. J. Pearce from his post in South Africa to Keta.[47] By 1912, the year when the African American missionary W. E. Shaw (who had replaced Pearce in 1909) was about to leave himself, the financial situation was as dire as it had been in 1905. In a report to the home church, Shaw noted that the Zion Church was alone among the missionary societies in failing to pay its ministers' and teachers' salaries.

With still no change by 1920, dismay and disgust with the church on the part of both the AME Zion's African members and their African American supporters reached such a level that complaints began to fill the pages of the various newspapers and journals that circulated throughout the black Atlantic. In 1920, for example, Shaw wrote to the official organ of the AME Zion Church, the *Star of Zion*, supporting Gold Coast letter writers who complained that the lack of financial support was costing them respect in the local communities in which they operated.[48] Five years later, F. A. Osam-Pinanko, one of Livingstone's first African graduates and the founder of the AME Zion Church in Cape Coast, led a group of ministers in secession from the American church.[49] Although they were convinced to return that same year, W. E. B. DuBois, founding member of the National Association for the Advancement of Colored People (NAACP) and editor of its official publication, *The Crisis,* was disturbed enough about the situation to print an editorial in 1926, a little less than a year after the crisis had ended, criticizing the church for its misguided, if well-intentioned, efforts to engage in missionary work in the first place.

> The A.M.E. Zion Church is trying to carry on missionary work in Liberia and on the Gold Coast of West Africa at the total expense of about $11,000 a year. . . . From

June 1924 to December 31st, 1925, the total expense was $21,496. Without further investigation it may be said flatly that no adequate mission work over a territory of a thousand miles or more in length, embracing between five and ten missions of people and situated three thousand miles from home base, can be carried on such a small sum of money. It means inadequate supervision, small salaries, or none and ineffective work.[50]

Especially effective in outlining the consequences of the church's financial neglect of its African missions was the secessionist leader F. A. Osam-Pinanko's own statement to the General Conference of the Gold Coast Zion Church, recorded by visiting AME bishop C. C. Alleyne and published in the *Star of Zion*.

[We] were among the first to espouse the cause of the struggling denomination. . . . Alas, [our] experience is that when [we] asked for bread, [we] were given a stone. When [we] pleaded for fish [we] were handed scorpions. [Our] prayers for tangible help brought only promises. These were observed more in the breach; they were made but to be broken. Finally goaded to desperation, [we] sent communications which were SOS signals. These were unheeded. Not even the courtesy of a reply was accorded them. . . . [We] cried out in despair, "carest thou not that we perish?" By way of answer, [we] were informed that the Mission Board had not entered into any contract with [us] and therefore owed [us] nothing. This was like piling on the agony. . . . What were [we] to do? The situation was unbearable. Debts were piling up; the preachers were being sued in the courts for the cost of the material with which they had erected school-chapels. [We] were objects of pity, ridicule and reproach.[51]

With the assistance of the Livingstone graduate and by then world-renowned J. E. K. Aggrey, the split between the Gold Coast African Methodist Episcopal Zion Church and its mother church in the United States was healed. But the infusion of financial resources that followed the reconciliation dried up shortly thereafter.[52] Problems continued.

In 1931, the British colonial government closed almost all the denomination's rural schools, and the ones in Keta were barely spared the ax.[53] In 1935, "A. Staunch Zionite" wrote to the home church to express his own great dissatisfaction with its record.

The white missionaries who began mission operations in Africa before Zion came have done more for the black man and are still doing it, they have numerous schools, both elementary and secondary, girls' training homes, seminaries for the training of teachers and ministers and industrial schools; what has Zion been able to accomplish during 37 years work in the Gold Coast—barely few schools where only elementary education is imparted, and no girls' schools therefore most girls

THE MISSIONARY SEER

HOLY BIBLE
THE MESSAGE OF
TRUTH AND SALVATION

GOSPEL LIGHT AFRICA

CHRISTIAN CIVILIZATION
KNOWLEDGE   POWER

OFFICIAL ORGAN OF DOMESTIC AND FOREIGN MISSIONS OF THE A.M.E. ZION CHURCH

Volume 31   MARCH, 1930   Number 3

SOME RESULTS OF OUR FOREIGN MISSION WORK
Reverend and Mrs. Pile appear at the right and left side of the bulletin respectively.

Published Monthly by the Department of Foreign Missions of the A.M.E. Zion Church, 1425 T Street
Northwest, Washington, D.C.

AME Zion in Keta. Photo from the *Missionary Seer* (1930).

go to attend the schools of other denominational churches and on completion of
their training become members of these churches . . .

Zionites in the United States may [also] be startled to hear that when Miss Charity Zormelo, B.Sc. a young woman from Keta . . . a Zionite by birth, who was taken to
the United States . . . for many years, returned to Africa, seeing the conditions of things

in her own Mission (Zion) she refused to teach in the Zion Mission School and joined the white Methodist Mission where she knows her pay will be sure.[54]

This particular letter is especially interesting. Many studies have commented on the fact that Western missionaries—like their colonial government counterparts at the turn of the century—engaged in fierce competition to recruit converts to their own denominations even as they attempted to lessen tensions by agreeing to work in different areas. In this letter we see this same sense of competition embraced by A. Staunch Zionite. His concerns, however, had to do with more than just a desire for the AME Zion Church to operate successfully in a crowded missionary field.[55] Weighing heavily on the minds of most Western-educated African Christians living in the Anlo district at the time was that the entire Western educational infrastructure in the region, as limited as it was, had recently been dealt a severe blow.

When World War One began in Europe, the British colonial government expelled the German missionaries associated with the Bremen Mission, who had organized the vast majority of schools operating in the Anlo area. From an educational perspective, this was disastrous. Since most of the ministerial and administrative positions had been filled with Europeans only, the expulsion forced upon the few Africans trained by the Bremen Mission as ministers the almost impossible task of managing a system over which they had little administrative experience.[56] Schools closed; teachers went unpaid. Even more disturbing was that this blow to the educational system came at a time when more and more villages were also competing among themselves to obtain the schools and churches they felt they needed to operate more effectively in the colonial world in which they now lived. It was this much broader set of concerns that probably compelled A. Staunch Zionite and others to write to the *Star of Zion* to express their concerns about AME Zion's lack of financial support for its missions on the Gold Coast and in Keta in particular. That the dire conditions faced by the congregations of the home church seem not to have tempered the criticism of these concerned Zionists is indicative of how deeply they felt their situation. For all were certainly aware, even if they read only the mission's publications, the *Star of Zion* and the *Missionary Seer,* that African Americans in the 1920s and 1930s were facing serious challenges of their own.[57]

Immediately after the war, as competition for jobs increased and returning African American soldiers began demanding respect for their sacrifices from a largely racist white public, the Ku Klux Klan exploded in membership. It organized two hundred public appearances in twenty-seven states and engaged in a reign of terror in the South, the Southwest, and the West. In the first year after the end of the war, 1919, more than seventy blacks, some returned soldiers still in uniform, were lynched. The summer of that year, known as "Red Summer," saw twenty-five race riots as whites attacked blacks on public beaches and in city streets and burned them out of their homes. The violence continued as blacks also used violence to defend themselves. Already suffering from high levels of under- and unemployment in the mid-1920s because of a recession, African Americans, including members of the AME Zion Church in the United States, faced even tougher times by the 1930s when the Great Depression forced businesses large and small to close their doors. The stress felt by all heightened tensions within the Zion Church in West Africa and the United States, as well as between the two regions. In writing to the *Star of Zion*, A. Staunch Zionite did more than express his dismay with the home church, however. He also indicated his continuing belief in race as a social category and its importance in the cause for black uplift. He goaded his racial brothers in America to do better by juxtaposing the successes of the white missionaries—their ability to pay their teachers on time, their establishment of secondary as well as elementary schools on the Gold Coast—against the AME Zion's failures to do the same. He sought to shame them by describing how a recently trained teacher, Charity Zormelo,[58] decided on her return from the United States not even to seek employment with the denomination with which she had been affiliated her entire life. Letters sent years earlier to the *Star of Zion* by Gold Coast Zion members indicated that Zormelo's decision was far from unique.[59] Racial feeling was simply not enough for many on the Gold Coast to remain members of a denomination that failed at that which other missionary societies were so successful.

Some, of course, never embraced the racial rhetoric of the church in the first place. As noted earlier and in the previous chapter, Paul Sands and other educated African citizens of Anlo found the church appealing because of their inability to counter the negative consequences of the racists attitudes held by the white missionaries, businessmen, and colonial officials with whom they worked closely. Unable to obtain the loans they needed to compete with larger European firms, stymied in their efforts to get the Bremen Mission to introduce at an earlier point in their educational curriculum instruction in the English language that was so important for conducting business in the region, having failed to persuade the Bremen Mission to be more accommodating to local cultural norms and to make available many more opportunities for higher education in the area, they looked to the AME Zion Church. The majority in Anlo, however, had no such experiences or aspirations. Their daily routines in the villages and hamlets, even in the major towns of the polity, required little direct interaction with whites. Yes, white British colonial officials had the power to and did fine and arrest. They interfered with long-held religious and cultural practices. They taxed and vaccinated despite local opposition. But their reach, even when assisted by a larger force of police and civil servants, was still quite limited. And even though all whites were called by the local term *yevu,* often translated as "cunning dog" (perhaps in reference to the distrust that characterized the Anlo's centuries-long trade relations with the Europeans), this was a term that was also used in reference to those defined as nonwhite or black in the West. Fellow West Africans, even family members, who were seen as having adopted aspects of European culture could be referred to as *yevu.* The same was true for mixed-race individuals and the many Diasporan blacks who lived in West Africa during this period. Color and culture (including oral and body language), sometimes together, sometimes separately, were the most salient characteristics the majority of Anlos used to distinguish themselves from strangers.[60] Yet race (as defined in the United States) was central to the AME Zion Church's means of distinguishing itself from the other missionary societies operating in the area. How did the local African supporters of the Zion Church deal with this? What did they do when faced with the obvious disconnect between the Zion Church's (and their own) emphasis on race and the way most Anlos used the term *yevu*? How did they adjust their rhetoric when addressing those in their communities who were unconvinced of the relevance of race in their own lives? What did they say to those who had come to believe—based on what they already knew of the relations between the local Zion denominations and their sister churches in the United States—that emphasizing racial consciousness would bring little to meet their educational needs? How did the local Ewe-speaking missionaries who traveled widely throughout the district for Zion handle these challenges: having to compete with the other missionary societies that were already well-established in the area; the meager support received from the home church; the limited extent to which race rhetoric spoke to the local population; and the precipitous decline in the size of their congregations, from a high of 9,933 in 1920 to a low of 1,771 in 1931?[61]

*   *   *

The response to the challenges faced by the Zion Church took a number of forms. Perhaps the most notable was a conscious decision taken on the part of several leaders of the Anlo Zion Church to lower expectations with regard to the support they could anticipate receiving from the home church.[62] One of these leaders was F. K. Fiawoo. A graduate of the Wesleyan Methodist schools in the Adangbe towns of Akuse and Kpong, he obtained a BA and BD in 1933 from a Presbyterian-affiliated Negro school, Johnson C. Smith University in North Carolina. On his return to the Gold Coast after graduation, he joined the AME Zion Church as pastor, presiding elder, and general manager over the Keta district (Zion's East Gold Coast Conference). He immediately threw himself into the work of recovering lost government funding for the Zion schools

Rev. F. K. Fiawoo
(right) with Rev.
Osabutey-Aguedze.

by adjusting the teachers' salaries. He instituted special classes to ordain more deacons and thereby expand the administrative capacity of the church. He requested and received additional ministerial support when the Anlo citizen and Livingstone graduate A. Amedzorgbenu Adjahoe agreed to leave his pastoral duties in North Carolina to join him in Keta. Together they considerably expanded school enrollments, held far more fund-raising events than before, and, with the assistance of Adjahoe's African American wife, Juanita, reinvigorated outreach efforts to the women of the region. In 1936, Fiawoo took a half-time leave of absence from this position to do what no other missionary in Keta had wanted or been able to do up to that point in time. He organized, in concert with his Johnson C. Smith University colleague Isaac D. Osabutey-

Aguedze, support for the founding of a secondary school in the Adangbe area where Fiawoo had completed his own early education; Fiawoo then organized another school in the town of Anloga, only six kilometers from his home village of Whuti.[63] More independently organized self-help initiatives had become the order of the day.[64]

The African ministers of the church, both in Anlo and elsewhere, did more than this, however. They also began to de-emphasize in their presentations to the local citizenry the importance of race as the basis for supporting the Zion Church, a concept that did not resonate with most of the people anyway. And it had already proved to be of limited value in obtaining the kind of support from the United States that the local congregations needed to maintain their churches and schools. Instead they highlighted the historic ties that connected Africans in West Africa with blacks in the Diaspora. These ties—defined as ones of kinship that had been severed several centuries earlier by the Atlantic slave trade—became the basis for encouraging the Gold Coast population to take a second look at the Zion Church. The many African American missionaries who had visited (and in the case of the Keta district had actually lived and worked there from 1906 through the 1930s) were not just any *yevuwo*. They were the descendants of those who had been forcibly removed from the area during the era of the Atlantic slave trade. In essence, they were kin. This was the message that resonated most with those Gold Coast citizens who operated largely within the traditional sectors of their society, as is evident from reports dating from the first two decades of the twentieth century. In 1925, for example, when C. C. Alleyne, the AME Zion bishop responsible for the church's West African missions, visited Keta and exchanged greetings with Chief Joachim Acolatse, this wealthy and influential Keta leader informed the fair-colored Alleyne that "when I saw you on Sunday [at the AME Zion Church service], I realized that we are but one family. It brought to my mind recollections of those who were carried away long years ago, and I could not but shed tears."[65]

Acolatse's remarks are particularly intriguing given that Anlo oral traditions retained memories of individuals from Atorkor who had been lost to the trade less than one hundred years earlier. But was this what Acolatse was referencing when he stated that the visiting bishop reminded him of those who had been carried away many years ago? Or was he simply alluding to the many slaves who had passed through the district from other, more distant locales? To what extent was the Atorkor incident even known outside the town in the 1920s? Its significance as a center of the slave trade had faded with the ending of the Atlantic slave trade in the early 1860s. It was never an important center for the domestic slave trade that continued in the Anlo area until at least the end of the nineteenth century, nor was it a place that had attracted any sustained interest by Bremen or Roman Catholic missionaries who might have found its oral traditions about the kidnappings worth recording and disseminating in their schools. There is no evidence, in fact, that this aspect of Atorkor history was ever mentioned in the local-language history texts used by the largest educational provider in the region, the Bremen Mission. Atorkor citizens themselves may have discussed with others this particular history while attending the cosmopolitan markets in the area or while visiting friends and relatives, but would they have connected the kidnapping of their relatives to the African American missionaries who lived in Keta? Answers to these questions remain elusive. What we do know is that the oral traditions like the one about the Atorkor kidnappings would have been particularly useful to the local ministers of the AME Zion Church. The poor reputation of the denomination in the area during the 1920s and 1930s, the push by Fiawoo and Adjahoe beginning in 1933 to reverse the church's decline, and Fiawoo's own background and interests suggest it may have been his efforts, in particular, that contributed significantly to the spread of the oral tradition well beyond Atorkor.

Born in 1891 and raised in the village of Whuti, only 1.6 kilometers east of Atorkor, Fiawoo came of age in the early twentieth century at a time when nationalism was clearly on the minds and in the hearts of many. In 1898, only eight years after his birth, the AME Zion Church established itself in Keta at the invitation of those interested in a religious organization that billed itself as a church "organized by negroes for negroes." In 1925, Fiawoo's life was touched directly by this emphasis on racial nationalism when AME Zion bishop C. C. Alleyne visited the Gold Coast and made arrangements for him and Osabutey-Aguedze to study at the Negro North Carolina school, Johnson C. Smith University. During this same period, especially prominent on the Gold Coast were the cultural nationalist ideas of the well-known Gold Coast lawyer J. E. Casely Hayford.[66] In the speeches delivered throughout the Gold Coast in the 1920s and in his book *Ethiopia Unbound,* published in 1911, Casely Hayford expressed disdain for the "bare imitator" of the West and implored the educated West African to "pursue [instead] a course of scientific enquiry which would reveal to himself the good things of the treasure house of his own nationality: his literature . . . his native tongue, . . . his manners and customs."[67] Both ideas—the AME Zion's racial nationalism and Casely Hayford's cultural nationalism—clearly resonated with Fiawoo.[68] Following Casely Hayford's insistence that it was important for Africans "to [take] command [of] the uses of his native tongue . . . to [produce] literature of his own," Fiawoo wrote in 1932 while still a student in the United States what would later become an Ewe-language classic, the play *Toko Atolia* (The Fifth Landing Stage). In this play, Fiawoo celebrated the Ewe language as it was actually spoken rather than as it was written and disseminated, in stilted form, by the Bremen Mission in their schools and churches.[69] He also used his play to respond to Casely Hayford's insistence that educated Africans should "respect the institutions and customs of [their] ancestors." In *Toko Atolia*, he extolled the value of the indigenous African legal system by describing how the Anlo practice of capital punishment worked to uphold the high moral values of the local community. He liberally sprinkled throughout *Toko Atolia* and in the two other plays he wrote subsequently, *Tuinese* (1945) and *Fia yi Dziehe* (1962),[70] local proverbs, sayings, and oral traditions to emphasize the existence and value of local wisdom in Africa itself. But *Toko Atolia* also reflected the influence racial nationalism had on Fiawoo's thinking. In this particular play, he described the plight of a young woman who had been captured by slave traders to be sold to any interested buyer. None of the potential buyers, however, was an indigenous or Euro-African slave trader even though they were just as active in the export slave trade to America as were Europeans. Rather, the girl was to be sold to a white slave trader based in Accra. Fiawoo's embrace of racial and cultural nationalism impacted more than just his literary works, however. It also affected his efforts as an educator.

In 1936, Fiawoo took a half-time leave of absence from his leadership of the Zion Church's Keta district or East Gold Coast Conference to found in 1937 his own private independent secondary school in Anloga, the New Africa University College. His dream was to provide for the first time in the region a secondary educational program that would operate according to principles defined not by an external body but rather in accordance with local Anlo and Ewe values and needs.[71] In 1940, he successfully petitioned the Anlo State Council, the traditional governing body of the polity, to tax the local population in support of the school. A year later, in 1941, he convinced the State Council "presided over by the paramount chief [to pass] a resolution in which the College was adopted as a State institution, [with] the Anlo State taking full ownership of the College." Funding, however, continued to be a problem. So in 1944, Fiawoo petitioned for and received financial support from the AME Zion Church in the United States. Thereafter, the school was known as Zion Secondary School. This change in name, however, did not alter local understandings that the school was organized to support their needs and that they had an ongoing commitment to provide funding for its operation. That such funding was still needed was evident in 1949. At that time, as reported by the visiting American AME Zion bishop H. T. Medford, "the main building of cement block . . . was two-thirds up, and the workmen still on the job. All the rooms on the first floor were in use, [but] several classes [were] being conducted under improvised shelters nearby."[72] The difficulty, however, was that opposition in Anloga and in some of the surrounding towns was growing rapidly as the local population began to rebel against the imposition of taxes, from which they saw little benefit in their own lives. It was in this context, in seeking support for his school, especially from the rank-and-file population resident in Anloga and from the nearby towns and villages in western Anlo, that Fiawoo resurrected and deployed the Atorkor history.

Zion College was portrayed as no ordinary school. It was founded by a local citizen who was intimately familiar with and respectful of the traditions and practices found in that part of Anlo. Funding came from abroad, but not from Europe or even from the descendants of those anonymous individuals who had been enslaved and shipped to America. No, support came from the descendants of their own kidnapped relatives, those who—like themselves—had been fishermen and farmers, and in agreeing to entertain the crew of a ship that had stopped off the coast of Atorkor, had been forcefully removed from their kith and kin. It was the descendants of these people, their own long-lost relatives, who were helping to help fund a "first class institution . . . for the benefit of the children of the Anlo State."[73] Given this, how could Anlo citizens themselves not also support such an endeavor? As an exhortation to the villagers in the Anloga area, Fiawoo's approach drew upon the rhetoric first deployed by the Zion Church in the late nineteenth and early twentieth centuries. Those speeches sought to distinguish the many African American missionaries and the visiting AME Zion bishops from other Westerners. But to what extent was this rhetoric effective or even known to the villagers in the Anloga area? AME Zion efforts to expand their work to the area had been unsuccessful throughout the early twentieth century. Not even the educated elite in the towns and villages of western Anlo had been supportive. Potentially more effective was a use of the traditions about the enslaved that were well-known both to Fiawoo and those who were so apprehensive about how the monies required to support the running of a secondary school would actually be used. These oral histories recorded the existence of enslaved individuals (anonymous victims of war and random violence) who had passed through the Anlo towns on their way to the European slave ships; they documented the Anlo's practice of selling to slave traders those from their own communities who had been convicted of crimes; they also recalled the Atorkor incident. In identifying African Americans as the descendants of those who had been kidnapped from the town in their very midst, Fiawoo used the history he thought would speak best to his fellow Anlo citizens as he sought their support for his school. This explains why this particular oral tradition, one that recorded an incident that was hardly unusual in the mid-nineteenth century, not only survived the ravages of time but was also remembered by others far from the site where the incident took place. As students from all over the region enrolled in his school, they were exposed to the Atorkor story reconfigured to connect Anlo citizens with their Diaspora kin. It is they who have carried the memory of this incident into the present century.[74]

CONCLUSION

Oral traditions serve a variety of purposes. They record memorable past events; they entertain; they offer lessons about life. For the AME Zion–trained minister D. K. Fiawoo and his supporters, the Atorkor oral tradition had the potential to do even more. It could become a basis for urging the citizens of Anlo to accept the financial obligation of supporting a school that had already received considerable support, both financial and inspirational, from those in America who were the descendants of their own kin: those who had been kidnapped from Atorkor and enslaved in the United States. Unfortunately, this particular effort failed. In January 1953, a riot erupted in Anloga as those opposed to the levying of the taxes that would have supported Fiawoo's school went on a rampage. The college sustained more than £2,000 in damage.[75] A temporary building that had served as an assembly hall was burnt to the ground. All the woodwork and many of the desks in the main school building suffered heavy damage. Fiawoo's own personal residences suffered as well, as noted in the AME Zion's publication the *Missionary Seer:*

> The house which Dr. Fiawoo was building for himself and family, the first story of which was finished but not occupied, was wrecked. What office furniture he had there was burned, and a large field of cassava cut to the ground. The rented house in which they were living was wrecked, [his] library was burnt, furniture damaged beyond repair, the 'well' choked with rubbish, and wife and children narrowly escaped being put to death."[76]

Deeply hurt, Fiawoo moved his school to a temporary site in Vui and only in 1967, fourteen years later, did the school return to Anloga.

In the long term, however, the efforts made by Fiawoo and his supporters made a tremendous impact on the area. In the 1980s, when I first visited the school, it had expanded to include many more buildings and students than when it was attacked in 1953; it had, in fact, become one of the top educational institutions in the region. Equally significant is that the connection Fiawoo had made between the kidnapped Atorkor citizens and their descendants as African Americans continued to live on as many Anlo citizens came to understand themselves as part of a larger black community, one that stretched across the Atlantic to the United States, where the descendants of those kidnapped from Atorkor were still living and actually returned periodically. It is this continued vitality that explains why the Atorkor incident is sometimes associated by Anlos not with Atorkor, but with Whuti, Fiawoo's hometown.[77] The connection Fiawoo and his supporters made between the kidnapped Atorkor residents and African Americans also explains an incident that I, as an African American, experienced in 1978. It was a market day in Anloga, and I had arranged to conduct an interview with a local elder at his house, not that far from the square where the market was held. As I passed the market square, several men, all of whom were inebriated to one degree or another, insisted that I stop and identify myself. They then proceeded to inform me that, no, I was not just an American researcher living in the town and conducting research on Anlo history, I was actually a descendant of people from Atorkor. They then offered to take me to the village and point out the very house from which my ancestors came. Having never heard about the Atorkor incident at the time, this came as quite a surprise. I had traveled and lived in various parts of Ghana since the mid-1970s, but this was the first time I had ever heard Ghanaians making a direct connection between African Americans and specific individuals who had once been residents of their own communities. Years later, I did indeed visit Atorkor, although the notion that the relatives of those kidnapped could still be identified proved to be apocryphal. More important, Fiawoo's emendations to the oral tradition—that African Americans were the descendants of the kidnapped residents of Atorkor—was accepted and repeated more than one hundred years later, to become the basis for local Anlos understandings of themselves as part of a larger Black Atlantic. Even though many other kidnappings had occurred during this period, it was the Atorkor incident that was recalled and reconstructed to fit the needs of more contemporary times.

9. Oral Traditions aboutIndividuals Enslaved: Preface and Texts

The oral histories and traditions presented here were recorded at different times by different individuals. The earliest account was documented by the Bremen missionary Carl Spiess in 1907. Because he collected it so close to the time of the Atorkor kidnapping, it can be considered an oral history since the elders with whom Spiess spoke probably had direct knowledge of the event. They were either children at the time or heard about the incident from their parents, who were themselves young adults when the kidnapping occurred. The other accounts included here were ones I recorded in the 1980s and can be considered oral traditions since those interviewed were far removed in time from the event. By the time these individuals had heard about the incident, many details had probably been forgotten and others probably added filler to make the story sensible and relevant to them.

Whether recorded closer to or more distant in time, the oral sources about the Atorkor kidnapping allow us to explore how and why local communities have retained memories of traumatic events from the past and who within these communities opted to retain these memories. Oral traditions and histories, however, are more than just the repositories of selective rememberings. What is recounted is also influenced by the identities of the individuals who shared their memories, the contexts in which they were recorded, and how those to whom the memories were being offered were perceived. Accordingly, I introduce each oral account with information about the individuals interviewed (where it is known) and the contexts that may have shaped the kinds and amount of information offered.

Anlo Oral Traditions about Atorkor and the Kidnapped and Enslaved Citizens of That Town

Togbi Awusu II, Chief of Atorkor: Interviewed by Sandra E. Greene
with K. A. Mensah, 29 March 1988, Atorkor

CONTEXT: *In this interview, Togbi Awusu discussed the history of the town and the role his grandfather, Ndorkutsu, played as slave trader. He was very forthcoming about this history. His willingness to speak may have been influenced by the fact that K. A. Mensah, who served as research assistant and translator, was a respected teacher in the area and that I was already known in the area as someone connected with the University of Ghana who had been collecting oral traditions and histories from many different individuals since the late 1970s. Years later, in 1992–93, when he was interviewed by Anne Bailey, he had become more circumspect as the Ghana government's focus on the European slave castles as possible sites of heritage tourism began to raise concerns about unearthing and disseminating traditions that could bring conflict between local families and well as between Africans and African Americans. While Awusu talked about it being an awful story in 1992–93, no such expressions of horror were offered in 1988. Instead, his tone in this earlier interview was quite matter-of-fact, offered with little emotion.*

In the past, Atorkor was the main trading center and we traded with the Danes. The place was formerly not under the British, but the Danes, and they brought their ships down here. The leader of this slave trade was Ndorkutsu, who was the father of Awusu and I am ruling on his stool as Awusu II. Ndorkutsu was my grandfather.

Before the slave trade started here, it was at Gbugbla [Prampram, a coastal town located west of Anlo and east of Accra]. It was transferred to this place. Ndorkutsu's brother, Gawuga, was buying a bird called *gakoe,* and another called *agbanyi.* He bought three as well as turkey and sold them at Prampram to the whites, who were slavers. They asked him if they came here, could they get them in large quantities. They asked if it was far and he said no, so they came down and when they came, they asked if they could get slaves. And that's when Ndorkutsu came in.

The Danes didn't go around to get the slaves. Rather it was the people here who sold them to the Danes. In every town they have some bad nuts. People would report them and he would send his men to get the person. Bad children were handled the same way. If a child was bad, you brought them here and sold them. Sometimes people were just captured without cause. Then the relatives would complain. If they were taken wrongly, [the Atorkor chief] Togbi Adaku would take care of the case. When they brought the slaves [to the collection centers], they were in fetters; one type was for a group of twelve, another for one. The fetters were put on the first person's neck and he carried the others on his head. When the second person was caught, they put one on his neck and that person would then carry the remaining ten. It would go on like that until you had finished. If a person proved troublesome when he arrived, they would put fetters on the ankles making them cross and holding them together so they couldn't escape. The fetters were removed after they put them on the ship.

Ndorkutsu had his own group. Besides, Ndorkutsu there was Gawuga and Gbele (Ndorkutsu's older brother). Ndorkutsu was the stronger so they all served under him. Ndorkutsu had a camp at Atsito, Atiavi, Heluvi (near Anyako), Asadame, and other areas. When they captured people, they kept them in these towns, and when they had many, they brought them here to Atorkor. At every station, the man in charge was given money to buy food to feed the slaves until they were brought here. If the ships weren't in they kept them in cells until the ships came. Ndorkutsu's slave cells were on the second floor [of his house], which was built of swish. There is a tradition that the first person to see the slave ships would be given a piece of cloth and a long-john (a large bottle with cane woven around it) or a cask of rum because they had to be loaded quickly.

In those days the Europeans were using sailing ships, *avuga*. They had so many sails. Even after the British came, they continued with the slave trade, smuggling. When the British would come, they would cut the anchor to get away quickly. We are now having trouble with those anchors interfering with the dragnet fishing. He had a camp at Atsito [where the slaves would be held] before transferring them to this place.

This [trade] continued until the Danes handed over [their trading rights and property] to the British. The British didn't like the trade so eventually they stopped it. Atorkor was the major center though and most were sent to America.

*   *   *

Togbi Tse Gbeku, Elder of the Amlade Clan: Interviewed by Sandra E. Greene with K. A. Mensah, 16 December 1987, Anloga.

CONTEXT: *Gbeku was identified by a number of elderly residents of Anloga as particularly interested in and knowledgeable about the history of the area. The interview began with queries about the history of his own clan, the Amlade, but then shifted to questions about the slave trade and slavery in Anlo.*

The slave trade began when the Danes were here. It started from Adina and Atorkor and Dzelukope. When the whites came, they saw our ancestors were interested in a type of drumming called Kpegisu. These whites invited the people to come and drum for them in their sailing ships. When the ships left, they took the people. That is how it started. It was a ploy for stealing human beings. At Adina, the whites were brought by Agbeno who was the intermediary. At Atorkor, it was Ndorkutsu.

Ndorkutsu definitely gained a lot. He would go to the interior, ask people to come and drum and the whites would take them away. He wasn't a slave trader as such; he just invited people to go to play on the boat. The whites brought rum, biscuits, and tobacco, which he used to lure the people to the boats.

* * *

Togbi Kosi Axovi: Interviewed by Sandra E. Greene with K. A. Mensah, 17 December 1987, Anloga.

CONTEXT: *Togbi Axovi was the brother of Seke Axovi, a renowned herbalist with whom I had had numerous interviews. After his brother's death, Kosi inherited Seke's clientele and had continued to provide services to those who sought indigenous medical assistance. He acknowledged that his own grandfather had been involved in the slave trade but went on to describe many others who were similarly involved in the trade in the surrounding towns, including Ndorkutsu of Atorkor.*

Ndorkutsu stayed at Atorkor. He was a wealthy trader who brought slaves from Kete Kratsi and sold them here to some of the chiefs in the area. The slaves were serving the chiefs. Some were fishing, trading, etc. Some of Ndorkutsu's main buyers were the whites. He could provide such a large number. He normally collected biscuits, gave them to the drummers, praised them, and sent them to the boats where they were taken away. Some were sent to America to work on farms.

* * *

William Tiordor Anum and Johnnie Victor Kwame Adzorlorlor: Interviewed by Sandra E. Greene and K. A. Mensah, 22 December 1987, Anloga, and 14 January 1988, Keta, respectively.

CONTEXT: *Mr. Anum was a retired history teacher living in Anloga. He was consulted at the suggestion of other elders in the town. He began by discussing the early history of his own clan, the Bate, but continued by describing the activities of some of the more contemporary members of this clan, including Ndorkutsu, who was his great-grandfather's brother. Mr. Adzorlorlor, seventy years old at the time, was interviewed separately. As a descendant, Adzorlorlor's account overlapped considerably with Mr. Anum's. They are combined here because of that fact but also because each discussed a few details not mentioned by the other.*

Our ancestors [the founders of the Bate clan] came from this town [Anloga]. When they settled here, our great-grandfather was Adeladza. The present paramount chief shares the same ancestry with me. Adeladza was a hunter and started [exploring] toward the River Volta. When he went there, he discovered an area inhabited by the original people who were here before the Anlo came. Some were thought to be spirits. One was a woman and followed him to this town. Then she vanished. He went to where he first saw her and found her. That's why she was thought to be a spirit. She was at a place now called Batefe. From the Srogboe junction toward Anyanui, you come to Dzita, then one mile further is Batefe. On their journeys to this place, my real great-grandfather noticed some groves around a pond which had fish. He established a village there and started to fish. Our great-grandmother would smoke them and bring them [here] to sell. The Akwamu would come down here and buy them. They bought them not [near their own home] on the river. Rather they would walk from Akwamu until they came to the coast. That small village became a fishing village where they would come to buy and sell. They called it *Mẹtor, mẹkor,* in Twi, I will buy and go. And it became the name of the place and was contracted into Atorkor. At that time, there was no Srogboe, no Whuti. It became a market center for Batefe and the other small villages in that area. Many moved to settle there from Anloga and that was the beginning of the village.

The population was said to have been fairly thick at that time. With the arrival of the Spanish and Portuguese, it became a trading center for them as well. Keta was big with the Danish presence, but Atorkor was next in importance. When Keta was bombarded, the people left . . . and it was desolate. Then Atorkor became the most important trading place. Later people came from Osu: the Quists, the Baetas, either the Europeans or their [African] descendants, selling their wares.

The Baetas still have a link with Atorkor. They were the first to sink wells in this area. They used barrels. They called it Baetawu or Baetawudor: Baeta's sunken well. They couldn't come to Anloga because it was taboo to wear European clothing. If they came, they would be killed, so when they traveled, they

used the beach. Most of Anloga was bush back then with the town very com-
pact. . . . No whites were allowed in the town because the [town's major] god
was white. The god rode a horse and a gown, so no one was allowed to wear
such clothing. Instead, they settled in Atorkor and Keta.

Then came the slave trade. Atorkor became one of the slave trading
grounds. The Akwamus helped a lot. Whenever they captured people, they
would sell them at Atorkor. The Adangmes also came, the Krobos, to be specific, those from Somanya. They came by the river and would sell at Ada and
Atorkor the people they had captured. There were some middlemen who bought
the slaves and sold to the whites. A special day was set for selling. Some were
whites and some were Africans; the whites were believed to be agents for their
own companies. The Africans were middlemen who bought and sold slaves.

Atorkor became an important trading place, and when people misbehaved,
they would be sold there. There was a traditional punishment called *toko atolia*.
Those who misbehaved were taken to Atorkor to be sold. The African who took
a keen interest in the trade was Ndorkutsu, a younger brother of Gbele.
Our ancestors are as follows:

Adeladza: Founder of the Bate clan
Adeladza's son: Adela Ko.
                          He used to go to Batefe with his father.
Adela Ko's son: Akume Geli
                          He founded the fishing village of Atorkor. He was my great-
                          grandfather.
Akuma Geli's
sons: Gbele
                          He was a general merchant trading in all kinds of things.
                          He was the first to go to Half Assini to get coconuts and to sell
                          coconut seedlings.
                          Ndorkutsu
                          He was younger than Gbele.
Gbele's son: Agbedanu
Agbedanu's son: Adzorlorlor
                          Our grandfather. He was a trader at places all along the
                          river with boats and wives there also. Every place where he
                          set up shop, he married a woman there, all the way to Akuse.
                          When my grandfather became wealthy, he made a stool to
                          symbolize his wealth. This was different from the war stool on
                          which they install you with a sword. The wealthy make the
                          hozi. Adjorlorlor was so wealthy he ordered a smoking pipe

from China. He was the only one who smoked the pipe and was carried around by slaves. No one ever said publicly, slaves, because it was taboo [by that time], but this is what they were secretly.

Gbele's younger brother, Ndorkutsu, took interest in the slave trade. He brought them to his house and kept them and sold them to the middlemen whites or directly to the whites. This is how the term, *ndǫkutsuviwo,* the children of Ndorkutsu, came about. All slaves were referred to as such. Ndorkutsu was the main dealer although there were smaller traders.

There was one interesting episode. Some of the whites there had an arrangement with the ships. They asked the people to come and drum, the women, children, and men. They went there, were given drinks. They got drunk and didn't realize the ship was sailing away. When this happened, the people [of Atorkor] were all offended. They didn't say anything, but they planned to retaliate. They went to the whites, not Ndorkutsu, and offered themselves for sale. Others came from the town at night and freed them after having collected the money for their compatriots. That was the retaliation. They didn't do this to Ndorkutsu because he would have been able to identify them.

After the slave trade stopped with the coming of the British, the people couldn't do anything and the trade stopped.

A Documentary Source about Atorkor
Derived from Oral Interviews

Memoir of the Days of the Slave Trade in West Africa
Missionary Carl Spiess
(1907)[1]

Translation by Rüdiger Bechstein

CONTEXT: *Carl Spiess was one of the longest-serving Bremen missionaries posted to work among the Ewe. He was also a prolific publisher of information about Ewe history and culture. His articles (which appeared in a number of different of journals between 1894 and 1933) covered a range of topics, from descriptions of the social and religious uses of various foodstuffs, to discussions about local history and legal practices, the worship of local gods, gender relations, and the meanings of Ewe place names. Typical of the times, these ethnographic descriptions also reflected his own negative attitudes about Africa and Africans. He doubted the cleanliness of Africans and advised against ordaining them as min-*

isters since no amount of training, in his opinion, could really prepare them to be an adequate replacement for himself or his fellow European missionaries. Nevertheless, because of his interest in spreading Christianity, he spent a considerable amount of time interviewing various individuals in Anlo to understand how members of this community understood their own history and culture. The excerpt below is based on interviews he had with various citizens of Anlo in the late nineteenth and early twentieth centuries about the history of the slave trade and Atorkor's role in that trade.[2]

On March 25th of this year, one century will have elapsed since the promulgation of the slave trade prohibition in the English colonies. Wilberforce pointed to this deep wound at that time. This remarkable day has been celebrated in West Africa, namely in Freetown, the capital of Sierra Leone. Yet on the Slave Coast, [this day] passed in silence even though the name of this place reminds us time and again of the terrible times, for the slave trade was carried on here the longest, secured by the dangerous ocean surf, hidden in inaccessible lagoons.

In Keta, I hinted about this remarkable deed [the abolition] in a lecture before the natives in Keta. . . . I don't have to repeat this lecture here, but it might not be without interest to take a look at the course of the slave trade, how it took place a hundred years ago and even earlier here in Keta and environs. I owe the greatest part of this information to elderly natives. One can rely on their excellent memory . . .

The Anlo District of the Slave Coast supplied a lot of slaves. Slave traders had branches in the coastal towns of Atorkor, Great Anlo, Woe, Keta-Dzelukope, Vodza, Blekusu, and Adina. The natives in the mentioned towns took many different ways to deliver the rich booty to the slave traders.

At the beginning, the Atorkor didn't buy the slaves from the interior of the country, as was the method of other towns, which then resold the slaves to the Europeans. They [the Atorkors] attacked their own tribesmen at night in the neighboring villages, caught them, and sold them at once to the slave traders. These indebted natives who had to serve the creditor [so the latter could] get [back] his money were men who had taken other men's wives, or were arrested for no special reason. At the beginning of the century, the value of a slave at Atorkor was 30 to 40 *ga* (that is 135 to 180 marks) according to their build or age.

In Atorkor, it was the Portuguese Baeta in particular who carried on a brisk slave trade. The so-called Baeta well is still in Atorkor. He had it built himself so that the slaves would not half die from thirst before they were shipped out. And the dilapidated walls of a big stone house near the well indicate that here was a place of untold misery.

When Baeta did not feel safe enough in Atorkor, he handed over the house to Chief Ndorkutsu, who also kept slaves in it until his death. Baeta fled to Blekusu, stayed there for a longer period, and founded the slave place called Gadome. Yet the English noticed him and drove him away so that he [in the end] preferred to return to his home [in Atorkor].

The walls of Baeta's slave factory in Atorkor are made from lagoon earth, blended with small shells. They show how robust such buildings are. If not, the heavy showers and storms would have already made them disappear long ago.

When the nightly assaults [against their fellow Anlos] became ineffective over the course of time, the Atorkor sold their own children to the Portuguese. If someone had two or three children, he handed over the ones who were less pleasant to him to the Portuguese. But as this did not yield enough sales for the trade, the elders of Atorkor sent messengers to the interior using bells: he who wants to earn money should bring human beings here. The white man asks for them. The Atorkor paid 30 to 60 *ga* to those in the interior, and resold them for 50 to 80 *ga,* with a profit of 20 *ga* = 20 marks.[3] Taleto near Atorkor was an important place for the embarkation of slaves. Natives told me the following: before the slaves were shipped, the Europeans took a red-hot iron and pressed it on their breasts in order to remember them and their number.

Conclusion

African narratives of slavery are rare. The continuing stigma associated with slave status, the desire on the part of the formerly enslaved and their descendants to focus not on the past but on the opportunities of the postemancipation present encouraged most to remain silent about a history that could be used by others to humiliate them. Silence was not universal, however. A few chose to record their memories. They recounted their experiences to an amanuensis or they documented them in their own diaries. They spoke with friends; they shared their recollections with family. Because they did so, we are better able to understand what Africans experienced as individuals enslaved in late nineteenth-century Africa. We can see which events they chose to remember and which they opted to forgot, why they spoke about their experiences as they did, and what experiences they preferred to consign to the recesses of their own memories. From the life history of Aaron Kuku, we know for example that he, and no doubt many others, were simply not prepared to forget their experiences as possible human sacrificial victims. Yet at the time his amanuensis recorded his life history, he would not discuss the suffering he and others had to endure on their forced march to their captor's homeland. Kuku found it especially important, however, to document the many efforts he made to reunite with his relatives and to record his successes in escaping the clutches of his enslavers. From the biographies of Lydia Yawo and Yosef Famfantor, we see how specific to each individual were the factors that led some after emancipation to return home and others to remain where they had been enslaved. Paul Sands's diary recounts in excruciating detail the anguish he felt on being continually teased because he was the descendant of a war captive, while the oral tradition from Atorkor reveals how memories of relatives kidnapped and enslaved could be passed from one generation to the next in ever expanding circles of remembering because the memories themselves served far more purposes than simply recounting past events. The texts presented and analyzed here allow us to focus on the personal and the particular. They speak about the lives of individual Africans. They help us "clothe the dry bones" of African slave studies with raiments stained with a lifetime of personal experiences. For although we know a great deal about the history of slavery in Africa, we still have precious little understanding of how individual Africans, the formerly enslaved or their descendants, experienced as well as remembered and talked about their lives. By reading biographies, autobiographies, diaries, and oral traditions that discuss the lives of specific men and women, we are better able to understand how a phenomenon that impacted so many millions was lived and remembered at the personal level.

Throughout my analyses of the five texts presented here, I have emphasized the importance of understanding them as more than simply the recording of a set of experiences. Each has been deeply influenced by a variety of factors: the decisions of the enslaved and their descendants to both remember and forget, the intentions of those who served as amanuenses, the literary and historical contexts that influenced the form and the very content of the narratives, the political concerns within particular communities that made remembering important. Equally significant for an informed reading is that all five narratives were produced by Christian missionaries, whether of African or European descent. The Bremen Mission–trained Ewe ministers G. K. Tsekpo and Samuel Quist produced the biographies of Yosef Famfantor and Aaron Kuku, respectively. Paul Sands was able to write his diary only because of his missionary education. Lydia Yawo's biography was penned by the Bremen missionary Johannes Merz, while F. K. Fiawoo, the most influential of the disseminators of the Atorkor tradition, was the product of three different missionary society's educational institutions: the Bremen Mission's Keta district elementary schools, the Wesleyan Mission's secondary schools, and the Presbyterian Church's higher educational institution in North Carolina. This connection between religious organizations and the production of narratives about slavery is far from unique. The narratives analyzed by Marcia Wright in her groundbreaking compilation of East and Central African texts, *Strategies of Slaves and Women,* were collected by a Moravian missionary. The slave narrative analyzed by Peter Haenger in his book *Slaves and Slave Holders on the Gold Coast* was produced by the Basel Mission. Missionary interest in the publication of African slave narratives was most often rooted in their desire to use the texts to solicit support for their evangelical efforts. Johannes Merz, for example, used his biography of Lydia Yawo to encourage German Pietist women to consider joining him and his Bremen Mission colleagues in West Africa as they sought to better serve their women converts. F. K. Fiawoo used the Atorkor oral tradition to urge his fellow Anlo citizens to understand the AME Zion Church as one founded by the descendants of their own fellow citizens enslaved in the United States. The West Africans who agreed to share their experiences did so, however, for their own reasons. Paul Sands wanted his descendants to be aware of their past so they could better protect their current and future social and political interests. Aaron Kuku sought to reconfigure in more positive terms both for himself and for others his reputation as a leader. The citizens of Atorkor remembered the kidnapping of their relatives, in part, because it didn't happen all that long ago, but also because it reinforced their belief that no Europeans, whether colonial officials or missionaries, could be trusted. These explanations address the individual motives of the enslaved and their descendants, and their amanuenses. But questions remain.

What allowed these individuals who had experienced enslavement to overcome the reluctance that prevented most others from speaking about their stigmatized status? Why did they opt to revive this aspect of their past at a time when they were now free? Answers to these questions can be found, in part, by examining the rhetoric about slavery deployed by the missionaries with whom many of the formerly enslaved lived and worked. If we focus specifically on the Bremen Mission, we see that this particular society refused to take a decisive stance on the issue throughout much of the nineteenth century.[1] Michael Zahn, the head of the Bremen Mission, offered theological justifications for refusing to condemn slavery, but he was almost certainly influenced by the fact that their already small West African congregations would have surely lost most of their slave-owning members if they prohibited the practice.[2] While this was the official stance of the mission, those in the field often took a much stronger position against the institution. In 1877, for example, when Noah Yawo, the husband of Lydia Yawo, whose biography is included in this study, converted to Christianity, he was publicly enjoined at his baptism to buy no new slaves, to free the children of those slaves he currently owned, and to allow his adult slaves "the opportunity to win their freedom."[3] Similarly, in 1884, when Rudolph Mallet, the first African ordained by the mission and a former slave himself, was confronted with a particularly recalcitrant slave-owning member of his congregation, he made sure to make mission headquarters aware of the extent to which slavery in West Africa could be quite cruel and inhuman. He spoke specifically about the Christian slave-owner Gideon Saba:

> One example of [Saba's] cruelty involves a slave girl named Martha who had run away because she suffered so much ill treatment and was then brought back; he flogged her so severely that she had wounds everywhere and then afterwards when he tied her up and had his wife rub her entire body with pepper, from head to foot, she nearly died. He said he could kill his slave whenever he liked and there was no one who would dare ask him about it.[4]

Mallet did more than write about this incident. He refused to allow Saba and his wife to participate in communion services and then exhorted them in public to "do better in the future."

Given the condemnation of slavery that a number of Bremen-trained missionaries directed at their Christian slave-owning co-religionists, it is likely that when these same missionaries spoke to the enslaved, they were no less condemnatory of the institution. That this was the case is evident in how a number of former slaves who converted to Christianity described those elements of the new faith that they found so compelling. In Yosef Famfantor's narrative we find sprinkled throughout his biography statements that describe slavery as a spiritual condition, not a social status. According to this perspective, even if a person was technically "free," that individual should nevertheless be considered a slave, held in bondage if he or she maintained allegiance to the false gods that required him or her to toil in fields for the devil. Only by becoming a Christian, only "by becoming a follower of Jesus," could one become "totally free," no longer stigmatized as a mere slave, taken advantage of and verbally abused. One could be accepted within the faith as an equal, since both "slaves and free people could come" to the faith; "there was no difference between them." One could even move from the status of a lowly slave to a respected leader by bringing others to Christianity. It was this missionary rhetoric that Famfantor and others embraced as they sought new ways of thinking about their identities while they simultaneously interacted with those in their communities who sought to shackle them with the stigma of their slave origins.

Not all self-identified Christians who recorded their experiences with the institutions of slavery found it necessary to embrace the rhetoric of equality before God. Aaron Kuku, for example, had no need to emphasize his equality with others. Despite being enslaved by Asante for approximately four years and then in Anfoe for another nine years, he was eventually able to return to his hometown and resume his life as a farmer. His former slave status was not seen by his fellow community members as a stain on his character. Instead they granted him grudging respect because of the knowledge and leadership abilities he claimed to have obtained during his years of enslavement. For others, the rhetoric of equality was not just ignored, it was rejected. The entries in Paul Sands's diary indicate that he was all too aware of the hypocrisy of a faith that preached equality but refused to treat African Christians as the equals of Europeans. Instead, he embraced the hierarchical frameworks that structured social relations in his own community. He then worked to reposition himself and his family at the top of that hierarchy. He insisted on distinguishing himself from those in his family who were of more recent slave origins. He reframed the ignoble aspects of his family background by acknowledging that his great-grandmother was indeed a war captive, but he insisted that she had been freed. Not only was he not a descendant of an unredeemed war captive, his family actually deserved more respect than the average citizen because of their kinship ties to the royal families of Ada and Agotime.

Whether the formerly enslaved and their descendants embraced Christian missionary rhetoric or opted instead to use other means to reposition themselves within the social and political hierarchies of their communities, mental maneuverings—establishing an identity different from those that stigmatized them as being of slave origin—were clearly important to them. A different or reconfigured framework allowed those individuals who sought to escape the stigma of their origins and experiences to reconceptualize their identities in their own minds. This in turn provided them with the foundation they needed to publicly assert themselves as dignified members of their communities, deserving of respect. Only by reading their stories can we understand how personal (as well as political, especially with regard to the Atorkor oral tradition) were the responses of those West Africans who sought to manage a history so deeply affected by slavery and the slave trade.

NOTES

INTRODUCTION

1. Narratives written by West Africans enslaved in the Americas include ones by James Albert Ukawsaw Gronniosaw, Ottobah Cugoano, John Jea, Olaudah Equiano, Venture Smith, Mahommah Gardo Baquaqua, Salim Aga, Boyrereau Brinch, John Joseph, Nicholas Said, Asa-Asa, Abu Bakr al-Siddiq, and Ayuba Suleiman Diallo. Many of these have been the subject of literary and historical studies. The narratives themselves can be found at http://docsouth.unc.edu or in Philip D. Curtin, *Africa Remembered: Narratives by West Africans in the Era of the Slave Trade* (Madison: University of Wisconsin Press, 1967).

2. Raymond Dumett and Marion Johnson, "Britain and the Suppression of Slavery in the Gold Coast," in *The End of Slavery in Africa,* ed. Suzanne Miers and Richard Roberts, 89 (Madison: University of Wisconsin Press, 1988).

3. Edward A. Alpers, "The Story of Swema: Female Vulnerability in Nineteenth Century East Africa," in *Women and Slavery in Africa,* ed. Claire C. Robertson and Martin A. Klein (Madison: University of Wisconsin Press, 1983); Marcia Wright, "Women in Peril: A Commentary on the Life Stories of Captives in Nineteenth Century East-Central Africa," *African Social Research* 20 (1975): 800–819; and Marcia Wright, *Strategies of Slaves and Women: Life-Stories from East/Central Africa* (New York: Lillian Barber Press, 1993).

4. Peter Haenger, *Slaves and Slave Holders on the Gold Coast: Towards an Understanding of Social Bondage in West Africa,* ed. J. J. Shaffer and Paul E. Lovejoy (Basel: P. Schlettwein, 2000), 181–91; John Hunwick and Eve Troutt Powell, *The African Diaspora in the Mediterranean Lands of Islam* (Princeton, N.J.: Markus Wiener, 2002).

5. Alpers, "The Story of Swema," 189.

6. Understanding African slavery from the perspective of the formerly enslaved based on their own testimonies is not easy. Very few texts exist. And those that do are often cryptic at best, recorded by European missionaries and government officials in the years immediately after abolition, not to document the workings of the institution from the perspective of the enslaved but rather to support their own goals. For missionary workers, this meant using information provided by the enslaved who had converted to Christianity to illustrate the mission's success in freeing the enslaved from the bondages of both slavery and heathendom. For government officials, this meant collecting just enough information to help them determine what to do with the enslaved they encountered and whether or not to prosecute their masters.

7. Audrey A. Fisch, "Introduction," in *The Cambridge Companion to the African American Slave Narrative,* ed. Audrey A. Fisch, 11–27 (Cambridge: Cambridge University Press, 2007).

8. William L. Andrews, "The Representation of Slavery and the Rise of Afro-American Literary Realism, 1865–1920," in *Slavery and the Literary Imagination,* ed. Deborah E. McDowell and Arnold Rampersad, 66, 68–69 (Baltimore: Johns Hopkins University Press, 1989).

9. The importance of exploring the contexts that influenced the production of slave narratives has been emphasized by a number of scholars. For representative discussions of these issues, see John W. Blassingame, ed., *Slave Testimony: Two Centu-*

ries of Letters, Speeches, Interviews and Autobiographies (Baton Rouge: Louisiana State University Press, 1977), xvii–lxv; and Paul D. Escott, *Slavery Remembered: A Record of Twentieth-Century Slave Narratives* (Chapel Hill: University of North Carolina Press, 1979), 3–17.

10. Wayne C. Booth, "The Rhetoric of Fundamentalist Conversion Narratives," in *Fundamentalisms Comprehended*, ed. Martin E. Marty and R. Scott Appleby, 372 (Chicago: University of Chicago Press, 1995).

11. On the format of the typical captivity narrative, see "The Slave Narrative," at http://www.wsu.edu/~campbelld/amlit/slave.htm. The classic study on captivity narratives is Alden T. Vaughan and Edward W. Clark, *Puritans among the Indians: Accounts of Captivity and Redemption, 1676–1724* (Cambridge, Mass.: Belknap Press, 1981). Since this book was published many others have also studied captivity narratives and have begun to challenge the notion that the captivity narrative is quintessentially American. They have done so by exploring the development of this genre in Europe long before it came to the Americas in the late seventeenth century and its continued popularity through the nineteenth century not only in the United States but also in Britain and in continental Europe. See, for example, Paul Baepler, *White Slaves, African Masters* (Chicago: University of Chicago Press, 1999); Joe Snader, *Caught between Worlds: British Captivity Narratives in Fact and Fiction* (Lexington: University of Kentucky Press, 2000); and Linder Colley, "Perceiving Low Literature: The Captivity Narrative," *Essays in Criticism* LIII, no. 3 (2003): 199–218.

12. Kuku's narrative actually appears in two different German-language versions, both published by Paul Wiegräbe. One appeared in the Bremen Mission's monthly journal, and as indicated by its title is reportedly a transcript of what Kuku actually said. This, in fact, is not true. Although it mirrors in large detail the original Ewe-language text composed by Samuel Quist—who is never acknowledged as the actual author of the narrative—Wiegräbe did make some small but significant changes. See Paul Wiegräbe, "Aus dem Leben aus des Afrikanischen Evangelisten Aaron Kuku-von ihm selbst erzählt," *Monatsblatt der Norddeutschen Missionsgesellschaft* 91 (1930): 51–57, 67–71, 186–89, 214–17. Wiegräbe also published a much abbreviated (and an even more seriously rewritten and edited) version of Kuku's narrative in pamphlet form. See Paul Wiegräbe, *Vom Sklaven zum Freigeborenen: Ein Lebensbild aus Westafrika* (Bremen: Bremen Mission-Schriften, 1930).

13. Werner Ustorf, *Bremen Missionaries in Togo and Ghana, 1847–1900* (Accra: Asempa Pub., 2002), 442, 467–68, 314, 349–83.

14. On Quist's role in the African-led church after the expulsion of the German missionaries, see Hans W. Debrunner, *A Church between Colonial Powers: A Study of the Church in Togo* (London: Lutterworth Press), 165.

15. On the clash during the interwar period between African and European ideas about educational goals for the Ewe-speaking areas that had been the site of Bremen Mission activity, see Ustorf, *Bremen Missionaries*, 471–72.

16. Quist and Tsekpo were probably inspired to take this particular approach by the cultural nationalist ideas of the late nineteenth- and early twentieth-century local political activists J. E. Casely Hayford and S. R. B. Attoh Ahuma. For although these individuals operated largely in the British colony of the Gold Coast, their ideas circulated widely throughout West Africa and were readily accessible to individuals like Quist and Tsekpo, who—if not literate in both English and German as well as in Ewe—would have still heard about these ideas from their interactions with family and friends who lived in the Ewe-speaking coastal area that was part of the Gold Coast. For more on Casely Hayford, see chapter 8. For more on Attoh Ahuma, see chapter 8, note 13. Note that while Quist remained committed into the 1920s and 1930s to working within

the boundaries of the Christian faith, Casely Hayford had long abandoned his trust in the ability of Christianity to bring development and respectability to the continent. On Casely Hayford's turn away from this faith, see David Kimble, *A Political History of Ghana: The Rise of Gold Coast Nationalism, 1850–1928* (London: Oxford University Press, 1963), 166.

17. On the limited attention to these questions by scholars of African slavery, see Dennis Laumann, "Laumann on Wright," unpublished paper.

18. John Sekora, "Black Message/White Envelope: Genre, Authenticity, and Authority in the Antebellum Slave Narrative," *Callaloo* 32 (1987): 510.

19. Sekora, "Black Message/White Envelope," 117.

20. Angelo Constanzo, "The Narrative of Archibald Monteith, A Jamaican Slave," *Callaloo* 13, no. 1 (1990): 118.

21. Constanzo, "The Narrative," 120, 127.

22. Dwight McBride, *Impossible Witnesses: Truth, Abolitionism, and Slave Testimony* (New York: New York University Press, 2001), 1–7.

23. Dan Doll and Jessica Munns, "Introduction," in *Recording and Reordering: Essays on the Seventeenth and Eighteenth Century Diary and Journal*, ed. Dan Doll and Jessica Munns, 9–21 (Lewisburg, Pa.: Bucknell University Press, 2006); Felicity Nussbaum, *The Autobiographical Subject: Gender and Ideology in Eighteenth-Century England* (Baltimore: Johns Hopkins University Press, 1989), 23–29.

24. Other West African examples of communities' memories commemorating the loss of citizens captured and enslaved are discussed in Sandra E. Greene, "Oral Traditions about Individuals Enslaved," in *African Sources on Slavery and the Slave Trade*, ed. Sandra E. Greene, Martin Klein, Alice Bellagamba, and Carolyn Brown (forthcoming).

1. ENSLAVEMENT REMEMBERED

1. Quist's manuscript was never published, but it can be found in the Bremen Staatsarchiv: 7, 1025–30/1. An edited version of this life history was published in two different forms by Bremen missionary Paul Wiegräbe. See his "Aus dem Leben." A second version, much fictionalized and reduced in size to pamphlet form, appeared as *Vom Sklaven.*

2. Much has been written on the 1869–71 Asante invasion of the territories east of the Volta, but perhaps the most detailed discussions can be found in Marion Johnson, "Ashanti East of the Volta," *Transactions of the Historical Society of Ghana* VIII (1965): 33–59; and Donna J. E. Maier, "Asante War Aims in the 1869 Invasion of Ewe," in *The Golden Stool: Studies of the Asante Center and Periphery*, ed. Enid Schildkrout, 232–323 (New York: American Museum of Natural History, 1987).

3. F. A. Ramseyer and J. A. Kühne, *Four Years in Ashantee* (New York: Robert Carter and Bro., 1875); Jules Gros, *Voyages, Aventures et Captivité de J. Bonnat chez les Achantis* (Paris: E. Plon, Courrit et Cie., 1884). See also Adam Jones, "'Four Years in Asante': One Source or Several?" *History in Africa* 18 (1991): 173–203, who discusses some of the problems with the English version of Ramseyer and Kühne's book. I use this version nevertheless given the lack of problems Jones notes with the passages I use. For the complete writings of Bonnat about his travels in West Africa, see Marie-Joseph Bonnat, *Marie-Joseph Bonnat et les Ashanti: Journal, 1869–1874*, ed. Claude-Hélène Perrot and Albert Van Dantzig (Paris: Société de Africanistes, 1994).

4. Wright, *Strategies*; Alpert, "The Story of Swema."

5. Debrunner, *A Church*, 97; Birgit Meyer, "Translating the Devil: An African Appropriation of Pietist Protestantism, The Case of the Peki Ewe in Southeastern Ghana,

1847–1992" (PhD diss., University of Amsterdam, 1995), 64. There were in fact so many converts after the war that new missions and out-stations proliferated rapidly thereafter: Kpenoe (1880); Gbadzeme (1881); Peki (1883); Anfoe and Vakpo (1888); Amedzofe (1890); and in present-day Togo, Tove (1893); and Agu Nyogbo (1895).

6. The first Ewe-language biography appears to have been written by Pastor Andreas Aku, who attended, as did Samuel Quist, the Ewe School in Westheim, Germany. He was ordained in 1910, served as head of the Bremen Mission in Lomé, and then became the first president of Ewe Evangelical Church when it became independent from the Bremen Mission in 1922. He published a biography of Helen Ayiku in 1909. Nothing seems to have been produced after this until 1929 and 1930. See Bremen Staatsarchiv: 7, 1025-29/5-30/1, for a list of Ewe-language biographies and autobiographies.

7. On the features of the standard conversion narrative as well as the particularities that characterized the conversion experience as written by Pietists (the form of Christianity practiced by those associated with the Bremen Mission and its descendant, the Ewe Evangelical Church, with whom Kuku was associated), see D. Bruce Hindmarsh, *The Evangelical Conversion Narrative: Spiritual Autobiography in Early Modern England* (Oxford: Oxford University Press, 2005), 7 and 57–59. For an example of a conversion narrative by a Bremen missionary in particular, see Meyer, *Translating*, 18–25. See also Elizabeth Reis, "Seventeenth Century Puritan Conversion Narratives," in *Religions of the United States in Practice, Volume One*, ed. Colleen McDannell, 22–31 (Princeton, N.J.: Princeton University Press, 2001); and Chanta M. Haywood, *Prophesying Daughters: Black Women Preachers and the Word, 1823–1913* (Columbia: University of Missouri Press, 2003), 34–50. On captivity narratives, see note 11 in the introduction.

8. Some of these tales can be found in Diedrich Westermann, *A Study of the Ewe Language* (London: Oxford University Press, 1930).

9. Carl Spiess, "Wie bestimmt der Evheer die Zeit," *Quartalblatt der Norddeutschen Missions-Gesellschaft* 2 (1894): 1–7.

10. Diedrich Westermann, *Ewefiala or Ewe-English Dictionary* (Berlin: Dietrich Reimer, 1928), 58; and on the use of the moon for calculating the passage of time, see 96. Similar "traditional" forms of calculating time among other African groups are discussed in Claudia Zaslavsky, *Africa Counts: Number and Pattern in African Culture* (Boston: Prindle, Weber and Schmidt, 1973), 62–64; 93–97. See also Ivor Wilks, *Forests of Gold: Essays on the Akan and the Kingdom of Asante* (Athens: Ohio University Press, 1993), 196–99.

11. James Olney, "'I Was Born': Slave Narratives, Their Status as Autobiography and as Literature," in *The Slave's Narrative*, ed. Charles T. Davis and Henry Louis Gates Jr., 149 (New York: Oxford University Press, 1985).

12. Many of the identified passages in Kuku's narrative come from the book of Psalms. They enjoin the reader to both praise God and to thank him for deliverance from a history of past difficulties. For a literary exegesis on the Psalms, including those cited by Kuku, see Bruce M. Metzger and Michael D. Coogan, eds., *The Oxford Companion to the Bible* (New York: Oxford University Press, 1993), 627–28.

13. Lynne Brydon, "Resettlement in Eastern Ghana: The Aftermath of a Pre-colonial Holocaust" (unpublished paper delivered at the 2003 African Studies Association annual meeting in Boston, Massachusetts).

14. On the killing of Ewe citizens in Kumase in 1900, see "Lichsrahlen aus dem Dunkel einer Heidnischen Mordthat in Ho," *Monatsblatt der Norddeutschen Missions-Gesellschaft* 12, no. 11 (1900): 92–93. On Asante attitudes toward strangers during this period, see Thomas J. Lewin, *Asante before the British: The Prempean Years, 1875–1900* (Lawrence: The Regents Press of Kansas, 1978), 216–22.

15. See Ustorf, *Bremen Missionaries*, 477–79, f. 29.

16. Jealousy was especially common in communities like Petewu, where the population had developed a system of social ethics that emphasized the importance of limiting differences in wealth accumulation.

17. This approach was deeply influenced by how the Ewe interpreted the Pietist ideas promoted by both the German missionaries still operating in the area and the local Ewe ministers. For a discussion of these Pietist ideas, see Birgit Meyer, *Translating the Devil: Religion and Modernity among the Ewe in Ghana* (Edinburgh: Edinburgh University Press, 1999); on the frustrations felt by local Ewe ministers with the continuing involvement of Christian converts in traditional beliefs and practices, see Elias Awuma, "Reste des heidentums in der christlichen Gemeinde," *Monatsblatt der Norddeutschen Missions-Gesellschaft* 88 (1927): 11.

18. Meyer, *Translating*, 86, 89.

19. Ibid., 89, 84, 99, and 97.

20. I would suggest that his detailed discussion of the actions he took when he suspected his wife did not die a natural death was also intended to reinforce his identity as a leader, in this case, of his family. He was prepared to take whatever action necessary to avenge the death of his wife.

21. Arthur Knoll, *Togo under Imperial Germany, 1884–1914: A Case Study in Colonial Rule* (Stanford, Calif.: Hoover Institution Press, 1978), 82.

22. On the migration of Africans from German Togo to the Gold Coast because of excessive labor demands, see Arthur Knoll, "Taxation in the Gold Coast Colony and in Togo: A Study in Early Administration," in *Britain and German in Africa*, ed. Prosser Gifford and William Roger Lewis, with the assistance of Alison Smith, 418–53 (New Haven, Conn.: Yale University Press, 1967); and D. E. K. Amenumey, "German Administration in Southern Togo," *Journal of African History* 10, no. 4 (1969): 623–39.

23. Paul John Eakin, *Fictions in Autobiography: Studies in the Art of Self-Invention* (Princeton, N.J.: Princeton University Press, 1985), 5.

24. Kratsi and its twin trading town of Kete emerged as a booming trade center in the late 1870s. See Donna Maier, "Competition for Power and Profits in Kete-Krachi, West Africa, 1875–1900," *International Journal of African Historical Studies* 13, no. 1 (1980): 33–50. It is possible that the owner of Kuku's mother moved to the town to take advantage of the new trade opportunities that had opened up with the British conquest of Kumase, since this freed those in Kratsi and the other Volta River towns to engage in the trade of a much greater variety and quantity of goods.

25. Similar efforts to reunite with lost relatives were taking place at exactly the same time in the United States with the abolition of slavery. See Leon F. Litwack, *Been in the Storm So Long: The Aftermath of Slavery* (New York: Random House, 1979), 229–47.

26. See chapter 6 on the life of Paul Sands, whose ancestors engaged in these kinds of efforts.

27. Far more is known about the efforts of former slaves in the United States to reconnect with lost family members. See, for example, Litwack, *Been in the Storm*, 229–47. There has been virtually no analysis, however, of the larger social context that may have produced more concern about certain relations but not others. What does exist in the African history literature tends to focus on whether or not slaves remained with their masters or migrated elsewhere either for new economic opportunities or to establish with other former slaves their own communities. The situation in what is now Ghana is discussed in Dumett and Johnson, "Britain and the Suppression," 3–68.

28. J. Spieth, "Von den Evhefrauen," *Quartal-blatt der Norddeutschen Missions-Gesellschaft* 4 (1889): 1–8.

29. On European images of "savage" women lacking maternal instincts, capable of eating, killing, or giving away their own children, see Felicity A. Nussbaum, *Torrid Zones: Maternity, Sexuality, and Empire in Eighteenth-Century English Narratives* (Baltimore: Johns Hopkins University Press, 1995), 50–52.

30. *Monatsblatt der Norddeutschen Missions-Gesellschaft* 20, no. 240 (1870): 1082.

31. *Monatsblatt der Norddeutschen Missions-Gesellschaft* 20, no. 239 (1870): 1077–78.

32. Ramseyer and Kühne, *Four Years*, 30, 31, 33, 65.

33. Ibid., 81, 83.

34. "Die Unruhen in Anglo-Gebiet," *Monatsblatt der Norddeutschen Missions-Gesellschaft* 3 and 4 (1885): 44–45.

35. John Illife, *Honour in African History* (Cambridge: Cambridge University Press, 2005), 71, 74, 87.

36. See Sandra E. Greene, *Gender, Ethnicity and Social Change on the Upper Slave Coast: A History of the Anlo Ewe* (Portsmouth, N.H.: Heinemann, 1996), 85–86.

37. Ivor G. Wilks, *Asante in the Nineteenth Century* (Cambridge: Cambridge University Press, 1975), passim; Maier, "Asante War Aims," 241.

38. Cynthia R. Pfeffer, *The Suicidal Child* (New York: Guilford Press, 1986), 13, 37.

39. See also http//www.cdc.gov/ncipc/dvp/Suicide/Suicide-def.htm.

40. On suicide attempts by those Africans being shipped to the Americas, see Robert Harms, *The Diligent: A Voyage through the Worlds of the Slave Trade* (New York: Basic Books, 2002), 261–62.

41. Samuel Ajayi Crowther also remembers considering suicide, as his 1841 autobiography indicates. His thoughts were prompted by his fear of being separated from his master and her son to be sold to the "Portuguese." See J. F. Ade Ajayi, "Samuel Ajayi Crowther of Oyo," in *Africa Remembered: Narratives by West Africans from the Era of the Slave Trade*, ed. Philip D. Curtin, 306–308 (Madison: University of Wisconsin Press, 1967).

42. On Asante views of suicide in the late nineteenth and early twentieth centuries, see R. S. Rattray, *Ashanti Law and Constitution* (New York: Negro University Press, 1911/1969), 299–301.

43. On how the Ewe in the area where Kuku came from viewed suicide and handled funerals for suicide victims, see Jakob Spieth, *Die Ewe Stämme* (Berlin: Dietrich Reimer, 1906), 272–77; and Matthaus Seeger, "Er soll die Straken zum Raube haven," *Monatsblatt der Norddeutschen Missions-Gesellschaft* 8, no. 9 (1896): 66–69.

44. Vera Lind, "The Suicidal Mind and Body: Examples from Northern Germany," in *From Sin to Insanity: Suicide in Early Modern Europe*, ed. Jeffrey R. Watt, 67, 75–77 (Ithaca, N.Y.: Cornell University Press, 2004).

45. Meyer, *Translating*, 25.

46. For a similar analysis of suicidal ideation as a nineteenth-century Christian conversion trope, see Haywood, *Prophesying Daughters*, 42.

47. Johnson, "Ashanti," 54. Note that the date of 1877 refers to the time a Mr. Dobson was said to have been traveling on the Volta River. In her "Ashanti East" article, Johnson gives the date of 1875 but appears to correct this with the revised date of 1877 as noted in Marion Johnson, "M. Bonnat on the Volta," *Ghana Notes and Queries* 10 (1968): 6.

48. On the Wusuta incident, see Wilks, *Asante*, 84–86; and Maier, "Asante War Aims," 237 and 240 (who lists other groups who suffered the same fate as the Wusutas).

49. Johnson, "M. Bonnat on the Volta," 8.

50. "Die Unruhen," 45.

51. "Lichsrahlen," 92–93. See also J. Spieth, "Reschtanschauungen der Eweer in Süd-Togo," *Koloniale Rundschau* 4 (1912): 345.

52. The widespread use of Akan names and words, as well as the development of certain political and military institutions among the northern Ewe, is often attributed to the influence of the returnees from Asante and Akwamu. See, for example, Kofi Baku, "The Asafo in Two Ewe States," *Transactions of the Historical Society of Ghana, New Series* 2 (1998): 21–28.

53. Wiegräbe, *Vom Sklaven*, 4–5.

54. Kwame Arhin, "The Ashanti Rubber Trade with the Gold Coast in the Eighteen-Nineties," *Africa: Journal of the International African Institute* 42, no. 1 (1972): 33, 36–37. For a more general discussion of the rubber trade, see Raymond Dumett, "The Rubber Trade of the Gold Coast and Asante in the Nineteenth Century: African Innovation and Market Responsiveness," *Journal of African History* 12, no. 1 (1971): 79–101. For information on the rubber trade in German Togoland (where Kuku lived after his escape) see Knoll, *Togo*, 150–52.

55. On Kuku's involvement in the rubber trade and his donation of three hundred marks, see the popularized version of Kuku's life that missionary Paul Wiegräbe published as a pamphlet *Vom Sklaven*. The information included therein incorporated this additional information about Kuku obtained from other ministers, both local and European, who knew him.

2. THE LIFE HISTORY OF AARON KUKU

1. Maier, "Asante War Aims," 237–38.

2. A. Wicke, "Die Blattern-Erkrankungen an der Westküste von Afrika, speziell im deutschen Togo-Gebiet," *Mitteilungen von Forschungsreisenden und Gelehrten aus den deutschen Schutzgebieten* 4 (1891): 184–88.

3. Maier, "Asante War Aims," 241.

4. See the map titled "Wege-aufnahmen in dem Gebiet der Deutschen Station Mishahoehoe ausgefürht von Hauptman von Francois, Premier Lieut. Herold und dem Planzer F. Goldberg," found in *Mitteilungen von Forschungsreisenden und Gelehrten aus den Deutschen Schutzgebieten*, V, 1890. The estimate of the number of houses in Petewu was made by Prem. Lieut. Herold, who passed through the village in his 1890 journey from Lomé to the interior of Togoland. See as well the map titled "Karte des Südlichen Teiles von Togo," published in *Mitteilungen von Forschungsreisenden und Gelehrten aus den Deutschen Schutzgebieten*, IX, 1896.

5. Translator's note: The silk-cotton tree is called ʷu-ti in Ewe.

6. Editor's note: The gender of the sibling is not specified and there is no indication in the original text as to whether the sibling was a boy or girl. I have edited the translation to indicate that Adanuvor was a girl, since preparing rice was traditionally a task assigned to girls, unless there were none in the household. The first person to translate this text from Ewe into German, Paul Wiegräbe, made the same decision.

7. Editor's note: Newborns were usually given a name only on the eighth day after their birth. Because the child died before this eighth day, the parents had not yet named the baby. Kuku makes reference to the fact that the Ewes in his area had not yet adopted the Akan day names to indicate that he also did not know what her Akan day name would have been.

8. Editor's note: Oil palms produce a nut that is processed to make palm oil, a substance used locally in food preparation and for fuel in oil lamps. By this date, 1870, there was also considerable demand in Europe for palm oil as well as palm kernel oil as a lubricant. Oil palms produce palm wine. To extract this substance, the tapper would have employed a process still in use today: "the tapper will first fell the tree. . . . They then cut a hole just below the crown of the fallen tree, creating a well in its trunk. At

the bottom of this well they punch a small hole right through the tree. A collecting pot is then placed underneath. The hole is fired to encourage the free flow of liquid from the tree. This is done using a large staff of tightly wrapped palm fronds, slowly burning at one end . . . finally, large leaves are placed over the top of the well to stop rain and insects from entering. When the tapper returns to collect the wine he will bore a new section inside the well. Fire is used once more and the process begins all over again. The tree is tapped continually until it produces no more wine." http://www.winesoftheworld.com/news/static/article_268.asp.

9. Editor's note: The meaning of this passage is unclear. Kokoro may have been one of the leaders of the three divisions that initially attacked the Ewes, or he could have been the leader of a division that was called to war as part of a third call-up of troops.

10. Editor's note: A sheep would have been offered for the average person, but because he was a man of stature, a military leader, it was appropriate to offer something more substantial, in this case a human sacrifice. Normally, a war captive belonging to the deceased would have been used for this purpose, but evidently because he was not a chief, he had not been allocated any by the chief under whom he had served.

11. Editor's note: Oaths served a variety of purposes in Asante. In this particular case, an oath was sworn to bring a case to the attention of the authorities that they might not normally hear. See Rattray, *Ashanti Law*, passim.

12. Editor's note: *Apā* is a fetter made of solid iron rather than of chain links.

13. Translator's note: This is a line from a Presbyterian hymn.

14. Editor's note: In the German translation of this text, Wiegräbe indicates that Salaga, a major trade town north of Asante, is used here as a way to refer to the realm of the dead. See Wiegräbe, "Aus dem Leben," 69. A similar practice exists among nineteenth- and early twentieth-century Anlo-Ewes. In their cultural discourse the town of Cotonu in the present Republic of Benin was often identified as the place of the dead.

15. Translator's note: The tradition at a palm wine drinking place is that after drinking, you pour the dregs on the ground. This is done in a special way to make a specific sound. Anyone who succeeded in doing this is congratulated with the expression *Eḍo afe*, meaning "you have reached home."

16. Translator's note: *Fufu* is a meal prepared by pounding boiled cassava and plantain or yam or cocoyam in a special mortar. It was originally a staple food of the Akans but has now become a popular food among most ethnic groups.

3. TO STAY OR GO

1. When the enslaved in Asante sang songs in praise of their royal masters, for example, they often composed songs that could also be interpreted as quite critical. Women enslaved in Anlo were remembered as regularly working harder to please their husband/masters than free wives and then manipulating their husband's affections to obtain an inheritance larger than that of the free wives. For additional examples of how African slaves responded to their situation, see Akosua Adoma Perbi, *A History of Indigenous Slavery in Ghana* (Accra: Sub-Saharan Pub., 2004); Jonathan Glassman, *Feasts and Riot: Revelry, Rebellion, and Popular Consciousness on the Swahili Coast, 1856–1888* (Portsmouth, N.H.: Heinemann, 1995); Frederick Cooper, *Plantation Slavery on the East Coast of Africa* (Portsmouth, N.H.: Heinemann, 1997); Martin Klein, *Slavery and Colonial Rule in French West Africa* (Cambridge: Cambridge University Press, 1998); various articles in Suzanne Miers and Richard Roberts, eds., *The End of Slavery in Africa* (Madison: University of Wisconsin Press, 1988); Paul Lovejoy, ed., *The Ideol-*

ogy of Slavery in Africa (Beverly Hills, Calif.: Sage, 1981); Claire Robertson and Martin Klein, *Women and Slavery in Africa* (Madison: University of Wisconsin Press, 1983); and Pier M. Larson, *History and Memory in the Age of Enslavement* (Portsmouth, N.H.: Heinemann, 2000).

2. Klein, *Slavery,* 173; J. S. Hogendorn and Paul E. Lovejoy, "The Reform of Slavery in Early Colonial Northern Nigeria," in *The End of Slavery in Africa,* ed. Suzanne Miers and Richard Roberts, 396 (Madison: University of Wisconsin Press, 1988).

3. Dumett and Johnson, "Britain and the Suppression," 89.

4. See Martin A. Klein, "Slave Resistance and Slave Emancipation in Coastal Guinea," in Miers and Roberts, *The End,* 203–219.

5. Miers and Roberts, *The End,* 33.

6. These issues and questions are drawn from a number of studies on biography, including Paula R. Backscheider, *Reflections on Biography* (Oxford: Oxford University Press, 1999), 3; Lindage Wagner-Martin, *Telling Women's Lives: The New Biography* (New Brunswick, N.J.: Rutgers University Press, 1994), 9; and Catherine N. Parke, *Biography: Writing Lives* (New York: Twayne Pub., 1996), xiii–xiv.

7. Efforts to avoid feuds involved fines or procedures that gave the family of the victim the right to inflict the same punishment using the same kind of weapon that the perpetrator inflicted on the victim. If, for example, a family was informed that one of its members had committed a murder with a gun, they would hand over the perpetrator to the family of the victim. The perpetrator would then be killed using the gun in the same way he had killed the victim. See Ernst Henrici, "Das Volksrecht der Epheneger und sein Verhältniss zur deutsche Colonisation im Togogebiete," *Zeitschrift für Rechtswissenschaft (Stuttgart)* II (1898): 146–47. See also Madeline Manoukian, "The Ewe Speaking People of Togoland and the Gold Coast," in *Ethnographic Survey of Africa,* ed. Daryll Forde, 38 (London: International African Institute, 1952).

8. On the racial attitudes found in nineteenth-century Germany, see Lisa Marie Gates, "Images of Africa in Late Nineteenth and Twentieth Century German Literature and Culture" (PhD diss., Harvard University, 1996); Hans Werner Debrunner, *Presence and Prestige: Africans in Europe—A History of Africans in Europe Before 1918* (Basel: Basler Afrika Bibliographen, 1979), 351–57. On attitudes within the Bremen Mission, see Ustorf, *Bremen Missionaries.*

9. This quote comes from the conversion narrative penned by the nineteenth-century Bremen missionary Jakob Spieth and is described as typical of those that all applicants wrote before being accepted as missionary trainees by the Bremen Mission. See Meyer, *Translating,* 19–21. On the Puritan precursors of the nineteenth-century Pietist conversion narrative, see also Reis, "Seventeenth Century Puritan Conversion Narratives," 22–24.

10. Booth, "The Rhetoric," 371–72.

11. For a fuller discussion of the influence of the captivity narrative format on Merz's biography, see the introduction to this study.

12. This upsurge in interest in Christianity after the 1870s, especially among the central Ewe-speaking peoples, is most often attributed to the many hardships that the Ewe experienced as one disaster after another overwhelmed the area in ways that the local priests could neither control nor adequately explain: an earthquake in 1862; a smallpox epidemic that erupted sometime between 1862 and 1869; and a devastating war that lasted from 1869 until 1871, followed by a famine.

13. For an indication of the significantly fewer women and girls affiliated with the mission even after the 1870s, when interest in conversion significantly increased among the Ewe, see Ustorf, *Bremen Missionaries,* 204–210. On the history of the conversion of

African women by the Bremen Mission in the town of Amedzofe, see Lynne Brydon, "A 'Religious Encounter' in Amedzofe: Women and Change through the Twentieth Century," in *Christianity and Social Change in Africa: Essays in Honor of J. D. Y. Peel*, ed. Toyin Falola, 471–88 (Durham, N.C.: Carolina Academic Press, 2005).

14. Prior to and after the publication of Merz's biography of Lydia Yawo, various missionaries penned a number of reports about Lydia, as well as her husband, Noah. See for example, Frau Illg, "Was Frau Illg von Ho erzählt," *Quartal-Blatt der Norddeutschen Missions-Gesellschaft* 74 (1875): 404–410; Letter from Stephan Kwami to Reverends and dear Gentlemen, 14 April 1883, Bremen Mission House, Ho-Statsarchiv, Bremen: 7, 1025–12/2.

15. It is because of the biographical elements included in his text that we can begin to hear Lydia herself.

16. For more information about Tsekpo, especially on his political work in the 1950s, see Kate Skinner, "Reading, Writing and Rallies: The Politics of 'Freedom' in Southern British Togoland, 1953–1956," *Journal of African History* 48 (2007): 123–47. About his life before the 1950s, little is known beyond the fact that he came from the Ewe-speaking town of Alavanyo and was known in central Eweland as "a German scholar" who had learned English. In other words, he received his education in the German schools run by the Bremen Mission prior to their expulsion by the British from the area with the outbreak of World War One. After the war ended, the League of Nations granted Britain the right to administer the western areas of German Togo as a mandated territory. Those who had been educated in German and Ewe were given an opportunity to learn English so as to continue to operate as a local educated elite. Some took advantage of this opportunity. Others did not. Tsekpo clearly did. He served as an elementary school teacher in the British-supervised schools that were once managed by the Bremen Mission but which were taken over by the Ewe church as local African ministers assumed control of all the works formerly run by the Bremen Mission. See Kate Collier, "Ablode: Networks, Ideas and Performance in Togoland Politics, 1950–2001" (PhD diss., University of Birmingham, 2003), 95–97, 109–115, 206–208. He was also probably ordained after 1936 since his name does not appear in the Bremen's list of Ewe ministers who were operating in the area by that date. See A. W. Schreiber, *Bausteine zur Geschichte der Norddeutschen Missions-Gesellschaft* (Bremen: Verlag der Norddeutschen Missions-Gesellschaft, 1936), 253.

17. On the history of early European funerary sermons, see Larissa Juliet Taylor, "Funeral Sermons and Orations as Religious Propaganda in Sixteenth Century France," in *The Place of the Dead: Death and Remembrance in Late Medieval and Early Modern Europe*, ed. Bruce Gordon and Peter Marshall, 224–39 (Cambridge: Cambridge University Press, 2000). See also pages 2–4, 12–16, and 29–30 in John M. McManamon, *Funeral Oratory and the Cultural Ideals of Italian Humanism* (Chapel Hill: University of North Carolina Press, 1989). On German discursive funerary practices among Moravian missionaries in East Africa, see Wright, *Strategies*, 23–24. Such writing traditions among the Bremen Pietists were known as memorial writing ("Gedächtnisschrift" in German). The first Bremen-trained Ewe minister to publish such a work was Andreas Aku. He was not only a religious leader in Lomé, Togo, affiliated first with the Bremen Mission and then with the Ewe Evangelical Church after it became independent in 1922, he was also a prominent leader of the business and political community in Lomé. It was he who authored the first two known memorial biographies, one of Christian Aliwodzi Sedode and the other on the life of Helena Ayiku, in 1909. The Sedode biography, written in German, was subsequently published with minor revisions by A. W. Schreiber under the title, *Lehrer Christian Aliwodzi Sedode, 1857–1907: Worte zu dessen Gedächtnis* (Bremen: Verlag der Norddeutschen Mission-Gesellschaft, 1908). I have not

seen the Ayiku biography, but the title, "Nkudozinya le Helene Ayiku nuti, 1851–1908. Enlola enye Andreas Aku, Lome, 1909," is on the list of Lebensbeschreibungen found in the Bremen Staatsarchiv: 7, 1025: 29/5–30/1. For more information on Aku, see Debrunner, *A Church*, passim; and Ustorf, *Bremen Missionaries*, passim, as well as information provided by his son in D. Westermann, "Martin Akou, de Lomé au Togo: Actuellement Étudiant en Médicine a Bale," in *Autobiographies d'Africaines*, ed. D. Westermann, 282–336 (Paris: Payot, 1943); and a biography about his life written by Pastor Robert Baeta, *Pastor Andreas Aku: Präses der Ewe-Kirke—50 Jahre Missonsdienst in Togo* (Bremen: Verlag der Norddeutschen Missions-Gesellschaft, 1934).

18. For a brief comparative description of the funerary practices of Ewe Christians and traditional believers as reported by a Bremen missionary, see Hedwig Rohns, "Sterben von Christen und Heider," *Monatsblatt der Norddeutschen Missions-Gesellschaft* 1 (1896): 7.

19. Kofi Anyidoho, "Death and Burial of the Dead: A Study of Ewe Funeral Folklore" (MA thesis, Indiana University, 1983), 96–100.

20. See Claude-Hélène Perrot and Albert van Dantzig, eds., *Marie-Joseph Bonnat et les Ashanti: Journal—1869–1874* (Paris: Société de Africanistes, 1994), 70–113; and "Völlingen Zerstörung unsrer Station Wegbe," *Monatsblatt der Norddeutschen Missions-Gesellschaft* 19, no. 225 (1869): 1006.

21. Spieth, *Die Ewe*, 53/54. In her article "Ashanti East of the Volta," 48, Marion Johnson indicates that the people of Ho reoccupied their town by 1876. Prior to that they were living in close proximity to it. The Ho king moved from Takla, which was about six and a half kilometers from Ho, to establish a number of farm villages outside of Ho at Yanyame. In 1873 the king moved to Agotime. In the meantime, many others had already returned to their farms surrounding Ho, including a number of Christians. See *Monatsblatt der Norddeutschen Missions-Gesellschaft* 20, no. 233 (May 1870): 1044; and Spieth, *Die Ewe*, 46/47–53/54. See also Bremen Staatsarchiv: 7, 1025–7/7: Aaron Onipayede, Waya, Letter to the Bremen Mission, ?Anyako.

22. They did so particularly to the male children because they suspected them of being spies for their fathers. Bremen Staatsarchiv: 7, 1025–12/2: Stephen Kwami to Mission House, Ho, 14 April 1883.

23. Attacks were directed against the citizens of particular polities because of their actions in the war, but travel in general was also simply unsafe. Bandits took advantage of the unsettled state of the region to rob travelers of their possessions and to kidnap and sell the women and children they encountered. See E. B. Asare, "Asante, Akwamu-Peki Relations in the Eighteenth and Nineteenth Centuries" (MA thesis, University of Ghana, 1973), 97–98, for a detailed description of the situation. Perhaps the most well known of these revenge attacks involved the town of Kwawu-Dukoman, an Asante ally some ninety-six kilometers from Taviefe. According to the historian H. Debrunner, the town "was completely destroyed and its inhabitants were either taken captive or killed. Only a remnant was able to escape." The polity of Teteman, about eighty kilometers north of Taviefe, also found itself completely isolated after the war. Towns in the immediate area forbade their citizens to have any social intercourse with them at all because Teteman residents had acted as guides, showing the Asante how best to attack their mountainous neighbor, Bowiri. Debrunner, *A Church*, 17, 18.

24. The people of Ho had only recently returned to their farm villages by May of 1872 after staying for a period of time in Agotime. They too were suffering from hunger. See Bremen Staatsarchiv, 7, 1025–7/: Aaron Onipayede, Waya, Letter to the Bremen Mission, ?Anyako.

25. On the legal position of enslaved women and their children among the Ewe, see H. Seidel, "Pfandwesen und Schuldhaft in Togo," *Globus* LXXIX, no. 20 (1901): 310,

n. 10; and Lieutenant Herold, "Bericht betreffend Rechtsgewohnheiten und Palaver der deutschen Ewe-Neger," *Mittheilungen von Forschungsreisenden und Gelehrten aus den Deutschen Schutzgebieten* V (1892): 168–70.

26. See Herold, *Bericht*, 168.

27. Safer travel began to emerge only in the 1880s. In 1884, a British envoy traveled with a number of prominent Anlos and a Bremen missionary to broker peace between Anlo, Ho, and Taviefe. For the most detailed description of this meeting, see "Die Unruhen," 42–46. In 1886, the British brokered a treaty between Anlo and Agotime, and they also signed a treaty of protection with Peki and a number of other polities in the region. All these treaties required the signatories to recognize British authority and to keep the trade roads open. See ADM 11/1/1107: Treaty of Peace and Friendship between Awoonah and Agotime, Quitta, 10 March 1886; and C. W. Welman, *The Native States of the Gold Coast: History and Constitution* (London: Dawsons of Pall Mall, 1969; Part One on Peki first published in 1925), 15. Hostilities emerged periodically nevertheless. In 1875 and 1888 war broke out involving Taviefe in conflict with Peki and Ziavi, respectively. Both had to do with continuing anger and sensitivities about the roles of these parties in the 1869–71 war.

28. The religious practices used by the Asante against the British are discussed in Wilks, *Asante*, 238–42, 506. Much of the emphasis by Wilks is on the Asantehene's consultations with Muslim advisors, but from Famfantor's account it is clear that at least equal attention was given to Asante's traditional religious priests.

29. The term *ɔkra* was used in this way in the late nineteenth and early twentieth centuries. See R. S. Rattray, *Religion and Art in Ashanti* (Oxford: Oxford University Press, 1927), 154. But it also referred to the soul in the context of the belief that the human soul exists prior to birth and continues to exist after death. See Rattray, *Religion*, 153–54.

30. On the events surrounding this death, see Wilks, *Asante*, 506. For background on the conflicts between the British and Asante during this period and for information on the general atmosphere in the capital that saw extreme food shortages, the muzzling of opposition, the suppression of news about the war in the south, and the murder of political opponents, see Lewin, *Asante before the British*, 41–47.

31. See Robin Law, "Human Sacrifice in Pre-colonial West Africa," *African Affairs* 84, no. 334 (1985): 53–55; Lewin, *Asante before the British*, 177–82; and Edmund Collins, "The Panic Element in Nineteenth Century British Relations with Ashanti," *Transactions of the Historical Society of Ghana* V, p. 2 (1962), 92–98.

32. Wilks, *Asante*, 638–43.

33. See Lewin, *Asante before the British*, 64–66; and Thomas C. McCaskie, "Death and the Asantehene: A Historical Meditation," *Journal of African History* 30, no. 3 (1989): 417–44.

34. The first two quotes in this passage, beginning with "a foreign-born slave" and "the real price" respectively are from Thomas McCaskie, *State and Society in Pre-Colonial Asante* (Cambridge: Cambridge University Press, 1995), 98; the last quote, beginning with "stigma of slavery" comes from A. Norman Klein, "The Two Asantes: Competing Interpretations of 'Slavery' in Akan-Asante Culture and Society," in *The Ideology of Slavery in Africa*, ed. Paul E. Lovejoy, 156 (Beverly Hills, Calif.: Sage Publications, 1981).

35. Wilks, *Asante*, 290–91, 280–81.

36. Jack Goody, "Introduction to Ashanti and the Northwest," in *Research Review—Supplement: Ashanti and the Northwest*, ed. Jack Goody and Kwame Arhin (University of Ghana, Institute of African Studies, 1965), 39.

37. Others who were known to trade from Cape Coast to Bonduku included a number of Asantes resident at the coast, Adu Gyasi, and the cousins of Asantehene Karikari, as well as people from the Asante province of Assin. According to their oral traditions, they purchased the same kinds of commodities mentioned by Famfantor (cloth, tobacco, and salt as well as guns and gunpowder) to trade in Bonduku. See Kwame Arhin, *West African Traders in Ghana in the Nineteenth and Twentieth Centuries* (New York: Longman, 1979), 9; and K. Y. Daaku, *Oral Traditions of Adanse* (Legon: Institute of African Studies, University of Ghana, 1969), passim. See also Dumett and Johnson, "Britain and the Suppression," 82–83, who comment on the continuing existence of the slave trade after 1875 in those districts like Assin that were part of the protectorate by that time, but which were on its periphery.

38. For a discussion of the civil wars in the northwest, which appear to have begun in 1878, the issues at stake, and the players involved, see Goody, "Introduction to Ashanti and the Northwest," 44–48. On the imposition of trade blockades, a consequence of the civil wars, and their impact on traders on the coast, see Arhin, *West African Traders*, 32. On the history of the market at Kintampo, see Arhin, *West African Traders*, 43–44.

39. For a discussion of and review of the debates about the use of slave labor in kola production, see Edmund Abaka, *Kola Is God's Gift: Agricultural Production, Export Initiatives and the Kola Industry of Asante and the Gold Coast, c. 1820–1950* (Athens: Ohio University Press, 2005), 112–19. See also Larry Yarak, "West African Coastal Slavery in the Nineteenth Century: The Case of the Afro-European Slaveowners of Elmina," *Ethnohistory* 36, no. 1 (1989), which mentions slaves being trained in carpentry, masonry, boat-handing, livestock rearing, coopering, and blacksmithing and used for work that required these skills. He also discusses their use in the production of cotton and coffee as commercial crops in the early nineteenth century.

40. Slave masters often preferred their slave children to their own sons and daughters because they could do as they wished with the former, but had to consult their own children's maternal uncle before pawning them. Rattray, *Ashanti Law*, 40.

41. The first three proverbs come from R. Sutherland Rattray, *Ashanti Proverbs: The Primitive Ethics of a Savage People* (London: Oxford University Press, 1916), 122, 128, and 121 respectively. The last proverb is from J. G. Christaller, *Three Thousand Six Hundred Ghanian Proverbs from the Asante and Fante Language* (Lewiston, N.Y.: Edwin Mellen Press, 1990), 288.

42. On normative social and legal practices among the northern Ewe, see Henrici, "Das Volksrecht," 135–36.

43. According to A. K. P. Kludze, *Ewe Law of Property* (London: Sweet and Maxwell, 1973), 61, if a northern Ewe child chose to affiliate with its maternal rather than its paternal family, it was most often under the influence of the child's mother.

44. On the inheritance of widows among the Ewe, see H. Klose, "Religiöse Anschauungen und Menschenopfer Togo," *Globus* (Braunschweig) LXXXI, no. 12 (1902): 190; and Henrici, "Das Volksrecht," 135.

45. See Herold, "Bericht," 161–62.

46. Other practices used to protect a person from the spirit of a deceased relative among the Ewe included burning strong-smelling plants and carrying a club during the mourning period. See Klose, "Religiöse," 190.

47. At the same time, in 1868, when the Asantes traveled to Wusuta, they had already begun to position troops in Akwamu. See "Anyako," *Monatsblatt der Norddeutschen Missions-Gesellschaft* 18, no. 215 (1868): 961; and "Anyako," *Monatsblatt der Norddeutschen Missions-Gesellschaft* 19, no. 220 (1869): 983.

48. These were the same tactics that Asante troops used when interacting with the Ewe communities with whom they were allied, the Anlo and the Adaklus. See "Anyako" (1869), 983; and "Der Ashanti-Krieg," *Monatsblatt der Norddeutschen Missions-Gesellschaft* 19, no. 226 (1869): 1010–11; and J. Merz, "Die Ashanteer in Waya," *Monatsblatt der Norddeutschen Missions-Gesellschaft* 20, no. 239 (1870): 1077–78.

49. Seidel, "Pfandwesen," 311.

50. On the rights of pawns among the northern Ewe in the mid-nineteenth to early twentieth century, see Seidel, "Pfandwesen," passim.

51. Rattray, *Ashanti Law*, 291, 323. See also John Mensah Sarbah, *Fanti Customary Laws: A Brief Introduction to the Principles of the Native Laws and Customs of the Fanti and Akan Districts of the Gold Coast* (London: Frank Cass, 1897/1968), 39.

52. On the *sunsum*, see Rattray, *Religion*, 154–55. On the fear of a husband's spirit in the event of a divorce and the responsibilities of fathers among the Akan, see Rattray, *Ashanti Law*, 9.

53. Rattray, *Ashanti Law*, 261.

54. *Royal Gold Coast Gazette and Commercial Intelligencer:* see reports printed in the 1823 issues of this paper on 21, 28 January; 18 March; 15 April; 6 May; 14, 21 June; 9, 16, 23, 30 August; 3 September; 25 October; 8, 22, 29 November; 13 December 1823. According to Rattray, *Ashanti Law*, 261, this war was waged because of the Wusuta's refusal to send troops to fight in Gyaman. Carl Reindorf, *History of the Gold Coast and Asante* (Basel, Missionsbuchhandlung, 1895), 311, asserts, however, that the Asantes invaded to assist the Akwamu who had been attempting to subdue the Ewe-speaking polities since they moved east of the Volta in 1730.

55. On those both assisting and opposing the Asantes in the Katamanso war and on the war itself, see Reindorf, *History*, 202–18.

56. E. Y. Aduamah, *Traditions from the Volta Basin (9): Ewes in the Afram Plains* (Legon, University of Ghana: 1965), 5.

4. COME OVER AND HELP US!

These dates are based on those found in the following primary and secondary sources: "Aus dem Innern," *Monatsblatt der Norddeutschen Missions-Gesellschaft* 23, no. 266 (1973): 1207–1208; "Völligen Zerstörung unsrer Station Wegbe," *Monatsblatt der Norddeutschen Missions-Gesellschaft* 19, no. 225 (1869): 1006; "Der Krieg," *Monatsblatt der Norddeutschen Missions-Gesellschaft* 20, no. 231 (1870): 1036; "Der Krieg," *Monatsblatt der Norddeutschen Missions-Gesellschaft* 20, no. 233 (1870): 1044; "Aus Afrika," *Monatsblatt der Norddeutschen Missions-Gesellschaft* 20, no. 236 (1870): 1062; "Der Afrikanische Krieg," *Monatsblatt der Norddeutschen Missions-Gesellschaft* 20, no. 238 (1870); Letter from Stephen Kwami to The Mission House, 14 April 1883: Bremen Staatsarchiv, 7, 1025–12/2; Letter from Aaron Onipayede to The Bremen Mission at Waya, 25 May 1872: Bremen Staatsarchiv: 7, 1025–7/7; *Royal Gold Coast Gazette*, 1823; Gros, *Voyages*, 106–107; ADM 39/5/73: Ho District Record Book, 40a, 231; Asare, "Akwamu-Peki Relations," 74–75; Welman, *The Native States*, 9–15; Gershon A. Sorkpor, "The Role of Awuna in the Triple Alliance Formed by Ashanti, Akwamu and Awuna during 1867–1874" (unpublished paper, Institute of African Studies, University of Ghana, Legon, 1966), 4; Josef Reindorf, "Ho und Taviewe," *Monatsblatt der Norddeutschen Missions-Gesellschaft* 25 (1875): 1364–65; Johann Daniel Illg, "Tafiewe und Ho," *Monatsblatt der Norddeutschen Missions-Gesellschaft* 25 (1875): 342–44.

1. ADM 39/5/73: Ho District Record Book, 1915, 232.

2. Translator's note: King James Bible, The Acts of the Apostles. 16:9: "And a vision appeared to Paul in the night; There stood a man of Macedonia, and prayed to

him, saying, Come over into Macedonia, and help us." http://king-james-bible.classic-literature.co.uk/the-acts-of-the-apostles/ebook-page-16.asp.

3. Translator's note: King James Bible, The Epistle of Paul the Apostle to the Romans. 3:15–18: "Their feet are swift to shed blood: 3:16 Destruction and misery are in their ways: 3:17 And the way of peace have they not known: 3:18 There is no fear of God before their eyes. http://king-james-bible.classic-literature.co.uk/the-epistle-of-paul-the-apostle-to-the-romans/ebook-page-03.asp.

4. Translator's note: the word "Mohrenland" quite literally means, "Land of the Moors." However, the expression is also used in the Old Testament for the land of Cush (located along the Nile). See in particular Isaiah 20:3–5.

5. Translator's note: from Acts 16:14.

6. Translator's note: Colossians 2:6.

7. Translator's note: Revelation 14:13. "Blessed are the dead who die in the Lord from now on."

8. Translator's note: Habakkuk 2:3, King James Version. http://www.biblegateway.com/passage/?search=Habakuk%202%20;&version=9.

5. *YOSEF FAMFANTOR*

Text from London: Longmans, 1948.

1. Editor's note: If Tskepo is correct in stating that Famfantor was about seven years old when the earthquake of 1862 occurred, Famfantor's year of birth would have been c. 1855, not 1851.

2. Editor's note: The correct date for this earthquake is 1862.

3. Editor's note: The Asante province of Nsuta and Wusuta had had contact with each from at least 1826, when the Nsutahene attacked Wusuta in that year for failing to send troops to Asante when the latter attacked Gyaman in 1816 and 1817. Wusuta and the other Ewe polities west of the Volta freed themselves of external control by Asante and its ally, Akwamu, in 1833. See Wilks, *Asante*, 173, 700.

4. Editor's note: A *hotu* is fifty strings of cowries with forty cowries to a string, a total of two thousand cowries. For more information on local cowry currencies among the Ewe and their equivalents in German marks at the beginning of the twentieth century, see Barbara Ward, "The Social Organization of the Ewe-speaking People" (MA thesis, University of London, 1949), 38.

5. Editor's note: Given the correction in his birthdate, Famfantor would have actually been about sixteen years old.

6. Editor's note: For more on Adu Bofo, see the Asante Collective Biography Project: Career Sheet—ACBP/2: Adu Bofo.

7. Editor's note: On the duties of the *ahenkwa*, their ambitions and opportunities for wealth and their self-image, see McCaskie, *State and Society*, 35, 83–84, 285–86.

8. Editor's note: This incident appears to have occurred in 1873. In that year, the British government—traditionally hostile to the Asante state—assumed control of the Dutch forts on the Gold Coast. Asante military forces that had been dispatched to the coast were withdrawn by Asantehene Kofi Karikari as he began to rely more on religious advisors on how best to avert the disaster that loomed as Asante confronted the British and their now unprecedented ability to deny Asante the weapons (previously purchased without difficulty from the Dutch) it needed to defend itself. Any ritual killings that may have been ordered by the Asante's religious advisors were also supplemented by the ritual sacrifices that were ordered on the death of the Asantehene's brother. See Wilks, *Asante*, 238–42; and Jones, "Four Years in Asante," 188–93.

9. Editor's note: According to Westermann, *Dictionary*, 121, these were made of either beans or plantain.

10. Editor's note: Mossi refers to the Mossi of present-day Burkina Faso. The term Grushi, also known as Grunshi, refers to decentralized communities that lived in what is now northern Ghana and southern Burkina Faso. According to Glenna Case, this is the area to the north and west of the confluence of the Kulpawn and White Volta Rivers and is bounded by the Mossi to the north, the Lobi country to the northwest, the Wa District to the southwest, and Gonja to the south. It also included the Kusasi area to the east of this area. For a discussion on the slave raiding in this area that produced so many slaves in the eighteenth and nineteenth centuries, see Glenna Case, "Wasipe Under the Ngbanya: Polity, Economy, and Society in Northern Ghana, Volumes I and II" (PhD diss., Northwestern University, 1979).

11. Editor's note: Given the earlier incorrect calculations about Famfantor's age (see notes 1 and 2), Famfantor would have actually been about sixteen in 1871.

12. Editor's note: On the wide circulation of Ewe textiles throughout the Gold Coast and Asante during this period, see Malika Kraamer, "Ghanaian Interweaving in the Nineteenth Century: A New Perspective on Ewe and Asante Textile History," *African Arts* 29, no. 4 (2006): 36–53, 93–95.

13. Editor's note: A demijohn is a large narrow-necked bottle of variable size, usually encased in wickerwork.

14. Editor's note: This is an Ewe term meaning military commander, borrowed from the Akan term *asafohene*. The suffix, *ga*, literally means big or the senior.

15. Editor's note: The British abolition of slavery and the domestic trade in slaves occurred in 1874.

16. Editor's note: The newborn baby was determined to be the reincarnation of his elder deceased brother.

17. Editor's note: The correct date is 1862.

18. Editor's note: Since the Basel Mission reported active work in Anfoe, Botoku, and Vakpo from 1888, one can assume that Famfantor had returned to Wusuta around this date. On Basel Mission activity in the mentioned three towns, see *Vierundsiebenzigster Jahresbericht der Evangelische Missions-Gesellschaft zu Basel*, I July 1889, p. xli.

19. Editor's note: The village of Botoku's first contacts with the Basel Mission probably came in 1882 and then in 1884 when the African Basel missionary David Asante was traveling through the area to encourage the local chiefs to consider hosting a catechist and/or a teacher. See David Asante, "Eine Reise nach Salaga und Obooso durch die Länder des mittlercrn Voltaflusse," Basel Mission Archives, Basel, Switzerland: D-10.S,7.

20. Editor's note: This visit occurred most likely in 1889. Peter Hall was the son of John and Mary Hall, two of the Jamaicans who were recruited for missionary work on the Gold Coast by the Basel Mission in 1843. For more information on the Jamaicans, see Dorothey Dee Vellenga, "Jamaican and Swiss-German Missionaries in the Basel Mission in the Gold Coast in the Mid-Nineteenth Century: Racial and Ethnic Conflict in a Christian Missionary Community," paper presented at the Annual Meeting of the African Studies Association, 1983 (available from the Schomberg Center for Research in Black Culture); and Peter A. Schweizer, *Survivors on the Gold Coast: The Basel Missionaries in Colonial Ghana* (Accra: Smartline Publishing, 2000), 50–53. On Peter Hall, see his autobiography, *Autobiography of Rev. Peter Hall: First Moderator of the Presbyterian Church of Ghana* (Accra: Waterville Pub. House, 1965).

21. Editor's note: According to D. Westermann, *Dictionary*, 2, this was a type of venereal disease.

22. Editor's note: The mentioned Otu was Cornelius Otu. Preparation for baptism took about twelve months. See Ustorf, *Bremen Missionaries*, 457, n. 4, who describes

the preparation time common for the Bremen Mission, which operated along the same lines as the Basel Mission. Given this fact and the date of his baptism in 1890, Famfantor probably began his catechism lessons in 1889. The Basel Mission was also interested at that time in establishing an elementary school in Botoku as early as 1888, when some residents first expressed interest in hosting a resident teacher as opposed to simply a catechist. At the time, however, the chief was concerned about the impact such a school would have on belief in the local god and its priest, a woman who was deeply hostile to the mission. See Paul Jenkins, "Abstracts of the Basel Mission, Gold Coast Correspondence" (Legon, 1970), 247.

23. Editor's note: Basel missionary Gottfried Martin was posted to Anum and worked in the area between 1890 and 1893 and then again from 1896. See *Jahresbericht* (1891) xliii; (1892) xliii; (1893) under the subtitle Goldküste-Anum; (1894) under the subtitle Goldküste-Anum; and (1897) under the subtitle Goldküste-Anum.

24. Editor's note: The first mention of a Basel school in Botoku and Wusuta is in the mission's yearly report for 1903 when the two towns were listed together as having nineteen students. See *Jahresbericht* (1894) under the subtitle Goldküste-Anum Anum and (1904), 119.

25. Editor's note: I have been unable to locate this particular document. Gottfried Stoevesandt was the inspector or head of the Bremen Mission from 1927 to 1933. He traveled to the then British Togoland in 1927–28. It would have been in that period that he met Famfantor. See Eva Schöck-Quineros and Dieter Lenz, eds., *150 Jahre Norddeutsche Mission, 1836–1986* (Bremen: Norddeutsche Mission, 1986), 141, 398–99.

6. OPEN SECRETS AND SEQUESTERED STORIES

1. Bayo Holsey, *Routes of Remembrance: Refashioning the Slave Trade in Ghana* (Chicago: University of Chicago Press, 2008), 74. Observations about the silences that surround domestic slavery as well as the slave trade in West Africa can be found in Martin Klein, "Studying the History of Those Who Would Rather Forget: Oral History and the Experience of Slavery," *History in Africa* 16 (1989): 209–217; Ralph Austen, "The Slave Trade as History and Memory: Confrontations of Slaving Voyage Documents and Communal Traditions," *The William and Mary Quarterly*, 3rd Ser., 58, no. 1 (2001): 229–44; and Rosalind Shaw, *Memories of the Slave Trade: Ritual and Historical Imagination in Sierra Leone* (Chicago: University of Chicago Press, 2002).

2. Holsey, *Routes*, 78.

3. Holsey also cites an instance of an individual who admitted being of slave origin, and she presents a particularly insightful analysis of why that person would be prepared to discuss their origins, but her principal informants are descendants of slave owners.

4. On the use of diaries by Pietists, see Stephan F. Miescher, "My Own Life: A. K. Boakye Yiadom's Autobiography—The Writing and Subjectivity of a Ghanaian Teacher-Catechist," in *Africa's Hidden Histories: Everyday Literacy and Making the Self*, ed. Karin Barber, 31 (Bloomington: Indiana University Press, 2006). Diaries written in the late nineteenth and early twentieth centuries by Africans that have been edited and introduced for use by historians include James H. Vaughn and Anthony H. M. Kirk-Greene, eds., *The Diary of Hamman Yaji: Chronicle of a West African Muslim Ruler* (Bloomington: Indiana University Press, 1995); and Adam Jones and Peter Sebald, eds., *An African Family Archive: The Lawsons of Little Popo/Anecho (Togo), 1841–1938* (Oxford: Oxford University Press, 2005). On early modern Western diary writing more generally, see Dan Doll and Jessica Munns, eds., *Recording and Reordering: Essays on the Seventeenth and Eighteenth Century Diary and Journal* (Lewisburg,

Pa.: Bucknell University Press, 2006); and Nussbaum, *The Autobiographical Subject,* 23–29.

5. Karin Barber, "Introduction: Hidden Innovators in Africa," in *Africa's Hidden Histories: Everyday Literacy and Making the Self,* ed. Karin Barber, 8 (Bloomington: Indiana University Press, 2006).

6. Ruth Watson, "'What is our intelligence, our school going and reading of books without getting money?' Akinpelu Obiṣẹsan and His Diary," in *Africa's Hidden Histories: Everyday Literacy and Making the Self,* ed. Karin Barber, 56 (Bloomington: Indiana University Press, 2006). See also Olufunke Adeboye, "Reading the Diary of Akinpelu Obisesan in Colonial Africa," *African Studies Review* 51, no. 2 (2008): 75–97.

7. Watson, "Akinpelu Obiṣẹsan and His Diary," 70, 71.

8. The name Paul Sands, whose diary is the subject of this study, is a pseudonym, as are the names Elijah Sands (Sands's father), Ama (Sands's mother), and Yao Mensah (Sands's maternal uncle). Although the use of pseudonyms is unusual in historical studies, it was deemed appropriate in this case given the general sensitivity about revealing the identities of those of slave origin in Ghana and given the particular concerns by Paul Sands's descendants that others in their community might use this historical information to harm their current social and political status. I have placed all events in the town of Keta, although this was not the hometown of Sands and his family. I have used the true names of most of the individuals with whom Sands and his family interacted (all of whom did operate in Keta) so that interested parties will be able to verify the accuracy of the actual events discussed. In keeping with my desire to protect their privacy, I have also omitted in the notes those sources about the life and work of Sands and his family that could be used to identify them.

9. Sands also never expressed any anxiety about his ability to handle the financial and political roles he had defined for himself. This was the case even though a British colonial officer stationed in Ada described Sands in a December 1904 letter to the secretary of native affairs as "an unsuccessful trader" and that "his only source of income [was] from his connection to the stool of Avenor." The officer wrote this after hearing with alarm that the chief of Avenor had handed over to Sands "full control of all stool lands [in] Avenor [with Sands having] received half of the profits of the land." See ADM 11/1/1113. See the author for additional information on this source. It is highly unlikely, however, that this was Sands's only source of income. He was known to have owned land in Keta and also was manager of his uncle's property, which was considerable. These comments about Sands should probably be understood as an example of the general hostility to "educated natives" that came to the fore at the end of the nineteenth century, when the British colonial government began to focus more on founding its indirect rule policy on the authority of local political leaders.

10. The term "mulatto" is used here because it is the term Sands used for himself and others. As noted by the historian Ray Dumett, this term did not refer exclusively to those of mixed parentage (African and European) but also was applied to those who adopted European names because of their affiliation with the European traders who operated on the coast. See Raymond Dumett, "African Merchants of the Gold Coast, 1860–1905: Dynamics of Indigenous Entrepreneurship," *Comparative Studies in Society and History* 25, no. 4 (1983): 669, n. 23. Other scholars, notably George Brooks and Roger Gocking, have opted to use the term EurAfricans or Euro-Africans, respectively, to emphasize the extent to which such individuals were culturally more connected to their home communities and cultures in Africa than in Europe. See George E. Brooks, *Eurafricans in Western Africa: Commerce, Social Status, Gender and Religious Observance from the Sixteenth to the Eighteenth Century* (Athens: Ohio University Press,

2003), xxi; and Roger Gocking, *Facing Two Ways: Ghana's Coastal Communities under Colonial Rule* (Lanham, Md.: University Press of America, 1999), 7. I do the same. See also John Parker, "*Mankraloi*, Merchants and Mulattos—Carl Reindorf and the Politics of 'Race' in Early Colonial Accra," in *The Recovery of the West African Past: African Pasts and African History in the Nineteenth Century—C. C. Reindorf and Samuel Johnson*, ed. Paul Jenkins, 31–47 (Basel: Basler Afrika Bibliographien, 1998).

11. See Greene, Field Notes 78: Interview with Dzobi Adzinku, 20 January 1988, Anloga. See as well Sorkpor, "The Role of Awuna," 12.

12. Parliamentary Papers, 1875 (London: Harrison and Sons, 1875): Correspondence relating to the Queen's Jurisdiction on the Gold Coast and the Abolition of Slavery within the Protectorate. Governor Strahan to Earl of Carnarvon (Received December 3, 1874), 25–26.

13. Prosecutions of individuals involved in slave trading and pawning and the abolition of slavery in the Keta area began in 1876, just two years after the abolition decree. These prosecutions could not have escaped the notice of the largest slaveholders since one of the most prominent cases in 1876 involved Amegashie, a particularly influential individual in Keta. Prosecutions continued in the 1880s with quite a few cases being brought to court in 1885. The prosecution of slave and pawning cases in Keta continued up to at least 1896. See ADM 41/1/2: passim; ADM 41/4/1–2: passim; and ADM 4/1/26: D. C. Kwitta to Acting Colonial Secretary, 17.6.96. On the kinds of adjustments in their business practices made by chiefs and so-called native merchants and educated natives in the coastal towns on the Gold Coast, see Susan B. Kaplow, "The Mudfish and the Crocodile: Underdevelopment of a West African Bourgeoisie," *Science and Society* XLI, no. 3 (1977): 317–33; and Dumett, "African Merchants," 661–93. These two articles focus largely on elites in Accra and Cape Coast. No comparable study has been made of those in Keta, although they too invested heavily in land and buildings as did their Accra and Cape Coast counterparts. On Akolatse, for example, see ADM 11/1/1885: Case No. 10/1920 and ADM 41/1/3: Contract between Mr. H. Randah on behalf of Messrs. Wober and Brohn of Hamburg, Germany and Chief Akolatse of Quittah. And R. Campbell, D. C. Quittah to the Honorable Colonial Secretary, Christiansborg, Accra, 5 January 1885.

14. In a 1913 court case about a matter that occurred in 1884 and which involved Sands working closely with Tamakloe on a land deal, Sands referred to the chief by the affectionate yet respectful term of "my old man Tamakloe." See Judicial Council Minute Book-1913; contact the author for additional information about this reference.

15. On which persons were considered appropriate occupants of such positions, see Greene, Field Note 70: Interview with K. Kpodo, 12 January 1988, Woe.

16. Greene, Field Note 72: Interview with Christian Nani Tamakloe, 13 January 1988, Keta.

17. Like the name Sands, this is a pseudonym. On the Euro-Africans or "mulattoes of Accra," and the history and politics surrounding their identities, see Parker, "*Mankraloi*, Merchants and Mulattos."

18. This disagreement had to do with Anlo opposition to Danish efforts to stop the slave trade at Keta.

19. Ustorf, *Bremen Missionaries*, 183.

20. According to Hans W. Debrunner, the reason the school was able to attract students from Accra in particular was because the British had bombarded Christiansborg in 1854 for refusing to pay a poll tax, so the Basel Mission that had operated in the Danish area of Accra was closed. Children were then sent to Keta to attend the Bremen school. See Debrunner, *A Church*, 84. For more information on the poll tax and the

conflict that erupted between the British and Christiansborg-Accra, see Kimble, *A Political History*, 168–91.

21. Ustorf, *Bremen Missionaries*, 184. See also Greene, Field Note 63: Interview with L. A. Banini, 5 January 1988, Anloga; and Field Note 93: Interview with Amegashi Afeku IV, 19 February, 1988 Acca-Nima.

22. Debrunner, *A Church*, 84.

23. See ADM 41/4/1–2: 3 June 1885: Regina v. Agboshie and 27 September 1888, D.C.'s Court, Genardoo v. Moshie. ADM 41/4/22: D. C.'s Court, Kwitta, 17 December 1889, Regina v. Amegashie. ADM 41/1/15: 28 December 1891, A. M. K. to the Honorable Colonial Secretary.

24. Studies of nineteenth-century slavery in what is now Ghana emphasize the distinctions that existed among slaves based on whether or not they were first- or later-generation slaves, bought or inherited. In the Anlo area, a further distinction was made between those captured in war and those who had been bought. See Haenger, *Slaves and Slave Holders*, 29. See also Rattray, *Ashanti Law*, 33–46.

25. Greene, Field Note 63: Interview with L. A. Banini, 5 January 1988, Anloga.

26. On the use of kinship terminology as a tool to encourage feelings of incorporation, see Lovejoy, *Ideology*.

27. Johannes Merz, *Ein Neger-Gehülte im Missionswerk: Das Leben des Katchisten Aaron Onyipayede* (Bremen: Norddeutsche Mission Gesellschaft, 1875), 14.

28. For a more complete description of the causes and outcome of this conflict, see Greene, *Gender*, 57–58.

29. In 1911, public accusations of being a slave were being prosecuted in local courts as defamation. See Judicial Court Record Book, 1911: Anyideme of Anloga, Complainant v. Akryra, Awoyo and Kodeku, of Anloga in the Native Tribunal of Fia Sri II, Anloga, 14/10/11.

30. Establishing kinship connections to distant homes and relatives (some of whom are remembered as royals) is a practice found today among many around the world. On this practice among Africans in late seventeenth- and eighteenth-century Europe, see David Northrup, *Africa's Discovery of Europe, 1450–1850* (Oxford: Oxford University Press, 2002), 143–44. See Holsey, *Routes*, 79–80, for a more recent example from Ghana.

31. On Ada trade and warfare, see C. O. C. Amate, *The Making of Ada* (Accra: Woeli Pub., 1999); see also Greene, *Gender*, passim; I. B. Sutton, "The Volta River Salt Trade: The Survival of an Indigenous Industry," *Journal of African History* 22, no. 1 (1981): 43–61; Trevor R. Getz, *Slavery and Reform in West Africa: Toward Emancipation in Nineteenth Century Senegal and the Gold Coast* (Athens: Ohio University Press, 2004), 171; and Dumett, "African Merchants," 671–76.

32. On Agotime's economic and military relations see Greene, *Gender*, passim; and Spieth, *Die Ewe*, 34–44.

33. On the decline in the status and influence of "mulattoes," see Gocking, *Facing Two Ways*.

34. On similar marital patterns in colonial Lagos, see Kristin Mann, *Marrying Well: Marriage, Status and Social Change among the Educated Elite in Colonial Lagos* (Cambridge: Cambridge University Press, 1985).

35. This is a pseudonym.

36. Bellois was still operating as a businessman in Keta, buying land, in 1881. See ADM 41/1/3: 11 February 1881.

37. See Dumett, "African Merchants."

38. According to Inspector Michael Zahn, the head of the Bremen Mission, "one could not demand [native Christians to give up their slaves] on the basis of scriptural

law . . . because 'Thou shall not keep any slaves' is not a commandment that follows from evangelical . . . truth . . .; Rather [the slaveholder] was to be shown the 'unseemliness' of slavery." Ustorf, *Bremen Missionaries*, 281, 282. Ustorf suggests that another possible reason behind Zahn's position was that "the still small congregations that had been won only with great sacrifice" might be lost if slaveholders were excluded.

39. On the history of Kru labor in West Africa, see George E. Brooks Jr., *The Kru Mariner in the Nineteenth Century: An Historical Compendium* (Newark, Del.: Liberian Studies Association in America, 1972); and Jane Martin, "Krumen 'Down the Coast': Liberian Migrants on the West African Coast in the 19th and early 20th Centuries," *The International Journal of African Historical Studies* 18, no. 3 (1985): 401–423. On the use of "Kruboys" by Euro-Africans or "mulattoes" in Keta, see ADM 41/4/21: 248, 404.

40. Ustorf, *Bremen Missionaries*, 213–14.

41. See Jones and Sebald, *An Africa Family Archive*, 28.

42. Sands recorded a number of incidents in which a slave murdered another person. One such incident involved his own family. He noted, for example that on 16 April 1874 his uncle's death was caused by "his [uncle's] own slave by the name Labidey."

43. As a maternal nephew operating in a patrilineal society, Sands may have found it necessary to emphasize the absence of genealogical connections between his uncle and the family's slaves as a means of reinforcing his own position within the family. Nephews did have inheritance rights in Anlo. They could inherit the self-acquired property of their maternal uncles. But some educated wealthy individuals in Anlo began to make wills that limited who would inherit their property. Sands might also have felt especially compelled to insist on his centrality to his maternal family because of the limited contacts he appears to have had with his father's relatives. Sands was able to identity his paternal grandfather and his father's siblings and a few of their children. But the information he was able to collect paled in comparison with the detailed accounts of his maternal family and his long association with them. For the historical origins of the matrilineal inheritance aspects of Anlo's otherwise patrilineal system, see Greene, *Gender*, 169–70.

44. The British government removed its troops from the Keta fort in 1856, but it should be noted that they continued to have direct contact with the Anlo in the 1860s because of concerns about the slave trade. In 1863, for example, the then British colonial governor, Richard Pine, even recommended to the Duke of Newcastle that they reoccupy Keta because "large parties of slaves are from time to time collected and kept within sight of the British fort ready for shipping." He indicates that "such a measure will enable me to defend this government from the charge of inactivity with respect to the slave trade on the river Volta so frequently of late leveled against it in some public print." ADM 1/2/12: Richard Pine, Governor, Cape Coast Castle to His Grace, the Duke of Newcastle, 7 May 1863. More active engagement prior to colonization in 1874 occurred in the late 1860s and early 1870s, when Britain was physically drawn back into the area because of conflicts between the Anlo-based trader Geraldo de Lima and the polity of Ada. For more on Geraldo de Lima, see Greene, *Gender*, 127–33. Britain signed treaties with the Anlo in 1867, 1868, 1871, and 1874, when the British finally reoccupied the fort at Keta. See ADM11/1/1246: History of the Awunas, Some Dates. See ADM 4/1/2: p. 250 for a copy of the 1868 treaty: "Treaty of Peace between Her Majesty and the Ahwoonlah and Addah Nations . . . 13 November 1868," which lists a series of treaties signed by the Anlo and Britain.

45. The first stipends were offered to the Keta and other Anlo chiefs in 1880. See ADM 11/1/1113: Chief Agbozo, Keta to C. Napier Curling, Esq. Commissioner of the Eastern Province, 14 July 1902. Technically, the relationship between the British government and the Keta chiefs was governed by the 1878 Native Jurisdiction Ordinance.

This law included no stipulation for stipends, but the practice of offering such monetary or material payments preceded the enactment of the 1878 ordinance on the Gold Coast, and the practice was eventually extended to Anlo.

46. On the history of the ordinances that pertain to the role of chiefs in the colonial administration, see Kimble, *A Political History,* 458–505. The Native Jurisdiction Ordinance of 1883 has been excerpted in G. E. Metcalfe, *Great Britain and Ghana: Documents of Ghana History, 1807–1957* (Legon-Accra, Ghana: University of Ghana, 1964), 390–93.

47. Traditional Council Minute Book, 1931–32: Awleshi Kwashikpui v. R. J. Acolatse and others, 87.

48. Ustorf, *Bremen Missionaries,* 211–13.

49. On the specific salaries and benefits offered and the debates about them during this period (1867–1890s), see Ustorf, *Bremen Missionaries,* 210–66. On the protests eventually waged by Africans employed by the mission, see Ustorf, *Bremen Missionaries,* 461–70, 349–59. See also Birgit Meyer, "Christianity and the Ewe Nation: German Pietist Missionaries, Ewe Converts and the Politics of Culture," *Journal of Religion in Africa* 32, no. 2 (2002): 167–99.

50. Ustorf, *Bremen Missionaries,* 182, 310.

51. See Ibid., 310–11.

52. At that time, there were seven Bremen missionaries in the field. Some were in Keta; the others were in stations distant from the coast. The majority were ordained ministers and those in Keta were certainly authorized to conduct baptisms.

53. Debrunner, *A Church,* 89.

54. Ustorf, *Bremen Missionaries,* 190–204.

55. Debrunner, *A Church,* 113.

56. Ustorf, *Bremen Missionaries,* 191–92.

57. See Kimble, *A Political History,* 63, 72, 84, 510–12; and F. L. Bartels, *The Roots of Ghana Methodism* (Cambridge: Cambridge University Press, 1965), 109–110.

58. On Hermann Yoyo's position, see Ustorf, *Bremen Missionaries,* 374–83.

59. *Gold Coast Aborigines,* 24 November 1898, p. 4.

60. On the history of this effort, which was largely successful, see Sylvia Jacobs, "The Impact of African American Education on 19th Century Colonial West Africa: Livingstone College Graduates in the Gold Coast," *Negro History Bulletin* 58, nos. 1–2 (1995): 5–13. See also Walter Ladell Yates, "The History of the African Methodist Episcopal Zion Church in West Africa, Liberia, Gold Coast (Ghana) and Nigeria, 1900–1939" (PhD diss., Hartford Foundation, 1967).

61. *Gold Coast Aborigines* 1 (25 February 1899), 3. This statement was made by Dr. Owen Smith, who was on an official visit to the Gold Coast as consul general for the United States and who agreed to attend the meeting at Keta as a presiding elder in the church.

62. On the role of the Methodist Mission in producing the vast majority of English-speaking clerks on the Gold Coast, see Kimble, *A Political History,* 72. According to. F. K. Fiawoo, "most Africans looked upon the two denominations [the AME Zion and the Methodist Mission] as one, each being an offshoot of the same ancestral stock." This was the case because the father of Rev. T. B. Freeman Jr., Rev. T. B. Freeman Sr., had been the founder of the British Methodism on the Gold Coast and throughout West Africa. See Yates, *The History,* 111–12. It is equally significant that even though the Roman Catholic Church had already established itself in Keta and had been teaching a significant number of its pupils in English since 1892 (as required by the British colonial government of those schools that received government subventions), Sands was still committed to bringing the AME Zion Church to Keta. We can only assume that he was

motivated in large part by its commitment not only to early English-language instruction, but also because he endorsed the idea of having African leadership in Christian churches. On the teaching of English in Keta's Catholic school, see ADM 11/1 1475 Report of the Acting Director of Education for the Year, 1892–93 (London: Her Majesty's Stationery Office, 1893), 36.

63. Kimble, *A Political History*, 510.

64. Stephanie Newell, *Literary Culture in Colonial Ghana* (Bloomington: Indiana University Press, 2002), 43.

65. Keta had documented trade ties with the interior since at least the eighteenth century. These links were periodically severed by war, the last of which—Asante's 1869–71 war against the communities that stretched from Awudome and Peki in the south to Buem in the north—saw Anlo's ties with the Ho area and a number of other polities cut because of its support for the Asante invasion.

7. THE DIARY OF PAUL SANDS

1. Editor's note: Camwood, also known as African sandalwood, is used to make a red dye that was highly valued for its use as a cosmetic for those involved in ritual activities.

2. Editor's note: This incident was widely reported in local histories. Sands no doubt obtained the entries here for 1839–40, 1842, and 1844 from Reindorf, *History*, 154–56. He may refer to this event as a revolution because in hindsight it was the beginning of the end of Danish presence in Keta.

3. Editor's note: As Keta grew in population, the demand for land—which was already scarce—grew tremendously. This information would have been important in land disputes as individuals and families vied for control over property that had become more valuable as Keta attracted increasing numbers of businessmen and women who needed accommodation and office and storage space.

4. Editor's note: The meeting between the Anlo *awǫamefia* and Hill involved Hill issuing the demand that the Anlo pay a poll tax to the British colonial government that had recently asserted claims over the area. The Anlo paid the tax once but refused thereafter.

5. Editor's note: The note that "he was delivered up to be killed" is a reference to the Nyiko custom, which involved the family's handing over their convicted relative to be executed in the Anlo capital; see Sandra E. Greene, *Sacred Sites and the Colonial Encounter: A History of Meaning and Memory in Ghana* (Bloomington: Indiana University Press, 2002), 112–14.

6. Editor's note: An account of this conflict appears in Pierre Bouché, *La Côte des Ésclaves* (Paris, 1885), 303, to which Sands may have had access, but it is most likely that much of the information about the Anlo participants in the war came from local Anlo oral histories.

7. Editor's note: On the Lawson family, see Jones and Sebald, *An African Family Archive*.

8. Editor's note: Frederich Plessing was a missionary associated with the Norddeutsche Missions-Gesellschaft (Bremen Mission) in Anlo from 1853 to his death in 1863.

9. Editor's note: The phrase "put into room" as part of a marriage ceremony is in reference to the practice among more wealthy Anlos of secluding the bride for several months in a room where she is pampered by being provided generously with food and prevented from doing any serious labor. After this period of seclusion, she is presented to the public.

10. Editor's note: This passage is a direct quote from Africanus B. Horton, *Letters on the Political Condition of the Gold Coast* (London: Frank Cass, 1970; 1870), 75.

11. Editor's note: See ADM 41/1/2: Ordinances Relating to H. M. Forts and Settlements on the Gold Coast, 1852–1870: Treaty of Peace between Her Majesty and the Ahwoonah and Addah Nations of the Protectorate, 3 March 1869, p. 250–51.

12. Editor's note: This entry is in reference to a major military expedition undertaken against the Anlo by the British because of reports that the Anlo were preparing to assist the Asante, who were facing a military invasion by the British. If the Anlo entered the war as an ally of Asante, they would have been in a position to attack the rear of the British forces that were preparing to attack Asante from the east. For more on this, see J. B. Yegbe, "The Anlo and Their Neighbors, 1850–1890" (MA thesis, University of Ghana, Legon, 1966), 88–92.

13. Editor's note: Amegashie was a major slave owner in addition to his position as Nyigbla priest in Keta on behalf of the Anlo political authorities who were based in the Anlo capital of Anloga. Quite a few of his slaves sought refuge in the Danish fort that was taken over by the British government. In this instance one of Amegashie's slaves, described here as a "domestic," encouraged others to seek refuge with the British, who had abolished slavery in 1874.

14. Editor's note: This incident occurred when Capt. Ellis and Capt. Laver of the Brig *Alligator* had traveled north by canoe across the Keta lagoon to shoot deer. The attack was launched in retaliation against the British confiscation of nontaxed goods being smuggled into the colony. Also known as the Lo war in Anlo, it was described by Ellis in one of his official reports. See ADM 41/1/2: A. B. Ellis, District Commissioner, Quittah to the Colonial Secretary, Christiansborg, Accra, 24 October 1878.

15. Editor's note: The assault on Kedzi occurred as part of the British campaign to suppress smuggling in the area.

16. Editor's note: On the Nyiko custom, see note 5 above.

17. Editor's note: The attack on Sands's employees probably occurred because of his association with the British government, which was seen as extremely hostile to Anlo because of government efforts to suppress the highly lucrative business of smuggling goods into the Gold Coast colony.

18. Editor's note: The date is difficult to read in the original. It could be 1887 or 1882.

19. Editor's note: This particular incident involved the Hausa troops used by the British to police the Keta district. They were often accused of abusing their authority by confiscating the property of Anlo residents and then using fire to intimidate the residents into not reporting their activities. The incident involving Chiefs Tamakloe and Akolatse is said to have involved a Hausa policeman beating one of Tamakloe's sons at the gate of the chief's house. According to G. A. Sorkpor, "Chief Tamakloe intervened and parted them. But soon after six other Hausas rushed on the house, broke his doors and windows and began to beat everyone with bayonets and clubs. Chief Acolatse rushed to the scene from his house, which was nearby. He too, like Tamakloe, was beaten and wounded on his head." G. A. Sorkpor, "Geraldo de Lima and the Awunas, 1862–1904" (MA thesis, University of Ghana, 1966), 101. On the activities of the Hausa troops in the area, see Francis Agbodeka, *African Politics and British Policy in the Gold Coast, 1868–1900: A Study in the Forms and Force of Protest* (Evanston, Ill.: Northwestern University Press, 1971), 69.

20. Editor's note: The closing of the market was related to the incident involving Tamakloe and Acolatse reported for the date Aug. 22. According to Sorkpor, the market was drawn into the conflict because "during the commotion [at Tamakloe's house], some of the Hausas and their women forcibly rushed into the market and frightened

the people away . . . and plundered whatever they could lay their hands upon." Sorkpor, "Geraldo," 101.

21. Editor's note: It is unclear why these individuals were arrested by the British and had to have bail posted for them.

22. Editor's note: This trip was organized to reopen trade relations between the coastal Anlo and the peoples of the interior, who had boycotted the markets in Anlo in protest over the Anlo's support of Asante's invasion of the interior between 1869 and 1871.

23. Editor's note: This attack was launched by a number of Anlos in retaliation for British actions taken against those they accused of organizing an attack against the 1884 British expedition, in which Paul Sands participated, to open trade ties between Keta coast and the Ewe-speaking interior. The opening of trade had been strongly supported by Chiefs Tamakloe and Acolatse, both of whom found the British colonial government's efforts to open trade useful for their own business interests. Many others, however, were deeply opposed to the British presence. Among this group was Geraldo de Lima, a wealthy trader who engaged in significant amounts of smuggling of firearms, ammunition, and liquor into the Gold Coast colony, all of which the British had made major efforts to stop. Chiefs Tenge and Tsitsi of Anyako were also deeply opposed to the British. On 13 January 1885, Geraldo was arrested by the colonial police for involvement in the attack on the 1884 British expedition into the interior. Shortly thereafter he was sent to Cape Coast for trial. After being sent by land from Keta through western coastal Anlo, however, he and his escort of four policemen were briefly detained in Whuti, Tamakloe's hometown. When Tamakloe heard this, he sent a message to his people that Geraldo and his police escort should be allowed to continue. He then traveled himself to Whuti with the British colonial district commissioner at Keta, Captain Campbell, in hopes of meeting Chiefs Tenge and Tsitsi, Geraldo's supporters, business partners, and friends. On hearing that Tenge was in Whuti, Capt. Campbell—who had invited Tenge to come to Keta many times to answer charges made against him with regard to the attack on the 1884 expedition—arrested Tenge as well as Tsitsi. During the march back to Keta, Tenge and Tsitsi managed to escape. Shortly thereafter, Tamakloe and Capt. Campbell were attacked. General Ahorloo [Axolu] was the head of the Anlo military and had not supported this attack. In protest against it, he removed the symbols of his office, a stool and a ritual sword, from Anloga, the Anlo capital, and moved them to Dzelukofe, a town more closely associated with support for the British colonial government. A first-person account of this incident by Tamakloe can be found in ADM11/1/166: 94–97. See also Agbodeka, *African Politics*, 68.

24. Editor's note: The 31 January and 2 February incidents reported here were in retaliation for the attack on Capt. Campbell and Tamakloe on 17 January.

25. Editor's note: This action was part of the antismuggling campaign by the British colonial government.

26. Editor's note: It is unclear what events prompted the need for a treaty between the Euro-African Williams and the communities of Mepe, Mlefi, and Bakpa.

27. Editor's note: As part of the Whuti war that saw a large contingent of Anlos attack Tamakloe and Capt. Campbell as they traveled from Whuti to Keta on 17 January 1885, Tamakloe's house in Whuti was also destroyed.

28. Editor's note: This was the second British colonial government–initiated effort to open the roads between the Anlo coast and the interior that had been closed to trade because of the hostilities that had continued after the 1869–71 war. The first agreement involved the people of Ho. See entry for 1884, Nov. 14.

29. Editor's note: So far, I have been unable to determine the circumstances surrounding this event.

30. Editor's note: On the background to this conflict over the stool and sword, see notes 23 and 24 above.

31. Editor's note: For the origins of this conflict, see note 23.

32. Editor's note: A *bokọ* is a diviner.

8. OUR CITIZENS, OUR KIN ENSLAVED

1. One sees this kind of forgetting about individuals in more recent times as well. Some three thousand Africans from the Gold Coast were recruited as soldiers by the Dutch between 1831 and 1872 to serve on the island of Java in the Netherlands East Indies. After their service, the majority returned to the Gold Coast and took up residence on Java Hill (named in recognition of where they had served) outside the coastal town of Elmina. Virtually all were forgotten by residents of Elmina, however, by the 1990s. Almost no one in Elmina even remembered the origins of Java Hill's name. I thank Larry Yarak (e-mail correspondence, 10 September 2008) for this information. On the history of the Dutch-recruited African soldiers, see Ineke van Kessel, "The Black Dutchmen: African Soldiers in the Netherlands East Indies," in *Merchants, Missionaries and Migrants: 300 Years of Dutch-Ghanaian Relations,* ed. Ineke van Kessel, 133–41 (Amsterdam: KIT Publishers, 2002); and http://elwininternational.com/elmina_java. html. Similarly, one Alfred Sam, who organized a well-publicized back-to-Africa movement that saw a number of Oklahoma residents return to the Gold Coast with him in 1915, was forgotten by the 1960s by everyone in southern Ghana except those relatives who in their youth had direct interactions with him. See William E. Bittle and Gilbert Geis, *The Longest Way Home: Chief Alfred C. Sam's Back-to-Africa Movement* (Detroit: Wayne State University Press, 1964), 208.

2. The ports mentioned—Atorkor, Vodza, and Cotonou—are noted in this particular oral tradition but do not necessarily coincide with the major sites from which slaves were shipped from this region. Vodza was never known as a major port. Cotonou is probably mentioned because it figures prominently in Anlo traditions as the point beyond which the spirits of the dead can be found. Atorkor was an export center in the early to mid-nineteenth century, but prior to this the major ports in the Anlo district were Keta and Woe.

3. Anne C. Bailey, *African Voices of the Atlantic Slave Trade: Beyond the Silence and the Shame* (Boston: Beacon Press, 2004). Bailey suggests that the incident was remembered because the people kidnapped, reportedly drummers, were affiliated with the chiefs and thus, because it affected the elite within Atorkor, they had special reason to remember. This argument is based on the notion that all drummers in Atorkor were affiliated with chiefs and headmen based on the pattern in Asante. Given that there are quite substantial differences between Asante and Anlo social and political organizational structures, this assumption seems ill-advised. She also suggests that their enslavement was unthinkable because of their association with the chiefs. This too is incorrect. People were kidnapped or enslaved all the time no matter their status. See Bailey, *African Voices,* 91.

4. A "cult house" is a compound constructed by the leaders and followers of a particular deity. It is used to house the god itself, to conduct that religious order's rituals and as a meeting place for members.

5. "West Africa," *Monatsblatt der Norddeutschen Missions-Gesellschaft* 11, no. 121 (1861): 518.

6. See Greene, Field Notes 56 and 99: Interviews with William Tiodo Anum, 22 December 1987, Anloga; and Togbi Awusu II, Chief of Atorkor, 29 March 1988, Atorkor,

respectively. See also Carl Spiess, "Ein Erinnerungsblatt an die Tage des Sklavenhandels in Westafrika," *Globus (Braunschweig)* 92 (1907): 205–208.

7. The dating of Ndorkutsu's death is based on the fact that when the Bremen missionary Friedrich Plessing visited Atorkor in April of 1855, he commented on the once important slave market that no longer existed and the decidedly dilapidated state of the trading post that had once been used by the resident slave traders. See Friedrich Plessing, "Theure und geliebte Väter!" *Monatsblatt der Norddeutschen Missions-Gesellschaft* 5, no. 57 (1855): 244–48. According to Anlo oral traditions, after Ndorkutsu's death a Euro-African of Danish descent, Major King, continued involvement in the slave trade east of Atorkor at the Tale Lagoon. This area became known as Matsikli or Matsikli Beach, Matsikli being a corrupted version of Major King. See Greene, Field Note 99: Interview with Togbi Awusu II, 29 March 1988, Atorkor.

8. Dumett, "African Merchants," 691.

9. Ibid., 661–93. See also Dumett's article, "John Sarbah, The Elder, and African Mercantile Entrepreneurship in the Gold Coast in the Late Nineteenth Century," *Journal of African History* 14, no. 4 (1973): 653–79; as well as Kaplow, "The Mudfish," 317–33.

10. See, for example, Adell Patton Jr., "Dr. John Farrell Easmon: Medical Professionalism and Colonial Racism in the Gold Coast, 1856–1900," *International Journal of African Historical Studies* 22, no. 4 (1989): 601–36; Adell Patton, *Physicians, Colonial Racism and Diaspora in West Africa* (Gainesville: University Press of Florida, 1996); Stephen Addae, *History of Medicine in Ghana, 1880–1960* (Edinburgh: Durham Academic Press, 1997), 140–47; Ramond Dumett, "The Campaign against Malaria and the Expansion of Scientific Medical and Sanitary Services in British West Africa," *African Historical Studies* 1, no. 2 (1968): 191–95; and Carina Ray, "Policing Sexual Boundaries: The Politics of Race in Colonial Ghana" (PhD diss., Cornell University, 2007).

11. All the missionary societies in Ghana at the time, including the Wesleyan Methodist Missionary Society, the Basel Evangelical Missionary Society, the Bremen Mission, and the Roman Catholic Church, relied heavily on local preachers and catechists to support their evangelical and educational efforts. But all were also infected by European racist attitudes about the educational and spiritual capabilities of their African colleagues and converts. For an overview on this issue, see Kofi Asimpi, "European Christian Missions and Race Relations in Ghana, 1828–1970" (PhD diss., Boston University, 1996). On the racist attitudes that Gold Coast Christians had to deal with specifically from Wesleyan missionary, see Bartels, *The Roots*, 139–41. On the attitudes of many Bremen missionaries, see Ustorf, *Bremen Missionaries*, 180–408; on attitudes within the Basel Mission, see Vellenga, "Jamaican and Swiss-German Missionaries." For the quite limited references to European Catholic missionary attitudes, see Hélè H. Pfann, *A Short History of the Catholic Church in Ghana* (Cape Coast, Ghana: Catholic Mission Press, 1970), 15, and Pashington Obeng, *Asante Catholicism: Religious and Cultural Reproduction among the Akan of Ghana* (Leiden: E. J. Brill, 1996), 104.

12. On local criticism of the Wesleyan Mission, see Raymond George Jenkins, "Gold Coast Historians and Their Pursuit of the Gold Coast Pasts: 1881–1917" (PhD diss., University of Birmingham, 1985), 234–35.

13. On the Mfantsi Amanbuhu Fekuw, see Kimble, *A Political History*, 150, and Gocking, *Facing Two Ways*, 73. On the role of such individuals as F. Egyir Assam and S. R. B. Attoh-Ahuma on "set[ting] a new fashion and [drawing] attention to the value of the African name," see Bartels, *The Roots*, 121–25. On how local elites used the writing of history to respond to the ideas discussed here, see Paul Jenkins, ed., *The Recovery of the West African Past: African Pastors and African History in the Nineteenth Century: C.C. Reindorf and Samuel Johnson* (Basel: Basler Afrika Bibliographien, 1998). On the

historical studies published in the Fante press, see Jenkins, "Gold Coast Historians," 236–93.

14. These sentiments emphasized valuing Western culture only if it could be blended together with local cultures and traditions to promote the development of the West Africa colonies. Such blending could not be achieved by just anyone, however. It required the leadership of an educated local elite, one that knew how to interact effectively within both the European and West African worlds. Who exactly constituted this local elite was a bone of contention at the time. Some promoted a Fante or Ga nationalism, others a Gold Coast nationalism, and still others a Pan-African one that included either only other West Africans or also Diaspora blacks. On the emergence of West African nationalism in the middle to late nineteenth century, see J. Ayodele Langley, *Pan-Africanism and Nationalism in West Africa, 1900–1945* (Oxford: Oxford University Press, 1973), 110–114; on Fante, Ga, and Gold Coast nationalism, see Jenkins, *The Recovery*, passim, and Jenkins, "Gold Coast Historians," passim. Advocates of a more broad-based Pan-Africanism expressed admiration for the work and views of Edward Wilmot Blyden, a West Indian by birth but long a Sierra Leone resident who identified himself as African rather than West Indian. On Blyden's identity, see Nemata Blyden, *West Indians in West Africa, 1808–1880* (Rochester, N.Y.: University of Rochester Press, 2000), 166–67, n. 9. Gold Coast Pan-Africanists also supported the development of a range of cooperative relationships, as seen in the attendance of the Gold Coast lawyer Harry Francisco Ribeiro at the First Pan African conference held in London, England, in 1900, and as seen in the establishment of the African Methodist Episcopal Zion Church. On Ribeiro and his attendance at this conference, see Michel Doortmont, *The Pen-Pictures of Modern Africans and African Celebrities by Charles Frances Hutchison: A Collective Biography of Elite Society in the Gold Coast Colony* (Leiden: Brill, 2005), 372–75; Gocking, *Facing Two Ways*, 70; P. Olisanwuche Esedebe, *Pan-Africanism: The Idea and Movement, 1776–1991* (Washington, D.C.: Howard University Press, 1994), 40–47; and Tony Martin, *The Pan African Connection: From Slavery to Garvey and Beyond* (Dover, Mass.: The Majority Press, 1983), 201–216. Of note is that local Gold Coast Pan-Africanist views often ran counter to the everyday tensions operating on the ground. According to Adell Patton, there were numerous complaints by Gold Coast elites about being discriminated against by those Sierra Leoneans and West Indians who felt themselves superior to the "natives" because of their greater exposure to and absorption of Western culture. See Patton, "Dr. John Farrell Easmon." On local Gold Coast Pan-African views expressed in the newspapers, see Bartels, *The Roots*, 141–42, 160–61. On similar developments in Nigeria, see J. Lorand Matory, *Black Atlantic Religion* (Princeton, N.J.: Princeton University Press, 2005), 57–61.

15. Bishop J. W. Hood, *One Hundred Years of the A.M.E. Zion Church: The Centennial of African Methodism* (New York: A.M.E. Zion Book Concern, 1895), 10–56.

16. See the list of administratively organized church groupings known as conferences listed by Hood, *One Hundred Years*, 92–96.

17. For more on Turner, on his appeal especially among southern blacks and on some of the other emigration schemes that developed during this period, see George M. Fredrickson, *Black Liberation: A Comparative History of Black Ideologies in the United States and South Africa* (Oxford: Oxford University Press, 1995), 74–80.

18. On the history of these recruitment efforts, and on Andrew Cartwright in particular, see Walter L. Williams, *Black Americans and the Evangelization of Africa, 1887–1900* (Madison: University of Wisconsin Press, 1982), xv–13, 33–41.

19. According to Yates, "The History," and Isaac Sackey, "A Brief History of the A.M.E. Zion Church, West Gold Coast District," *Ghana Bulletin of Theology* 1, no. 3

(1957): 16–20 (a copy of which also appears in the AME Zion publication *The Missionary Seer* 51, no. 11 [1953]: 6–9), these acquaintances included Charles Arthur Albert Barnes, his sister Mrs. Christine Selby, James and John Hockman, and the Reverend James Egyir Asaam. Given that Barnes and Egyir Asaam were only born in 1862 and 1864, respectively, it's likely that Small may have known their parents in the 1860s, but he would have only come to actually meet the children, Albert Barnes, his sister Christine Selby, and James Asaam on his return to the Gold Coast in 1897. Information on Barnes, an engineer, can be found in Doortmont, *The Pen-Pictures*, 120. According to Jacobs, "The Impact," 8, a son of either James or John Hockman, William Hockman, was among the first four Gold Coast students enrolled at Livingstone College in 1897. According to Sackey, "A Brief History," 6–7, it was Barnes and Selby who gave land to the church on which it built its first chapel. Prior to this, the church held services in the Hockman's Hotel. For more on Egyir Asaam, see note 26.

20. On the activities of the West Indian Regiments in West Africa during this period, see Brian Dyde, *The Empty Sleeve: The Story of the West India Regiments of the British Army* (St. John's, Antigua: Hansib Caribbean, 1997), 176, 191–98.

21. On life in Barbados and the ideas about immigration to Africa to which Small would have been exposed, see Melanie J. Newton, *The Children of Africa in the Colonies: Free People of Color in Barbados in the Age of Emancipation* (Baton Rouge: Louisiana State University Press, 2008), 256–82; and Hilary Beckles, *A History of Barbados: From Amerindian Settlement to Caribbean Single Market*, 2nd ed. (Cambridge: Cambridge University Press, 2006), chapter 6.

22. Whether or not Small actually knew Freeman Sr. is unclear, but Freeman Jr. was certainly well known to him. When Small left the Gold Coast after his brief visit in 1898, he left Freeman Jr. to take responsibility for supporting the expansion of the Zion denomination to the Keta District. See Yates, "The History," 104–105. On the wide respect shown Freeman Sr. by many West Africans, see Allen Birtwhistle, *Thomas Birch Freeman: West African Pioneer* (London: Cargate Press, 1950), 97.

23. *Gold Coast Aborigines*, 26 November 1898, p. 4. In his political history of Ghana, David Kimble argues that the Basel and Wesleyan Missions (and one could include the Bremen Mission as well in this group) were not hostile to African culture, but Africans who attended the schools run by these missionary societies certainly felt otherwise, as even Kimble acknowledged. See Kimble, *A Political History*, 159–61.

24. Quoted from the 14 December 1883 issue of the *Gold Coast Times* in Jenkins, "Gold Coast Historians," 230, n. 3. Hostility toward mulattos and Euro-Africans existed not only among Africans and other dark-skinned blacks in the Americas because of the privileges they were accorded by the white power structures in Africa and the Americas, as so clearly articulated by Edward Wilmot Blyden, but increased as well among Europeans as the century progressed and British colonial policy began to give preference in their administrative structures to the chiefs as "pure native Africans."

25. *Gold Coast Aborigines*, 26 November 1898.

26. The first editor of the *Gold Coast Aborigines* was Kobina Fynn Egyir-Asaam, who was deeply critical of the Wesleyan Mission and strongly supported the AME Zion Church. He was appointed the Gold Coast representative for the church by Bishop Small during his trip to the Gold Coast in 1897 and held that position until Frank Ata Osam-Pinanko took over the leadership of the church on his return from his studies at Livingstone College in 1903. Another Aborigines Rights Protection member who was very supportive of the AME Zion Church was Samuel Richard Brew Attoh-Ahuma. For more information on these men, see Magnus Sampson, *Makers of Modern Ghana* (Accra: Anuwuo Educational Publications, 1969), 92–101; and Kimble, *A Political History*, 163. On Attoh-Ahuma's often fractious relations with the Wesleyan Methodist

Mission and his support of the AME Zion Church, see Kimble, *A Political History,* 159–60, 518–19; Yates, "The History," 183–90.

27. For a more detailed history of the Aborigines Rights Protection Society, see Kimble, *A Political History,* 330–403.

28. The italics are my emphasis.

29. Hollis R. Lynch, *Edward Wilmot Blyden: Pan-Negro Patriot 1832–1912* (New York: Oxford University Press, 1967), 61–62.

30. Cited in Esedebe, *Pan-Africanism,* 164.

31. Blyden went even further by distinguishing the "pure Negro" from the mulatto. See Lynch, *Edward Wilmot Blyden;* and V. Y. Mudimbe, *The Invention of Africa: Gnosis, Philosophy and the Order of Knowledge* (Bloomington: Indiana University Press, 1988), 98–134.

32. J. E. Casely Hayford, *Ethiopia Unbound: Studies in Race Emancipation* (London: Frank Cass, 1969/1911), 165.

33. Casely Hayford, *Ethiopia,* 174. Casely Hayford emphasized African cultural nationalism not only in his writings but also in his interactions with African Americans. When the AME Zion bishop C. C. Alleyne visited Cape Coast in 1925, he was confronted by Casely Hayford, who in his remarks made it clear that he did not regard Alleyne as an African. This in turn prompted a retort from Alleyne, who stated that "his great grand parents had been abstracted from West Africa and taken to America and that the burden of proof was upon Mr. Casely Hayford to show that he, Bishop Alleyne, was not a Fanti." See "Zion Reunion," *The Gold Coast Leader,* 14 February 1926; reprinted in *The Star of Zion* 49, no. 14 (2 April 1925): 1, 8.

34. Edwin William Smith, *Aggrey of Africa: A Study in Black and White* (New York: Doubleday, Doran and Co., 1930), 61, 117–42; see also Leonard S. Kenworthy, "James K. Aggrey: Reconciler of Races," *Journal of Negro Education* 15, no. 2 (1946): 181–90; as well as Sylvia M. Jacobs, "James Emman Kwegyir Aggrey: An African Intellectual in the United States," *Journal of Negro History* 81, no. 1/4 (1996): 47–61.

35. *The Gold Coast Nation* II, no. 86 (6 November 1913): 457; *The Missionary Seer* 30, no. 2 (February 1929): 1.

36. On the history of government aid to Gold Coast schools, see Philip Foster, *Education and Social Change in Ghana* (London: Routledge and Kegan Paul, 1965), 48–51, 80–86. For examples of local AME Zion Church anxieties about the loss of government aid when their schools were unable to meet government requirements, see "Anonymous Letter from British West Africa, Winneba, Gold Coast Colony," *The Missionary Seer* 27, no. 1 (January 1926): 5–6; Rev. Isaac C. Cole, "Our Mission Schools," *The Missionary Seer* XXXII, no. 3 (March 1931): 6–8; and *The Missionary Seer* XXXIV, no. 2 (February 1933): 1.

37. *Gold Coast Aborigines* 1, no. 1 (26 November 1898): 4. Italics are my emphasis.

38. *The Gold Coast Nation,* 31 December 1914, p. 792.

39. *The Gold Coast Leader* XX, no. 1 (21 January 1922): 8. Pomeyie was also at this time the official chief registrar of the Native Tribunal of Anloga and often conveyed to this body information about political activities within the region, whether it was government action or the activities of the British Congress of West Africa. See *Gold Coast Leader,* 3 February 1923, p. 6.

40. That the residents of the polity of Anlo, for example, did indeed make such distinctions among the different European and Euro-African groups operating there is evident from the history of their relations with different groups resident in the area. By the late nineteenth century, for example, the Anlo had long known that the Germans who worked in their midst as missionaries were not the same as the English who gov-

erned the area as colonizers. In 1854, for example, when the German missionaries made their first official visit to the Anlo capital of Anloga, they found it necessary to distinguish themselves not from the English but rather from the Danes, who had operated as traders in the area since the early eighteenth century. Once this distinction was made, however, it was understood and accepted. See Friedrich Plessing, "Station Quittah in West-Afrika," *Norddeutschen Missions-Gesellschaft* 4, no. 42 (1854): 176–78.

41. It is unclear which Johnson from Sierra Leone this may have been since several Johnsons lived in Keta at the time, among them B. P. Johnson and a Mr. and Mrs. J. J. or J. G. Johnson.

42. Freeman's leadership of the new church began in 1899 and lasted until 1902, when the Livingstone graduate and Cape Coast native J. Drybauld Taylor assumed the position. Taylor resigned c. 1905 and was replaced by a series of African American missionaries to head the Keta Mission and to oversee the work of both the church, its local ministers, and schools: J. J. Pearce (1906–1909); W. E. Shaw (1909–1912); the Peters (1914–125); the Francises (1925–1926), and the Piles (1926–1930). This list is based on Yates, "The History," passim; and *African Methodist Episcopal Zion Church Year Book, 1944*, p. 117. On the use of race for recruitment efforts by Taylor, see E. Eldern, "Dr. J. D. Taylor Visits Mission and Aggrey College [Arochuku, Nigeria]," *African Methodist Episcopal Zion Church Year Book* XXXV, no. 12 (December 1935): 1.

43. Among the church's strongest supporters (after some early misunderstandings) was the local Keta priest, Amegashie. See Greene, Field Note 56 and 96: Interviews with William Tiodo Anum, 22 December 1987, Anloga, and J. W. Kodzo-Vordoagu, 24 February 1988, Tegbi. See also "Der Krieg," *Monatsblatt der Norddeutche Missions-Gesellschaft* 20, no. 232 (April 1870): 1039–40. Support for greater missionary involvement in providing commercial opportunities to the local population is evident in the remarks made in 1925 by Fia Sri II, Anlo paramount chief, when he met with the visiting AME Zion bishop, C. C Alleyne. Sri informed him that "commerce was the greatest need of his country," and then stated, "I know the missionaries are not commercial, yet I hope that they will use their influence to induce commercial experts to come to Africa" at the same time that they built "more schools for the training of the people." Bishop C. C. Alleyne, "Crusading for African Redemption: Our Landing, Luggage and Mammy Chair," *Star of Zion* 49, no. 9 (26 February 1925): 1, 8. On Bremen work to educate local Anlo women, see "Diakonissenarbeit in Keta," *Monatsblatt der Norddeutschen Missions-Gesellschaft* 3 (1904): 22–24, and Charles M. K. Mamattah, *The Ewe of West Africa, Volume One* (Accra: Advent Press, 1979), 286–88. Much of this education involved preparing women to be the dutiful wives of mission-educated men and maintaining a Christian home. In the schools for girls, the Bremen deaconesses, as the German missionary women were called, taught reading, writing, and math as well as singing and needlework. It was this last skill that many women used to supplement their incomes. The hat worn by local men known as an "ear warmer" or *togbenya* is remembered as being produced by women who had learned to knit from the Bremen Mission women. The Bremen Mission, however, did little to challenge and actually strengthened patriarchal values among the Anlo by emphasizing the importance of a wife being her husband's helpmate rather than also working for her own economic well-being. In contrast, the AME Zion Church emphasized the kind of education that would allow women to hold leadership roles. This included training them for the ministry, an occupation traditionally reserved in the West for men.

44. On the history of the Roman Catholic Church in Keta, see A. K. Deku, *Historical Sketch of the Keta-Ho Catholic Diocese: May 24, 1890–May 25 1990, Centenary Edition* (Keta: Accra Committee, 1990), as well as http://www.ghanacbc.orga/ketahistory.html.

45. Resistance by educated Anlos to the AME Zion Church became most clearly evident in 1922, when many in the literate community refused to attend an AME Zion meeting. See *Gold Coast Leader,* 29 April 1922.

46. On changes in the economy in the Anlo area during this period, see Greene, *Gender,* 160–68.

47. Yates, "The History," 106–107, 110, 120–28.

48. Dr. W. E. Shaw, "Our African Missions," *Star of Zion* 42, no. 15 (1920): 1, 6. Another major complaint was the lack of a resident bishop to supervise the church's work.

49. Involved as well in this secessionist effort, according to Yates, "The History," 151–52, were J. Drybauld Taylor and J. E. K. Aggrey, both Livingstone graduates.

50. W. E. B. DuBois, "Opinion," *The Crisis: A Record of the Darker Races* 32, no. 2 (June 1926): 63. DuBois was made aware of the problems of the church by Phillip Jao Djan of the Gold Coast, who sent a letter to *The Crisis* for publication. For Djan's letter, see his piece titled "Zion in Africa: An Open Letter on Missions in West Africa by a Native Christian, Secondee, Gold Coast, West Africa," *The Crisis: A Record of the Darker Races* 31, no. 6 (April 1926): 293–94.

51. C. C. Alleyne, "Crusading for African Redemption: The Withdrawal Withdrawn," *Star of Zion* 49, no. 14 (2 April 1925): 1, 8.

52. According to Yates, "The History," 201, the AME Zion Church in the United States raised and distributed more money to its African missions between 1914 and 1928 than at any time in its history. But this sum, which had to be distributed among its many churches and schools in Liberia, Gold Coast, Ivory Coast, and Nigeria, amounted to very little going to the Gold Coast in comparison with the monies the churches and schools in that British colony raised for themselves.

53. Cole, "Our Mission Schools," 7.

54. A Staunch Zionite, "The Needs of the African Methodist Episcopal Zion Church in Africa," *The Missionary Seer* XXXVI, no. 4 (April 1936): 1, 4.

55. In a letter written to the then AME Zion bishop, William W. Matthews, three Anlo citizens expressed concern specifically about the Roman Catholic Church. In seeking more missionaries from the home church, they emphasized that "the Roman Catholic[s] must not occupy the whole field for they have so many priests landed here [in Keta] lately and 2 bishops (both) of them in the Gold Coast." Yates, "The History," 154. The great rivalry that developed among the different Christian denominations has also been well remembered in oral traditions. See Theophelus W. Adjorlorlor, "The History of Education in Anlo with Special Reference to Keta, from 1850–1960" (BA long essay, History Department, University of Ghana, Legon, 1977), 9, 12–13.

56. See Ustorf, *Bremen,* 343; and Debrunner, *A Church,* 146.

57. Local newspapers also carried considerable news about the racial situation in the United States. See, for example, *The Gold Coast Independent,* 31 January 1925, which contained the article "Black and White: Race Relations in the States," and *The Gold Coast Leader,* 3 February 1923, which published a piece titled "Racial Movements."

58. Zormelo studied at the Negro school, Hampton Institute, in Virginia. After her return, she married F. K. Fiawoo, whose affiliation with the AME Zion Church is discussed later in this study. She is also profiled, under the name of Charity Akoshiwo Tornyewonya Zormelo-Fiawoo, in D. E. K. Amenumey's *Outstanding Ewe of the 20th Century: Profiles of Fifteen Firsts* (Accra: Woeli Pub. Services, 2002), 162–69.

59. See, for example, "Anonymous Letter," 5–6; Cole, "Our Mission Schools"; K. A. Osam-Pinanko Jr., "African Methodist Episcopal Zion Church—West Gold Coast Conference, West Africa," *The Missionary Seer* XXXV, no. 10 (October 1935): 1, 3–4.

60. That the American concept of race (in which "one drop of African blood" in a person or that person's family background defined him or her as black) was largely

absent among the majority of the Anlo population is given support by an observation made by C. C. Alleyne, an AME Zion Church bishop responsible for church's West African missions. During his visit to Keta in 1925, he was informed by the African American missionary stationed there at the time, Henrietta Peters, that "she had to withdraw a mulatto child from [the] school [because] the other children made life miserable for her because they said she had bad hair that wouldn't wrap." This incident, involving a mixed-race child, would suggest that the local community in Keta did not define individuals according to the "one drop" rule. C. C. Alleyne, *Gold Coast at a Glance—Specially Adapted to Mission Study Class* (New York: Hunt Printing Co., 1931), 80.

61. Yates, "The History," 148. P. D. Ofosuhene, "Paving the Way," *The Missionary Seer* 29, no. 2 (February 1928): 11–12. Alleyne, *Gold Coast*, 118.

62. According to Yates, "The History," 233, increased support did arrive from the United States starting in 1936, but this did not alter local decisions to rely as much as they could on self-help.

63. On Fiawoo, see Frederick Baldwin Kwami, *Living Aphorisms II: Selected Kakabiku's, 1960–68-Wayside Wisdom* (Agbozume, Ghana: Kakabiku Enterprises, 1970), 5; C. L. Acolatse, "Rev. A. A. Adjahoe, B.A., S.T.B. Holds Quarterly Conference," *The Missionary Seer* XXXVII, no. 32 (February 1937): 6; Herrmann Jungraithmayr, "Enleitung," in Ferdinand K. Fiawoo, *Tuinese-Fiayi Dziehe; Two Plays in Ewe and English*, v–xi, German introduction by H. Jungraitmayr (Marburg an der Lahn: Im Selbstverlag, 1973); Alleyne, *Gold Coast*, 126, as well as Greene, *Gender*, 144–45. See also Felix Kwabena Ofosu, "The History of the African Methodist Episcopal Zion Church in Ghana" (BA Honors long essay, Department for the Study of Religions, University of Ghana, Legon, 1981), 37; and V. K. Ametewee, "The Development of Education," in *A Handbook of Eweland: Volume I: The Ewes of Southeastern Ghana*, ed. Francis Agbodeka, 219–24 (Accra: Woeli Publishing Services, 1997). On Adjahoe, see A. K. Mensah, "Missionary Day Celebration in Keta A.M.E. Zion Church, East Gold Coast Conference, West Africa," *The Missionary Seer* XXXVI, no. 12 (December 1936): 1; Acolatse, "Rev. A. A. Adjahoe," 6; and Andrades Brown, "Our Work with the Women in West Africa," *The Missionary Seer* XXXVII (July 1937): 1–2. The school Fiawoo and Osabetey-Aguedze founded in Adidome was called the Gold Coast People's College. Osabetey-Aguedze later moved the school to Dodowa, where it is known today as Ghanata Secondary School. The other school founded in Anloga was known as the New College of West Africa.

64. This is not to suggest that appeals by Gold Coast Zion members for assistance ceased. That was not the case. See, for example, F. K. Fiawoo, "Letters from the Field," *The Missionary Seer* XXXVI, no. 5 (May 1935): 4.

65. Alleyne, "Crusading" (26 February 1925), 1, 8. The recently returned Asante king Prempeh made similar remarks when Alleyne visited him as well. See C. C. Alleyne, "Crusading for African Redemption—Comments on Cooomassie," *Star of Zion* 49, no. 30 (23 July 1925): 7. Several years earlier, when Alfred C. Sam worked to have a group of African Americans settle in the Gold Coast, they were welcomed "to the home of their ancestors" by the editor of *The Gold Coast Nation* and the leaders of the Aborigines Rights Protections Society. See Kimble, *A Political History*, 542.

66. Fiawoo was exposed to Casely Hayford's ideas in the first two decades of the twentieth century when he was completing his studies and working for the business firm F. & A. Swanzy.

67. Casely Hayford, *Ethiopia*, 170–74.

68. The Bremen Mission was a strong advocate of valuing local-language education, but for their own very different reasons. See Meyer, "Christianity," 167–99. One can assume that this was an additional influence on Fiawoo, although he took a different approach to the Ewe language than did the Bremen Mission.

69. For a literary analysis of Fiawoo's plays, see Kofi Awoonor, *The Breast of the Earth: A Survey of the History of Culture and Literature of Africa South of the Sahara* (Garden City, N.Y.: Anchor Press/Doubleday, 1975), 132–36.

70. Fiawoo, *Tuinese-Fia yi Dziehe*.

71. The desire for such an independent institution was fueled, in part, by conflicts and disagreements over a range of issues between the Africans and African Americans affiliated with the Zion Church starting in the 1920s. Among the concerns were the level of financial support from the United States, the lack of administrative oversight, and the unwillingness of the home church to appoint an African bishop to oversee the West African missions. But cultural issues were of concern as well. In 1925, when AME Zion bishop C. C. Alleyne spoke at a general conference of the denomination at Cape Coast, he presented AME Zion as the national church of all Africans. But the editor of the *Gold Coast Leader* expressed concern about such an expansive definition of the term "Africans." He opined that "we watch with some degree of anxiety the career of this National Church among us . . . [for] we should like to feel that as Africans we can support and maintain *our own* Church organizations, and so develop them as to be in conformity with *our* national genius. . . . We should like to feel that Bishop Alleyne will come in time to realize that the African abroad has much to unlearn and that the only culture worth developing is not necessarily European or American culture." "Zion Reunion," *Gold Coast Leader,* 14 February 1925. Italics are my emphasis.

72. The amount received, as authorized by then AME Zion bishop E. B. Watson, was $2,800. See H. T. Medford, "Laboring for Africa," *The Missionary Seer* 47, no. 6 (June 1949): 8–10.

73. ADM 39/1/120: Memorandum from the Chiefs, Linguists and Hanua of Anlo to His Excellency Sir Alan Cuthbert Maxell Burns . . . Governor and Commander-in-Chief of the Gold Coast, Accra, 13 November 1944.

74. The larger political movement launched by Kwame Nkrumah, who like Fiawoo was educated at a U.S. Negro college, in this case Lincoln University, may have also facilitated the longevity of this oral tradition. Nkrumah embraced Pan-Africanism and African Americans as part of his drive to free the Gold Coast from British colonial rule and to inaugurate the first African colonized country in sub-Saharan Africa to win its independence. On Nkrumah's exposure to and embrace of Pan-Africanism, see Marika Sherwood, *Kwame Nkrumah: The Years Abroad, 1935–1947* (Legon, Ghana: Freedom Publications, 1996); Kevin Gaines, *African-Americans in Ghana: Black Expatriates and the Civil Rights Era* (Chapel Hill: University of North Carolina Press, 2006); and Ahmad A. Rahman, *The Regime Change of Kwame Nkrumah: Epic Heroism in Africa and the Diaspora* (New York: Palgrave Macmillan, 2007).

75. Sophia Amable, "'The 1953 Riot in Anloga and Its Aftermath'" (BA long essay, History Department, University of Ghana, Legon, 1977), 29.

76. D. C. Pope, "A Survey Report of Zion in Africa," *The Missionary Seer* 51, no. 6 (June 1953): 4–5, 12.

77. Awoonor, *Breast*, 12.

9. ORAL TRADITIONS ABOUT INDIVIDUALS ENSLAVED

The oral traditions excerpted here can be obtained from the author.

1. C. Spiess, "Ein Erinnerungsblatt."

2. A listing of Spiess's articles can be found in Christine Seige and Wolfgang Liedtke, *Bibliographie Deutschesprachiger Literatur zur Ethnographie und Geschichte der Ewe in Togo und Südostghana, 1840–1914* (Dresden: Staatliches Museum für Völkerkunde-Forschungsstelle, 1990); and Krzysztof Zielnica, *Bibliographie der Ewe in*

Westafrika, published as part of the series *Acta Ethnological et Linguistica Nr. 38,* ed. Engelbert Stiglmayr (Wien: Institute für Völkerkunder der Universität, Wien. 1976). For information on Spiess's attitude toward Africans, see Ustorf, *Bremen Missionaries,* passim.

3. The term *"ga"* in Ewe refers to metal, in this case, coinage. Using such a term makes it difficult to determine exactly which currency Spiess was referencing. During the early to mid-nineteenth century, several metal currencies circulated in Anlo, all of Western origin: American, German, Spanish, and British. What is particularly striking about Spiess's account is the drop in value of *"ga."* In the first few decades of the nineteenth century, he indicates a slave cost 40 *ga* or the equivalent of c. 180 marks. But when Ndorkutsu gained control of the trade in Atorkor in the 1840s the value of 20 *ga* (or 40 as stated in the text) had dropped to the equivalent of c. 80 marks. In the absence of information about which metal currencies (*ga*) Spiess is talking about, it is difficult to explain this drop in the currency exchange rates. For information on what currency exchange rates and the prices of slaves we do know about for the period between 1817 and the late nineteenth century as it involved gold and British pounds (with a few equivalencies for marks and dollars), see Gareth Austin, *Labour, Land and Capital in Ghana: From Slavery to Free Labour in Asante, 1807–1956* (Rochester, N.Y.: University of Rochester Press, 2005), 128–34.

CONCLUSION

1. The Bremen Mission's decision on how to handle the issue of slavery stands in contrast to the position taken by its sister missionary society, the Basel Mission, which had forbidden slavery among its congregations as early as 1861.

2. Ustorf, *Bremen Missionaries,* 278–84.

3. *Monatsblatt der Norddeutschen Missions-Gesellschaft* 2, no. 1 (1877): 10–12.

4. Staatsarchiv Bremen: 7, 1025–12/2—Breife von Lehrern in englischer Sprache, 18 June 1884.

BIBLIOGRAPHY

BOOKS AND ARTICLES

Abaka, Edmund. *Kola Is God's Gift: Agricultural Production, Export Initiatives and the Kola Industry of Asante and the Gold Coast, c. 1820–1950.* Athens: Ohio University Press, 2005.

Acolatse, C. L. "Rev. A. A. Adjahoe, B. A., S. T. B. Holds Quarterly Conference." *The Missionary Seer* XXXVII, no. 32 (February 1937): 6.

Addae, Stephen. *History of Medicine in Ghana, 1880–1960.* Edinburgh: Durham Academic Press, 1997.

Adeboye, Olufunke. "Reading the Diary of Akinpelu Obisesan in Colonial Africa." *African Studies Review* 51, no. 2 (2008): 75–97.

Aduamah, E. Y. *Traditions from the Volta Basin (9): Ewes in the Afram Plains.* Legon: University of Ghana, 1965.

African Methodist Episcopal Zion Church Year Book, 1944.

"Der Afrikanische Krieg." *Monatsblatt der Norddeutschen Missions-Gesellschaft* 20, no. 238 (1870): 1070–72.

Agbodeka, Francis. *African Politics and British Policy in the Gold Coast, 1868–1900: A Study in the Forms and Force of Protest.* Evanston, Ill.: Northwestern University Press, 1971.

Ajayi, J. F. Ade. "Samuel Ajayi Crowther of Oyo." In *Africa Remembered: Narratives by West Africans from the Era of the Slave Trade,* ed. Philip D. Curtin, 289–316. Madison: University of Wisconsin Press, 1967.

Alleyne, Bishop Cameron Chesterfield. "Crusading for African Redemption: Our Landing, Luggage and Mammy Chair." *Star of Zion* 49, no. 9 (26 February 1925): 1, 8.

———. "Crusading for African Redemption—Comments on Cooomassie." *Star of Zion* 49, no. 30 (23 July 1925): 7.

———. "Crusading for African Redemption: The Withdrawal Withdrawn." *Star of Zion* 49, no. 14 (2 April 1925): 1, 8.

———. *Gold Coast at a Glance—Specially Adapted to Mission Study Class.* New York: Hunt Printing Co., 1931.

Alpers, Edward A. "The Story of Swema: Female Vulnerability in Nineteenth Century East Africa." In *Women and Slavery in Africa,* ed. Claire C. Robertson and Martin A. Klein, 185–219. Madison: University of Wisconsin Press, 1983.

Amate, C. O. C. *The Making of Ada.* Accra: Woeli Pub., 1999.

Ametewee, V. K. "The Development of Education." In *A Handbook of Eweland: Volume I: The Ewes of Southeastern Ghana,* ed. Francis Agbodeka, 219–24. Accra: Woeli Publishing Services, 1997.

Amenumey, D. E. K. "German Administration in Southern Togo." *Journal of African History* 10, no. 4 (1969): 623–39.

———. *Outstanding Ewes of the 20th Century: Profiles of Fifteen Firsts.* Accra: Woeli Pub. Services, 2002.

Andrews, William L. "The Representation of Slavery and the Rise of Afro-American Literary Realism, 1865–1920." In *Slavery and the Literary Imagination,* ed. Deborah E. McDowell and Arnold Rampersad, 62–80. Baltimore: Johns Hopkins University Press, 1989.

"Anonymous Letter from British West Africa, Winneba, Gold Coast Colony." *The Missionary Seer* 27, no. 1 (January 1926): 5–6.

"Anyako." *Monatsblatt der Norddeutschen Missions-Gesellschaft* 18, no. 215 (1868): 961.

"Anyako." *Monatsblatt der Norddeutschen Missions-Gesellschaft* 19, no. 220 (1869): 983–84.

Anyidoho, Kofi. "Ewe Verbal Art." In *A Handbook of Eweland: Volume I: The Ewes of Southeastern Ghana,* ed. Francis Agbodeka, 123–52. Accra: Woeli Publishing Services, 1997.

Arhin, Kwame. "The Ashanti Rubber Trade with the Gold Coast in the Eighteen-Nineties." *Africa: Journal of the International African Institute* 42, no. 1 (1972): 34–43.

———. *West African Traders in Ghana in the Nineteenth and Twentieth Centuries.* New York: Longman, 1979.

"Der Ashanti-Krieg." *Monatsblatt der Norddeutschen Missions-Gesellschaft* 19, no. 226 (1869): 1009–1011.

A Staunch Zionite. "The Needs of the African Methodist Episcopal Zion Church in Africa." *The Missionary Seer* XXXVI, no. 4 (April 1936): 1, 4.

"Aus Afrika." *Monatsblatt der Norddeutschen Missions-Gesellschaft* 20, no. 236 (1870): 1062.

"Aus dem Innern." *Monatsblatt der Nord-deutschen Missions-Gesellschaft* 23, no. 266 (1973): 1207–1208.

Austen, Ralph. "The Slave Trade as History and Memory: Confrontations of Slaving Voyage Documents and Communal Traditions." *The William and Mary Quarterly,* 3rd Series, 58, no. 1 (2001): 229–44.

Austin, Gareth. *Labour, Land and Capital in Ghana: From Slavery to Free Labour in Asante, 1807–1956.* Rochester, N.Y.: University of Rochester Press, 2005.

Awoonor, Kofi. *The Breast of the Earth: A Survey of the History of Culture and Literature of Africa South of the Sahara.* Garden City, N.Y.: Anchor Press/Doubleday, 1975.

Awuma, Elias. "Reste des heidentums in der christlichen Gemeinde." *Monatsblatt der Norddeutschen Missions-Gesellschaft* 88 (1927): 11.

Backscheider, Paula R. *Reflections on Biography.* Oxford: Oxford University Press, 1999.

Baepler, Paul. *White Slaves, African Masters.* Chicago: University of Chicago Press, 1999.

Baeta, Robert. *Pastor Andreas Aku: Präses der Ewe-Kirke-50 Jahre Missonsdienst in Togo.* Bremen: Verlag der Norddeutschen Missions-Gesellschaft, 1934.

Bailey, Anne C. *African Voices of the Atlantic Slave Trade: Beyond the Silence and the Shame.* Boston: Beacon Press, 2004.

Baku, Kofi. "The Asafo in Two Ewe States." *Transactions of the Historical Society of Ghana, New Series,* 2 (1998): 21–28.

Barber, Karin. "Introduction: Hidden Innovators in Africa." In *Africa's Hidden Histories: Everyday Literacy and Making the Self,* ed. Karin Barber, 1–24. Bloomington: Indiana University Press, 2006.

Bartels, F. L. *The Roots of Ghana Methodism.* Cambridge: Cambridge University Press, 1965.

Beckles, Hilary. *A History of Barbados: From Amerindian Settlement to Caribbean Single Market,* 2nd edition. Cambridge: Cambridge University Press, 2006.

Birtwhistle, Allen. *Thomas Birch Freeman: West African Pioneer.* London: Cargate Press, 1950.

Bittle, William E., and Gilbert Geis. *The Longest Way Home: Chief Alfred C. Sam's Back-to-Africa Movement.* Detroit: Wayne State University Press, 1964.

Blassingame, John W. ed., *Slave Testimony: Two Centuries of Letters, Speeches, Interviews and Autobiographies.* Baton Rouge: Louisiana State University Press, 1977.

Blyden, Nemata. *West Indians in West Africa, 1808–1880.* Rochester. N.Y.: University of Rochester Press, 2000.

Bonnat, Marie-Joseph. *Marie-Joseph Bonnat et les Ashanti: Journal, 1869–1874.* Edited by Claude-Hélène Perrot and Albert Van Dantzig. Paris: Sociéte de Africanistes, 1994.

Booth, Wayne C. "The Rhetoric of Fundamentalist Conversion Narratives." In *Fundamentalisms Comprehended,* ed. Martin E. Marty and R. Scott Appleby, 367–95. Chicago: University of Chicago Press, 1995.

Bouché, Pierre. *Sept ans en Afrique Occidentale: La Côte des Esclaves.* Paris: E. Plon, 1885.

Brooks, George E. *Eurafricans in Western Africa: Commerce, Social Status, Gender and Religious Observance from the Sixteenth to the Eighteenth Century.* Athens: Ohio University Press, 2003.

———. *The Kru Mariner in the Nineteenth Century: An Historical Compendium.* Newark, Del.: Liberian Studies Association in America, 1972.

Brown, Andrades. "Our Work with the Women in West Africa." *The Missionary Seer* XXXVII (July 1937): 1–2.

Brydon, Lynne. "A 'Religious Encounter' in Amedzofe: Women and Change Through the Twentieth Century." In *Christianity and Social Change in Africa: Essays in Honor of J. D. Y. Peel,* ed. Toyin Falola, 471–88. Durham, N.C.: Carolina Academic Press, 2005.

Casely Hayford, J. E. *Ethiopia Unbound: Studies in Race Emancipation.* London: Frank Cass, 1969/1911.

Christaller, J. G. *Three Thousand Six Hundred Ghanian Proverbs from the Asante and Fante Language.* Lewiston, N.Y.: Edwin Mellen Press, 1990.

Cole, Rev. Isaac C. "Our Mission Schools." *The Missionary Seer* XXXII, no. 3 (March 1931): 6–8.

Colley, Linder. "Perceiving Low Literature: The Captivity Narrative." *Essays in Criticism* LIII, no. 3 (2003): 199–218.

Collins, Edmund. "The Panic Element in Nineteenth Century British Relations with Ashanti." *Transactions of the Historical Society of Ghana* V, p. 2 (1962): 79–144.

Constanzo, Angelo. "The Narrative of Archibald Monteith, A Jamaican Slave." *Callaloo* 13, no. 1 (1990): 115–30.

Cooper, Frederick. *Plantation Slavery on the East Coast of Africa.* Portsmouth, N.H.: Heinemann, 1997.

Curtin, Philip D. *Africa Remembered: Narratives by West Africans in the Era of the Slave Trade.* Madison: University of Wisconsin Press, 1967.

Daaku, K. Y. "Oral Traditions of Adanse." Legon: Institute of African Studies, University of Ghana, 1969.

Debrunner, Hans W. *A Church Between Colonial Powers: A Study of the Church in Togo.* London: Lutterworth Press.

———. *Presence and Prestige: Africans in Europe—A History of Africans in Europe Before 1918.* Basel: Basler Afrika Bibliographen, 1979.

Deku, A. K. *Historical Sketch of the Keta-Ho Catholic Diocese: May 24, 1890–May 25, 1990, Centenary Edition.* Keta: Accra Committee, 1990.

"Diakonissenarbeit in Keta." *Monatsblatt der Norddeutschen Missions-Gesellschaft* 3 (1904): 22–24.

Djan, Phillip Jao. "Zion in Africa: An Open Letter on Missions in West Africa by a Native Christian, Secondee, Gold Coast, West Africa." *The Crisis: A Record of the Darker Races* 31, no. 6 (April 1926): 293–94.

Doll, Dan, and Jessica Munns. "Introduction." In *Recording and Reordering: Essays on the Seventeenth and Eighteenth Century Diary and Journal,* ed. Dan Doll and Jessica Munns, 9–21. Lewisburg, Pa.: Bucknell University Press, 2006.

———, eds. *Recording and Reordering: Essays on the Seventeenth and Eighteenth Century Diary and Journal.* Lewisburg, Pa.: Bucknell University Press, 2006.

Doortmont, Michel. *The Pen-Pictures of Modern Africans and African Celebrities by Charles Frances Hutchison: A Collective Biography of Elite Society in the Gold Coast Colony.* Leiden: Brill, 2005.

DuBois, W. E. B. "Opinion." *The Crisis: A Record of the Darker Races* 32, no. 2 (June 1926): 63.

Dumett, Raymond. "African Merchants of the Gold Coast, 1860–1905: Dynamics of Indigenous Entrepreneurship." *Comparative Studies in Society and History* 25, no. 4 (1983): 661–93.

———. "The Campaign against Malaria and the Expansion of Scientific Medical and Sanitary Services in British West Africa." *African Historical Studies* 1, no. 2 (1968): 153–97.

———. "John Sarbah, The Elder, and African Mercantile Entrepreneurship in the Gold Coast in the Late Nineteenth Century." *Journal of African History* 14, no. 4 (1973): 653–79.

———. "The Rubber Trade of the Gold Coast and Asante in the Nineteenth Century: African Innovation and Market Responsiveness." *Journal of African History* 12, no. 1 (1971): 79–101.

Dumett, Raymond, and Marion Johnson. "Britain and the Suppression of Slavery in the Gold Coast." In *The End of Slavery in Africa,* ed. Suzanne Miers and Richard Roberts, 71–116. Madison: University of Wisconsin Press, 1988.

Dyde, Brian. *The Empty Sleeve: The Story of the West India Regiments of the British Army.* St. John's, Antigua: Hansib Caribbean, 1997.

Eakin, Paul John. *Fictions in Autobiography: Studies in the Art of Self-Invention.* Princeton, N.J.: Princeton University Press, 1985.

Eldern, E. "Dr. J. D. Taylor Visits Mission and Aggrey College [Arochuku, Nigeria]." *African Methodist Episcopal Zion Church Year Book* 35, no. 12 (December 1935): 1.

Esedebe, P. Olisanwuche. *Pan-Africanism: The Idea and Movement, 1776–1991.* Washington, D.C.: Howard University Press, 1994.

Escott, Paul D. *Slavery Remembered: A Record of Twentieth-Century Slave Narratives.* Chapel Hill: University of North Carolina Press, 1979.

Fiawoo, F. K. "Letters from the Field." *The Missionary Seer* XXXVI, no. 5 (May 1935): 4.

———. *Tuinese-Fia yi Dziehe: Two Plays in Ewe and English.* German introduction by H. Jungraitmayr. Marburg an der Lahn: Selbstverlag, 1973.

Fisch, Audrey A. "Introduction." In *The Cambridge Companion to the African American Slave Narrative,* ed. Audrey A. Fisch, 11–27. Cambridge: Cambridge University Press, 2007.

Foster, Philip. *Education and Social Change in Ghana.* London: Routledge and Kegan Paul, 1965.

Fredrickson, George M. *Black Liberation: A Comparative History of Black Ideologies in the United States and South Africa.* Oxford: Oxford University Press, 1995.

Gaines, Kevin. *African-Americans in Ghana: Black Expatriates and the Civil Rights Era.* Chapel Hill: University of North Carolina Press, 2006.

Getz, Trevor R. *Slavery and Reform in West Africa: Toward Emancipation in Nineteenth Century Senegal and the Gold Coast.* Athens: Ohio University Press, 2004.

Glassman, Jonathon. *Feasts and Riot: Revelry, Rebellion and Popular Consciousness on the Swahili Coast, 1856–1888.* Portsmouth, N.H.: Heinemann, 1995.

Gocking, Roger. *Facing Two Ways: Ghana's Coastal Communities under Colonial Rule.* Lanham, Md.: University Press of America, 1999.

Goody, Jack. "Introduction to Ashanti and the Northwest." In *Research Review—Supplement: Ashanti and the Northwest,* ed. Jack Goody and Kwame Arhin, 1–110. University of Ghana, Institute of African Studies, 1965.

Greene, Sandra E. *Gender, Ethnicity and Social Change on the Upper Slave Coast: A History of the Anlo Ewe.* Portsmouth, N.H.: Heinemann, 1996.

———. "Oral Traditions about Individuals Enslaved." In *African Sources on Slavery and the Slave Trade,* ed. Sandra E. Greene, Martin Klein, Alice Bellagamba, and Carolyn Brown (forthcoming).

———. *Sacred Sites and the Colonial Encounter: A History of Meaning and Memory in Ghana.* Bloomington: Indiana University Press, 2002.

Gros, Jules. *Voyages, Aventures et Captivié de J. Bonnat chez les Achantis.* Paris: E. Plon, Courrit et Cie., 1884.

Haenger, Peter. *Slaves and Slave Holders on the Gold Coast: Towards an Understanding of Social Bondage in West Africa.* Edited by J. J. Shaffer and Paul E. Lovejoy. Basel: P. Schlettwein, 2000.

Hall, Peter. *Autobiography of Rev. Peter Hall: First Moderator of the Presbyterian Church of Ghana.* Accra: Waterville Pub. House, 1965.

Harms, Robert. *The Diligent: A Voyage through the Worlds of the Slave Trade.* New York: Basic Books, 2002.

Haywood, Chanta M. *Prophesying Daughters: Black Women Preachers and the Word, 1823–1913.* Columbia: University of Missouri Press, 2003.

Henrici, Ernst. "Das Volksrecht der Epheneger und sein Verhältniss zur deutsche Colonisation im Togogebiete." *Zeitschrift für Rechtswissenschaft (Stuttgart)* II (1898): 131–52.

Herold, Lieutenant. "Bericht betreffend Rechtsgewohnheiten und Palaver der deutschen Ewe-Neger." *Mittheilungen von Forschungsreisenden und Gelehrten aus den Deutschen Schutzgebieten* V (1892): 160–75.

Hindmarsh, D. Bruce. *The Evangelical Conversion Narrative: Spiritual Autobiography in Early Modern England.* Oxford: Oxford University Press, 2005.

Hogendorn, J. S., and Paul E. Lovejoy. "The Reform of Slavery in Early Colonial Northern Nigeria." In *The End of Slavery in Africa,* ed. Suzanne Miers and Richard Roberts, 391–414. Madison: University of Wisconsin Press, 1988.

Holsey, Bayo. *Routes of Remembrance: Refashioning the Slave Trade in Ghana.* Chicago: University of Chicago Press, 2008.

Hood, Bishop J. W. *One Hundred Years of the A.M.E. Zion Church: The Centennial of African Methodism* New York: A.M.E. Zion Book Concern, 1895.

Horton, Africanus B. *Letters on the Political Condition of the Gold Coast.* London: Frank Cass, 1970; 1870.

Hunwick, John, and Eve Troutt Powell. *The African Diaspora in the Mediterranean Lands of Islam.* Princeton, N.J.: Markus Wiener, 2002.

Illg, Frau. "Was Frau Illg von Ho erzählt." *Quartal-Blatt der Norddeutschen Missions-Gesellschaft* 74 (1875): 404–410.

Illg, Johann Daniel. "Tafiewe und Ho." *Monatsblatt der Norddeutschen Missions-Gesellschaft* 25 (1875): 342–44.

Illife, John. *Honour in African History.* Cambridge: Cambridge University Press, 2005.

Jacobs, Sylvia. "The Impact of African American Education on 19th Century Colonial West Africa: Livingstone College Graduates in the Gold Coast." *Negro History Bulletin* 58, no. 1–2 (1995): 5–13.

———. "James Emman Kwegyir Aggrey: An African Intellectual in the United States." *Journal of Negro History* 81, no. 1/4 (1996): 47–61.

Jenkins, Paul, ed. *The Recovery of the West African Past: African Pastors and African History in the Nineteenth Century: C.C. Reindorf and Samuel Johnson*. Basel: Basler Afrika Bibliographien, 1998.

Johnson, Marion. "Ashanti East of the Volta." *Transactions of the Historical Society of Ghana*. VIII (1965): 33–59.

———. "M. Bonnat on the Volta." *Ghana Notes and Queries* 10 (1968): 4–17.

Jones, Adam. "'Four Years in Asante': One Source or Several?" *History in Africa* 18 (1991): 173–203.

Jones, Adam, and Peter Sebald, eds. *An African Family Archive: The Lawsons of Little Popo/Anecho (Togo), 1841–1938*. Oxford: Oxford University Press, 2005.

Jungraithmayr, Herrmann. "Enleitung." In Ferdinand K. Fiawoo, *Tuinese-Fiayi Dziehe; Two Plays in Ewe and English*. Marburg an der Lahn: Im Selbstverlag, 1973.

Kaplow, Susan B. "The Mudfish and the Crocodile: Underdevelopment of a West African Bourgeoisie." *Science and Society* XLI, no. 3 (1977): 317–33.

Kenworthy, Leonard S. "James K. Aggrey: Reconciler of Races." *Journal of Negro Education* 15, no. 2 (1946): 181–90.

Kessel, Ineke van. "The Black Dutchmen: African Soldiers in the Netherlands East Indies." In *Merchants, Missionaries and Migrants: 300 Years of Dutch-Ghanaian Relations*, ed. Ineke van Kessel, 133–141. Amsterdam: KIT Publishers, 2002.

Kimble, David. *A Political History of Ghana: The Rise of Gold Coast Nationalism, 1850–1928*. London: Oxford University Press, 1963.

Klein, A. Norman. "The Two Asantes: Competing Interpretations of 'Slavery' in Akan-Asante Culture and Society." In *The Ideology of Slavery in Africa*, ed. Paul E. Lovejoy, 149–67. Beverly Hills, Calif.: Sage, 1981.

Klein, Martin. "Slave Resistance and Slave Emancipation in Coastal Guinea." In *The End of Slavery in Africa*, ed. Suzanne Miers and Richard Roberts, 203–219. Madison: University of Wisconsin Press, 1988.

———. *Slavery and Colonial Rule in French West Africa*. Cambridge: Cambridge University Press, 1998.

———. "Studying the History of Those Who Would Rather Forget: Oral History and the Experience of Slavery." *History in Africa* 16 (1989): 209–217.

Klose, H. "Religiöse Anschauungen und Menschenopfer Togo." *Globus* (Braunschweig) LXXXI, no. 12 (1902): 187–94.

Kludze, A. K. P. *Ewe Law of Property*. London: Sweet and Maxwell, 1973.

Knoll, Arthur. "Taxation in the Gold Coast Colony and in Togo: A Study in Early Administration." In *Britain and Germany in Africa*, ed. Prosser Gifford and William Roger Lewis, with the assistance of Alison Smith, 418–53. New Haven, Conn.: Yale University Press, 1967.

———. *Togo under Imperial Germany, 1884–1914: A Case Study in Colonial Rule*. Stanford, Calif.: Hoover Institution Press, 1978.

Konrad, Zinta. *Ewe Comic Heroes: Trickster Tales in Togo*. New York: Garland, 1994.

Kraamer, Malika. "Ghanaian Interweaving in the Nineteenth Century: A New Perspective on Ewe and Asante Textile History." *African Arts* 29, no. 4 (2006): 36–53, 93–95.

"Der Krieg." *Monatsblatt der Norddeutschen Missions-Gesellschaft* 20, no. 231 (1870): 1036.

"Der Krieg." *Monatsblatt der Norddeutschen Missions-Gesellschaft* 20, no. 232 (April 1870): 1039–40.

Der Krieg." *Monatsblatt der Norddeutschen Missions-Gesellschaft* 20, no. 233 (1870): 1044.

Kwami, Frederick Baldwin. *Living Aphorisms II: Selected Kakabiku's, Wayside Wisdom 1960–68*. Agbozume, Ghana: Kakabiku Enterprises, 1970.

Langley, J. Ayodele. *Pan-Africanism and Nationalism in West Africa, 1900–1945.* Oxford: Oxford University Press, 1973.

Larson, Pier M. *History and Memory in the Age of Enslavement.* Portsmouth, N.H.: Heinemann, 2000.

Law, Robin. "Human Sacrifice in Pre-colonial West Africa." *African Affairs* 84, no. 334 (1985): 53–87.

Lewin, Thomas J. *Asante before the British: The Prempean Years, 1875–1900.* Lawrence: Regents Press of Kansas, 1978.

"Lichsrahlen aus dem Dunkel einer Heidnischen Mordthat in Ho." *Monatsblatt der Norddeutschen Missions-Gesellschaft* 12, no. 11 (1900): 92–93.

Lind, Vera. "The Suicidal Mind and Body: Examples from Northern Germany." In *From Sin to Insanity: Suicide in Early Modern Europe,* ed. Jeffrey R. Watt, 64–80. Ithaca, N.Y.: Cornell University Press, 2004.

Litwack, Leon F. *Been in the Storm so Long: The Aftermath of Slavery.* New York: Random House, 1979.

Lovejoy, Paul, ed. *The Ideology of Slavery in Africa.* Beverly Hills, Calif.: Sage, 1981.

Lynch, Hollis R. *Edward Wilmot Blyden: Pan-Negro Patriot 1832–1912.* New York: Oxford University Press, 1967.

Maier, Donna J. E. "Asante War Aims in the 1869 Invasion of Ewe." In *The Golden Stool: Studies of the Asante Center and Periphery,* ed. Enid Schildkrout, 232–323. New York: American Museum of Natural History, 1987.

———. "Competition for Power and Profits in Kete-Krachi, West Africa, 1875–1900." *International Journal of African Historical Studies* 13, no. 1 (1980): 33–50.

Mamattah, Charles M. K. *The Ewe of West Africa, Volume One.* Accra: Advent Press, 1979.

Mann, Kristin. *Marrying Well: Marriage, Status and Social Change among the Educated Elite in Colonial Lagos.* Cambridge: Cambridge University Press, 1985.

Manoukian, Madeline. "The Ewe Speaking People of Togoland and the Gold Coast." In *Ethnographic Survey of Africa.* Edited by Daryll Forde. London: International African Institute, 1952.

Martin, Jane. "Krumen 'Down the Coast': Liberian Migrants on the West African Coast in the 19th and early 20th Centuries." *The International Journal of African Historical Studies* 18, no. 3 (1985): 401–423.

Martin, Tony. *The Pan African Connection: From Slavery to Garvey and Beyond.* Dover, Mass.: Majority Press, 1983.

Matory, J. Lorand. *Black Atlantic Religion.* Princeton, N.J.: Princeton University Press, 2005.

McBride, Dwight. *Impossible Witnesses: Truth, Abolitionism and Slave Testimony.* New York: New York University Press, 2001.

McCaskie, Thomas C. "Death and the Asantehene: A Historical Meditation." *Journal of African History* 30, no. 3 (1989): 417–44.

———. *State and Society in Pre-Colonial Asante.* Cambridge: Cambridge University Press, 1995.

McManamon, John M. *Funeral Oratory and the Cultural Ideals of Italian Humanism.* Chapel Hill: University of North Carolina Press, 1989.

Medford, H. T. "Laboring for Africa." *The Missionary Seer* 47, no. 6 (June 1949): 8–10.

Mensah, A. K. "Missionary Day Celebration in Keta A.M.E. Zion Church, East Gold Coast Conference, West Africa." *The Missionary Seer* XXXVI, no. 12 (December 1936): 1.

Merz, Johannes "Die Ashanteer in Waya." *Monatsblatt der Norddeutschen Missions-Gesellschaft* 20, no. 239 (1870): 1077–78.

———. *Ein Neger-Gehülte im Missionswerk: Das Leben des Katchisten Aaron Onyi-payede*. Bremen: Norddeutsche Mission Gesellschaft, 1875.

Metcalfe, G. E. *Great Britain and Ghana: Documents of Ghana History, 1807–1957*. Legon-Accra, Ghana: University of Ghana, 1964.

Metzger, Bruce M., and Michael D. Coogan, eds. *The Oxford Companion to the Bible*. New York: Oxford University Press, 1993.

Meyer, Birgit. "Christianity and the Ewe Nation: German Pietist Missionaries, Ewe Converts and the Politics of Culture." *Journal of Religion in Africa* 32, no. 2 (2002): 167–99.

———. *Translating the Devil: Religion and Modernity among the Ewe in Ghana*. Edinburgh: Edinburgh University Press, 1999.

Miers, Suzanne, and Richard Roberts, eds. *The End of Slavery in Africa*. Madison: University of Wisconsin Press, 1988.

Miescher, Stephan F. "My Own Life: A. K. Boakye Yiadom's Autobiography—The Writing and Subjectivity of A Ghanaian Teacher-Catechist." In *Africa's Hidden Histories: Everyday Literacy and Making the Self*, ed. Karin Barber, 27–51. Bloomington: Indiana University Press, 2006.

Mudimbe, V. Y. *The Invention of Africa: Gnosis, Philosophy and the Order of Knowledge*. Bloomington: Indiana University Press, 1988.

Newell, Stephanie. *Literary Culture in Colonial Ghana*. Bloomington: Indiana University Press, 2002.

Newton, Melanie J. *The Children of Africa in the Colonies: Free People of Color in Barbados in the Age of Emancipation*. Baton Rouge: Louisiana State University Press, 2008.

Northrup, David. *Africa's Discovery of Europe, 1450–1850*. Oxford: Oxford University Press, 2002.

Nussbaum, Felicity. *The Autobiographical Subject: Gender and Ideology in Eighteenth-Century England*. Baltimore: Johns Hopkins University Press, 1989.

———. *Torrid Zones: Maternity, Sexuality and Empire in Eighteenth-Century English Narratives*. Baltimore: Johns Hopkins University Press, 1995.

Obeng, Pashington. *Asante Catholicism: Religious and Cultural Reproduction among the Akan of Ghana*. Leiden: E. J. Brill, 1996.

Ofosuhene, P. D. "Paving the Way." *The Missionary Seer* 29, no. 2 (February 1928): 11–12.

Olney, James. "'I Was Born': Slave Narratives, Their Status as Autobiography and as Literature." In *The Slave's Narrative*, ed. Charles T. Davis and Henry Louis Gates Jr., 148–75. New York: Oxford University Press, 1985.

Osam-Pinanko, K. A. Jr. "African Methodist Episcopal Zion Church—West Gold Coast Conference, West Africa." *The Missionary Seer* XXXV, no. 10 (October 1935): 1, 3–4.

Parliamentary Papers, 1875. London: Harrison and Sons, 1875.

Parke, Catherine N. *Biography: Writing Lives*. New York: Twayne, 1996.

Parker, John. "*Mankraloi*, Merchants and Mulattos—Carl Reindorf and the Politics of 'Race' in Early Colonial Accra." In *The Recovery of the West African Past: African Pasts and African History in the Nineteenth Century—C.C. Reindorf and Samuel Johnson*, ed. Paul Jenkins, 31–47. Basel: Basler Afrika Bibliographien, 1998.

Patton, Adell Jr. "Dr. John Farrell Easmon: Medical Professionalism and Colonial Racism in the Gold Coast, 1856–1900." *International Journal of African Historical Studies* 22, no. 4 (1989): 601–36.

———. *Physicians, Colonial Racism and Diaspora in West Africa*. Gainesville: University Press of Florida, 1996.

Perbi, Akosua Adoma. *A History of Indigenous Slavery in Ghana*. Accra: Sub-Saharan Pub., 2004.

Perrot, Claude-Hélène, and Albert van Dantzig, eds. *Marie-Joseph Bonnat et les Ashanti: Journal—1869–1874*. Paris: Société de Africanistes, 1994.

Pfeffer, R. *The Suicidal Child*. New York: Guilford Press, 1986.

Pfann, Hélè H. *A Short History of the Catholic Church in Ghana*. Cape Coast, Ghana: Catholic Mission Press, 1970.

Plessing, Friedrich. "Station Quittah in West-Afrika." *Norddeutschen Missions-Gesellschaft* 4, no. 42 (1854): 176–78.

———. "Theure und geliebte Väter!" *Monatsblatt der Norddeutschen Missions-Gesellschaft* 5, no. 57 (1855): 244–48.

Pope, D. C. "A Survey Report of Zion in Africa." *The Missionary Seer* 51, no. 6 (June 1953): 4–5, 12.

Rahman, Ahmad A. *The Regime Change of Kwame Nkrumah: Epic Heroism in Africa and the Diaspora*. New York: Palgrave Macmillan, 2007.

Ramseyer, F. A., and J. A. Kühne. *Four Years in Ashantee*. New York: Robert Carter and Bro., 1875.

Rattray, R. S. *Ashanti Law and Constitution*. New York: Negro University Press, 1911/1969.

———. *Ashanti Proverbs: The Primitive Ethics of a Savage People*. London: Oxford University Press, 1916.

———. *Religion and Art in Ashanti*. Oxford: Oxford University Press, 1927.

Reindorf, Carl. *History of the Gold Coast and Asante*. Basel: Missionsbuchhandlung, 1895.

Reindorf, Josef. "Ho und Taviewe." *Monatsblatt der Norddeutschen Missions-Gesellschaft* 25 (1875): 1364–65.

Reis, Elizabeth. "Seventeenth Century Puritan Conversion Narratives." In *Religions of the United States in Practice, Volume One*, ed. Colleen McDannell, 22–31. Princeton, N.J.: Princeton University Press, 2001.

Robertson, Claire, and Martin Klein. *Women and Slavery in Africa*. Madison: University of Wisconsin Press, 1983.

Rohns, Hedwig. "Sterben von Christen und Heider." *Monatsblatt der Norddeutschen Missions-Gesellschaft* 1 (1896): 7.

Sackey, Isaac. "A Brief History of the A.M.E. Zion Church, West Gold Coast District." *Ghana Bulletin of Theology* 1, no. 3 (1957): 16–20.

Sampson, Magnus. *Makers of Modern Ghana*. Accra: Anuwuo Educational Publications, 1969.

Sarbah, John Mensah. *Fanti Customary Laws: A Brief Introduction to the Principles of the Native Laws and Customs of the Fanti and Akan Districts of the Gold Coast*. London: Frank Cass, 1897/1968.

Schöck-Quineros, Eva, and Dieter Lenz, eds. *150 Jahre Norddeutsche Mission, 1836–1986*. Bremen: Norddeutsche Mission, 1986.

Schönhärl, Josef. *Volkskunliches aus Togo*. Dresden: C. A. Kochs Verlagsbuchhandlung, 1909.

Schreiber, A. W. *Bausteine zur Geschichte der Norddetuschen Missions-Gesellschaft*. Bremen: Verlag der Norddeutschen Missions-Gesellschaft, 1936.

———. *Lehrer Christian Aliwodzi Sedode, 1857–1907: Worte zu dessen Gedächtnis*. Bremen: Verlag der Norddeutschen Mission-Gesellschaft, 1908.

Schweizer, Peter A. *Survivors on the Gold Coast: The Basel Missionaries in Colonial Ghana*. Accra: Smartline Publishing, 2000.

Seeger, Matthaus. "Er soll die Straken zum Raube haben." *Monatsblatt der Norddeutschen Missions-Gesellschaft* 8, no. 9 (1896): 66–69.

Seidel, H. "Pfandwesen und Schuldhaft in Togo." *Globus* LXXIX, no. 20 (1901): 309–313.

Sekora, John. "Black Message/White Envelope: Genre, Authenticity, and Authority in the Antebellum Slave Narrative." *Callaloo* 32 (1987): 482–515.

Shaw, W. E. "Our African Missions." *Star of Zion* 42, no. 15 (1920): 1, 6.

Shaw, Rosalind. *Memories of the Slave Trade: Ritual and Historical Imagination in Sierra Leone.* Chicago: University of Chicago Press, 2002.

Seige, Christine, and Wolfgang Liedtke. *Bibliographie Deutschesprachiger Literatur zur Ethnographie und Geschichte der Ewe in Togo und Südostghana, 1840–1914.* Dresden: Staatliches Museum für Völkerkunde-Forschungsstelle, 1990.

Sherwood, Marika. *Kwame Nkrumah: The Years Abroad, 1935–1947.* Legon, Ghana: Freedom Publications, 1996.

Skinner, Kate. "Reading, Writing and Rallies: The Politics of 'Freedom' in Southern British Togoland, 1953–1956." *Journal of African History* 48 (2007): 123–47.

Smith, William. *Aggrey of Africa: A Study in Black and White.* New York: Doubleday, Doran and Co., 1930.

Snader, Joe. *Caught between Worlds: British Captivity Narratives in Fact and Fiction.* Lexington: University of Kentucky Press, 2000.

Spiess, Carl. "Wie bestimmt der Evheer die Zeit." *Quartalblatt der Norddeutschen Missions-Gesellschaft* 2 (1894): 1–7.

———. "Ein Erinnerungsblatt an die Tage des Sklavenhandels in Westafrika." *Globus (Braunschweig)* 92 (1907): 205–208.

Spieth, J. *Die Ewe Stämme.* Berlin: Dietrich Reimer, 1906.

———. "Reschtanschauungen der Eweer in Süd-Togo." *Koloniale Rundschau* 4 (1912): 339–54.

———. "Von den Evhefrauen." *Quartalblatt der Norddeutschen Missions-Gesellschaft* 4 (1889): 1–8.

Sutton, I. B. "The Volta River Salt Trade: The Survival of an Indigenous Industry." *Journal of African History* 22, no. 1 (1981): 43–61.

Taylor, Larissa Juliet. " Funeral Sermons and Orations as Religious Propaganda in Sixteenth Century France." In *The Place of the Dead: Death and Remembrance in Late Medieval and Early Modern Europe,* ed. Bruce Gordon and Peter Marshall, 224–39. Cambridge: Cambridge University Press, 2000.

"Die Unruhen in Anglo-Gebiet." *Monatsblatt der Norddeutschen Missions-Gesellschaft* 3 and 4 (1885): 42–46.

Ustorf, Werner. *Bremen Missionaries in Togo and Ghana, 1847–1900.* Accra: Asempa Pub., 2002.

Vaughan, Alden T., and Edward W. Clark. *Puritans among the Indians: Accounts of Captivity and Redemption, 1676–1724.* Cambridge, Mass.: Belknap Press, 1981.

Vaughn, James H., and Anthony H. M. Kirk-Greene, eds. *The Diary of Hamman Yaji: Chronicle of a West African Muslim Ruler.* Bloomington: Indiana University Press, 1995.

"Völlingen Zerstörung unsrer Station Wegbe." *Monatsblatt der Norddeutschen Missions-Gesellschaft* 19, no. 225 (1869): 1006.

Wagner-Martin, Lindage. *Telling Women's Lives: The New Biography.* New Brunswick, N.J.: Rutgers University Press, 1994.

Watson, Ruth. "'What is our intelligence, our school going and reading of books without getting money?' Akinpẹlu Obiṣẹsan and His Diary." In *Africa's Hidden Histo-*

ries: *Everyday Literacy and Making the Self,* ed. Karin Barber, 52–77. Bloomington: Indiana University Press, 2006.

Welman, C. W. *The Native States of the Gold Coast: History and Constitution.* London: Dawsons of Pall Mall, 1969; Part One-Peki. First published in 1925.

"West Africa." *Monatsblatt der Norddeutschen Missions-Gesellschaft* 11, no. 121 (1861): 518.

Westermann, Diedrich. *Ewefiala or Ewe-English Dictionary.* Berlin: Dietrich Reimer, 1928.

———. "Martin Akou, de Lomé au Togo: Actuellement Étudiant en Médicine a Bale." In *Autobiographies d'Africaines,* 282–336. Paris: Payot, 1943.

———. *A Study of the Ewe Language.* London: Oxford University Press, 1930.

Wicke, A. "Die Blattern-Erkrankunen an der Westküste von Afrika, speziell im deutschen Togo-Gebiet." *Mitteilungen von Forschungsreisenden und Gelehrten aus den deutschen Schutzegebieten* 4 (1891): 184–88.

Wiegräbe, Paul. "Aus dem Leben aus des Afrikanischen Evangelisten Aaron Kuku-von ihm selbst erzählt." *Monatsblatt der Norddeutschen Missions-Gesellschaft* 91 (1930): 51–57, 67–71, 186–89, 214–17.

———. *Vom Sklaven zum Freigeborenen: Ein Lebensbild aus Westafrika.* Bremen: Bremer Mission-Schriften, 1930.

Wilks, Ivor. *Asante in the Nineteenth Century.* Cambridge: Cambridge University Press, 1975.

———. *Forests of Gold: Essays on the Akan and the Kingdom of Asante.* Athens: Ohio University Press, 1993.

Williams, Walter L. *Black Americans and the Evangelization of Africa, 1887–1900.* Madison: University of Wisconsin Press, 1982.

Wright, Marcia. *Strategies of Slaves and Women: Life-Stories from East/Central Africa.* New York: Lillian Barber Press, 1993.

———. "Women in Peril: A Commentary on the Life Stories of Captives in Nineteenth Century East-Central Africa." *African Social Research* 20 (1975): 800–819.

Yarak, Larry. "West African Coastal Slavery in the Nineteenth Century: The Case of the Afro-European Slaveowners of Elmina." *Ethnohistory* 36, no. 1 (1989): 44–60.

Zaslavsky, Claudia. *Africa Counts: Number and Pattern in African Culture.* Boston: Prindle, Weber and Schmidt, 1973.

Zielnica, Krzysztof. *Bibliographie der Ewe in Westafrika.* Published as part of the series *Acta Ethnological et Linguistica Nr. 38.* Edited by Engelbert Stiglmayr. Wien: Institute für Völkerkunder der Universität, Wien.

"Zion Reunion." *Gold Coast Leader,* 14 February 1925.

DISSERTATIONS, THESES, LONG ESSAYS, AND UNPUBLISHED PAPERS

Adjorlorlor, Theophelus W. "The History of Education in Anlo with Special Reference to Keta, from 1850–1960." BA long essay, History Department, University of Ghana, Legon, 1977.

Amable, Sophia. "The 1953 Riot in Anloga and Its Aftermath." BA long essay, History Department, University of Ghana, Legon, 1977.

Anyidoho, Kofi. "Death and Burial of the Dead: A Study of Ewe Funeral Folklore." MA thesis, Indiana University, 1983.

Asante Collective Biography Project: Career Sheet—ACBP/2: Adu Bofo.

Asare, E. B. "Akwamu-Peki Relations in the Eighteenth and Nineteenth Centuries." MA thesis, University of Ghana, 1973.

Asimpi, Kofi. "European Christian Missions and Race Relations in Ghana, 1828–1970." PhD diss., Boston University, 1996.

Brydon, Lynne. "Resettlement in Eastern Ghana: The Aftermath of a Pre-Colonial Holocaust." Unpublished paper delivered at the 2003 African Studies Association annual meeting in Boston, Massachusetts.

Case, Glenna. "Wasipe Under the Ngbanya: Polity, Economy, and Society in Northern Ghana," Volumes 1 and II. PhD diss., Northwestern University, 1979.

Collier, Kate. "Ablode: Networks, Ideas and Performance in Togoland Politics, 1950–2001." PhD diss., University of Birmingham, 2003.

Gates, Lisa Marie. "Images of Africa in Late Nineteenth and Twentieth Century German Literature and Culture." PhD diss., Harvard University, 1996.

Jenkins, Paul. "Abstracts of the Basel Mission, Gold Coast Correspondence." Legon, 1970.

Jenkins, Raymond George. "Gold Coast Historians and their Pursuit of the Gold Coast Pasts: 1881–1917." PhD diss., University of Birmingham, 1985.

Laumann, Dennis. "Laumann on Wright." Unpublished paper.

Meyer, Birgit. "Translating the Devil: An African Appropriation of Pietist Protestantism, The Case of the Peki Ewe in Southeastern Ghana, 1847–1992." PhD diss., University of Amsterdam, 1995.

Ofosu, Felix Kwabena. "The History of the African Methodist Episcopal Zion Church in Ghana." BA long essay, Department for the Study of Religions, University of Ghana, Legon, 1981.

Ray, Carina. "Policing Sexual Boundaries: The Politics of Race in Colonial Ghana." PhD diss., Cornell University, 2007.

Sorkpor, Gershon. "Geraldo de Lima and the Awunas, 1862–1904." MA thesis, University of Ghana, 1966.

———. "The Role of Awuna in the Triple Alliance Formed by Ashanti, Akwamu and Awuna during 1867–1874." Unpublished Paper. Institute of African Studies, University of Ghana, 1966.

Vellenga, Dorothy Dee. "Jamaican and Swiss-German Missionaries in the Basel Mission in the Gold Coast in the Mid-Nineteenth Century: Racial and Ethnic Conflict in a Christian Missionary Community." Paper presented at the African Studies Association Annual Meeting, 1983. Available at the Schomberg Center for Research in Black Culture.

Ward, Barbara E. "The Social Organization of the Ewe-Speaking People." MA thesis, University of London, 1949.

Yates, Walter Ladell. "The History of the African Methodist Episcopal Zion Church in West Africa, Liberia, Gold Coast (Ghana) and Nigeria, 1900–1939." PhD diss., Hartford Foundation, 1967.

Yegbe, J. B. "The Anlo and their Neighbors, 1850–1890." MA thesis, University of Ghana, Legon, 1966.

NEWSPAPERS AND PERIODICALS

Gold Coast Aborigines
Gold Coast Independent
Gold Coast Leader
Gold Coast Nation
Gold Coast Times
Jahresbericht der Evangelische Missions-Gesellschaft zu Basel
The Missionary Seer
Mitteilungen von Forschungsreisenden und Gelehrten aus den Deutschen Schutzgebieten

Monatsblatt der Norddeuteschen Missions-Gesellschaft
Royal Gold Coast Gazette and Commercial Intelligencer
The Star of Zion

WEBSITES

http://www.biblegateway.com/passage/?search=Habakuk%202%20;&version=9
http:/docsouth.unc.edu
http://elwininternational.com/elmina_java.html
http://www.ghanacbc.orga/ketahistory.html
http://king-james-bible.classic-literature.co.uk/the-acts-of-the-apostles/ebook-page-16.asp
http://www.winesoftheworld.com/news/static/article_268.asp
http://www.wsu.edu/~campbelld/amlit/slave.htm
http//www.cdc.gov/ncipc/dvp/Suicide/Suicide-def.htm

ARCHIVAL AND ORAL SOURCES

NATIONAL ARCHIVES OF GHANA, ACCRA
ADM 11–
ADM 39–
ADM 41–
ADM 4–

DISTRICT COURT GRADE II, ANLOGA, GHANA
Judicial Court Record Book, 1911
Judicial Council Minute Book, 1913

ANLO TRADITIONAL COUNCIL OFFICE, ANLOGA, GHANA
Traditional Council Minute Book, 1931–32

STAATSARCHIV, BREMEN, GERMANY
Bremen Staatsarchiv: 7,1025–

BASEL MISSION ARCHIVES, BASEL, SWITZERLAND
David Asante. "Eine Reise nach Salaga und Obooso durch die Länder des mittlerern
   Voltaflusse." D-10.S,7.

ORAL INTERVIEWS
Greene, Sandra E. Field Notes 56: Interview with William Tiodo Anum, 22 December
   1987, Anloga.
———. Field Note 63: Interview with L. A. Banini, 5 January 1988, Anloga.
———. Field Note 70: Interview with K. Kpodo, 12 January 1988, Woe.
———. Field Note 72: Interview with Christian Nani Tamaklo, 13 January 1988, Keta.
———. Field Note 78: Interview with Dzobi Adzinku, 20 January 1988, Anloga.
———. Field Note 93: Interview with Amegashi Afeku IV, 19 February, 1988 Acca-Nima.
———. Field Note 96: Interview J. W. Kodzo-Vordoagu, 24 February 1988, Tegbi.
———. Field Note 99: Interview with Togbi Awusu II, Chief of Atorkor, 29 March 1988,
   Atorkor.

INDEX

Page numbers in italics refer to illustrations.

Sandra E. Greene is a
professor of history at Cornell
University. She is author of
*Sacred Sites and the Colonial
Encounter* (IUP, 2002).